EKA 1

Weinrich, James D.
    Sexual landscapes : why we are what we
are, why we love whom we love / James D.
Weinrich. -- New York : Scribner's, 1987.

306.7
WEINRICH

    xii, 433 p. : ill. ; 25 cm.

    Bibliography: p. 405-420.
Includes index.
ISBN 0-684-18705-1

    1. Sex (Psychology) 2. Love--
Psychological aspects.   I. Title.

87-4423

SEXUAL
LANDSCAPES

"Let's hope, Lucille, that our decision hasn't been too hasty."
DRAWING BY ZIEGLER; © 1979 THE NEW YORKER MAGAZINE, INC.

SEXUAL
LANDSCAPES

Why We Are What We Are
Why We Love Whom We Love

JAMES D. WEINRICH, PH.D.

CHARLES SCRIBNER'S SONS
NEW YORK

Charles Scribner's Sons
Macmillan Publishing Company
866 Third Avenue, New York, NY 10022
Collier Macmillan Canada, Inc.

Library of Congress Cataloging-in-Publication Data
Weinrich, James D.
Sexual landscapes.
Bibliography: p.
Includes index.
1. Sex (Psychology)   2. Love—Psychological aspects.
I. Title.   [DNLM: 1. Identification (Psychology)—
popular works.   2. Love—popular works.   3. Sex
Behavior—popular works.   HQ 21 W424s]
BF692.W335   1987   306.7   87-4423
ISBN 0-684-18705-1

Macmillan books are available at special discounts for bulk purchases for sales promotions, premiums, fund-raising, or educational use. For details, contact:

Special Sales Director
Macmillan Publishing Company
866 Third Avenue
New York, NY 10022

10 9 8 7 6 5 4 3 2 1
Book design by The Sarabande Press
Printed in the United States of America

To my parents,
Albert James Weinrich
and
Helen Lautz Weinrich,
who provided me with all of my genes,
most of my early environment,
and far more than the average number
of the facts of life

CONTENTS

Contents

PREFACE

L et me begin with some comments about scientists writing books that, like this one, are addressed both to scientists and to lay people.

Building a scientific theory is like building a house. If you are a house builder, you start by digging and pouring a careful concrete foundation. Each subsequent stage literally builds on those completed previously, and when it's all done, you step back, take a look at everything, and—if you've done your work right—feel pretty proud.

But most of the people who will use and admire the house really don't care about the steps you took to construct it. They don't look at the house's foundations, they don't give any thought to the plumbing, and they plug in appliances until they blow a fuse. If you had built the house from the roof down instead of from the basement up, they'd be just as happy. You know that's impossible, and so do they, but you're the only one for whom that fact really matters.

Moreover, even though a good house *has* to start with a good foundation, that's not the part of the house the architects planned first. They began by thinking about how the house should look, how its owners would use it, and how the land around it was arranged. That is, first they drew up a *design*. The design then dictated what form the foundation would have to take, taking into account the other technical details such as groundwater, subsoil, and so on.

Science is the same. It is scientists who must carefully do their digging, build a foundation for their theories, then assemble (by experiment and deduction) the higher constructs the rest of the world will have to live with. Scientists care deeply about these steps and look closely at them when they examine theories being constructed by others. But most people who use science care only about the final results.

They are largely justified in this narrow interest, because the foundations and the experiments used to build the theory all flow from the design thought out first.

This book cannot be all things to all people. The foundations of my theories are laid bare in scientific journals. What I will focus on here are the plans I used to construct the theory and a sketch of the final product. Accordingly, if you are a scientist, you may find yourself irritated by the fact that I don't seem to be progressing, as I would in a good review paper, from fundamentals through deductions to conclusions. I'm sorry about that, but that's why I have footnotes.

Some other readers of early drafts have also been worried about the way I flow back and forth between science and politics, or science and social concerns that are not strictly scientific. Again, in building a house, there are social and political concerns that have little or nothing to do with the question of soundness of the house itself: Will the neighbors complain about the extra story? Will the permit board allow a different kind of fire escape? Will the Historic District Commission approve the color of paint? Some users of the house are more concerned with these matters than they are with whether the roof will collapse (sometimes, mind you, to their discredit). But many of these concerns are legitimate, and some of them relate to fascinating problems with clever solutions. Again, in reality the architects are concerned with such matters throughout the process of design and construction, and they influence the final form the house will take. And so in this book I, too, will allow readers to see how social and political concerns affect my construction of reality, scientifically speaking.

Now some comments about the plan of the book itself. The chapters are connected in a way that resembles the circulatory system. Chapters 1–4 are the arteries: the vessels from which all others flow; you should read them first. Chapters 5–13 are the capillaries; they function pretty much independently of each other, so you can skip around in them if you wish. Chapters 14 and 15 are the veins, returning the flow to the heart; in order to understand them fully, you need to be familiar with all the chapters in between.

Finally, a note on the book's title. Although it was conceived independently of the title of a book by John Money—*Lovemaps*—there seems to be an obviously similar metaphor. In fact, however, the metaphors are different. A Money lovemap belongs to an individual, it's his or her own scheme of erotic attraction. The sexual landscape we'll explore in this book, in contrast, is common property. We'll tour it together, mostly using sources that are publicly available to anyone who knows where to look for them. A lovemap, in contrast, is available only to the person who has it and, typically, to the very few other people by whom the owner permits it to be seen.

ACKNOWLEDGMENTS

There are plenty of people I need to thank, without whom this book would never have happened or taken the form that it did.

If you can read this book, thank a teacher, and I have many to thank: Peter Drees for the logic and the sense of humor; Charles Buell, Jay Horschak, and Mary Campbell for the introduction to the levels below the surface; Robert Trivers for the sociobiology and the strategy; John Money for the sexology, more strategy, and the theory of the levels below the surface; Sarah Hrdy for suggesting I write a book in the first place; Richard Pillard for the vocational interest and the job; and many others far too numerous to name. If you borrowed this book from a library, thank a librarian; and I would like to thank the phone-query answerers in the Humanities Reference Department at the Boston Public Library and at the general-reference desks at Widener Library (Harvard University) and Mugar Memorial Library (Boston University). I thank Mitzel for additional help in references.

For consistent encouragement I thank Edward O. Wilson; for constant inspiration, Charles Darwin and Alfred Kinsey.

For money, I thank (besides anyone who buys a nonremaindered copy of this book) the National Science Foundation, Harvard University's Society of Fellows, the National Institutes of Health, and my various employers.

For personal computer advice, I thank the Macintosh User's Group of the Boston Computer Society, and for the computer itself I thank the greatly insane Steve Jobs and the entire Macintosh team at Apple. I'm looking forward to what's NeXT. I thank Ric Ford for the LaserWriter.

Several people read drafts of chapters (some of which never made it, alas, into the final version) or listened to excerpts read over the phone and gave helpful comments: Ray Blanchard, David S. Carter, Mark L. Cohen, Gregg Edwards, Kurt Freund, George Goethals, Richard Green, June Werlwas Hutchison, Ariadne Kane, Peter Nardi, Jeffrey Nickel, Timothy Perper, James Saslow, Paul Schalow, Herman Schornstein, Robert Trivers, Tyll van Geel, Sherwin Wine, Katherine Williams, and my parents. Roger Swain was the first reader, and my editor, Elizabeth Rapoport, the last.

Several people have influenced me through their written works, although they may not yet know how much I appreciate their insights: Richard W. Smith, Leonore Tiefer, George Goethals, Evelyn Hooker, David Finkelhor, Martin Gardner, Lawrence Mass, Boyd McDonald, Plato, and pseudo-Lucian. Paul Robinson and Kurt Freund get credit in the text, but I'll mention them here again, anyway.

Besides contributing in most of the categories above, John Boswell and Ralph Hexter generously answered innumerable questions I've had over the years about the classics, often at far greater length than I deserved.

Of course, everyone who's helped me out gets some of the credit for the things I did right in this book. I think it only fair, then, to try to blame them somehow for any mistakes that may have crept in along the way. I don't think I can get away with this, however, so I guess I'll have to admit that if there's a mistake somewhere, it might even be my fault. Although I doubt it, let me nevertheless state that I take the responsibility for any errors that remain.

If I've forgotten anyone in any of the above categories, I hereby apologize and offer a special discount on the purchase of multiple copies.

And thank you all!

S E X U A L
LANDSCAPES

SEXUAL
LANDSCAPES

1

THE POWER OF LOVE

Let me tell you 'bout the birds and the bees
And the flowers and the trees
And the moon up above
And a thing called love.
  Jewel Akens, "The birds and the bees"
  © Dominion Entertainment, Inc.

Said seventeen-year-old Allen Little . . . "We want to know what's happening. Don't treat us like jerks."
  Wall Street Journal News Roundup (29 January 1986) Lessons from space: Children in schools witness a tragedy. *The Wall Street Journal* 207(20):1,24.

The power of love, as Huey Lewis and the News say, is "curious." Rock stars sing about it, comedians tell jokes about it, and just about every advice columnist writes about it. Scientifically, however, just *how* curious love is is still an open question. When scientists write up proposals to study love, tenure committees get skittish, and senators start cranking out press releases. Everyone may know that love makes the world go round, but it seems people don't want to figure out why.

"Love" is a four-letter word not only in the scientific community but also in the broader community of scholars. As a specialty, it's intellectually offbeat and risky. It's not safe and respectable—like cancer

1

research, accountancy, or literary criticism—and it's not at the center of a discipline with endowed chairs and old money.

"Sex," in turn, is the shortest four-letter word. Sex is also curious in our society, but it's even more taboo than love is. Cyndi Lauper may bop, and the owner of a brand-new pair of roller skates may be looking for a key, but only the brashest Princes of rock sing openly about sex—lucrative though the results might be when they do.

No one seems to know whether sex is like love or unlike love. Dr. Ruth Westheimer's phone-in radio show is called "Sexually Speaking," but "love" never seems far from her mind. And critics of sex research are fond of pointing out how wide-ranging studies of sex—the famous Kinsey Institute studies published after World War II, for example—fail to range widely enough and ignore love altogether.

It's my task in this book to tell you what I know about love, sex, and science. My strategy is to do this in two ways: specifically, by telling you some facts and experiments about sex I think are interesting, and generally, by setting out some theories that can explain these facts. I'll introduce you now to some of the most important concepts I'll discuss throughout the book. The first of these is the question of why people should be allowed to study sex and love in the first place.

Frankly, I go beyond "allowing"; scientists have an *obligation* to study love and sex. Not everyone agrees with me, so first I'll explain why, using examples in plants and animals (since I was originally trained as a biologist). Some of the lessons drawn from these examples apply to humans, as I explain in later chapters. Next, I'll explain the two kinds of question biologists answer when they want to understand a behavior: "proximate" questions and "ultimate" questions. This distinction will be important every time I talk about an explanation for something. Finally, I'll take aim at Western dualistic thought (a common hobby these days) and illustrate the attack by describing psychological femininity and masculinity. Since masculinity and femininity are involved in the definition of the gender transpositions (see chapter 2), this attack raises issues that will be important throughout the book.

SEX IS SPECTACULAR

My first task is to point out the obvious: sex and love are spectacular. What you might not understand is just how spectacular they are, why they are spectacular, and how curious it is that everyone goes around pretending they are not spectacular at all.

I do some of this pretending myself. When people ask me what my specialty is, I tell them "human reproductive strategy" when I'm feeling discreet and "love and sex" when I'm not. I am, in short, a "sexologist" (as well as a psychobiologist and many other things), and if the term strikes you as funny, remember that so did "speleologist," "humoralist," and "gymnosophist" until you got used to them. There are lots of people doing similar research, and many of them are supported by government money or university endowments, as I have been throughout most of my career. This raises an important question.

A certain member of the Senate Foreign Relations Committee,[1] and some of you taxpayers, might wonder why U.S. citizens and distinguished alumni contributors should be paying for all this sex research. After all, the fellowships and salaries I've received in the past fifteen years or so might have been better spent on something else—decreasing the federal deficit, perhaps, or covert operations in developing countries, or maybe paying the expenses of our finer university marching bands. Why make a fuss about this sex-and-love stuff? Better for us scientists to leave well enough alone and let sex return to its proper place in life, right?

Well, then, just what exactly *is* the proper place of sex (or love) in human life? Consider the following facts:

- **Universality:** Love and sex are responsible, in the proximate sense, for 100 percent of the human births on the face of this earth.[2] In contrast, federal deficits, undercover operations, and marching bands are not universal human experiences and are only incidentally associated, if at all, with the beginnings of life.[3]
- **Intensity:** Human beings—young or old, female or male—have the capacity to experience the most addicting human response—orgasm—and the most powerful human bond—love.[4] This is reflected in the fact that soon after someone first experiences love or orgasm, the lyrics of popular songs suddenly make sense. In contrast, only a fraction of the world's population has had the experience of a halftime show, a tax return, or the *Christian Science Monitor* editorial page, and few popular songs refer to these activities.

[1] The Honorable "Golden Fleece" himself, Sen. William Proxmire.

[2] Nowadays, of course, we'd have to make that "nearly 100 percent." Test-tube fertilization is on its way, but it'll be a while before its use in conceptions approaches that of, say, the rarest position listed in the Kama Sutra.

[3] I realize that the "nothing is certain but death and taxes" crowd will disagree with part of my analysis here. But anthropologists insist that there are remote cultures that get along without any taxation whatsoever. None get along without birth.

[4] By which, to be precise, I mean "limerence," which will be defined in chapter 5.

- **Adaptation:** Nearly all human beings have parts of their bodies specially adapted for sexual intercourse—body parts that have benefited from a research and development history of millions of years of evolution by natural selection. In contrast, tax collectors do not have specially evolved sticky fingers, trumpeters' lips have not evolved so as to make mouthpieces obsolete, and superpower interventions in developing countries have not been perfected by millions of years of R & D. The result is that none of these behaviors—delightful though some people find them to be—are quite as delightful as sexual intercourse, watching your kid smile, or murmuring in your lover's ear.[5]
- **Self-reinforcement:** Sexual matters are so important that they are carefully scrutinized in every society on the face of the earth, and every culture restricts or encourages sex in some ways. It's so compellingly human an activity that many people in any society would engage in it without any encouragement from society whatsoever. But undercover operations, trumpet playing, and foreign relations sometimes require substantial rewards to encourage people to participate in them.

Frankly, it's no contest. The evidence is clear that given a free choice, people will choose under-covers copulation, strumpet paying, or outlandish relations substantially more often than the corresponding nonsexual activities. So I suppose we do agree with each other, after all. Sexologists should help other citizens get the *proper* perspective on human sexuality—a perspective placing it at the center of human life.[6] Come and join me for a good close look.

BUT FIRST, SOME OTHER SPECTACULAR THINGS

But before we start talking about human sexuality, let's take a stroll around the block and take a look at the lay of the land. As a biologist, I tend to notice biological things when I walk. There are some beautiful daisies in bloom just down the street—so let's talk about flowers.

---

[5] Or—to make my bias more explicit here—*I* don't think they are. I'll talk about my biases, and why I let them get involved with my arguments, later on.

[6] Which is not to imply that it is the *only* topic that belongs at the center of human life. Surviving the nuclear age belongs there, too, along with the First Amendment and chickens in every pot. In the surrounding circle, almost as important, we should probably put freshly picked corn, *Casablanca*, and Macintosh personal computers.

4

Flowers

Everyone loves flowers, and for good reason: flowers are spectacular. But there's a reason *why* flowers are spectacular, and it has to do with sex. Forgive me for pointing this out, but . . . flowers are the sexual parts of plants.

Pollinators—the agents that move pollen from one flower to another—are nature's matchmakers. For millions of years plants have used[7] their blossoms to lure pollinators into moving pollen from one flower's stamen to another's pistil.[8] As a result, flowers display some spectacularly clever adaptations. For example, insect-pollinated flowers can attract just the right set of pollinators by the patterns they display on their petals, using ultraviolet (UV) pigments that insect eyes can see but bird eyes cannot.[9] Seen with UV-sensitive eyes, these blossoms display striking patterns—a sort of bull's-eye pattern in one species, say, and something like an asterisk in another—which show insects exactly where the nectar and pollen lie. But to birds, these flowers all look roughly alike (e.g., white petals with a yellow center). Because insects can see UV, while birds cannot, the result is a set of flowers that look different to honeybees but alike to hummingbirds—different to the species that pollinate those particular flowers, alike to the hummingbirds that don't.

Bird-pollinated flowers are a different story. For example, plants pollinated by hummingbirds often have striking patterns involving red—a color invisible to an insect, which can't see that wavelength of visible light, but not to a bird.

If I were a botanist, I could give you lots of examples like this one. Why? Because sex is important to plants, so there's a lot to be discovered about flowers—the structures that embody plants' reproductive strategies. But this isn't a book about flowers; it's about humans. So let's leave the flowers behind and cruise on over around the corner.

But wait—is that a whippoorwill I hear singing? Let's talk about birds.

---

[7] Here I use the language of intention to describe the behavior of unconscious organisms. Whenever I do this, consider it to be a shorthand for saying, for example, "Plants have evolved responses that act *as if* the plants used their blossoms to lure pollinators."

[8] The stamen is the flower's male reproductive system; the pistil is the female. Like sperm, pollen, the male gametes (sex cells) of plants, is designed to seek its way to the female gametes that in plants become seeds.

[9] Actually, it's not just birds that are blind to UV. The UV light is visible to invertebrates (without backbones) such as insects and invisible to vertebrates (with backbones) such as birds, bats, humans, and a few other pollinators.

Birds

Everyone loves birds, and for good reason: birds are spectacular. Such beautiful feathers! Such cheerful melodies!

But there's a reason *why* birds' feathers and songs are spectacular, and it has to do with sex. Forgive me for pointing this out, but . . . feathers and song are used when birds prepare for sexual relations.

Bird-watchers and ornithologists know that the birdsong you hear on a lovely spring morning is sexual posturing: a member of one sex [10] telling other members of its sex to stay away, at the same time suggesting to members of the other sex that this turf could be theirs, too, if they pair up with the singer. Birdsong is spectacularly complex. For example, many species have local song dialects—which other birds use to identify first where the singer came from and then who the singer is—and experts have the impression that a lot more is going on with birdsong than human ears have managed to figure out. For example, in at least one species, the part of the brain in charge of singing degenerates and regrows over the course of each year—an astonishing fact in a group of species (vertebrates) previously thought to have little or no brain growth after infancy. This suggests that the song-singing parts of birds' brains are extremely important.

Spectacular feather patterns are also used in courtship. A good example is the sage grouse. Usually, sage grouse look and act like ordinary, large brown birds. But during the mating season, males in this species assemble and stake out territories on a *lek,* an open-field mating ground. As females move from territory to territory on the lek, the males—each in his own territory—literally strut their stuff in a weird-looking posture that looks even weirder from a bird's-eye view (which in this case is on the ground). They puff up their chest feathers and hold their wings open in a way that shows off the feather patterns. This is all undertaken at a substantial cost: the male sage grouse go without food when they are "lekking," and they are more likely to get eaten by predators because they spend so much time out in the open where they are easy to find.

If I were an ornithologist, I could give you hundreds of examples like this one. Why? Because sex is important to birds. That means there's a lot to be studied in feathers and songs, which embody birds' reproductive strategies. But this isn't a book about birds; it's about humans. So let's head back to civilization.

But look out! There's a bee buzzing around your elbow! So let's talk about honeybees.

[10] Usually, but not always, male.

6

Bees

Everyone knows about honeybees, and for good reason: beehives have spectacular forms of cooperation and social organization.[11] But there's a reason *why* the social organization of bees is spectacular, and it has to do with sex.

Forgive me for pointing this out, but . . . most honeybees are celibate. Not merely celibate, mind you, but sterile: they couldn't reproduce even if their bee brains were capable of wanting to. No, instead of having sex, most female bees are abuzz with the Protestant work ethic beloved by their Social Darwinist fans.[12] Meanwhile, the males—which are usually born only as the mating season approaches and are always fertile—drone on, waiting for fertile females available from other hives before they set off on a mating flight—after which they conveniently die.

Sociobiology is the study of behavior from the point of view of its evolution by natural selection. One of sociobiology's triumphs has been to show that the incredibly spectacular forms of social cooperation in the social insects might have resulted from a silly little fact about sex determination: female bees have twice as many chromosomes as males do.[13] *Chromosomes* are the microscopic, spindly-looking things located in the nucleus of every cell in your body.[14] Chromosomes consist of lengths of DNA (deoxyribonucleic acid) looped and folded into the spindle shapes by certain proteins. Logically, chromosomes can be divided into shorter sections called *genes*; roughly speaking, a gene is the repository for one particular set of genetic instructions passed from parent to offspring in reproduction. A cell's chromosomes thus resemble a multivolume instruction manual on how to build an organism, and the genes resemble the logical divisions (sections) of the manual that explain how to manufacture each part.

Now if you think back to what you learned when you were *first* told about the birds and the bees, you will recall that two of the chro-

---

[11] The fact that bees make honey may also contribute to their good reputation. Honey is food—not sex or love, alas—and this distracts from my theory. I'll leave it to others to decide if food and sex have something to do with each other. . . .

[12] Please note that here I'm just pointing out that Social Darwinists use evolution to draw lessons for human behavior. I'm not implying that people ought to draw such lessons or that the lessons are the logically correct ones to draw.

[13] There are many details of the social insects' social arrangements that are *not* explainable directly in terms of this silly little fact. But most experts now agree that the broad outlines—and some of the most puzzling details—are well explained by the kin-selection hypothesis I'm about to discuss, and not by any competing theory. Kin selection itself will be discussed in a later chapter.

[14] With some exceptions, such as red blood cells.

7

mosomes human beings have are called *sex chromosomes,* which determine the sex of the offspring.[15] Boys typically get an X chromosome from their mother and a Y chromosome from their father and thus have the combination XY, and girls typically get an X chromosome from both parents and thus have the combination XX. The other forty-four human chromosomes (called *autosomes*) make a total of forty-six chromosomes in twenty-three pairs.

Well, in the Hymenoptera—also known as ants, bees, and wasps—sex is determined not by sex chromosomes but by whether an individual has a single set of chromosomes (is *haploid*) or a double set of chromosomes *(diploid).* In particular, males are haploid, and females are diploid. (If humans worked this way, then women would have forty-six chromosomes per cell and men would have twenty-three.) This system is called *haplodiploidy.*

Haplodiploidy has an unexpected consequence for the honeybee family: full sisters are genetically more closely related to each other than they are to their own offspring.[16] This fact in turn influences nearly every one of the deductions that sociobiologists make in working out the theories that underlie social evolution in honeybees. The bottom line is this: bees have evolved spectacular social arrangements because they have a particular sex-determination system that predisposes them to do so.

If I were an entomologist (an expert on insects), I could go on and on. Why? Because sex is important to ants, bees, and wasps, celibate though so many of them be. But this isn't a book about insects; it's about humans. So let's move on—this time, for real.

THE SEX TABOO

Why have I been spending so much time on the birds and the bees and the flowers? Because these topics are, of course, the traditional detours taken by American parents as they explain sexual reproduction and human sexuality to their children. I took these detours on purpose. First, I wanted to remind you what it's like to be treated like a kid and thus to get you angry or bored. Second, I wanted to show you what your educators might have missed telling you about the

---

[15] The sex chromosomes "determine" the sex of the offspring in most cases but not in all. Entire careers have been built around dealing with the situations in which, due to transsexualism, birth defects, or whatever, there is not a direct relationship between chromosomal sex (XX versus XY) and gender assigned at birth or taken up in adulthood.

[16] The mathematics of this consequence are worked out in most introductions to sociobiology. See, for example, Wilson 1975.

birds and the bees that was really interesting. And third, I wanted to back up my assertion that sex really is spectacular when you understand it well.

The fact that these detours are taken so often shows that our society has a *sex taboo*[17]—it insists that sex and love are so important that we must pretend that they are unimportant and so emotionally loaded that they are dangerous to think about. And that's a shame, because these things are so interesting!

One aspect of the taboo is that parents believe that children need to be told about sex through stories rather than through plain facts because children are not ready to understand sex in all its gory detail. Or, when they do, they use words like "gory" that have such bad connotations that kids get the idea that sex and love are supposed to be unpleasant.[18] In fact, telling children about birds, bees, and flowers—instead of about wombs, penises, love, and sexual feelings—delays their understanding of sex instead of advancing it.

> Children are misled and confused by many of the analogies used to explain the origin of babies. Seed in soil, eggs and chicken, and sperm as tadpoles . . . appear to be taken so literally that they retard understanding for some time. Similarly the vague use of stomach or tummy to indicate uterus or womb appears to block the child's thinking.[19]

Optimist though I generally am, there are times when I think the birds/bees/flowers detour is undertaken in the hopes that kids will lose interest in the explanation long before the grown-ups get to the good stuff.

But deciding that the sex taboo is a bad thing doesn't make breaking it any easier. Here is an exchange between a ten-year-old girl and her uncle—a sex researcher who dislikes the sex taboo and has taught plenty of parents how to explain sex to their children without guilt, shame, or hesitation:

[17] My discussion of the sex taboo—and especially my insistence on its importance—owes a great deal to John Money, the medical psychologist and sexologist at Johns Hopkins University.

[18] Or, as one author wrote (in jest), that sex is a natural function: just as natural as vomiting and a lot more fun. I am sorry that I have not been able to locate the source of this delightful way of putting it; if my memory serves me correctly, it was either Mary Breasted or M. S. Kennedy.

[19] Goldman and Goldman 1982, p. 386.

Evening newscaster: Local police tonight apprehended a man they say is responsible for the rape of at least a dozen women, including the—
10-year-old girl: Uncle Jim, what's "rape"?
Uncle Jim: (A pause) Uh . . . (A longer pause) Well, you see . . .

And Uncle Jim proceeded briskly to a discussion of "mating" in animals and (indirectly) humans.[20]

SEX AND SCIENCE

Obviously we're going to have to break the sex taboo to get anywhere in this book. As it turns out, that's not such a bad thing to do, intellectually speaking. There are important scientific reasons to look into sex—reasons that make the taboo indefensible, and so all the more fascinating.

The most important reason to study sex in evolutionary biology is to analyze *reproductive success* (RS). By definition, evolutionary biologists are interested in how an animal's behaviors and body structures evolved by natural selection. Evolution is defined as any change in genes (and gene frequencies) from generation to generation, and natural selection is an agent of this change. Since reproductive success is the measure of which genes are passed along to the next generation, reproductive success is the key variable of natural selection and evolution.

Suppose that evolutionary biologists want to study a particular structure or behavior in a species. First, they find *variation* in that structure or behavior; then they think about what effects the variations might have on reproductive success. They do this by constructing a logical argument linking a change in the structure or the behavior to a change in reproductive success.

For example, faster legs (or better strategies for finding escape routes) enable animals to escape predators better; this means they will die later in life rather than sooner, which extends their reproductive lives and thus increases reproductive success. Here is how this argument would be represented in a diagram (fig. 1.1) that makes every step in the chain explicit:

---

[20] I regret to report that "mating" was the actual word he used. I'll return to this example in chapter 3.

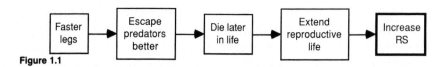

Figure 1.1

Or: stronger jaw muscles (or better cooperation in hunting) enables predators to capture prey better, which means they will have more food to support a larger brood, which amounts to a higher reproductive success (fig. 1.2):

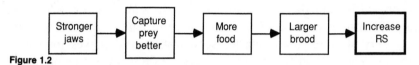

Figure 1.2

And so on. The further removed from reproductive success that the structure or the behavior may be, the more links there are in the causal chain scientists construct to explain it. And so the more uncertain the entire chain of deduction becomes. For example, why would an animal avoid predators better *after* it ends its reproductive life? What about the conflicts engendered by *dividing* the spoils among individual animals cooperating in a hunt, which solo hunters don't have to worry about? Each of these questions raises doubts about the interpretation of a link I just put forth; the more links there are, the more chances for doubt.

The beauty of studying *sexual* behaviors and sexual structures in evolution is that the logical chain from a sexual trait to its effect on reproductive success is very short, since by definition sexual things are those involved in reproduction.[21] That means that uncertainties about them should be fewer and less troublesome than explanations involving longer logical chains. That means sexual behaviors and structures are ideally suited for tests of evolutionary theory.

So sex is not just a kinky sidelight of interest mostly to animal breeders and hormone manufacturers; it is central to the study of ev-

[21] This definition is incomplete and too strict. Once a structure or act is classified as "sexual" under this strict definition, it is permissible to continue regarding it as "sexual" even if particular instances involving it do not result in reproduction. (Otherwise, sex acts involving sterile individuals could not be considered sexual, nor could homosexual sex acts, and so on.) Of course, this opens up another complication; is a woman's breast a "sexual" organ if she's using it in nursing? This complication is minimized as soon as we admit that any organ or behavior can have more than one function; the penis is a sexual organ used in urination, and it is also an excretory organ used in copulation. But the complication isn't completely resolved. Some women describe sensations during breast-feeding that others believe are those of sexual arousal, but those women might object if they were told that breast-feeding is sexually arousing to them. Definitions are always a problem.

olution. If you'll permit me an exaggeration, evolutionary biologists really ought to be studying sex most of the time.

Notice, however, that this argument only explains why sex should be of interest to my particular discipline. What about the social sciences, such as psychology and sociology, which are not necessarily as interested in reproduction? Sex is not strictly necessary in transmitting culture or to socializing children, so psychologists and sociologists might be excused if they pay less attention to sex than biologists do, mightn't they?

Probably so, but there are reasons why these disciplines should be more interested in sex than they seem to be. The sex taboo sets up some very strange conditions for socialization and makes for some Alice in Wonderland psychology. These conditions are so important that I will devote much of chapter 4 to them. Here I will simply point out that children learn the sex taboo without being specifically told what this taboo consists of, that people grow up to do particular things sexually (homosexuality, for example) even though they have never been overtly socialized to do those things, and so on. Some theories of human development have taken these puzzling facts and tried to make sense of them, but in my opinion not enough.

PROXIMATE AND ULTIMATE CAUSES

So: many disciplines, including biology, *ought* to be interested in explaining human sexuality. But what kinds of explanations should we look for? In evolutionary biology especially, we'll have to distinguish between *proximate* and *ultimate* causes.

The difference can be illustrated by answering two questions about watches:

Why is this watch so thin? Because people who buy the watches want them to be thin. This is called an *ultimate* answer. It takes the form "We did it this way because that's the way somebody asked us to do it," that is, somebody other than the watchmakers specified the feature, and that's why it's there.

Why is this watch so thick? Because watchmakers figured out that watches had to have batteries and there were no inexpensive thinner batteries that could do the job. This is called a *proximate* answer. It takes the form "We did it this way because that's the cheapest way," the only physically possible way, or the fastest way.

Evolutionary biology makes similar distinctions between ultimate and proximate causes. Here's an example that will be important in later chapters.

Why are most people heterosexual? The ultimate reason most people are heterosexual is that heterosexual acts are required to pass on genes to the next generation and the genes of members of a society that fails to provide for this die out. So from this point of view it is not surprising that most people are heterosexual; Mother Nature must have found a way or our species would not be around.[22] Notice how this answer zips past all the technical details of how heterosexuality comes about, heading directly for the ultimate evolutionary logic of reproduction. Homosexuality, however, is not as easy to figure out in ultimate terms, because its reproductive function, if any, is not obvious; in the ultimate sense, it might be considered a puzzle.

Why are most people heterosexual? To obtain the proximate reason, restate the question this way: "By what mechanism do most people become heterosexual?" Here the answer is *not* obvious. Saying that it's "instinct" is just a cop-out, of course. Maybe it has something to do with hormones, socialization, the circuits built into the brain and the genitalia, or all of the above. It would make sense to assume that Mother Nature had taken care of this, too, but this wouldn't tell you just *how* she took care of it. To find out, you'd need to know a lot about science—physiology, neurology, socialization, genotype/environment interaction, and so on. Not coincidentally, you'd need to know all these things to answer the question "How do people become homosexual?," too. So proximately speaking, homosexuality and heterosexuality are both puzzling.

One of the goals of this book is to explain sexual orientation in evolutionary terms: both proximately and ultimately. In my ultimate explanation, I'll spend more time on homosexuality than on heterosexuality, because homosexuality is more puzzling from an ultimate viewpoint.[23] But my proximate explanation will give equal treatment to each sexual orientation, because from the point of view of proxi-

[22] I said it's not surprising—instead of obvious—because, strictly speaking, heterosexual acts are required to pass genes on to the next generation only *from time to time*. Remember, for example, that most honeybee females are celibate and sterile, not heterosexual in any meaningful sense of the term. And as you'll read in a subsequent chapter, there are human cultures in which homosexuality is required for just about everybody at certain stages of life—and these are not societies that are about to disappear from underpopulation.

[23] I should qualify this, because sexuality and heterosexuality are not quite as inevitable in the ultimate sense as they might seem. First, *some* heterosexuality is required, but not very much, as I pointed out in the previous footnote. Second, the question of why sexual reproduction evolved and replaced simple cell division, budding, or other forms of parthenogenesis is one that biologists have not yet answered satisfactorily. They've worked out sophisticated mathematical models, plugged values into equations, and found that things don't add up right. I don't have the space or expertise to explain this puzzle in detail, but there are good introductions in many sociobiology textbooks.

mate causes, homosexuality and heterosexuality are equally puzzling. Knowing the answer to the ultimate question doesn't help much in answering the proximate one.[24]

DUALISTIC THOUGHT

Besides breaking the sex taboo, we're also going to have to break out of the venerable Western tradition of dualistic thought. Dualistic thought is a big help to Western science; it sets up hypotheses that can be tested to help explain our world. I used it in the last section, for example, to distinguish between ultimate and proximate causes. But dualistic thought gets troublesome sometimes.

By "dualistic thought" I mean the tendency we Westerners have to see things in terms of *pairs* of *opposites:* black and white, right and wrong, proximate and ultimate, male and female, homosexual and heterosexual. There are two faulty extremes to which this dualism can be taken. First, the members of the pair can be incorrectly viewed as in competition with each other: the more black you have, the less white you have; the more masculine you are, the less feminine you are. Second—and worse—these opposed pairs can be misconstrued as all-or-nothing: a little bit wrong means you're 0 percent right; or a little bit homosexual means you're not at all heterosexual. Let's call these two extremes the *competition* extreme and the *all-or-nothing* extreme; the all-or-nothing extreme is even more extreme than the competition extreme.

Consider the ancient Chinese symbol of yin and yang. It is conventionally illustrated by a diagram such as the one on the left in figure 1.3, but sometimes, in order to stress the bit of yin in the yang and yang in the yin, it is illustrated as on the right. This right-hand version shows that the ancient Chinese were not making the all-or-nothing mistake. On the other hand, both diagrams seem to exhibit the competition extreme: they imply, by their eating-each-other's-tail arrangement, that the more black you have, the less white, and vice versa.

Yin/yang is often interpreted in terms of masculinity and femininity. In this case, the figure on the right is used to stress that every man has some femininity in him and every woman has some masculinity

---

[24] In fact, knowing the ultimate answer can slow you down in trying to figure out the proximate one. For example, you might naively assume that "opposites attract" and thus that it's a simple fact of nature that "different things" would be intrigued by each other. Of course, this is nonsense; in nature, there is no general mechanism causing opposites to attract. Yes, a north magnetic pole attracts a south magnetic pole. But birds of a feather flock together, right? The best generalization you can expect to come up with is that opposites attract—except when they don't. And that, of course, is not a generalization at all.

Figure 1.3

in her. Until recently, this view was way ahead of the Western view of a strict separation between the masculine and the feminine. But recently we Westerners have gotten a leg up: the most modern theory of sex roles does even better than yin/yang does and rejects not only the all-or-nothing extreme but also the competition extreme. Here's how.

Sex-role psychologists love to construct "tests"—checklists, actually—of masculinity and femininity. They administer these checklists to the students in their classes, then write learned papers about the results and send copies to their tenure committees. Back in the bad old days, femininity and masculinity were embodied in these tests as opposites: if you answered "true" to the statement

Windstorms terrify me

then your masculinity/femininity score took a step in the "feminine" direction; if you answered it "false," then it took a step in the "masculine" direction. Your score on such a test was represented by a single number that put you at some point on a single scale (fig. 1.4, *left*).[25]

The more modern masculinity/femininity scales, in contrast, are *two-dimensional*. Nowadays, masculinity and femininity each have their own independent scales, and so you get assigned two scores: one for masculinity and one for femininity. Thus, in the good new days, if you rate yourself highly as "compassionate," then your femininity score is raised, but your masculinity score is unaffected. And if you rate yourself highly as "forceful," then your masculinity score is raised, but your femininity score is unaffected.

Your answers on such a test are summarized by *two* numbers that put you at some point on a plane (fig. 1.4, *right*).

Here there's room for four different kinds of people: the entirely

---

[25] In defense of these scales, let me point out that they were an advance from an even worse situation beforehand. In the really *really* bad, *really* old days, supposedly your sex role existed at only one end or the other of this scale: you were either masculine or you were feminine. Period. There was no in-between.

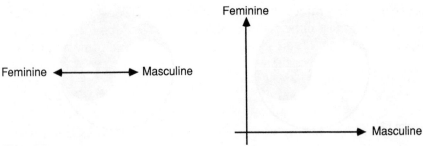

Figure 1.4

masculine (and not feminine—John Wayne?), the entirely feminine (and not masculine—Zsa Zsa Gabor?), the androgynous (Kate Hepburn? Alan Alda?), and the undifferentiated (who so rarely become famous that I can't think of any). To oversimplify a bit, think of someone who is forceful but not compassionate; that's the masculine stereotype. Someone who's compassionate but not forceful is the feminine stereotype. An androgynous person is both forceful and compassionate (not a contradiction!), and the undifferentiated person is neither forceful nor compassionate.

An important fact about these ideas is that they have empirical support. Thousands of people have now been tested with these two-dimensional checklists. If the bad old view were correct, scores on the new masculinity and femininity scales would be *negatively correlated* (see fig. 1.5, *left*). But it turns out that statistically speaking, these masculinity and femininity scores are *uncorrelated*—that is, the points that plot them fall all over the map (see fig. 1.5, *right*). It didn't have to turn out this way—after all, the world might have turned out to be composed of John Waynes and Zsa Zsa Gabors. But it isn't—luckily for Alan Alda, Kate Hepburn, and many of the rest of us.

This two-dimensional view will be extremely important when I discuss theories of sexual orientation. As you can imagine, it has

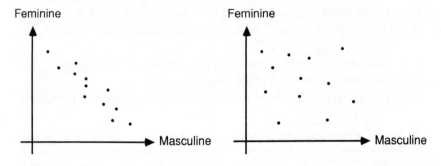

Figure 1.5

crossed people's minds that heterosexuality and homosexuality might not be opposites, either, and might also best be described in a two-dimensional way. If you scored high on a scale of heterosexuality *and* on a scale of homosexuality, you'd be called bisexual; if you scored low on both, you'd be called asexual. It also turns out that the body's genitalia, and the brain's sexuality circuits, are probably better described by two dimensions rather than one. So these scales, which were developed by psychologists to answer psychological questions, may turn out to have a basis in anatomy and physiology, as well. More on this in later chapters.

THE POWER OF SCIENCE

This last example is a good illustration of the power of science—and of science's limitations. The two-dimensional theories of masculinity and femininity were supported by feminist scholars,[26] and feminism, in turn, rose to prominence during the counterculture revolution of the sixties and seventies. Accordingly, scientists woke up to the fact that social belief (in masculine *versus* feminine terms) had been keeping them from seeing a second dimension in their data. But once awakened, scientists could phrase the possibility in testable terms and then gather data to test the suggestion. Now that these data show statistical independence (lack of correlation), the point is made: masculinity and femininity are not opposites, and forcing them to be opposites oversimplifies the way things really are.

The implication is clear: social beliefs are not firm grounding for scientific conclusions, but they are fertile ground for scientific suggestions. Even if future social scientists decide that these experiments are incomplete or even wrong, they cannot thereby conclude that the experiments shouldn't have been performed or that it was "obvious" that the experiments would fail (after initially succeeding). It is clearly necessary to allow a model with at least two dimensions for sex roles—even if there turns out to be only one—and this is essentially established for all time.

It is this intellectual certainty that makes science so powerful and so interesting—in a word, spectacular. It is also what makes scientists so insufferable, because this certainty can be exaggerated and manipulated, and scientists sometimes act as if their method is the only reliable one to use to get to the truth.

Sex, too, is spectacular—whether it turns up in the birds, the bees,

[26] See, for example, Constantinople 1973.

17

the flowers, or people; whether it's studied as evolutionary biology, psychology, sociology, or physiology; whether it's thought of proximately or ultimately and one-dimensionally or two-dimensionally. And if you doubt me on this point, then go turn on the radio.

So here is a syllogism: Sex is spectacular. Science is spectacular. Ergo, sex and science together are especially spectacular.

An insufferable opinion, especially coming from a sexual scientist? Yes, but it's also true. If we follow this opinion where it leads us, a spectacular vista opens up in front of us—with hills and valleys, musky caves and jutting promontories, secret hideouts and spectacular viewpoints. Come with me and tour as I explore the power of sexual science.

Our first stop? The *gender transpositions*—also known as bisexuality, homosexuality, transvestism, transsexualism, and that old standby, heterosexuality. Everyone's a foreigner somewhere here.[27] You don't understand your own language until you've learned about someone else's, and you don't understand your own sexual feelings until you've learned about someone else's. So at least some of the people I describe in the next chapter will be unfamiliar to you. Let's get on down the road!

---

[27] After all, you aren't *all* bisexual fetishistic transvestisexuals with decided preferences for sadomasochistic cuddling, are you? Good!

2

MEET THE
GENDER
TRANSPOSITIONS

You ask [homosexuals], "What is your role in the sex act—is it male or female?" They say, "Well, sometimes it's male, sometimes it's female."

Anita Bryant, quoted on p. 85 of Kelley 1978.

. . . much butch/femme role-playing stopped at the bedroom door (where butches could suddenly become very "feminine" and vice versa) . . .

Sisley and Harris 1977, p. 60.

Don't own a single record by Barbra, Bette or Judy
Heard of Bette Davis, but never saw her movies
Guess I'm irresponsible; it seems I've shirked my duty
What kind of self-respecting faggot am I?
"What Kind of Self-Respecting Faggot Am I?"
© 1983 by Romanovsky and Phillips

For most of the chapters in this book, you'll need to be familiar with the gender transpositions. Gender transpositions are covered in any decent introductory course in sexology, so if you've taken and passed Sexology 101, you may skip to the next chapter. What's that, you say? Your college didn't *have* an introductory sexology course?[1] Then you'd better read on below.

To understand the gender transpositions (put aside for the moment the definition of just exactly what they are), you need to understand the three components of gender identity: core gender identity, gender role, and sexual orientation. So first I'll define these three components, and then I'll describe and classify the gender transpositions in terms of these three components.

First, *core gender identity*. This is the innermost experience of oneself as male or female. Usually it goes along with the appearance of the genitals: most people who have a vagina and labia consider themselves female; most people with testicles and a penis consider themselves male. (This component is sometimes just called "gender identity.")

Next, *gender role*. This is the set of social roles that a particular society at a particular time prescribes for females and for males. Most societies, for example, expect that men and women will dress differently and perform different tasks—although what these differences will consist of varies quite a bit from society to society. (This component is sometimes called "sex role" or "social sex role.")

Finally, *sexual orientation*. This is the readiness particular people have to pair erotosexually with a member of their own sex or a member of the other sex. It includes the possibility that one might pair with members of either sex. Most people in our society expect to fall in love with, or be sexually attracted to, members of the sex whose genital shapes don't look like their own. (This component is sometimes called "sexual preference.")

Taken together, these three concepts are called *gender identity*.[2] The fine points of gender identity can be illustrated with examples from the gender transpositions. A *gender transposition* is a particular pattern of adherence to or differentiation from the typical patterns of gender identity; the differentiation consists of a transposition of masculine and feminine in comparison with the typical pattern. As you'll see, transsexuals are transposed on core gender identity, transvestites on gender role, and homosexuals on sexual orientation.

It's much easier to understand these points by way of some specific

[1] What's a liberal education coming to, anyway? Aren't students required to learn *anything* universal these days??

[2] Or *gender identity/role* by sexologists such as John Money of Johns Hopkins University. Money also has a different definition of gender role: in his scheme, it is the public presentation of core gender identity, which may or may not be in accord with what society expects from a person with a particular core gender identity.

examples. It will also help if I can be frank in describing each group's strengths and weaknesses. Ladies and gentlemen—meet the gender transpositions!

THE GENDER TRANSPOSITIONS

Sexologists nowadays think of the gender transpositions as being composed of five different groups: heterosexuals, homosexuals, bisexuals, cross-dressers, and transsexuals. I'll discuss each in turn.

Heterosexuals

Here I'm talking about heterosexuals whose sexual behavior is discreet and respectful of the rights of others—not the ones who expose themselves in shopping malls, not the ones who rape and kill. Many famous people are, reputedly, heterosexual: Dr. Ruth Westheimer, Norman Mailer, Wally Simpson, Donna Summer, Mao Tse-tung, Anita Bryant. . . . The list is long and distinguished. There are also, however, some infamous heterosexuals—such as Richard Speck and Adolf Hitler.

Ordinary heterosexuals are ordinary on all three components of gender identity. They come in two flavors: female and male. If they have labia and a vagina, they think themselves female, wear clothes (corsets, saris, whatever) that their culture thinks acceptable for females (even if they feel a bit uncomfortable doing so), and plan to put their vagina around a penis from time to time.[3] If they have testes and a penis, they think themselves male, wear clothes that their culture thinks acceptable for males (a coat and tie, a Buckingham Palace guard's uniform, whatever), and plan to put their penis into a vagina from time to time. In short, typical heterosexuals exhibit the *null transposition*—the gender transposition in which none of the three components of gender identity is transposed.

It is heterosexuals who traditionally take on most of the responsibility for producing and rearing the next generation of children. Most social scientists use terms to describe this trait that suggest that these behaviors are altruistic—sacrifices performed by the parents to benefit their offspring. Many sociobiologists, in contrast, use terms that describe this trait as selfish—acts performed that result in an increased distribution of the parents' genes in the next generation.

Heterosexuals are very common—a majority, in many societies,

---

[3] Note that, following John Money, I did not say "have a penis put into their vagina," which would imply that the receptive act was a passive one.

sometimes a large majority—and most heterosexuals consider it natural that penis and vagina should fit together. Many heterosexuals also believe it natural that certain activities (cooking, lawn mowing, etc.) be performed only by members of a particular sex. And all societies have formalized institutions—ours is called *marriage*—in which such beliefs play a central role.

So you may be surprised to learn that male and female heterosexuals sometimes don't get along with each other. Many[4] heterosexual husbands and wives get angry at each other—sometimes violently so—and our society formalizes this possibility in an institution called *divorce*. Sometimes the arguing continues even after a divorce, as formalized in institutions called *alimony, child support,* and *child custody.* But even happily married heterosexuals have been known to be surprised by the strange behavior of members of the other sex. In fact, the theme of male and female heterosexuals misunderstanding one another is a common one in heterosexual literature.

Homosexuals

Ordinary homosexuals are transposed on sexual orientation but not on either of the other two components of gender identity. That is, their core gender identity is in accord with their genitalia, and they are not particularly unusual in gender role. But they are sexually attracted to members of their own sex.

Homosexuals are a minority but not rare. They come in two flavors: female and male. As it turns out, many[5] homosexuals have childhoods characterized by sex-role nonconformity—cross-dressing, playing house in the role of the opposite sex, and so on. In adulthood, however, homosexuals generally don't cross-dress, except maybe for Halloween or when they want to make a point.

You may have heard, for example, of a fellow in San Francisco named Sister Boom Boom. He was a member of the Sisters of Perpetual Indulgence (S.P.I.), a group that described itself as an order of gay male nuns. As nuns, these men claimed that it was important for them to do good works, which typically had to do with alleviating sexual guilt or misinformation: exorcising demons from Virginia's Rev. Jerry Falwell, for example, or handing out literature describing how to avoid contracting AIDS.[6] But as far as I know, no member of the S.P.I. ever

[4] Not all.

[5] Not all.

[6] The sisters have disbanded, because they found that not enough people could understand the complex message they were sending; they were both deadly serious and com-

got into his habit because he felt he was really a woman.

So for ordinary homosexuals, gender nonconformity is more a memory than an actuality. Robin Tyler, a lesbian comic, gives a perfect example. In one of her routines, she bemoans the number of high school girlfriends of hers who have gotten heterosexually married and remarks with a sigh, referring to herself, "Always the bridesmaid, never the groom!" (This is also the title of one of her albums.) This kind of joke makes sense if you understand a gender-nonconforming childhood; it would not be funny if Tyler still really wanted to be male.

Homosexuals often do not accept the fit of penis and vagina as necessary or natural. In fact, they sometimes consider such a fit distasteful to talk about, although usually they find it simply uninteresting. Likewise, they are relatively unlikely to consider it natural for someone with particular genitalia or particular preferences in bed to perform particular roles about the house or on the job. The one who mows the lawn may well be the same one who cooks the food, and both gay sexes can be found in jobs such as computer programming or library administration.

Only a few decades ago, many homosexuals took on the responsibility of caring for distant relatives' children when the parents of those children were no longer able (through death or illness) or willing (through desertion) to care for them. Nowadays this sometimes still happens. Some famous (or infamous) homosexuals are Sappho, Walt Whitman, Lorena Hickok, John Wayne Gacy, Horatio Alger, and Willa Cather.

Most social scientists use terms to describe homosexuality that suggest that these behaviors are selfish—acts performed to benefit the actors. Many sociobiologists, in contrast, use terms that describe this trait as altruistic—acts performed that result in an increased distribution of someone else's genes in the next generation.

It may come as a surprise to you, but sometimes male and female homosexuals don't get along with each other. Some gay bars cater to both sexes, of course, and plenty of gay bars catering to one of them tolerate the other should it walk in the front door. But there are gay men's bars that have taken the doors off the toilet stalls in the (legally required) women's restrooms. And there are lesbian bars that have placed potted plants in the (dry) men's urinals.

------

pletely entertaining. The cross-dressing was often misinterpreted as merely weird, silly, threatening, or pointless. The sisters tried various strategies to get their messages across more accurately, but the cross-dressing continued to interfere with their reception. So they decided to pack it in. Nevertheless, a couple of the sisters (including Sister Boom Boom) continue their work.

Bisexuals

Ordinary bisexuals are *partially* transposed on sexual orientation. They might find themselves falling in love with their own sex sometimes and with the other sex at other times. Or they might find that they have purely sexual fantasies about one sex and purely romantic fantasies about the other. Bisexuals need not be transposed on any other aspect of gender identity.

Bisexuals come in two flavors—female and male. Female bisexuals are apparently more common than male, but the exact figures depend on the way the classifications are set up. If sexual arousal throughout life is taken as the criterion, then most people are bisexual. If current sexual fantasy is taken as the criterion, then most people are not.

Bisexuals get flack from both gay people and straight people challenging their bisexuality. This criticism has an interesting skew. Many heterosexuals seem to believe that any homosexual activity, even by a bisexual person, implies homosexuality. This belief is commonly shared by homosexual men, many of whom went through a phase in which they pretended they weren't gay by saying they were bisexual. But when bisexual women are criticized by lesbians, it is often because the lesbians suspect that a bisexual's heterosexual component is all too likely to be genuine.

It may come as a surprise to you, but bisexual men and bisexual women aren't always interested in meeting one another. The Boston Bisexual Women's Network, for example, which prefers that only women attend its meetings, was formed long before the Boston Bisexual Men's Network was, and has a far larger mailing list. The two groups are cordial, but they usually meet separately (except at conferences).

Cross-Dressers (Including Transvestites)

Transvestites are transposed on gender role, especially as it pertains to clothing. But the transposition often covers other aspects of gender role, too—usually the role of breadwinner (see below). By definition, the so-called classic or fetishistic transvestite is (or was at one time) sexually aroused by wearing clothes society prescribes for members of the other sex. So these transvestites are a subcategory of *cross-dressers,* who by definition wear clothes of the other sex but are not necessarily sexually aroused as a result.

Cross-dressers also come in two flavors, but these are heterosexual and homosexual, not male and female; for all practical intents and purposes, the classic, fetishistic transvestites are always men.[7] No one really knows how common heterosexual transvestites are. If you had X-ray eyes, it might be easier to pick some of them out; they number among them the men wearing panties, bras, or girdles under their three-piece suits. A typical transvestite has alternating periods in two sex-role personas, masculine and feminine,[8] bringing home the bacon like the stereotype of a good husband much of the time but slipping into his feminine persona for hours, days, or weeks at a time.

During these "femme" periods, the experience of being cross-dressed is typically more important to transvestites than how they appear (although appearance is not ignored entirely). If you photograph them dressed en femme, they will probably want copies, even if the photos aren't of very high quality or aren't flattering.[9] And among understanding friends, they usually speak in an ordinary masculine voice.

When a transvestite's feminine side is coming to the fore, wearing male clothing becomes extremely uncomfortable. The discomfort is psychological, not physical; it has nothing to do with the discomfort felt while wearing an ill-fitting three-piece suit, say. Those men wearing a bra or panties *under* their three-piece suits are trying to relieve their anxiety about being dressed as men ordinarily dress.[10] Thus, unlike cross-dressing in order to make a sociopolitical point or for old times' sake (as in homosexuality), heterosexual transvestites usually cross-dress in order to feel comfortable or to accompany sexual arousal.

To transvestites themselves, the sexual aspects of their situation are sometimes not the most important ones. This is true, incidentally, of most people, not just transvestites. When an ordinary heterosexual man walks over to talk to an attractive woman, he usually doesn't have an erection, and he wouldn't think that sexual arousal is what's causing him to go over and talk; he's "interested," not "turned on." So it is for transvestites and all the gender transpositions. What transvestites do notice is that they *want* to put on women's clothing, just as an ordinary heterosexual man notices that he *wants* to talk to a

---

[7] For the *three* exceptions, see Stoller 1982.

[8] Dr. Virginia Prince, herself a transvestite, makes a careful distinction between *masculine* and *feminine* on the one hand and *male* and *female* on the other. A sex role can be characterized, she says, as masculine or feminine, but a sex role itself cannot be male or female; after all, sex roles don't copulate. The point is well taken but (for me) difficult to observe in practice.

[9] I suppose the same could be said of those cute little packets of reproductive success you see in holiday pageants at school.

[10] Of course, heterosexual transvestism is not confined to the three-piece-suited class; there are construction workers and career military officers (and, for all I know, guards at Buckingham Palace) who wear feminine underfrills.

pretty woman at a party. So some transvestites prefer to describe their cross-dressing as an expression of a *gender shift*. This term stresses the gender-role aspects, not the sexual ones, that are more salient to the transvestites themselves. It has the added benefit of implying that the shift might not be permanent; one can shift back to an ordinary gender role, or one can shift further in the direction of transsexualism. "Transvestite," on the other hand, seems to stress that it is a situation that is fixed and unchangeable.

There is another flavor of cross-dresser: men who are sexually attracted to males but who also cross-dress. These men are commonly called *drag queens*. (In order to avoid a thorny sexological debate, I will reserve the term "transvestites" for heterosexual cross-dressers.) Drag queens are transposed both on gender role and on sexual orientation. Nobody really knows how common they are, either.

Drag queens are doing rather well these days, professionally and financially; some are appearing on Broadway; while others are writing hit songs and thanking America for its good taste in internationally televised awards shows. By contrast with heterosexual cross-dressers, drag queens typically have an androgynous appearance when they are just being themselves; they seem to dichotomize the masculine and feminine parts of the personality somewhat less.[11] When drag queens present themselves unequivocally as one sex rather than the other, they do so mostly because our society wants cut-and-dried distinctions[12] or because they are appearing in a show in which the point is to make the feminine illusion as perfect as possible.

It may come as a surprise to you, but heterosexual and homosexual cross-dressers don't necessarily get along with each other. There are organizations and publications for heterosexual transvestites that specifically exclude homosexual ones. And there are drag queens known for expressing their displeasure at this loudly and often. Indeed, some cross-dressers are famous for not getting along with *anybody*.

It may also surprise you that drag queens and ordinary homosexual men sometimes don't get along with each other. Some ordinary gay men had tried to keep drag queens out of gay-pride marches and in return have had their masculinity stingingly challenged by the drag queens in question.[13]

[11] Boy George is a good example of someone who aims for an appearance that's in between.

[12] There are people who, while walking down the street, want to be able to discern the sex of any person they encounter. Some of them also want to be able to make this distinction instantaneously at fifty paces. These people are usually the ones most upset when they encounter drag queens, who require—indeed, insist upon—more than a passing glance.

[13] The usual cross-dresser's rejoinder to criticism from heterosexual men is "Honey, I'm

Transsexuals

Transsexuals are transposed on core gender identity and usually also on gender role but not necessarily on sexual orientation (see below). That is, a person with a normal penis and testes is a male-to-female transsexual if convinced of or obsessed with the notion that those organs must be removed in order to bring the body parts into line with the inner experience of the self as female. (A few sexologists apply the term only to people who have actually had a transsexual operation, but most do not.) Transsexuals are rare; estimates range from less than 1 in 40,000 all the way up to 1 in 10,000.

With transsexuals the standard taxonomy gets complicated. Some sex researchers claim that there are only two flavors of transsexual: male-to-female and female-to-male. Others claim that there are homosexual transsexuals, heterosexual transsexuals, bisexual transsexuals, and asexual transsexuals;[14] supposedly, the latter two types only exist among genetic males, while the homosexual type exists among both males and females.

Are you confused by applying words like "heterosexual" and "homosexual" to someone in the process of changing sex? Don't worry; so are many sexologists. One camp uses "heterosexual" and "homosexual" in reference to the original (preoperative) state of the genitalia of the two partners. The other camp uses them by reference to the desired state of the genitalia. Hence, a male-to-female transsexual sexually attracted to women (whether before or after the sex-reassignment operation) is a heterosexual transsexual according to the first camp but is a lesbian transsexual according to the second.[15]

Many transsexuals simply want to spend the rest of their lives in their preferred sex, in as many respects as society, the law, and surgical science will permit, and some are very successful in this respect. Some other transsexuals, especially those of the male-to-female variety, are not at all successful or succeed only at prostitution. Female-to-male transsexuals, it seems, are more successful in adjusting to society's requirements. Although either direction of transsexual can occur in any social class, there seems to be a preponderance of male-

---

more of a man than you'll ever be and more of a woman than you'll ever get!" No longer original, mind you, but usually effective.

[14] For example, Blanchard 1985, although he then collapses these four categories into two. The Diagnostic and Statistical Manual of the American Psychiatric Association (DSM-III) recognizes three kinds of male-to-female transsexual, omitting the bisexual group.

[15] Got it? If so, then you're ready for the next methodological quibble: whether the term should be spelled "transsexual" or "transexual."

to-female transsexuals in the lower classes and of female-to-male transsexuals in the middle or upper classes.

Some transsexuals state that their genitalia are hermaphroditic or their sex-hormone levels intermediate even when there is no evidence in their medical histories to confirm this. Not all transsexuals have complete sex-change operations; many only take hormones to alter the parts of the body visible with clothes on.[16] This is especially likely to be true for female-to-male transsexuals, who often obtain a hysterectomy (removal of the womb), mastectomy (the breasts), and vaginectomy (vagina) but stop short of a phallus-constructing operation.

It may come as a surprise to you, but sometimes transsexuals and their doctors don't get along very well. A few transsexuals are so convinced of the necessity of their request for surgery that they will insist on operations that cannot be done—a uterine transplant, for example, so that the former male can become pregnant and have a baby, or a penile transplant so that a former female can acquire a penis that becomes erect in the ordinary way.[17] Much of the conflict results from those transsexuals who want the operation as soon as possible (preferably yesterday) or as cheaply as possible (preferably free) and from the gatekeeping psychologists and psychiatrists (who want to postpone the operation, possibly forever[18]) or the surgeons (who don't want to be sued if the postoperatives want their original equipment back[19]).

Some of this conflict arises because applicants for the operation don't necessarily match the gatekeepers' notions of what kind of person a transsexual ought to be. Some male-to-female transsexuals remain sexually attracted to women after their operation, but some gatekeepers believe that "true" male-to-female transsexuals can only be sexually attracted to men. Accordingly, some transsexuals misrepresent the sex they are attracted to; one sex researcher reported, only partly

[16] These transsexuals can resemble certain male cross-dressers—those who take female hormones in order to grow breasts but still want to retain their male genitalia.

[17] An original-equipment penis becomes erect when blood pools in the three vessels—"corpora"—designed for this purpose. Penile prostheses cause a penis (whether constructed from scratch, reconstructed, or original equipment but damaged) to become erect in different ways: in one, by simply straightening a surgically implanted hinge; in another, by opening a valve that causes a liquid in an implanted reservoir to fill a balloon structure. There are doubtless other devices under development; this is a rapidly expanding field.

[18] I have been told of one psychiatrist, who has counseled dozens if not hundreds of transsexuals, who charged them double what he charged anyone else for a particular procedure and who privately vowed never to recommend *any* transsexual for surgery.

[19] There *have* been postoperative transsexuals who wanted to change back; I don't know if any of them sued.

in jest, that such transsexuals know his publications better than he himself does.[20]

By now it will probably not come as a surprise to you that some[21] gay people and transsexuals don't get along with each other. Male-to-female transsexuals are told to use men's restrooms when they visit certain lesbian bars and are forbidden to attend certain all-women's music festivals (to which heterosexual and bisexual women are freely admitted). And some transsexuals get the operation, find a partner interested in their new self, then fade invisibly into the heterosexual world, lashing out every now and then at those "perverts" who fall in love with members of their own sex.

CONCLUSIONS

The most important thing to understand about the gender transpositions is that each has a particular pattern of core gender identity, gender role, and sexual orientation. Before these three components were understood, people commonly believed that they had to be interconnected: that is, that a lesbian really wanted to become a man, that someone who wanted to change sex really wanted to behave homosexually, that a man who wanted to put on a dress wanted to fall in love with a man, that a man who fell in love with men wanted to put on a dress. Not so! In fact, there is no necessary connection between any of these three components.[22]

Another generalization about gender-transposed people (including heterosexuals) is that they don't necessarily get along with each other. Remember that just because some people are atypical in one way doesn't mean they will understand people who are atypical in another. In this respect, alas, gender transpositions are no different than other traits on which humans differ. It is probably easier for someone atypical in one way to understand another's atypicality, but each still needs to be educated in the ways of the other.

These conflicts and misunderstandings arise for several reasons. First, members of each kind of gender transposition view themselves in a particular way. Their emotions appear perfectly normal to themselves,

---

[20] See Blanchard 1985 and Stoller 1973.

[21] Not all.

[22] As I've indicated, there are particular transpositions that are likely to be associated with other transpositions. But these associations are not required in theory; in practice they occur only in a statistical sense. The particular pattern is observed, not deduced, and has important consequences for theories of gender-identity development I'll describe in later chapters.

and thus they find it easy to project these emotions onto others. Many heterosexuals think that penis and vagina fit together perfectly and cannot understand why someone wouldn't want to fit them together if they had the opportunity. Nor can such heterosexuals understand how someone could try fitting the two together and not find the experience delightful. Many heterosexual transvestites think that women's underclothes are inherently attractive and that any man would want to put them on. Many gay men presume that there must be something homosexual about the men who engage in the sort of nude horseplay common in locker rooms. Many lesbians believe that any woman could fall in love with a woman if given the social permission to do so.

Second, members of the different gender transpositions don't talk very much with each other. This has to do with the sex taboo, of course, through which society makes some of the gender transpositions unspeakable. The result is that everyone falls back on his or her own experience, projects it onto everyone else, and gets puzzled or angry when people don't act the way they expect them to. Some heterosexuals, for example, remember their own anxiety when first encountering the other sex in bed and can only understand homosexuality (incorrectly) as a fear of the other sex.

At this point, I could sit back and play the ultrascientist and tell you that these questions—who understands whom and so on—are social questions, not scientific ones. But besides getting me into hot water with sociologists (who are, after all, social *scientists*), such a statement is nonsense. These questions are a different kind of scientific question, but they are definitely scientific, and scientists ought to address them. *The fact that group A doesn't get along with group B is an observation* and itself has scientific significance (and social significance, too, of course), especially if we can figure out a pattern to the conflict. In short, we have no alternative but to address the political, scientific, and social all at once. It's a tough job, but somebody's got to do it, and I'm going to give it a try.

The core of my argument will be given in the next three chapters, so let me describe briefly each one (in reverse order).

In chapter 5, I'll discuss the validity of the definitions of the gender transpositions themselves. After all, so far I've just asked you to take my word for everything: that there are these different kinds of people and this is what they are like. There is a danger in following me blindly. The scientists who make up these definitions were raised in Western societies and could conceivably have been too influenced by Western notions of gender identity. The result would be a classification that merely reflects Western prejudices and doesn't tell us anything more lasting or profound about human nature. Likewise, adopting the point of view of any particular gender transposition risks a corresponding danger[23] and doesn't necessarily free us from the Western view, anyway. This is the reason why cross-cultural studies are so important to gender-identity research; they help us decide whether our definitions make sense in the first place.

You may have noticed while reading this chapter that there were some things about the gender transpositions you had been misinformed about. In chapter 4, I'll discuss in depth one of the reasons for your misinformation: the sex taboo. Perhaps in no other area of sexology are the social, political, and scientific interwoven so tightly— and therefore in no other area of sexology is thinking clearly so important.

In chapter 3, I'll give you more reasons to be interested in my theory in the first place: puzzles about sex that are begging to be solved. With your new knowledge of the gender transpositions, I hope you've already discovered that there's a lot of nearly virgin territory out there to be explored. The territories' Departments of Tourism have put out some brochures to attract you there, and I've done all the hard work for you: whittling down the attractions into a single compact list. A really good theoretical tour de force, of course, should fit all the gender transpositions together and explain the major puzzling features of each of them—including heterosexuality. I think I know which way to go in search of such a theory (see chapters 6 and 7), but first you need to know some more of the puzzles.

---

[23] I only mean to imply, by the way, that members of particular gender transpositions are "biased" in the sense that everyone is biased.

3

SEXUAL AROUSAL: TEN UNSOLVED PROBLEMS

By and large, calls involving two or more girls and one client were about as exotic as we would get. . . . Because being with two women at once is the most common male fantasy, . . . more than one man told us that an evening he spent with two of our girls constituted the greatest sexual thrill of his life.

Barrows 1986, pp. 166–167.

S cience seems straightforward—find a puzzle, then figure out a solution. The hard part seems to be the figuring. But *figuring out what the puzzles are* is what separates good scientists from mediocre ones. In fact, some of the most famous theories in science started out as solutions to puzzles no one thought were puzzling except the person who solved them.

A scientific revolution begins when an old theory is faced with too many puzzles it can't solve, according to science historian Thomas Kuhn, famous for establishing the importance of "paradigms" in science. A new paradigm—a new way of looking at facts—begins when someone finds puzzles that can only be explained in a new way. The new paradigm succeeds if it comes to explain most of the facts in a given area of knowledge and when it is generally accepted that it explains those facts better than the old one. It ends when an even newer set of puzzles pops up and requires an even newer paradigm.

This book is built around ten sexological puzzles that I find fascinating, because they don't seem to be well explained by the theories we already have about human sexuality.[1] The purpose of this chapter is to get you puzzled by them, too, by explaining each one. Many of these will at first seem unrelated to each other. But like the separate maps for a territory's roads, geography, and political boundaries, each piece of the puzzle eventually fits in with the others to make a unified whole.

Some of the puzzles require more explanation than others. Don't worry about that; all the puzzles will be solved (tentatively, I assure you) later on in the book.

So let's get on with it. The study of sex is spectacular, eh? Let's see some of the reasons why.

1. THE TECHNIQUE PUZZLE

Pioneering St. Louis sex therapists William Masters and Virginia Johnson found that coupled gay men and women have better technique making love with their lovers than do uncoupled gays—and also better than coupled or uncoupled heterosexuals. Why?

It wouldn't be too surprising if *in*experienced gays had better sexual techniques than *in*experienced straights, since people know bodies of their own sex better than the bodies of the other sex. Likewise, gays and straights did equally poorly in a related study in which Masters and Johnson paired people up randomly, then asked them to make love.[2] It was definitely a surprise, however, when they observed that

---

[1] Magnus Hirschfeld, the famous German sexologist, was my inspiration for this chapter. He wrote a paper entitled (roughly translated), "Twelve reasons supporting the inborn nature of homosexuality" (Hirschfeld 1912). However, I won't confine myself just to homosexuality or inborn natures, and I'll also try to avoid another problem. Over the years, you see, Hirschfeld published these ideas more than once (see, for example, Hirschfeld 1936). The twelve reasons he gave varied a bit from paper to paper—but the total number was always twelve. This is a bit unbecoming by the standards of modern science.

[2] Masters and Johnson thought their so-called assigned couples were too direct in their lovemaking: they didn't seem to take their time or to care much about feedback from their assigned partner about what felt good and what didn't. Here they did find that the same-sex assigned couples were better at communicating their immediate sexual needs and responses, but it was not by much.

heterosexual married couples usually did little better than those randomly assigned couples.

Masters and Johnson took their observations seriously. Here is their description of what it meant to do poorly:

> Close observation has suggested that there were many times when women were made physically uncomfortable by their husbands' approaches to the breast. Although frequently admitting later in private that the observer's impression of cyclic [menstrual-cycle] breast tenderness had been correct, the women simply did not inform their husbands at the time. The usual stated reason was because "he likes to play with my breasts so much I didn't want to distract him." When the husbands were queried separately, they expressed surprise at their wives' cyclic distress, and the unanimous reaction was, "Why didn't she tell me . . ."[3]

> When husbands were interviewed, their most frequent complaint was that their wives did not grasp the shaft of the penis tightly enough. Yet not one man with this complaint had ever taken the initiative and suggested this specific technical improvement to his wife.[4]

And here is their description of how gay couples did:

> When the committed lesbian couple did turn to breast play, it was significantly prolonged compared to similar activity during heterosexual interaction. . . . As much as 10 minutes were sometimes spent in intermittent breast stimulation before genital play was introduced. The stimulatee always evidenced copious vaginal lubrication during these protracted periods of breast stimulation, and, on many occasions, the stimulator also was well lubricated. . . .

> The focus of lesbian breast play was directed toward the subjective pleasure of the recipient. During the lengthy "play periods," the stimulator usually responded to the stimulatee's nonverbal communication of pleasure and expended specific effort to enhance the recipient's experience of the moment rather than forcing her rapidly toward higher levels of sexual excitation.

[3] Masters and Johnson 1979, p. 68.
[4] Masters and Johnson 1979, p. 74.

In the sexual play of married couples, female breast stimulation was far more casual. Husbands apparently spent time in stimulating their wives' breasts as much, if not more, for their own immediate arousal as specifically to enhance the female partner's sexual pleasure. In most cases the man became so involved in his own sexual tensions that he seemed relatively unaware of the degree of his female partner's sexual involvement. . . . It was no surprise, then, that in contrast to lesbian interaction, the heterosexual women lubricated moderately at most during breast play. . . .[5]

So this finding was not a casual one. Indeed, you can practically see Masters and Johnson's eyes widening as they watch. Gay people seem pleased by the compliments paid them by Masters and Johnson, even if they feel a little overpraised.[6] How can we explain Masters and Johnson's finding?

Possibility 1 is that heterosexuals and homosexuals are about equal in their lovemaking technique—*equally bad.* Perhaps everyone is nervous when having sex in the lab, and perhaps it was by good luck that Masters and Johnson got a group of proficient homosexuals. If this is true, then other workers will fail to confirm what Masters and Johnson found, because they will not have such good luck when recruiting their sample.

Possibility 2 is that heterosexuals and homosexuals are about equal in their lovemaking technique—*equally good.* This suggests that it's not difficult to get used to Masters and Johnson's lab environment and that it was by bad luck that Masters and Johnson got a group of incompetent heterosexuals. If this is true, then other workers will fail to confirm what Masters and Johnson found, because they will not have such bad luck.

Possibility 3 is that the finding is *real.* This possibility suggests that other workers would usually reach the same conclusion.

Scientists have not rushed out to try to replicate these results, so for the moment we're limited by what Masters and Johnson have reported. One clue is that so-called ambisexuals didn't do well in these sessions. (In Masters and Johnson's terminology, ambisexuals are people

---

[5] Masters and Johnson 1979, pp. 66–67.

[6] I still remember the look in the eyes of one gay man to whom I read the quotes above; he said, astounded, "That sounds like propaganda!" Masters and Johnson worry that their data might be used as "an effective recruiting argument for lesbianism" (Masters and Johnson 1979, pp. 227–228)—a weak argument at best and, frankly, a bit queer.

who don't seem to care much whether it is a man or a woman they are having sex with.[7]) Frankly, this isn't surprising; if you don't choose your own partner, you're not likely to be especially turned on. Indeed, the sex the ambisexuals had in the lab appeared mechanical. This pattern also seemed to be at work for those homosexual and heterosexual couples who had been together for less than a year; it really does take time to get to know someone intimately, sexually.

But none of this really explains the puzzle. With the long-term heterosexual and homosexual couples, we're not talking about a few fumbling gropes versus a lot of fumbling gropes; we're talking about a major difference in communication in and around the marriage bed. It is reasonable to suppose that in the right circumstances heterosexuals can have sexual relationships as rewarding as homosexual relationships can be. It is reasonable to suggest that somewhere out there are heterosexuals who would make Masters and Johnson proud. Indeed, some such heterosexuals did make their way in to the lab.[8] But if those heterosexuals are out there in proportions not too different from what Masters and Johnson found among the homosexuals, then why not find them, recruit them, get them to the lab, and get them to ham it up in front of the camera in about the same proportions? Masters and Johnson did not succeed in doing this. And so we return to the question, Why not?

The beginning of the answer may lie in Masters and Johnson's observation that too many husbands and wives simply didn't tell each other what was pleasant and unpleasant. The conclusion Masters and Johnson themselves reach is that there is an American, cultural, heterosexual norm that appoints the husband as the chief sexual expert:

> The man initiates the mounting process when he is ready, presuming that if his partner is lubricated, she is ready. Usually he hunts for, finds the vaginal outlet, and inserts the penis; yet, the woman could have accomplished the insertion with greater facility, for she certainly would not have had to hunt and find. He selects coital positioning, usually without consultation as to his partner's preference, and she almost always defers to his decision. He predominantly sets the thrusting pattern and presumes that she will respond and will be pleased. And usually she makes every effort to cooperate with his thrusting pattern whether she is pleased or not.

[7] This definition of the term "ambisexual" is nonstandard.
[8] Masters and Johnson 1979, p. 230.

One wonders by what divine gift of providence the human male is endowed with such infinite knowledge of woman's sexual anatomy and sexual needs. When reflecting on the degree of male dominance in coital interaction, we have a better understanding of the many pitfalls that the culture has placed in the way of an enduring heterosexual partnership for unsuspecting men and women.[9]

Masters and Johnson are on the right track. This cultural pattern—a script, if you will, about how married couples are supposed to go about sexual relations—exists for heterosexual couples but usually does not exist for homosexual couples. Homosexual couples seem freer to create their own relationship patterns—including sexual ones.

This explanation suggests that it is *equally uncommon* for homosexual and heterosexual couples to have a good-communication sexual relationship. Relationships tend to break up among homosexuals if this communication is lacking, but heterosexual marriages lacking it need not break up. Experimentally speaking, the requirement that the couples had to have been together for over a year probably biased the sample so that a higher proportion of the homosexuals willing to be studied had good-communication relationships. I elaborate on this possible explanation in chapter 4. The empirical evidence that men really do follow a social script for being the expert in sexual matters—and that women let them get away with it—is given in chapter 12.

This explanation is quite believable. But I have some bad news for it: there seems to be evidence that something similar happens in other species. That is, homosexual relationships sometimes seem to be more emotionally or physically satisfying than heterosexual relationships—even in animal species that do not have a social script that says that males are supposed to take the sexual initiative. Read more about this in chapter 13.

2. THE EROTICA PUZZLE

Heterosexual men and heterosexual women act as if they are sexually aroused by very different types of erotica. But when tested with actual erotica, the differences sharply decrease or disappear. Why?

When pollsters ask people face-to-face whether they are sexually aroused by particular types of erotica—sexually explicit magazines, movies, novels, or narratives—very strong sex differences emerge. Alfred

[9] Masters and Johnson 1979, p. 220.

Kinsey, the Indiana University biology professor who conducted America's first large-scale sex survey, found that most men said they were turned on by visual stimuli (as seen nowadays in magazines like *Playboy* or *Torso*), but women usually said that they were aroused by narratives (like modern romance novels and stories).[10] These surveys are supported by statistics on people's actual behavior: men are overwhelmingly the more common buyers of visual erotica, and women the more common buyers of romance novels and what has been called "women's pornography."[11]

But nowadays scientists are less certain how to interpret these data. Back in the 1960s, a couple of West German sexologists decided to actually *try out* some sexually explicit materials on men and women and then look at what differences there were in sexual arousal patterns. These two sexologists, Gunter Schmidt and Volkmar Sigusch, recruited West German college students, took them to the lab, and showed them one of three things: a set of nice,[12] sexually explicit slides, a nice movie that included scenes of a man and a woman having sex with each other, or some nice stories that included accounts of a woman and a man having sex. Then the students answered a questionnaire asking for their opinions of what they'd seen or read and rated their sexual arousal. The students also came back the next day to fill out a questionnaire about what they'd done and felt sexually in the twenty-four hours after the experiment took place; these answers were compared with what the students had reported the previous day.[13]

Was there a sex difference in these students' reports? Did more men say they were turned on and more women say they weren't? Or did the men say they were more turned on by the visual stimuli than by the stories and the women more by the stories than by the visuals?

In a phrase, the answer was "Maybe—but if so, not by much." Basically, the two sexes (see fig. 3.1) reported about the same level of erotic arousal in response to any of the materials.

Schmidt and Sigusch asked about much more than just sexual

[10] Kinsey, Pomeroy, Martin, and Gebhard 1953.

[11] See Radway 1984 for a general discussion of the purchasers of romance novels. Romance novels are often sexually arousing to the women who buy them. For example, one study showed that romance novels are bought more often by women who are more, not less, sexually responsive than women who do not purchase them (Coles and Shamp 1984). They are not, as some people might claim, unsexy stories that substitute for supposedly sexier visual publications.

[12] I call them "nice" in order to emphasize that they were otherwise ordinary accounts of situations that became explicitly sexual. This was not red-light-district porno. It was "erotic" rather than "pornographic," if you will; Laird Sutton rather than Linda Lovelace.

[13] Schmidt and Sigusch 1973.

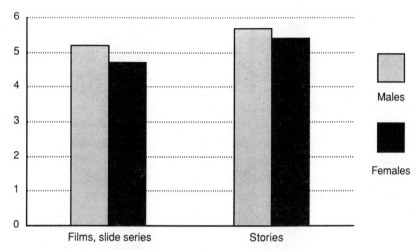

Figure 3.1. Self-Ratings of Sexual Arousal Immediately after Exposure

arousal. Concerning specific sexual behaviors and feelings in the twenty-four hours after the experiment, there were some sex differences, but they were relatively small (see fig. 3.2). Reported coitus differed between men and women only by 4 percentage points, for example, after the slides experiment; sexual tension, only by 6 percentage points. It seems the men did a bit more to relieve their sexual tension (especially in masturbation), but the fact remains that the women *were* aroused, just as the men were. In fact, the 6-percentage-point difference on sexual tension was not, as scientists say, "statistically signifi-

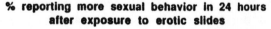

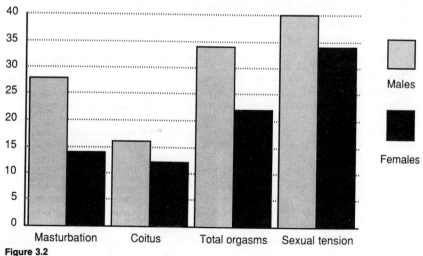

Figure 3.2

cant''—meaning that this difference might easily be the result of chance.[14]

Results like this are not just confined to West Germany in the 1960s. It is a pattern that holds true in many other studies: when you ask people if they are aroused by sexually explicit stimuli in general, you get strong sex differences, with men reporting far more often that they are aroused. And men also act more arousable. But when you actually put people in an arousing situation and then observe or ask how aroused they are by a particular stimulus, men and women respond much more alike—although not identically.

So that's the puzzle; what's going on here? My answer is in chapter 6.

3. THE ''HOW COMMON?'' PUZZLE

Some gender transpositions are more common in one sex than the other, and the pattern of which is more common in which sex doesn't seem to make much sense. This is probably the most important puzzle about the gender transpositions. Since there are several gender transpositions, we can break this puzzle into several others:

- *The homosexuality puzzle:* homosexuality seems more common in men than in women, but it is not rare in either sex. Why?
- *The bisexuality puzzle:* bisexuality seems more common in women than in men and may or may not be rare. Why?
- *The transsexualism puzzle:* male-to-female transsexualism seems more common than female-to-male transsexualism. Transsexualism is a very rare trait, but it does exist in both male-to-female (m–f) and female-to-male (f–m) forms. Why?
- *The transvestism puzzle:* Fetishistic heterosexual transvestism is not rare in men, but it seems not to exist in women.[15] Why?

[14] For the group of experiments as a whole, there was one interesting pattern that showed some sex differences: total orgasms, compared in a particular way. Each person was asked whether he or she had had more orgasms in the twenty-four hours *before* the experiment or in the twenty-four hours *after*. All groups reported more orgasms afterward (not surprising); males, more orgasms than females. However, in order to obtain the *net* effect of the stimuli, we should subtract the percent saying they had more orgasms before from the percent saying they had more after. When we do that, it turns out the stories had a bigger effect on the women than on the men. Moreover, the before/after difference is significant among the men for the slides and the films *but not the stories*, and it is significant among the women for the films and stories *but not the slides*.

[15] Even the three female fetishistic transvestites described by Stoller (1982) all had bisexual or homosexual aspects to their personalities. So female *heterosexual* fetishistic transvestism seems nonexistent, while female *homosexual* fetishistic transvestism is merely extremely rare.

Any single one of these statements isn't so puzzling by itself. The trouble comes when you try to fit the various explanations together. For example, suppose we notice that men tend to be more sexually atypical than women are. That would explain the homosexuality puzzle, the transsexualism puzzle, and part of the transvestism puzzle. But it doesn't explain the bisexual puzzle and would only suggest that female transvestites would be rare, not nonexistent.[16] So let's explore each of these puzzles in turn to see if we can do better understanding them.

The Homosexuality Puzzle

No one really knows why male homosexuality is more common than lesbianism—but that seems to be the case. The Kinsey researchers found, for example, approximately 4 percent exclusive homosexuality among men and about 2 percent among women.[17] A larger percentage, of course, is predominantly homosexual at some time during adulthood, but the sex difference probably still holds. The surveys conducted by feminist sexologist Shere Hite show a disparity in the same direction.[18] Moreover, lesbians on average "come out"[19] later in life than male homosexuals do, so if there were equal percentages over a lifetime, the percentages at any given age would still be quite different.

The Bisexuality Puzzle

That bisexuality is more common in women than in men is true in three slightly different senses—each of them complicated by the fact that defining "bisexuality" is a confusing matter (see chapter 6).

---

[16]The hypothesis would explain why male transvestites are more common than female transvestites but not why no heterosexual female transvestites exist.

[17]See the revised figures in Gebhard 1972.

[18]Hite 1981, p. 395, gives 8 percent of her female sample preferring sex with women. Hite 1982, p. 822, gives 11 percent of her male sample preferring sex with men. Hite's samples were less scientific than Kinsey's. But would they be biased about the *relative* incidence of homosexuality in the two sexes? Probably not; if both these percentages are really the same in men as in women, why would fewer lesbians volunteer for Hite's female sample or so many male homosexuals volunteer for her male sample? There may be an answer to this question, but it also ought to explain why Hite's difference wouldn't be an *under*estimate. Some people would guess—admittedly with little direct evidence—that lesbians would be more likely to answer a questionnaire written and analyzed by a woman than male homosexuals would.

[19]"Come out" is the slang term—short for "coming out of the closet"—that refers to the critical moments in gay people's lives when they more openly deal with their sexual feelings. The term can obviously be adapted to any trait that people have difficulty coming to terms with.

First, higher proportions of women identify themselves as bisexual than men do. As it happens, the Kinsey surveys are not much help here.[20] In the Hite surveys, about 4 percent of the women identified themselves as bisexual. Another 5 percent had had sexual encounters with both men and women but did not state that they thought of themselves as bisexual. (This is one of the complications about defining bisexuality mentioned above.) But only 4 percent of Hite's men had had sex with both men and women (more often with women), with an additional 2 percent predominantly homosexual but enjoying sex with women.[21]

The second sense in which women are more bisexual than men is that heterosexual women seem to have more homosexual experience than heterosexual men do. For example, in group-sex encounters or among so-called swingers, husbands often discourage homosexual advances even when they do not mind bisexuality in their wives.[22]

A third sense is that lesbian women have more heterosexual experience than homosexual men do. Several kinds of studies find significant levels of bisexual behavior and fantasy among lesbian women. Lesbians as a group have their first *heterosexual* coitus at lower ages than heterosexual women do and report much higher frequencies of heterosexual fantasy and behavior than gay men do.[23] It is easy to find bisexual women when researching the gay community, but it is difficult to find bisexual men.[24]

[20] The figures for bisexuality printed in the original Kinsey *Male* volume (Kinsey et al. 1948) are too high, since they included a disproportionate number of prisoners (who have disproportionately bisexual histories); see Gebhard 1972. Revised totals published thirty years later (Gebhard and Johnson 1979) correct this problem, but they don't break down the figures the same way they were broken down in the *Male* volume.

[21] Hite 1981, p. 395, and Hite 1982, pp. 822 and 858. Again, Hite's samples were less scientific than Kinsey's. But why would they be biased about the *relative* incidence of bisexuality in the two sexes in comparison with the incidence of homosexuality? We can calculate the ratio of bisexuals to homosexuals among Hite's men and women using the percentage figures given in the text. For the sake of a rough estimate, assume that "bisexual" means "anyone who identifies consciously as a bisexual or reports experience with both sexes in a survey like Hite's." For women, the ratio is $(4+5) \div 8$, a ratio greater than 1; among the men it is $(2+4) \div 11$, or just over $\frac{1}{2}$. So the bisexual/homosexual ratio is quite a bit bigger for the women in Hite's sample than for the men. Both questionnaires were widely distributed in the gay and bisexual communities, so if the ratio really is equal for the two sexes, why would more bisexual women volunteer for Hite's female sample or so few male bisexuals volunteer for her male sample? There may be an answer to this question, but if so, it's difficult for me to figure out.

[22] Fang 1976. Technically, this statement applies to acceptance of bisexual *behavior*, not to acceptance of a bisexual *identity*.

[23] Saghir and Robins 1973; Schäfer 1976, 1977; Bell et al. 1981b, p. 159.

[24] For example, psychiatrist Richard Pillard (my colleague at Boston University Medical School) and I conducted a study that recruited men through advertisements in gay and general-audience newspapers (Pillard and Weinrich 1986). Detailed sex-history interviews

The Transsexualism Puzzle

Some people think that transsexualism is what happens when someone is too gender rigid to admit his or her homosexual impulses. People attracted to their own sex who are flexible in their approaches to life, according to this theory, eventually come out and call themselves homosexual, but others who think that only members of opposite sexes should fall in love with each other notice "homosexual" impulses in themselves and think that what's wrong is not the sex of the person they're attracted to but the sex they themselves are.[25]

This explanation has never satisfied me, for it makes a prediction that turns out to be wrong. As social options for women grow, this theory predicts that we should be seeing relatively less female-to-male (f–m) transsexualism—because fewer women would feel that they are not feminine if they are attracted to women. But in fact, we've seen more f–m transsexualism, not less, as feminist beliefs have become more accepted in society.[26]

Indeed, gender rigidity has changed in transsexuals, as it has in the rest of us. On a recent visit to Los Angeles, for example, I went to a meeting of a support group attended by examples of just about every single one of the gender transpositions. One of the announcements was of an upcoming softball game between the m–f transsexuals and the f–m transsexuals. (Since both preoperatives and postoperatives were welcome on either team, this was to be one match at which sportscasters would certainly need a scorecard.)[27] If Los Angeles transsexuals were really as gender rigid as some people say all transsexuals are, this lighthearted announcement would have been impossible.

---

identified only a handful of men who could be considered neither predominantly homosexual nor heterosexual. Only one of these men seemed clearly to fall into this bisexual category, and that was judging by his report of his fantasy life; he was still a virgin in behavior. We are also finishing a study of women similar to this men's study, with ads placed in similar kinds of newspapers. Although analysis is not complete, it is already easy to identify clear-cut bisexuals among the women in our sample.

[25] This theory is especially popular among some homosexuals. But it is in a way adopted by people who feel that postoperative transsexuals' sexual behavior is acceptable but that of preoperative transsexuals (and that of homosexuals) is not. These people approve of gender nonconformity only in individuals who publicly reinforce (via an operation) the social rule that men should have sex only with women and vice versa.

[26] Please note that this does not necessarily imply that the spread of feminism is the cause of the increased transsexualism.

[27] Please do not take this as a slap at transsexuals. It is, in fact, a slap at sportscasters.

The Transvestism Puzzle

The very existence of transvestites—who are heterosexual[28]—is plenty puzzling to some people, but it's much easier to understand if you think about the nature of male sexuality. Heterosexual men find some women's clothing erotic. They like to see women scantily clad, presumably because it suggests that nudity and sex are on the way. All you need to realize is that transvestites have eroticized women's clothing so much they like having it on themselves. If a man masturbates while cross-dressing, it is almost as if his masculine component—the part of him that is in control of the decision to masturbate—is aroused by his feminine component—the part of him that is wearing the dress. In fact, many if not most transvestites view themselves as men with a feminine side.

In order to solve all these subpuzzles, you need to know quite a bit more about the gender transpositions. I'll come back to them toward the end of the book.

4. THE "WHAT IS BI ABOUT BISEXUALS?" PUZZLE

The amount of bisexuality found in any given survey depends crucially on how we define it. As I explained above, bisexuality is rare or absent among men but not rare among women. Defined in another way, it is not rare in either sex. Why?

Part of the answer has to do with an important scientific controversy. Like a lot of controversies, it hinges on a definition: what "is" a bisexual? And as you may have guessed by now, there are dozens of answers.

The first answer was provided after World War II by—you guessed it—the Kinsey researchers, using what they called the *heterosexuality/homosexuality rating scale* (see fig. 3.3), which was designed to measure sexual responsiveness to one's own sex in comparison to one's responsiveness to the other. Nowadays, this scale is simply called the

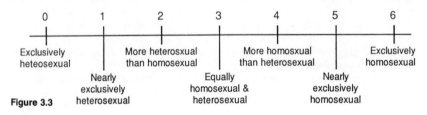

Figure 3.3

| 0 | 1 | 2 | 3 | 4 | 5 | 6 |

Exclusively heteosexual

More heterosxual than homosexual

More homosxual than heterosexual

Exclusively homosexual

Nearly exclusively heterosexual

Equally homosexual & heterosexual

Nearly exclusively homosexual

---

[28] See chapter 2 for the distinction between a (heterosexual) transvestite and a (homosexual) drag queen.

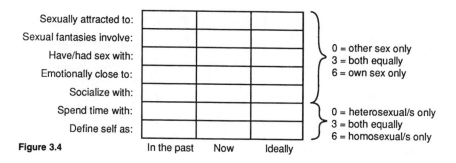

	In the past	Now	Ideally	
Sexually attracted to:				
Sexual fantasies involve:				
Have/had sex with:				
Emotionally close to:				
Socialize with:				
Spend time with:				
Define self as:				

0 = other sex only
3 = both equally
6 = own sex only

0 = heterosexual/s only
3 = both equally
6 = homosexual/s only

Figure 3.4

Kinsey Scale. This scale arranges people according to their sexual orientation along a continuum from entirely heterosexual to entirely homosexual, with every conceivable degree of bisexuality in between. (The numbers from 0 to 6 are just convenient benchmarks.)[29] People were rated on this scale, year by year, by interviewers who had just conducted sex-history interviews with them. Usually a person's sexual desires and/or fantasies were within a point or two of their actual behavior but not always.[30] For this reason, some of the later studies conducted by the Kinsey Institute used the scale to make separate ratings of these separate components.

Well, sexology marches on, and some sexologists have gone even further than Kinsey did. San Diego psychiatrist Fritz Klein, for example, wants to replace the Kinsey Scale with what is now called the *Klein Grid* to describe twenty-one different aspects of one's sexual personality (see fig. 3.4). In each of the twenty-one cells, the person is given a rating from 0 to 6: 0 corresponding to the response "pure" heterosexuals would give and 6 being the response "pure" homosexuals would give.

Examples are obviously called for. Let me describe a fellow who could be found in any modern urban gay ghetto; I'll call him Butch. Butch is nowadays sexually attracted only to men, has fantasies only about men, has sex only with men, tells his most intimate problems only to men, socializes with homosexual men almost all the time, and definitely considers himself homosexual. These patterns are also his

[29] Kinsey himself did not use the terms "homosexual" and "heterosexual" as nouns—only as adjectives (sometimes in the clumsy phrases "the homosexual" and "the heterosexual," used in the same way as "the tall" and "the short"). He did not, as far as I know, use the term "bisexual" at all, a tradition carried on today by some of his co-workers. What most sexologists would call a "bisexual" would have been viewed by Kinsey as a person situated at a particular position along the homosexuality/heterosexuality continuum. Now it is a rough convention to call Kinsey 2s, 3s, and 4s bisexual.

[30] When they were not, it is not entirely clear what rating resulted. Apparently, the most important criterion was clear evidence of a person's *responsiveness*: to what extent did the person sexually respond to (become sexually aroused by) men versus women?

	In the past	Now	Ideally	
Sexually attracted to:	6	6	6	
Sexual fantasies involve:	6	6	6	0 = other sex only
Have/had sex with:	4	6	6	3 = both equally
Emotionally close to:	2	6	6	6 = own sex only
Socialize with:	2	6	6	
Spend time with:	1	6	6	0 = heterosexual/s only
Define self as:	0	6	6	3 = both equally / 6 = homosexual/s only

Figure 3.5

ideal for his future. But in the past, although he was only sexually attracted to men and only fantasized about men, he had sex with both men and women, had a lot of women friends until he moved to the gay ghetto, socialized with lots of heterosexuals and women and for a long time denied he was gay. How Butch's Klein Grid would look is shown in figure 3.5.

Now consider a college woman I'll call Mary.[31] Mary has sex only with women, is usually, but not always, sexually attracted to women, but has sexual fantasies involving a higher proportion of men. It wasn't always that way; in high school she was sexually attracted only to women and had sex only with women, because women were (and are) her closest friends. But in spite of attending an all-women's college, she finds herself nowadays identifying as a bisexual and would like to become equally sexually attracted to both sexes, have sex with both about equally, and enjoy fantasies about the two in equal proportions. Her closest friend now is a man she is starting to spend a lot of time with; she hopes to find more such men in the future but believes she will probably always have more women friends. She socialized with both sexes in high school and hopes to do the same in the future, although now she spends most of her time socializing with heterosexual women, feeling a strong bond among women regardless of their sexual orientation. In high school, she thought of herself as a lesbian, now thinks herself bisexual, and wants to be bisexual in the future. How Mary's Klein Grid would look is shown in figure 3.6.

Are you confused? Don't worry. There are sexologists who believe the Klein Grid goes too far, giving more information than anyone really needs to know. There are other sexologists who believe it doesn't go far enough; they believe the only valid description of a person's sex life is a complete sex history. It's a conflict, really, between the lumpers and the splitters: splitters stress everyone's delightful peculiarities,

[31] Credit where credit is due: It was a store in Provincetown, Massachusetts, called "Butch and Mary's" from which I got the names.

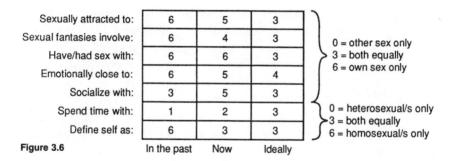

	In the past	Now	Ideally	
Sexually attracted to:	6	5	3	
Sexual fantasies involve:	6	4	3	0 = other sex only
Have/had sex with:	6	6	3	3 = both equally
Emotionally close to:	6	5	4	6 = own sex only
Socialize with:	3	5	3	
Spend time with:	1	2	3	0 = heterosexual/s only
Define self as:	6	3	3	3 = both equally
				6 = homosexual/s only

Figure 3.6

and lumpers stress the similarities that bind people together.

So what is it, then, that is "bi" about bisexuality? Are bisexuals more like homosexuals or like heterosexuals? Or are they halfway in between? The answer, I believe, is very complicated—and it's in chapter 6. Is "bisexuality" even a logically valid category to put people into?[32] For that matter, are "homosexuality" and "heterosexuality" logically valid categories? The answer to that, too, is complicated—and the answer is in chapter 5.

5. THE "PSEUDOLESBIAN PORN" PUZZLE

Heterosexual men can be aroused by pictures of women having sex with other women. Why?

On the face of it, this makes no sense—because as a rule, men and boys are not socialized into being aroused by lesbian stimuli. Let's face it, folks. How many teenaged boys boast about how many lesbians they've deflowered recently? How many parents do you know who slyly let their sons know that it's okay if they have sex with lesbians? How many advertisements have you seen that show lesbians as sex objects in the eyes of heterosexual men? Even if your answer is "more than you think," you won't succeed in showing that many males have been overtly socialized to become aroused by lesbians. I call this the *"pseudo*lesbian porn" puzzle because most of the images heterosexual men see of two women making love are not pictures of lesbians, nor are they photos taken by lesbians. Rather, they are pictures of models posed and photographed by heterosexual men.

Social-science sexologists do explain these facts, but they don't sound very convincing. If I may put words into their mouths, they would argue something like this: socialization leading to the eroticization of

---

[32] After all, there are tall people, short people, and middle-height people, and you can talk about "the tall" and "the short." But can you really talk about "the middles"? And if so, can you really say anything interesting about them other than that they are, well, middling in height?

pseudolesbian porn is indirect. Sex is taboo in our society, so what is secret or shameful is exciting. When boys or young men discover erotica portraying two women, it at first falls under the taboo. They become sexually excited by its forbidden nature and thus eroticize the pictures.

There may be some truth in this argument, but as a general principle it stinks. After all, our society says talking about feces is taboo and is even dimly aware that feces are an erotic turn-on for some people. But far fewer males eroticize feces than eroticize lesbians.[33] How many men would cancel their *Playboy* subscriptions if they came across a photo spread on feces? I don't know, but I'll bet it's a lot. How many men would cancel their *Playboy* subscriptions if they came across a photo spread on lesbians? Very few.[34] No, the "it's taboo" argument doesn't do very well.

There's a sociological variation on this argument. Sociologists explain that society has "scripts" for sexual interactions. When a boy calls a girl for a high school date (and not vice versa), he is following a script he has consciously learned from his culture. These scripts can be very detailed and very subtle and do not always result from overt socialization. (Recall, for example, that I used a script concept when I was explaining the Technique Puzzle earlier in this chapter.) But as far as I know, there are no scripts for heterosexual men enjoying pseudolesbian porn. It is certainly the case, if such scripts exist, that society spends far less effort socializing men into them than it spends on socializing men into other sexual scripts. That means, in turn, that sociologists have to explain why the pseudolesbian porn script is learned with so little attention from society but other scripts fail to be learned even though there is far more overt socialization concerning them. Think, for example, about the script that says that men and women are not supposed to live together and have sex with each other unless they plan to get married (or act as if they were married, as in common-law marriage). In about one decade (the 1960s), college-age women and men went from almost no one living together before marriage[35] to a great many of them doing so—and it was certainly not

---

[33] Please note here that I am not saying that feces and lesbians are alike. Nor do I usually think of feces when I think of lesbians. To the contrary, I'm comparing heterosexual men's *responses* toward the two (and conclude that these responses are different).

[34] And, as I'll explain later on, there is even evidence that some (many?) heterosexual men are *more* aroused by pictures of two naked women than by pictures of a naked woman with a naked man.

[35] The very phrase "living together *before marriage*" is deceptive, for it implies that one only "lives together" if one plans to marry one's roommate/lover. But of course this happens only some of the time. Even with the alleged end of the sexual revolution, I don't see youth moving back to the standards of the 1950s.

as the result of their parents' socializing them into the new pattern. Social scripting theory has lots to offer but not enough to offer here.

I have encountered only two answers to this puzzle I like:

1. Heterosexual men are aroused by way of projecting themselves into the scene depicted in pseudolesbian porn. A picture of a woman having sex with a woman represents not just one but two women, sexually aroused, waiting for a man to fulfill them. The heterosexual man viewing the picture projects himself into it and thinks consciously or unconsciously that he is the man who will make the women become heterosexual.
2. One naked woman is arousing. Two naked women is twice as arousing. Two naked women having sex is more arousing still.

I am happy to report that sexologists have been hard at work solving this puzzle—sometimes even when they didn't know they were working on it. The solution lies in constructing a *general* theory of sexual arousal—which I attempt in chapters 6 and 7. The key to testing the theory is a technique called *penile plethysmography*—which I describe in question 6 (below) and discuss in chapter 8.

6. THE LITTLE-GIRLS/TEENAGED-MALE-BUTTOCKS PUZZLE

Heterosexual men can be aroused (a bit) by looking at pictures of naked little girls or pictures of teenage males' buttocks. Why?

To answer this question, we need the experimental data provided by penile plethysmography. "Penile" is the adjectival form of "penis," and "plethys-" comes from the Greek word meaning "volume" or "balloon." So a penile plethysmograph is a penis-volume measurer; when it's hooked up enclosing a penis, it squiggles out a moment-by-moment record telling the good doctor how much of an erection the man has. I'll let you discover more about this technological marvel in chapter 8; here I just want to single out a couple of findings.

The inventor of the plethysmograph, Kurt Freund, a sexologist at the Clarke Institute of Psychiatry in Toronto, found that the most exciting stimulus he could show an ordinary heterosexual man was—surprise!—a picture of a naked woman. A picture of a naked teenage female was a little less arousing, on average, and one of a naked girl (aged nine to eleven or so) even less. He did find a little bit of arousal, too, to even younger girls (aged eight to ten or so)—more than the landscapes (the so-called control stimulus).[36]

When testing homosexuals, he found a mirror-image pattern of arousal: homosexual men found pictures of naked adult men most arousing, teen males next, older boys third, and younger boys last. But not quite a perfect mirror image; in this case, the average arousal to younger boys was *not* significantly more than to landscapes.[37]

Frankly, I don't know why little girls are more arousing to heterosexual men than little boys are to homosexual men, but I do suspect that it accounts for friction between otherwise well-meaning homosexuals and heterosexuals (see puzzle 9). This finding intrigued Freund enough that he conducted another experiment to check it out.

This experiment Freund conducted on heterosexual men only. Instead of using photos of people naked from head to toe, he used photos of body parts: the head, the chest, the pubic region, the buttocks, and the legs. For each of these 5 categories, he had pictures of the 2 sexes and of 3 different age categories (adult, adolescent, just preadolescent), for a total of 30 ($= 5 \times 2 \times 3$) different kinds of photos. He showed these combinations to the heterosexual men, along with some more landscapes as controls.[38]

Virtually all the pictures of females were arousing to these men, and all but one of the male categories were not. That one category was teenaged males' buttocks. On average, this category aroused these ordinary heterosexual men a bit more than landscapes did. These findings show that the men's penises were capable of some remarkable discriminations. Little girls' buttocks somehow must have looked different from little boys' buttocks, for example, because the first category was more arousing than landscapes and the second category was not. So it's difficult to argue that the teenaged males' buttocks looked too much like teenaged females' buttocks; all the more so because it's in the teen years that the hips widen in girls and stay slim in boys.

There are two things that interest me about these puzzles: the solutions and the consequences. The solutions, I suspect, have to do with our primate heritage, some of which I address in chapter 13. The consequences are some conflicts among us—ranging from when homosexuals and heterosexuals misunderstand each other all the way to

---

[36] There is no evidence for the existence of landscapophiles—people sexually aroused by the viewing of pictures of landscapes. If there were, let me assure you that Freund would have found them by now.

[37] This and other experiments are described in Freund 1974.

[38] This experiment is described in Freund, McKnight, Langevin, and Cibiri 1972.

child abuse and molestation. These questions are addressed in several places in the book, especially chapters 4 and 8.

7. THE EXHIBITIONISM PUZZLE

Fetishistic, repetitive exhibitionism to strangers occurs almost exclusively in heterosexuals. Why?

There's an old joke among sexologists that goes like this:

> When a woman sees a man who is undressing in a window, the man is arrested for exhibitionism. When a man sees a woman who is undressing in a window, it's still the man who gets arrested—this time, for voyeurism!

Mind you, by "exhibitionism" I'm not talking about hogging the stage during the holiday pageant or that time you rented an instant-picture camera to take some hot shots of your spouse. I'm talking about *paraphiliac exhibitionism* which is something much more specific.

A *paraphilia* is (roughly speaking) a particular sexual turn-on in which something not inherently sexual is added to the process of sexual arousal—and then becomes an essential or extremely (and unusually) important component of sexual arousal. For example, a shoe fetishist is only profoundly aroused when a person wears particular kinds of sexy shoes. Sometimes he is only aroused by the shoes and can dispense with the partner. Most paraphilias exist in homosexual and heterosexual versions: for example, there are straight shoe fetishists and there are gay shoe fetishists. Many paraphilias are echoed in the nonparaphiliac population as preferences or partialisms—some people are "partial" for breasts, say, and Chinese men in the foot-binding era supposedly were "partial" for small feet.

A partialism for sexual self-display is common in our own and in many other societies. It becomes a paraphilia when it becomes so much of a turn-on in people that they don't really want to consummate the act with the person being exhibited to. It is paraphiliac exhibitionism, for example, when a man deliberately shows off his genitals to passing females who are strangers. Usually he does this repeatedly—dozens or hundreds of times in a couple of hours.

The women viewing exhibitionists' displays sometimes report them to the police. That's not surprising, because many women worry that if a guy is kooky enough to show off so publicly, he might be kooky enough to go on to something like rape.

But many women don't report exhibitionists to the police. That's also not surprising, because the act of exhibitionism in and of itself, without complications, harms no one, and case histories of paraphiliac exhibitionists show that they typically remain harmless.

Harmless or not, exhibitionism is the most commonly repeated (or *recidivistic*) sex offense. Why? Because the number-one turn-on for these men is showing off. If they're married, they may expose themselves a dozen times during the afternoon (supermarket parking lots seem to be a favorite location); when they have sex with their wives that evening, they turn on by thinking back to earlier in the day. Mind you, exhibiting in front of their wives is no fun—the fantasy always requires a stranger.

All right, guys, now think: you've done the grocery shopping every now and then. When was the last time some *man* caught your eye in the parking lot and then dropped his trousers? Raise your hand now. . . . Anyone?

No, someone just being forward doesn't count; even if you prefer that men approaching you be backward, propositions don't constitute paraphiliac exhibitionism. No, showing off in the locker room doesn't count, either. No, I'm talking about somebody who likes the shocked look of fascination when a stranger—a *male* stranger—sees he's nude.

Until very recently I thought that men like that didn't exist. I now know of one such man, and the Dutch therapist (Dr. Joost Dekker) who told me about him confirmed that he knows of no other similar cases. That is, homosexual exhibitionism practically doesn't exist. Heterosexual exhibitionism certainly does. So, once again, why?

Most theories of exhibitionism aren't much help. They typically trace the problem back to childhood, when the preexhibitionist got his childhood sex play interrupted by Mommy. Although there are some compelling case histories that support this theory, I can't help but wonder (1) what happens if the boy gets interrupted by Daddy instead and (2) why Mommy gets transformed (psychodynamically) into a stranger rather than a wife—or, for that matter, a Mommy.

The best theory—and even it is incomplete—is the "courtship disorder" theory of psychiatrist Kurt Freund.[39] Freund's theory begins by sketching out a script for sexual interaction, then asks what can go wrong with it. The script won't win any awards for originality, but it'll do (at least until we get to chapter 12, which is about courtship). Since there are no known female paraphiliac exhibitionists, the script is presented from the man's point of view.

[39] Freund's theory is shared by his colleague Ron Langevin (see Langevin 1983) and somewhat independently developed by Timothy Perper (see Perper 1985).

- Boy sees girl.
- Boy is attracted to girl.
- Boy and girl meet.
- Boy discovers that girl is attracted to him.
- Boy and girl date, and their attractions deepen.
- Boy makes pass at girl.
- Boy discovers that girl responds.
- Boy becomes sexually excited by prospects.
- Boy and girl remove some clothes.
- Boy is thrilled by his sexual arousal.
- Boy and girl pull curtain on further sexological investigation.

Freund groups exhibitionism with voyeurism and rape. For Freund, all three of these traits are a short-circuiting of the ordinary stages of heterosexual meeting, dating, and mating. The exhibitionist short-circuits directly to undressing himself, the voyeur short-circuits directly to undressing his partner, and the rapist short-circuits directly to coitus.

Now on the face of it this theory doesn't really help solve the puzzle. If you postulate that gay and straight "circuits" are mirror images of each other, then there ought to be significant numbers of homosexual exhibitionists, but there aren't. (Since heterosexuals are more common than homosexuals, we would expect more heterosexual exhibitionists than homosexual ones. But we would still expect a decent percentage of homosexuals to fall into this category.) But if gay and straight are not mirror images, then perhaps the gay path leads away from exhibitionism and the straight one goes closer to it.

This is not an entirely satisfactory answer. But it gets us back to another important question posed in chapter 1: what is sex *for*? In particular, what are homosexuals and heterosexuals *for*? What is the ultimate evolutionary logic of the gender transpositions? And specifically, what might be the ultimate evolutionary logic of sexual display in males and in females? Answering these questions requires understanding some theories of homosexual and heterosexual behavior (explained in chapter 13) and theories of courtship and sexual dimorphism (explained in chapter 12).

8. THE APPROVAL PUZZLE

Surveys show that on average heterosexuals judge male homosexuals more negatively than lesbians. But there's a bias concerning which people disapprove of which kind of homosexual. The bias is that heterosexual men

Percent responding that they would allow a homosexual to join their campus social organization:

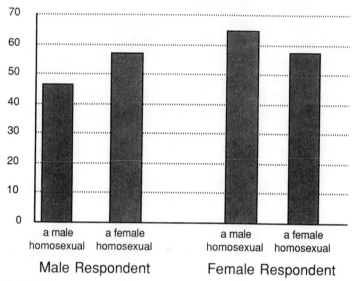

Figure 3.7

tend to disapprove of male homosexuality much more than they do of lesbianism, but heterosexual women tend to disapprove of lesbianism about the same as they do of male homosexuality[40] (see fig. 7).

Part of the answer is *gender empathy*: it's easy for heterosexual men to see why women could be found attractive and for heterosexual women to see how men could be found attractive. So heterosexual men can understand lesbians (woman-lovers) more readily than they can understand homosexual men (man-lovers), and vice versa for heterosexual women.

But this doesn't explain the difference in the size of the effect—why the sex of the homosexual in question makes less difference for heterosexual women than for men. This can be explained if we add onto the gender-empathy hypothesis the additional assumption that lesbianism is (for whatever reason) more widely accepted in general than male homosexuality is. I call this *lesbian sympathy*—it adds points to the approval ratings directed at lesbians in these surveys. The result is that heterosexual women disapprove of the two gay sexes about equally,

---

[40] Or perhaps a little more; see Steffensmeier and Steffensmeier 1974. The Steffensmeiers asked heterosexual students several questions about acceptance of homosexuals; the graphed responses are typical of those for questions eliciting medium rates of acceptance. Needless to say, respondents were far more likely to "allow a homosexual to live in my nation" and less accepting of inviting a homosexual "home for Easter vacation."

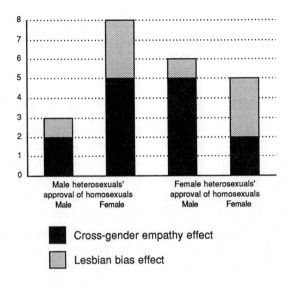

Figure 3.8

but the preference heterosexual men show for gay women over gay men increases (see fig. 3.8).

The dark bars indicate the effect of gender empathy, the light bars the lesbian-sympathy effect. The theoretical result above is similar to the first chart, which reflects data from an actual survey.

Now what happens if we ask about acceptance of homosexuals in particular situations—from situations in which the cross-gender empathy factor is more important to situations in which the lesbian-sympathy factor is? Clearly, as we move from one extreme to the other (fig. 3.9), we'll move from patterns in which the dark bars account for the shape of the graph (only a tiny bit affected by the light bars) to patterns in which the light bars account for the shape of the graph (only slightly affected by the dark bars):

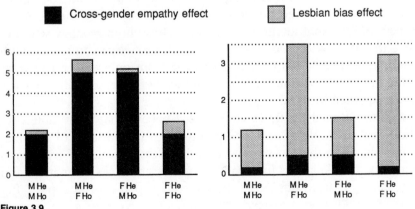

Figure 3.9

All this mathematics is interesting, but what does it mean? We still have the two underlying factors to explain: gender empathy and lesbian sympathy. For my answer, see chapter 5.

9. THE "GRASS IS GREENER ON MY SIDE" PUZZLE

Heterosexual and homosexual are far more alike than different; so why is there such a misunderstanding between the two? This is, of course, a difficult question—and it applies to all the gender transpositions, although it is best studied along the homosexual-heterosexual dimension.

I can hint at some of the answer, which boils down to communication problems in one way or another. For example, as I mentioned earlier, Freund's experiments suggested that some heterosexual men are aroused a bit by the sight of naked little girls. Presumably, many of these men will assume that homosexual men are aroused a bit by the sight of naked little boys. But Freund showed that homosexual men as a rule are not aroused by this. So when accused by heterosexuals of being especially dangerous around small children, homosexual men react not only with the anger of being prejudicially accused but also in ignorance of one of the reasons why they were accused in the first place.

Likewise, research suggests that homosexuals have a strong sense of sexual identity, because they see so clearly how different they are from the majority. It is patently obvious to homosexuals that they are attracted to different things than heterosexuals are, because the icons of heterosexuality are displayed everywhere. But many heterosexuals do not have such a strong sense of sexual identity, presumably because they implicitly think of themselves as "normal" and so do not possess any particular identity in relation to their normality. (After all, if you are not an exhibitionist, do you have a "nonexhibitionist" identity?) If this is so, then heterosexuals may overestimate the extent to which one's sexual identity is a choice. Those homosexuals who believe that their sexual identity is not a choice, when confronted with the opinion that it is a choice, might react not only with anger from being misunderstood but also in ignorance of the reason why they are misunderstood in the first place.

As I mentioned briefly in chapter 2, I believe that the simple psychological principle of *projection* accounts for a great deal of the miscommunication that goes on surrounding sexual issues. If we have a sex taboo that keeps us from talking openly about sexual matters and that keeps us from observing the ways in which other people differ fundamentally from ourselves, then our own experience is the most common way—sometimes the only way—to understand other people. Fill in the gaps with a bit of folklore and you have trouble.

10. THE PAIN-AND-PLEASURE PUZZLE

I've saved the worst and most puzzling puzzle for last. Why is it that things as delightful as sex and love can get intertwined with pain? With things as horrible as serial murder and nonconsensual sado-masochism?

The facial expressions of sexual arousal are easy to confuse with those of discomfort or pain. This is one of the reasons why children supposedly are disturbed if they stumble upon their parents having sexual relations: they confuse people having sex with each other with people hurting each other. But the puzzle is deeper and more disturbing than that. When I read of a serial killer—somebody who kills a series of strangers, often in horrifyingly ritualistic ways—I assume as a matter of course that sex is involved. I am sorry to say that, as far as I know, I have never been wrong in this assumption. Serial killers kill the kind of people they are sexually attracted to: heterosexual killers like Richard Speck kill women or girls; homosexual killers like John Wayne Gacy kill men or boys. The only people who kill more than a couple of people for nonsexual reasons do it for financial reasons: hit men for the Mafia or for the KGB, say. But even in these cases I suspect the killers have to some degree chosen their jobs with their personal tastes in mind.

This puzzle I will lump with another having to do with sado-masochism, or "S & M" (the intentional infliction of pain in order to produce sexual arousal), and bondage and discipline, or "B & D" (the acting out of power, domination, and physical-restraint games in erotic arousal, not necessarily involving pain). The puzzle is Why are there more masochists than sadists? Why are there more people who want to be tied up than who want to tie others up? Why are there more people who want to take orders and be humiliated than those who want to give orders and humiliate?

True, we live in a society that idolizes power. Yes, we live in a country in which the majority of the population worships a God who revealed His love for the human race by suffering a masochistic punishment, the crucifixion. But these facts really don't explain the puzzle.

After all, when it comes to ordinary affairs, there are plenty of people out there ordering and obeying, dominating and being dominated, and the majority seem to enjoy the "top" role to the "bottom." Most business people try to make money rather than lose money. Most people think they would prefer to be the boss rather than the employee. Most people prefer to work toward a pension rather than try to be fired. Most people like to give orders rather than just take them.

One of the things that ordinary people don't like about B & D and S & M when they hear about their existence is what they assume about their balance of power. It comes as a big surprise to most people (well, it did to me!) to find out that the masochists have trouble finding enough sadists to spank them or whip them. It was surprising to find "bottoms" running around looking for a really good "top"—one willing to take control of what would be done ·sexually for an evening.

Because, after all, when it comes to the more commercial aspects of all this, people are capable of making perfectly rational decisions. Call girls—female prostitutes with a regular clientele and no pimp to tell them what to do—are very careful to play only the "top" role with their customers who enjoy sexual power games. They'll tie their customers up but never let themselves be tied, because to allow the latter is too dangerous to their livelihoods, not to mention their lives.

So what's going on here? The answer, I believe, has to do with the way these preferences get set: in childhood. Although S & M, when consensual, has nothing to do with child abuse, my explanation flows most naturally from a discussion of child abuse, which I examine in chapter 10.

Sadomasochism and child abuse are, of course, two extremely sensitive topics. As I mentioned in chapter 2, in the sex taboo the social, political, and scientific are interwoven most tightly. With any sensitive topic it would be nice to be able to discuss each of these three aspects separately—science and the facts first, of course, then society, and then politics, in a logically deductive sequence—but when it comes to sex, that's impossible.

For example, it is my experience that if I talk dispassionately about people who murder for sexual kicks, listeners get *very* nervous unless I mention along the way that I consider such behavior morally wrong. In fact, they seem to get nervous unless I mention *over and over* that I consider it morally wrong. Yet people don't seem to get nervous if murder-mystery writers don't come out against murder or take a position on the death penalty. It's as if people always assume the worst, or worry about whether they ought to assume the worst, when it comes to sexologists. (Sexologists are not the only ones who face this problem, of course.)

The result is that if I keep my scholarly neutrality and don't say anything one way or the other about whether I consider lust murder to be morally wrong, I have to worry about whether I'll be seen as having a hidden agenda in favor of lust murder. Likewise, if I don't mention any political considerations until the end of the book, those opposed to my politics are going to assume the worst about them in the meantime. And frankly, although sexologists can be just as scientifically objective (or unscientifically biased) as any other kind of scientist, some of my best ideas come from my politics or my social views. Likewise, although I pretend that it pains me to admit it, some of my best ideas come from seeing the truth in political or social views I *dis*agree with! So why bother to conceal the truth in these matters?

What's that? Can you believe what I just wrote so innocently? I wrote, *why bother to conceal the truth?* Now that's a stupid question, because the answer is obvious: people always conceal the truth when it comes to **sex.** Oops! I said it: the world's shortest four-letter word. Let's get explicit and talk about the s*x taboo.

4

THE S*X TABOO

It seems ludicrous that after scientists have been seriously searching for extraterrestrial intelligence for a decade, basic research into the physiology of the female vagina on this planet . . . has just begun.

Peter Hoon 1979, p. 22.

But what is it for some people of genuine good will that makes it so difficult to accept our sexuality? I come increasingly to believe that they haven't accepted their own. . . . . If straight people have the decency to be modestly ashamed of their own sexual natures, what right have we to be proud of ours? Marriage is for them not a flaunting but a legalizing of their sexuality. They don't think of children as a celebration of their sexuality, but as its redeeming result. . . . . Everyone is *supposed* to be ashamed.

Jane Rule (January 1985). Straights, come out. *The Body Politic*, p. 16. Also in: *A hot-eyed moderate*, Naiad Press, 1985, p. 118.

Never had the Emperor's clothes been such a success.
"But he hasn't got anything on!" said a little child. "Goodness gracious, do you hear what the little innocent says?" cried the father; and the child's remark was whispered from one to the other. . . .
"Well, but he hasn't got anything on!" the people all shouted at last. And the Emperor felt most uncomfortable, for it seemed to him that the people were right. But somehow he thought to himself: "I must go through with it now, procession and all." And he drew himself up still more proudly, while his chamberlains walked after him carrying the train that wasn't there.

Hans Christian Andersen, "The Emperor's New Clothes."
R.P. Keigwin, transl. *The Little Mermaid and Other Fairy Tales.*
Flensted, Odense (Denmark), 1960.

One has opinions in England, but they are formed in private and clung to in public despite everything, despite their often being quite wrong. There is real defensiveness and insecurity, a Victorian fear of revealing so much as a genital of an idea, the nipple of a notion or the

sex of a syllogism. Where sexual exhibitionism and the discussion of positions and emissions is fashionable, indeed orthodox, thinking and argument are avoided.

> Hanif Kureishi (1986). *"My beautiful laundrette"* and *"The rainbow sign."* p. 33. Faber and Faber, London/Boston.

The s*x taboo is the notion that s*x and love are so important that we must pretend that they are unimportant and so emotionally loaded that they are dangerous to think about. It is a widespread belief in Western culture, and in the age of birth control it is a self-contradiction. Like all self-contradictions, it will eventually fall of its own weight. But that doesn't mean we can afford to wait until it does, because in the meantime it's doing a lot of damage.

When I see the s*x taboo in action, I find myself wanting to react in various ways. The disciplinarian in me wants to snap, "Shut up," the parent in me wants to say, "Grow up," the teenager in me wants to throw up, and the pragmatist in me wants to give up.[1] The author in me wants to write it up, of course, and it is the author that won—at least for the duration of this chapter. But of course simple ridicule won't untie the tongue-tied, nor will simple education; remember that Uncle Jim got pretty tongue-tied back in chapter 1.

You may wonder why I'm putting an asterisk into a poor, defenseless little three-letter word. Younger readers may be forgiven for asking this question, because the custom of s*xual asteriskizing comes from before their time.[2] But it's a perfect example of the pointlessness of the s*x taboo itself. After all, writing the word as "s*x" fools only the retarded and the least inquisitive of the very young.[3] So why bother? Short of sheer perversity—and when it comes to the s*x taboo, we do want to avoid perversity—the only answer is that it has a latent function: a nod in the direction of the taboo, a way to say, "This is the word you shouldn't say."

Or is that the only reason? Let's see.

Much of this chapter reflects issues I first heard raised by John Money.

[1] Of course, anyone who really believes Americans grow up must have been watching too much of "The Love Boat." How can we expect people to learn a decently s*x-positive attitude if we can't even mass-market a realistic plot?

[2] It was also before mine, but scholars are expected to know history.

[3] And frankly, it only fools some of those. There are only twenty-six logical possibilities for the asterisk, and less than a moment's thought will narrow them down to the six vowels, at which point a dictionary can be consulted to rule out misspellings, saxophones, the numeral, and east-of-the-Mississippi baseball teams.

MUMMY AND JOHNNY

I know of no better illustration of the s*x taboo than the following quotation from an actual conversation between a mother and her little boy:

> The mother saw the boy rubbing his penis. She said: "Johnny, what are you doing?"
> "Nothing, Mummy."
> "Well, stop it, then."
> "O.K.," and he stopped.[4]

Now this conversation is extraordinary from the point of view of sociology, psychology, or indeed any theory that takes human language to be about the overt communication of plainly stated information. Let's analyze this conversation in excruciating detail.

Mummy sees Johnny doing something she doesn't want him to do (in this case, rubbing his penis)—or worse yet (and more precisely), rubbing his penis in her presence. Her desire to get him to stop is okay, I suppose; we don't want Johnny picking his nose in public, either, now do we?

But if we see Johnny picking his nose in public, we tell him, out loud and directly, "Johnny, don't pick your nose in public; that's disgusting." Chances are he will learn this custom about our culture because we told him about it literally: "in so many words." Is this what Mummy did in this case? Did Mummy tell her son, "Johnny, don't rub your penis in front of me; people don't do that in public"?

Of course not; when it comes to s*x, the s*x taboo keeps us from doing what comes naturally. Mummy's first reaction is to ask Johnny what he's doing. This is a question that she already knows the answer to, so logically it makes no sense at all.

Now think of Johnny. Johnny has been seen doing something his mother won't name. Does he reply to Mummy's nonquestion with a question? Does he ask, for example, "Stop doing what, Mummy?"

Of course not; he replies to Mummy's nonquestion with a nonanswer: he says he's doing nothing even though he knows he's doing something—although he might not yet know what to call it. (He is about to learn that he's not supposed to call it anything at all.) And it will be years before he learns what the polite word for this behavior is.

[4] Sears, Maccoby, and Levin 1957, p. 190.

So now Johnny has been boxed into an untruth: he said he's not doing anything, but in fact he's been rubbing his penis. Does Mummy next tell Johnny to tell the truth next time? To say, in response to a similar question, "I'm rubbing my penis, Mummy"? Does Mummy confront Johnny and say something like, "But Johnny—I just saw you playing with your penis!" No, Mummy breezes right past Johnny's falsehood and tells him to stop doing "it"—even beginning her sentence with the word "Well," as if to suggest that her sentence logically followed from his.

Now it's Johnny's turn to doublespeak. He has denied doing anything, then was told to stop doing it. "Okay," he says, to report that he's gotten the message, which he then demonstrates by stopping the rubbing.

To put it mildly, the overt communication of plainly stated information is not what's going on here. Mummy is telling Johnny what he is doing is unacceptable and *literally unspeakable.* At the same time, Johnny is learning how people talk about what it is he shouldn't do—without even talking about it. Just think of the problems Johnny would face if someone at his day-care center came along and rubbed his penis for him; it should not be surprising that Johnny might find such an incident indescribable and unspeakable, too.

The people who originally reported the Mummy and Johnny incident, psychologists Robert Sears, Eleanor Maccoby, and Harry Levin, had their own suggestion about how to handle the Johnnies of the world—although they made it indirectly. Theirs was a study of child-rearing practices in the United States (published in 1957, it's remarkably current thirty years later), and they simply noted that *no* family in their study gave their Johnny an *emotional* explanation of his s*xual responses—not even the families that named the genitalia correctly. Not one of them said, in response to a question, "Because you're feeling s*xy, that's why"—or anything remotely related to emotions instead of plain facts. The authors point out that Johnny has his anger, his joy, and his jealousy pointed out to him from time to time—but why not his s*xy feelings?

This kind of incident is not the way reinforcement is illustrated in freshman psychology classes. Instead, frosh put up with examples of little girls being approved for playing with dolls and little boys encouraged to play with trucks. The Mummy/Johnny kind of example is avoided not only because it's s*xual but probably also because it's counterintuitive and a bit disturbing. That's too bad, because the Mummy/Johnny interaction is so much more interesting.

Please note that I am not implying that this example is "biological" or is an embarrassment to socialization theory.[5] (*Socialization theory* is the theory that people do what they are *socialized* to do—explicitly through instruction in so many words or implicitly through subtle variations of speech or body language, or sometimes in even more subtle ways.) Since I was first trained as an evolutionary biologist and use biology often, I am sometimes interpreted as being anti-social-science, or biologically deterministic. This can even happen when I describe a theory that is environmentalistic; it's as if people stereotype me so firmly as a biologist that nothing I say with a more social-science flavor registers. Worse, it sometimes happens when I'm criticizing socialization theory on grounds having nothing to do with biology.

So let me make it crystal clear: Mummy is socializing Johnny, all right, and socializing him in ways that social scientists need not resort to biology to explain. But socialization theory too often suggests simplistically that the socializee is *passively* socialized by the socializer—Johnny by Mummy in this case. This is clearly not happening with Johnny; if he wants to avoid going bonkers with a Mummy like this one, he must *actively* work to figure out the complicated mixed message Mummy is sending him. Most kids accomplish this amazingly well, because they have Mummies exactly like this one. I wish introductory textbooks would give messy but real cases like this one—Kafkaesque though they may be. These Alice in Socialization Land examples could make psychology more interesting and less tautological than it usually seems in those texts. We would also learn that being socialized is an active, strategic process that requires the cooperation of the person being socialized in order to take place.

And that is a conclusion with important consequences. Let's take a look at what happens when the recipients of our gift of information do *not* have the chance to decide whether to cooperate in the decision about what we tell them.

"NASA BANS SEX FROM OUTER SPACE"

That was the headline in *Science* magazine a few years ago.[6] I read it back when I was an impressionable young Ph.D., and it brought back fond memories of when I had been an impressionable young graduate student. During both periods, the National Aeronautics and Space Administration (NASA) had plans to send some "smut" off into the cosmos, and people were complaining.

[5]It may be an embarrassment to the way socialization theory is *taught*, but it is not an embarrassment to socialization theory itself.
[6]Wade 1977.

The first fracas was about a plaque on the *Pioneer* spacecraft.[7] Cornell astronomer Carl Sagan and his wife had designed the plaque back in the early 1970's. It depicted a naked man and woman, to show the aliens what we looked like in case they had managed to miss the reruns of "The Love Boat" we'd been sending heavenward in the meantime. I remembered a cartoon showing some residents of Jupiter wearing three-piece Brooks Brothers suits looking it over. "Gosh, earthlings look exactly like us," the caption read, "except they don't wear any clothes!"

In short, the Sagans had gotten away with disseminating some cosmic s*x education, and as it happened, someone else at Cornell was trying to get away with it again in the late 1970s. Hence, the article. When it came time to put something cultural onto the *Voyager* spacecraft (*Pioneer*'s successor), NASA chose the Sagans' collaborator, Frank Drake, to coordinate the effort.[8] Drake put together a creditable package—*Science* called it "curiously moving"—that included pictures of cultural artifacts from all over the globe, ready for encoding and engraving onto a copper phonograph record. As a biologist, I was proud to read that these sky gazers decided advanced civilizations ought to know that human beings are a s*xually reproducing species.[9]

To this end, Drake and his committee planned to include a drawing of human genitalia and a photograph of a naked heterosexual couple—among the thousands of other illustrations already scheduled for the copper disk. To make the picture as unerotic as possible—I kid you not—they planned to use a woman model who was slightly pregnant. They also pondered whether to use models who were conventionally attractive—whatever that is—or "just dumpy, average human beings."

Alas, this overt concession to anti-erotic tastes was a tactical error. It gave NASA a target (targets are part of NASA's job), and NASA seemed afraid that someone who didn't like the illustrations would get hold of them and send copies to all the newspapers in protest. Well, you can't have a protest without explaining what it is you're protesting about, and so I presume some of the newspapers would have to show what all the fuss was about. NASA perhaps would have

[7] This particular Pioneer mission was the first destined to leave the solar system and fly off into deep space; previous ones remain orbiting the sun.

[8] In fact, Drake had helped the Sagans out with the Pioneer plaque.

[9] Sexual reproduction is related to species variability, and variation is the raw material of evolution, and evolution is one of the reasons why someone like you exists to read words like these. Although the theorists haven't gotten all the details worked out, most biologists are betting that the variety created by sexual reproduction was required for the evolution of higher forms of life.

been willing to keep its smut limited to the aliens, but the protesters, by their actions if not their words, would effectively insist that the aliens be excluded and give everyone else a look. This would neatly sabotage their supposed goal of making explicitly s*xual pictures as unavailable as possible. Sounds just as crazy as Johnny and Mummy to me.

A NASA public relations person told *Science*, "There are some who believe that naked pregnant women are extremely erotic"; when the reporter pointed out that the pictures would be seen, if ever, by aliens unfamiliar with earth eroticism, he replied that the message "was going to become the property of NASA and would be reflecting on NASA and the federal government."[10] Indeed, it would reflect on NASA and the federal government, and very well, but apparently NASA was ashamed when it should have been proud. So the pictures were canned.

By the way, NASA insisted, at the last moment, that Drake add something else to the recording: "the names of all the congressmen on the House and Senate space science committees." From ashamed to shameless in one short step!

And so it came to pass that when the aliens finally did recover the spacecraft and played back the disk, they said, bewildered, "Gosh, earthlings act exactly like us—except they don't have any s*x!"

Well, now, wait a moment; I seem to be overlooking the theory that it is s*xual repression itself that enables a society to create great culture. If that Victorian notion is true in outer space, too, then consider the possibility that the aliens capturing the *Voyager* will be just as erotophobic as we are. Maybe even more so. Maybe NASA was right!

An insane fantasy? Not at all. Stranger things have happened in the name of the s*x taboo. Let me tell you some more.

TWO ORIFICES

I know of two dark, wet, delightful, and fleshy orifices that are abused in the course of some of the most disgusting s*x crimes known to humankind. There are doctors whose solemn duty it is to know everything there is to know about these orifices. They probe every corner and take every measurement seeking to relieve human misery. Into them they insert instruments, wires, light sources, and practically everything but the kitchen sink in order to figure out how the blood

---

[10] *Science* gave no explanation of this puzzling non sequitur, with the implication that none had been given. And so there we are with a "Mummy and Johnny" again.

vessels work, where the secretions come from, how to clear up infections—all that good physiological stuff.

You can probably guess the two orifices I'm talking about—one of them has flaps of skin on the outside called "lips"; the other has flaps of skin on the outside called "labia."[11] When the doctors in question are called "dentists" and trained at dental schools, no one questions the doctors' morals or mutters about the size of their schools' endowments. But when the doctors in question are called "plethysmographers" and the plethysmographers are trained at graduate schools, critics start questioning the graduate schools' morals and the doctors' endowments.[12]

This impulse is utterly unmerited. It has nothing to do with the relative merits of the two orifices; it merely has to do with the existence of a taboo. Indeed, there but for the grace of God go dentists.

If you made it your business to ridicule saliva research—let's say you give out the Golden Dribble Award—a little ingenuity could get you a lot of press. You could make invidious comparisons with Pavlov's dogs, pointing out how those inhuman saliva experiments treat human beings like animals,[13] what with all those electrodes and wires and computers hooked into some poor volunteer with his mouth clamped open. Or you could say that saliva is a substance best left in the mouth—where it belongs, after all—and should not be openly described in medical textbooks where an impressionable child might run across a description. Children drool, yes, but why throw information at them about carbohydrate breakdown that they can't understand?

The problem is that your objections wouldn't get very far after you were òn the Phil Donahue show opposite a patient who was unable to salivate. And you might not feel very good after you talked to kids whose parents beat them up every time they drooled on the carpet. A society that made salivation such a big taboo would itself be plagued, I suspect, by eating disorders. Some of these disorders—not all—would arise because society had raised its kids to be uptight about salivation. But good luck trying to convince people of that! You'd have Johnny Carson and Ed McMahon dissolving into fits of giggles at the very mention of a juicy steak—just as they do now when radio s*xologist Dr. Ruth Westheimer starts talking about s*xual intercourse.

---

[11] Which, as you classics majors know, is the Latin word for lips.

[12] Plethysmography is the physiological measurement of sexual arousal. See chapter 8.

[13] Here you might even get some support from the more extreme animal-rights proponents, who would complain that these experiments treated animals like . . . well, animals. Not even a dog should be treated like a dog, right?

IT'S OK TO SAY NO

The s*x taboo has strange effects even in some of the areas where those effects are very destructive. S*xual child molestation is a terrifying crime that strikes fear into the heart of everyone who cares for children. And rightly so, because there are people out there who want to do unbelievably atrocious things to kids. It is, of course, impossible to train children to be able to recognize these situations perfectly; after all, we can't even train professionals to do so. Nor can we explain to kids why child molesters want to have s*x with them, because we don't really understand why ourselves.

But efforts to teach kids how to say "no" to a s*xual advance are crippled by the s*x taboo. It is deeply ironic and dangerous that a movement trying to reduce children's ignorance of the dangers of a s*xual approach can itself be complicit with keeping children ignorant of s*xual matters in general. How can we teach kids to avoid s*x in certain situations without telling them what s*x is all about?

It's OK to Say No is a valiant attempt to do exactly this. It does a better job than any other attempt I know that uses its strategy—and yet it fails. *It's OK to Say No* is a coloring book designed for parents to give and read to their children. Although the book can help prevent kids from nons*xual dangers like simple kidnapping, most of it is directed at avoiding s*xual molestation. But children reading the book will get no help at all in understanding why the bad people mentioned in the book would want to do these bad things. For example, without being told why, kids read that people "shouldn't touch your private parts"—and then learn a definition:

Private parts is the area that is covered by your bathing suit.

I have a lot of trouble with this definition.[14] It's illustrated by a drawing of a little girl in a one-piece bathing suit that covers a lot of the girl's body that it's perfectly okay to touch. The suit goes over the girl's shoulders, for example, and completely covers her midriff. (On a preceding page a fully clothed boy standing on a street corner is shown being touched on his shoulder by a bizarrely grinning man to illustrate the phrase "They shouldn't touch your private parts.") Moreover, the words defining "private parts" are adjacent to an arrow presumably pointing to the private area; it points, in fact, to some vague spot in the middle of the girl's back, or (arguably) just above the top of her buttocks.

---

[14] Beginning, of course, with its grammar; the error is in the original.

The authors are aware of this imprecision; in a short introduction, parents are told to make sure their children "know what 'private parts' means. Many families use different terms and you should identify this page of the book with the terms your child is most familiar with." Although this is true as far as it goes, I fear it is an evasion of a far more important fact: that people like Mummy and Johnny don't have any terms they use regularly at all.

How can you expect children to understand why they should say no if you don't tell them what it is the bathing suit is covering up? And even if you belong to one of the families in which children do know those words, what if they have no idea what those private parts are used *for*? It's like telling kids not to play with matches but not telling them that matches can start fires or that fires can burn down houses.

S*x is spectacular—sometimes spectacularly fun and sometimes spectacularly dangerous. So is fire. Young children cannot possibly understand all the ramifications of love and s*x. Neither can they understand phosphorus, which causes matches to catch fire, but that doesn't stop their parents from telling them about the dangers of playing with matches. Because children are told more or less what matches are used for, they'll have some common sense about what to do if tempted to play with them even if they don't understand physics or how to use kindling and a bellows to get a fire going. In our society, however, they are often not told what s*x organs are used for, so they lack common sense about what to do if tempted to play with the fire down below. If girls and boys are taught, more or less, what penises and vaginas will be used for later in life, they'll have at least some common sense about what to do when a grown-up approaches them s*xually—just as they do when someone suggests they play with matches. Of course, children don't always heed advice not to play with matches, and they probably won't always heed advice not to let strangers touch them s*xually. Until we turn children into robots, this will always be true—but this doesn't invalidate my argument.

Adults are fascinated with s*x a lot. Kids will be fascinated with s*x, too—probably not as much as adults are, but fascinated they will be, sooner or later, and certainly sooner than you think. If grown-ups go around pretending that s*x is *un*spectacular, sooner or later some children are going to call their bluff—just as the little innocent did with the Emperor's new clothes. It would be better if those kids didn't call the bluff by responding to a lust murderer.

By being so closed about s*x, society not only plays into the hands of those who want to exploit children s*xually, it also increases the likelihood of accidental inflammation. A little girl squirming around in the lap of the wrong brother-in-law or great-uncle may be playing with matches, s*xually speaking. If she doesn't know what effect her squirms are having on such men, she has been deprived of one more way to help prevent any molestation that may follow. This is not to imply that she is responsible for arousing him; it's just to say that it might help her to understand how her behavior influences others. She doesn't know what a penis is, and she doesn't know what an erection is, and she doesn't know what erections are used for. And she certainly doesn't know that scientists have shown that ordinary heterosexual nonpedophilic men can be s*xually aroused by little girls like her.[15]

It disturbs me deeply that the s*x taboo keeps her from learning these vitally important facts. Of course, the younger she is, the more difficult it will be for her to understand them. But who ever said you only tell her about playing with matches once in her life? Who ever said you shouldn't discuss fire in front of children until they're old enough to understand all the issues involved in arbitrating a fireman's strike?

A five-part television program,[16] widely praised for its sensitivity and effectiveness in dealing with child s*xual abuse, nevertheless couldn't avoid the contradiction inherent in the s*x taboo. One critic, while praising the show generally, pointed out that the show only addressed the case in which the child was forced or tricked into having s*x. Said the critic, "The possibility that a child might willingly enter into and enjoy a sexual relationship with someone is never explored, or even denied. It appears to have been deliberately ignored." In fact, kids themselves have been known to see through this one-sidedness.

> Midway through the show, an obvious question popped out of the mouth of a curious boy [during a filmed classroom session].
> "But what if you like it?"
> She [a rape counselor] didn't give him an answer. She said most people don't like it when they are tricked or forced into something.

Goodness gracious, did you hear what the little innocent said? This little fellow homed right in on the s*x taboo—and he didn't even know

[15] If you don't either, then see chapter 8 or the brief account in chapter 3.

[16] Produced by WTTW-TV in Chicago for PBS. The information about the program, and quotations from it, are taken from a description printed in the Canadian gay newspaper *The Body Politic*, January 1985, pp. 29–30.

it. If society really were structured the way it is in Hans Christian Andersen's fairy tale, this little boy would have been rewarded for his honesty—but he wasn't. And frankly, Hans's little boy might not have been either. Some parents, after all, would have taken the little brat home and washed out his mouth with soap. How dare he embarrass his family in front of the Emperor?

Consider now the following press release:

FOR IMMEDIATE RELEASE

New York—The Kid's Television Edventure, Inc., announced that it has begun production of a new children's program, "The Baby Boom," for release through the Public Broadcasting System beginning in fall 1987.

" 'The Baby Boom' is KTE's first foray into sex education," said Susan Larkin Marconi, executive director of Edventure. "We're extremely excited by the prospects." Pointing out that several studies have shown that children up through the high school years receive inadequate information about human sexuality, Marconi and TBB's producer, Marla Williams, said that "The Baby Boom" will use the techniques so successful on competing PBS programs like "Sesame Street" and "The Electric Company."

"Research over the past ten years has shown beyond any reasonable doubt that in sex education—as in reading—children do not need an organized, sequential method in order to learn," said KTE's educational consultant, Burton Riley. "On 'Sesame Street' children hear the alphabet before they know what letters are; on 'The Electric Company' kids deal with one reading skill one day, another the next, in an order entirely different from what would be used in a traditional setting like a school. We know that the nonsequential method is the way children actually learn language, social skills, and a huge number of the most important things in life. Children are not confused by this; only adults are."

"After all," joked Marconi, "it's not as if they learn about sex in an orderly way on the street corner! And most studies show that that's exactly where they get most of their information today."

FOR MORE INFORMATION CONTACT: The Kid's Television Edventure, 100 Lincoln Plaza, New York, NY, or call (212)555-3456.

Now the first thing I have to say about this press release is that it is entirely fictitious. A 100 percent fake. I made it up—every word.

But be honest, now: as you read it and realized that every word made sense, didn't it strike a little terror into your heart? Did images of Big Bird talking about condoms flash through your head? Of Bert and Ernie holding hands? Of Oscar complaining that he never seems to be able to get a date?

If so, welcome to the oh-so-advanced Western world.

THE MYSTERY OF THE MUTILATION OF THE VATICAN HERMS

I had learned what herms are just a couple of weeks before I visited the Vatican Museum. They sounded fascinating. It turned out that the Vatican owned lots of herms, and so I was eager to see them. But much to my dismay, those on exhibit had been severely damaged. None were displayed in a state even remotely resembling the proudly erect one in which they had stood, centuries ago, guarding the homes of the best families in Athens. Stranger still, all the herms in the museum had suffered exactly the same damage. And even more dismaying, there was not the slightest indication that the Vatican regretted the mutilation their statues had undergone.

If you know what herms are, you know why. The Vatican knows why, too, so let's let everyone else in on the secret. A *herm* is a particular kind of Greek statue. It consists of a plain column of marble with two adornments: a head of the god Hermes at the top of the column (hence, the name) and a set of erect male genitals sticking out the front of the column about halfway up (hence, the problem). Were you wondering? It was the genitals that were missing from every single one of the museum's herms I saw.

When the ravages of time happen to sever a herm between the head and the genitals, I'm downright generous. I'll let museum curators remount the head on a plain base, even at some cost to s*x education. After all, *Venus de Milo* is charming just the way she is, and her arms were presumably quite unpornographic. But when the column of a herm is clearly unbroken, when the educated eye finds the spot where the genital portion had been attached, when there is a scar there (sanded smooth and then partially covered by the sticker keying the work to its listing in the catalog), and when the catalog identifies the work as a "bust of Hermes"—well, something is amiss.

I call it the Great Herm Castration Project, because I like to imagine that someone in the Vatican, long ago, specifically ordered that these "pornographic" statues be made proper for the public to see. I have no proof of this, of course, and I doubt that the Vatican's records indicate the precise state in which they received these statues. The Vatican's collection started life as the private collection of various popes, who presumably obtained these objects in various states of disrepair. Although heaven only knows what the various barbarians and middlemen did to the herms before the popes acquired them, I still suspect that not all the herms arrived with genital scars neatly sanded down to flatness.

The resultant des*xed statues constitute, fundamentally, a lie. It was one lie to alter the appearance of a statue in such a way as to obliterate what (to modern eyes) is an extremely interesting feature—although, as I indicate above, I do not know who did the obliteration. It is another lie to describe the result merely as a "bust of Hermes."

After all, how would the Vatican feel about a thirty-third-century religious group that acquired thousands of the relics of second-millennium Christianity and put them on public display with some crucial aspect obliterated? Suppose, say, that this group believed that resurrection is impossible—and downright blasphemous—yet it possessed hundreds of paintings portraying the days between Jesus' resurrection and ascent into heaven. A painting in which Jesus was surrounded by disciples and friends, let us say, will have been retouched to remove Jesus from the picture. Then the painting would be hung in a museum, and the catalog would identify it as "a portrait of Jesus' friends after his death."

That would be a lie. If someone other than the thirty-third-century religious group did the obliteration, it would reduce the size of the lie, but as long as people in charge of the relics knew what the truth was, they would share in the lie. And a lie it would be if the Shroud of Turin were to be displayed, after suitable alteration, then described as "a piece of cloth of mystical significance to second-millennium Christians." The truth represented by the herms, then, must be an extremely threatening one.

Finally, the lie is extreme, in a disturbing and pathological way. In order to explain this, I'll have to make a digression about fig leaves.

Fig Leaves

There are dozens, if not hundreds, of nude statues at the Vatican Museum. Many (not all) have had their genitalia covered by fig leaves—fig leaves "invented," according to Columbia University art historian James Saslow, in the mid-1500's. Supposedly, the fig leaf's function is to conceal the indelicate parts of the body and keep one's thoughts from wandering to them. But the plaster used to cover up the indelicate parts has become discolored, so that it no longer matches the surrounding stone. And so exactly the opposite effect is produced:

everyone's gaze is drawn to precisely the part of the anatomy they are supposed to look away from. Accordingly, the fig leaves function—whether intended to or not—as a lesson in the s*x taboo. They say, in effect, "Look down here: this is the part of the body you cover up."

Actually, the precise form of a fig leaf depends on whether it was installed as original equipment by the sculptor or as an option at extra cost by the owner. The fig leaves on display in the Vatican are usually of the latter variety[17] and as a result can increase the size of the problem. In Italy, an original-equipment fig leaf on a male statue generally replaces the penis; if you screw up the courage to look behind it, you'll usually see the scrotum represented accurately. The optional/additional fig leaves owned by the Vatican, however, do not replace; they cover up and enclose. That means the plaster bulges out in front and the leaf curves around underneath; the tip of the leaf ends at the center of the perineum.[18]

Now imagine trying to put a fig leaf onto a herm. Erections on real people have an insistence of their own impossible for owners and viewers to ignore. The erection of a herm has its own aesthetic insistence; the result is that fig-leaf installers cannot go about their business as usual. A herm's fig leaf would have to be enormous and obviously misshapen. The only alternative seems to be the hacksaw and sandpaper.

The Pathology

And so the marble clean-up went from the passably discreet to the actively destructive. It is for that reason that it is disturbing and pathological. Those who think that uncovered female breasts on statues are unseemly have several options open to them. If they want to cover up the breasts, people might titter—that's all. But what if they wanted to cut off the breasts and sand down the scars? *Those* people would get arrested. If penises are different, please explain why.

The tragedy in all this is that herms are spectacularly interesting items. Herms were important religious objects and were taken deadly seriously by their owners. They appear on much of the other artistic work from ancient Greece (the vase paintings, for example). A story about the famous Greek politician Alcibiades shows just how seriously Greeks took their herms.

One morning the citizens of Athens awoke to find that someone

[17]In this case, it was the Church itself that installed them, according to Saslow.

[18]The perineum is that netherland of skin between the legs, behind or aside the external genitalia.

had gone around the city the night before and mutilated its herms.[19] Alcibiades and his crowd were suspected, especially after one of their number (named Andocides) confessed to being a party to the crimes (which had also included some profane parodies of religious rites). Citizens believed that Athenian democracy itself was in danger as a result of these crimes, and the confessor felt it wise to banish himself from Athens. Alcibiades was recalled from a military campaign to face his trial but escaped and fled. The *Oxford Classical Dictionary* rates him as "outstandingly able as a politician and later as a military leader, but . . . [he] aroused the distrust of the Athenians, who twice discarded him when his leadership might have been a decisive factor." I doubt the Athenians ever forgot what he did to the herms any more than the Vatican will ever forget what that fellow with the hammer did to the *Pietà*.

So what else is new? What would I expect the Vatican to do with their embarrassing statues—use them for s*x-education classes? Everyone knows that some churches are, or have been markedly erotophobic. The castrations themselves are in the past. Why keep harping on them?

Well, of course, not everything is a fait accompli; the fig leaves, at least, can be taken off as soon as the museum orders them taken off. An optional/additional fig leaf was removed a couple of decades ago from Michelangelo's *David,* for example.

More to the point, although it is boring to harp on an evil that is widely known, it is important to be reminded of the evil every now and then. For example, Communist oppression in Poland is real and continuing, and we Westerners get bored worrying about it every day, since we do not experience it every day. But it is not boring to Poles, and it is healthy for the rest of us to be reminded of it from time to time, to freshen our outrage.

Most important of all, however, the mutilation of the herms is tragic because there were always decent alternatives for a museum befuddled by the conflict between its morals and its collection. If the Vatican couldn't come to grips with this aspect of Greek religion and s*xuality, they could have sold or given away their herms, or at the very least kept them in some back room somewhere.[20] But this the

---

[19]The story doesn't say just how the herms were mutilated, but I think we can presume that the offenders saved some curators, censors, or vandals some subsequent work.

[20]Nowadays, for example, the Kinsey Institute would happily accept anything like this coming their way and even ensure that the prurient be kept at a decent distance. Although the institute has only been around for a couple of decades, there are doubtless many secular museums, universities, and collectors that would have welcomed such gifts even before then.

museum did not do; instead, they put them on display and lied.

Of course, many other museums "lied," too. According to a conversation I had with Columbia University art historian Beth Cohen, in the Victorian era genitals from male statues were actually cut off many of the statues in museums across Europe. At some later point, she said, the British Museum found some severed parts and restored them to their rightful owners. (After all, in a museum things are rarely actually thrown away.) Then she led me to a book that has even more fascinating information.

Taste and the Antique: The Lure of Classical Sculpture, 1500–1900, by Francis Haskell and Nicholas Penny (Yale University Press, 1981), catalogs the history of the statues in Europe thought to be masterpieces in the sixteenth through nineteenth centuries. According to this book, the tastemaking began with François I, king of France in the first half of the 1500s, whose court artist, Primaticcio, began making plaster casts of the ancient world's surviving master statues. Alas, the statues got a bad reputation from the start, for François "enjoyed exploiting the titillating effects of the nudity of the statues on the ladies of his court"—the exact nature of the titillation, of course, left to our imagination.

Soon antique statuary was all the rage, and the Vatican was but one of many states vying for possession of each new discovery. This all changed with the election as pope, in 1566, of an "emaciated Dominican friar" named Pius V. According to Haskell and Penny, the reverence shown to the ancient statues was far too reverent for Pius's comfort—they were of pagan origin, of course, and idealization can too easily be converted into idolization. And so Pius began dispersing the collection. Art-lovers beseeched him to keep the best ones, however, and "despite a campaign of unprecedented violence against courtesans and sodomites," he consented—but closed the famous Belvedere statuary courtyard to the public. It was only after his death, in 1572, that others could be assured that the very best statues had not been disposed of.

The erotic questions raised by these and other nude statues continued to bedevil the following centuries. A "brazen" fig leaf was attached to the so-called Farnese Hercules by 1802, supposedly because the statue's " 'large, brawny limbs' were disconcerting many ladies." Casts were made for museums in the New World in the early 1800s, and they, too, aroused heated passions of the antisexual variety. Statues of Venus (naked, of course; she was the goddess of erotic love) on display in New York and Philadelphia were "indecently disfigured" near the beginning of the 1800s; railings were set up around the ones in New York in 1818. In Philadelphia, one female commentator reported that men and women were not supposed to view the nude statues in mixed company. And by 1875 a nude *Discobolus* had been "relegated . . . to a lumber room in the Museum of Natural History in Montreal."

The only relief from this seemingly unremitting erotophobia, as far as I could find, was the reaction to the Louvre's *Hermaphrodite*. True, sometimes it was reproduced without its penis, but one comment from Lady Townshend makes up for it all. She said that this statue depicted "the only happy couple she ever saw"!

In short, not only the Vatican but also many other museums had to face quite strong erotophobic responses to their collections over the centuries, and although I wish they had had more backbone in dealing with them, realistically speaking they may be excused. On the other hand, I consider *modern* fig-leafing and herm-castrating practices inexcusable.

Charming little innocent that I am, during that visit to the Vatican Museum I informed them of my opinion as soon as I discovered one of their many suggestion boxes. I pointed out the splendid precedent offered by the de-fig-leafing of Michelangelo's *David* and recommended the same policy be pursued with their statues. Haven't gotten a reply though.

MASTERS AND JOHNSON AND THE STATE OF MATRIMONY

Masters and Johnson are the last ones I would accuse of worshiping the s*x taboo. They must have their hang-ups, as we all do, but writing about s*x is not one of them. But one of their puzzling findings can be explained, I think, if we are aware of the effect the s*x taboo has on American s*xual relationships.

Recall the "technique puzzle" from chapter 3: according to Masters and Johnson's studies, homosexual male and lesbian couples demonstrated far better s*xual technique in their s*xual relationships than heterosexuals did—an average difference that showed up the best in the relationships of the longest duration. I think that Masters and Johnson's finding could have resulted from a biased sample—but the bias came by way of the s*x taboo and was reinforced by the way our society idealizes marriage. Masters and Johnson endorse this idealization to some extent, and that may be why they fell into this trap.

Children learn the s*x taboo very well. Masters and Johnson's cases of s*xual dysfunction show that if children don't unlearn it as adults—

at least a bit—they won't have rewarding s*xual relations of the sort that impress s*xologists. But married people get married for social as well as for s*xual reasons. So heterosexuals do not *have* to come to terms with the s*x taboo in order to put themselves into a situation in which s*xual behavior is expected—namely, marriage.

Neither do homosexuals; there are plenty of homosexuals who have not come to terms with the taboo against their s*xuality, yet who go out and have s*x, anyway. Among them are vast numbers of deeply closeted people, with defenses so rigidly effective that they can be having gay s*x and nothing but gay s*x and still say they love their spouse and are heterosexual. But Masters and Johnson could not possibly get such people into their labs, because they don't consciously consider themselves homosexual. If they did, on average these people's s*xual technique would be rather poor, for they do not permit themselves to have the long-term intimacy that would let them get to know a lover's every nook and cranny.

Instead, Masters and Johnson got homosexuals who had come to terms with being gay. Those are people who by definition have overcome the s*x taboo, since coming out means being able to admit to yourself that you are homosexual, and that means that you are no longer pretending that your s*xual feelings are unimportant and not worth talking about.

Therefore, all or nearly all of Masters and Johnson's homosexuals would have overcome the single most important roadblock to s*xual satisfaction. It would follow that they could (not necessarily would) have learned to communicate s*xually with their partners as they got to know them over the space of the year of living together required to qualify them for the study.

But only those heterosexuals who *have* dealt with the s*x taboo and overcome it would have done as well. As Masters and Johnson pointed out, some heterosexuals did perform well sexually. But they seemed to miss the point that marriage alone does not ensure this.

No, the s*x life of open homosexuals is not paradise; it wasn't even paradise before AIDS came on the scene. But coming out requires getting in touch with one's s*xuality—and this has never been guaranteed by marriage in our society. Accordingly, one year of heterosexual marriage is not at all equivalent to one year of homosexual mateship. The s*x taboo allows or encourages s*xually dysfunctional heterosexual marriages to limp along while ensuring that openly homosexual mateships can use s*x as a very effective bonding mechanism. The task—bonding—is the same for homosexuals and heterosexuals. But our society encourages people to assume that marriage leads inevitably to bonded bliss when there is nothing inevitable about it. I conclude that the s*x taboo is very damaging to the s*xual majority.[21]

HOMOSEXUALITY, SEDUCTION, AND GAY RIGHTS

The s*x taboo also is bad news for members of the s*xual minorities, for it allows misunderstandings between them and the typical heterosexual majority to fester. Psychotherapists call such misunderstandings *unfinished business,* and unfinished business is one of the commonest causes of psychological problems. Sociopolitically speaking, it gums up the normal process of debate and resolution of conflict.

Every year since the early 1970s, a gay-rights bill has been introduced into the Massachusetts House of Representatives. In many of those early years, one particular representative voted against the bill because—as he carefully explained in public debate on the bill—he was s*xually molested by a (male) dean when he was in college.[22] Apparently, this one incident was all the evidence he needed to allow discrimination against every homosexual in Massachusetts to continue. I infer that this incident left him with unfinished business and that the s*x taboo was one of the things that kept him from finishing it off. The result was that he looked foolish—every year.

Very probably there are other people like him. How many people's only direct, personal experience of homosexuality was when someone of their own s*x approached them s*xually when they were young? Obviously, everyone meets heterosexuals who do not begin the meeting with a grope, but for some people such a s*xual approach forms the only in-the-flesh picture of homosexuals they have. It is the s*x taboo that keeps them from knowing other kinds of homosexuals personally, and it is the s*x taboo that keeps them from talking about their being approached. Gay-rights advocates can explain—quite accurately, mind you—that such a sample is biased and the representative's logic is twisted. They can explain this until they're blue in the face, but if people can't talk about their molestation, they'll harbor their unfinished business a long time.[23]

---

[21] There is another explanation of Masters and Johnson's finding, which I will address at the beginning of chapter 13.

[22] This particular representative is no longer in politics, according to the U.S. congressional aide who refreshed my memory of this incident, Joseph Martin.

[23] Many gay-rights advocates know this problem very well. They are right to point out that there is little they can do about it; after all, denying a negative stereotype just tends to publicize it and remind the bigots that other people share it.

THE CONTRADICTION

So here's the question I wish I could answer: why on earth is something as natural, as delightful, as dangerous, and as spectacular as human s*xuality deemed so embarrassing that children are lied to about it, universities can't teach it, and even aliens 20,000 years in the future can't be told about it? Logically, it just doesn't make sense. At some level, one hopes, it had better make sense, or we might just as well go read existentialist novels or write science fiction. But if it does make sense, how?

The s*x taboo *used* to make sense, apparently, according to some people whose theories I admire (see chapter 12). But scientifically speaking, the s*x taboo's days are numbered. How many days are left is still unclear. In the meantime, the contradictions between s*x truth and s*x taboo will, like a logical contradiction in mathematics, continue to cause the whole house to collapse at unpredictable times.

In fact, it is this contradiction that has made it possible for me to provide you with so many entertaining stories in this chapter. A logical contradiction in a system of logical deduction, formally speaking, implies that anything whatsoever is true.[24] All I have been doing in this chapter is taking the logical contradiction embodied in the s*x taboo and following deductions to their bizarre conclusions.

The contradiction between s*x truth and s*x taboo, in fact, makes some people act crazy (see chapter 10). The reactions to s*x with which ordinary people in Western culture have been inculcated have sometimes been so bizarre that they deserve a psychiatric diagnosis. For example, *masturbatory insanity*—the notion that too much masturbation drives you insane—was widely believed as recently as the early 1900s, as evidenced by the early Boy Scout manuals, and was literally as American as Kellogg's cornflakes.[25] This belief had seriously waned by the beginning of World War II, but a mild version of it—that masturbation led to a neurotic disorder called neurasthenia—was believed by many experts at least through 1936.[26] It did incalculable damage

---

[24] The logician would prove the following statement:

IF *(A & −A)* THEN *B*

—which translates as, "If *A* is true and *A* is false, then any statement at all *(B)* is true." So if a contradiction is presumed true, then anything at all can be proved true.

[25] Cornflakes—and graham crackers—were originally developed to calm the sexual instincts and prevent masturbation; see Money 1985. For a good summary of the theory of masturbatory insanity, including precise documentation of many of the points I present here, see Hare 1962.

[26] Hare 1962, p. 9.

during the centuries it held sway and continues to do damage today. And that's not pleasant to think about.

Frankly, the s*x taboo makes me deeply angry. I hope, by the way, that by now you are angry at me for forcing you to put up with all those asterisks. If so, may I suggest you direct your anger and write your congressperson—or your local school board, or anybody—about sex? After all, don't you think that the next *Voyager* spacecraft should include some selections from the Kama Sutra? No? How about that famous liquor ad with "SEX" spelled out in the ice cubes? Still no? Hmm . . . Would you settle for some of the illustrations from *It's OK to Say No*? Well, maybe NASA would, but I wouldn't; I don't want those aliens to think I can't write good.

More seriously, don't you think that kids have a right to be protected not only from grown-ups who want to force them to have sex but also from parents (or statue owners!) who want to lie to them about sex? That's what they think in Sweden, and that's why Swedish schools give children a good sex education even if some children's parents think they are better off ignorant. Don't you think society should encourage attitudes that permit sex to cement a relationship rather than cause difficulties that require sex therapy to fix? That's what more people could have if socialization were set up to discourage the formation of a sex taboo. Don't you think that people ought to get to know others sexually unlike themselves on a down-to-earth basis rather than as the result of stereotypes created by gropes in the dark rows of movie-theater balconies? That's what could happen if sexual preferences could be discussed, and people's sexual options explored, as openly as their other preferences are.

Taboo or not taboo—that is the question. Are members of different sexual orientations going to venture out of their sexual homelands to try to understand each other? Or are they going to stay at home, sexually speaking, and go on assuming the worst about those people living over in Sodom or Gomorrah, or San Francisco, or for that matter, Scarsdale? If we decide to venture forth, then we have to understand sexual arousal and sexual development—the processes by which individuals decide that they prefer the customs of one sexual locale over another. We need a theory that applies to everybody, that specifies what's universal and what's specific about the different kinds of people we see. I've got some ideas that might help—about women and men, about bisexual, gay, and straight. But first we have to be sure that it's really okay to talk about "bisexual," "gay," and "straight." Read on.

5

REALITY OR SOCIAL CONSTRUCTION?

Playboy: So a homosexual is not a homosexual until he commits a physical homosexual act?
Anita Bryant: That's what I consider a homosexual to be.

Kelley 1978, p. 85.

Like berdaches, "drag queens" are known to dress like women, or with a mixture of male and female clothing, but they are still queens even if they dress like men.

Williams 1986, p. 125.

Both realists and nominalists must lower their voices. Reconstructing the monuments of the past from the rubble of the present requires quiet concentration.

Boswell 1982, p. 113.

Are things like "homosexuality" and "transvestism" real entities that exist out there somewhere rather than just in the mind? Or are they made-up concepts that only have meaning within the boundaries of a society? Just what *is* a drag queen? Why do we make all these distinctions, anyway?

This chapter is about the hottest philosophical controversy to hit psychology in years: the social-constructionist/realist debate. Since "the social-constructionist/realist debate" is a mouthful, for the rest of this chapter I'll just call it "the Debate."

The Debate is so important that I have included both sides of it, implicitly, in the subtitle of this book. "Why we are what we are" implies that an *identity* or an *essence* is important in the ups and downs, the ins and outs, that form the human sexual landscape. "Why we love whom we love" implies that it is the *people* we love and the *meanings* we assign to the *acts* we perform with them that are the important things to study. Social constructionists tend to argue that all that objectively exists are sexual acts and that identities are constructed by societies out of those acts. They argue, geographically speaking, that "Nevada" is a social construction; it exists only because our culture says it exists. Their opponents argue that sexual identities are not arbitrarily constructed out of sexual acts but are to some extent "really there" in the structure of the acts or the relationships themselves. They argue, geographically speaking, that "Mount Baldy" has a reality that transcends the name a society gives to it.

The Debate is important for several reasons. First, it's socially important. If gender transpositions aren't real entities, then laws dealing with them don't make sense. For example, "silliness" and "ghosts" are pure social constructions (or pure nonsense)—so laws against just acting silly or laws protecting the rights of ghosts are absurd. Likewise, if homosexuality is purely a social construction, then laws against it or laws protecting the rights of homosexuals might be absurd.

Second, the Debate is important to gender transposees themselves. Some gay people, for example, like the idea that homosexuality is "real" because it contributes to their feeling that their struggle to achieve a gay identity is necessary and productive. Other gay people like the idea that homosexuality is a social construction, because it suggests that people can change the boundaries of the construction and thereby change—or escape entirely—the social consequences of what it means to be gay. After all, "define and conquer" is a strategy used at least since the time of Adam; by taking for granted the existence of categories like "homosexual" and "heterosexual," people give power to those who made the definitions in the first place.

And third, the Debate is scientifically important, because some theories depend on particular answers to it. In biology, for example, if the Debaters conclude that homosexuality isn't a real entity, then it's hard to justify genetic theories about its origin, since genetic theories have to model objectively "real" traits, not ones like "silliness" or "Nevadaness."

The Debate has been hottest when applied to homosexuality, so that's the gender transposition I'll talk about in this chapter. But the Debate concerns all the gender transpositions. Indeed, it questions the whole idea of a gender transposition in the first place.

The Debate asks the following question: is each gender transposition an essential (or real) trait, or is each a social construction? Let me illustrate the question with one of my pet examples: cat-lovers and dog-lovers.

CAT-LOVERS AND DOG-LOVERS

The realist: Frankly, there are only two kinds of people in this world: cat-lovers and dog-lovers. Cat-lovers (the scientific term for them is *feliphiles*[1]) are, as we all know, an oppressed class. Since most people are dog-lovers *(caniphiles),* cat-hating *(feliphobia)* has become part of our culture. It's even part of our language: "catty," for example, not to mention "filibuster" and "philippic." Some countries even have laws that make feliphiles felons!

Much as caniphiles would deny it, the only real difference between caniphiles and feliphiles is their *petual orientation.* Petual orientation is the preference, in ownership and/or desire, for a particular kind of pet in one's petual relationships. No one knows what causes people to have particular petual orientations, although most specialists believe that it usually begins in childhood.[2] It is *not* a choice, and it is very difficult to change one's petual orientation. Although there are instances in which a feliphile has gone out and bought a dog, either the relationship doesn't last, or the person wasn't really a feliphile in the first place. In short, petual orientation reflects an underlying reality; a feliphile who owns a dog is still a feliphile, and a caniphile who owns a cat is just slumming.

The taboo surrounding petual orientation is so severe, incidentally, that many careers have been seriously hurt when people showed too much interest in human petuality. The usual reaction is to ignore it; failing that, to trivialize it. And it used to be much worse; some people interested in petual orientation have been hounded until they resigned in disgrace.

[1] Those of you up to date with your Latin and Greek will note that, like some other terms used in this book, "feliphile" has a hybrid etymology. The *feli* part comes from the Latin for "cat," the *phile* part from the Greek for "love." This may rub you the wrong way—*feliphile* could be confused with *philiphile,* or "lover of love"—but so be it. I find the term felicitous.

[2] The theory that one becomes a feliphile by having overtly *sexual* relationships with a cat, while perhaps true in certain tragic clinical cases, is no longer considered applicable to the vast majority of feliphiles.

The social constructionist: I agree that feliphiles are an oppressed class in our modern society, but they are not an objectively "real" category. Rather, the category is a social construction. All that exists objectively is pet ownership; what it means to own a particular pet is socially constructed. There is lots of evidence from other cultures that proves this is so.

For example, there once was a society in which petual preference was no big deal. In the United States, back in the twentieth century, society was so accepting of human petual diversity that *they didn't even have words* for petual orientation. Words like "feliphobia," "caniphilia," and even "fidophobia" were not listed in their dictionaries. Laws regulating pet ownership were few. Although there were rules (seldom enforced) about which kinds of pets could be kept in particular apartments and laws about registering and caring for pets, that was all. Most importantly, there were no words that specifically meant anything like what we now mean when we say "feliphilia" or "petual preference."

I say "petual preference" rather than "petual orientation" because "orientation" is too essentialistic. It implies that what one likes petually is an eternal—a given—and will never change. But society makes a choice to enforce the felic taboo, and particular feliphobic people make a choice to participate in particular antifeliphilic actions. Likewise, even if it's true that some people have an unchangingly felic preference, that doesn't mean that others don't change. As I said, the only concrete, observable variable is pet ownership; everything else is an epiphenomenon of cultural interpretation.

For example, what about bipetuals—people who have both feliphilic and caniphilic feelings? It's true that some people who call themselves bipetual later come out openly as feliphiles, but everyone is at least a little bit bipetual. Think back to your childhood; can't you remember times when you played innocently both with cats *and* with dogs? It was just social conditioning that got you thinking that you had to choose between the two. The only reason you feliphiles are so insistent about this "petual orientation" stuff is that you think your profelic feelings mean you don't have any caniphilic ones!

The realist replies: Well, it's true that the twentieth century was the golden age for freedom of petual orientation and that cultures nowadays differ in the way they think about petual orientation. But that doesn't mean that petual orientation is just a figment of the imagination. If you look carefully enough, even people living in the golden age recognized the distinction.

I know it's hard to believe, but back in 1985 there was a book published entitled *Dogs Are Better than Cats*.[3] It's important to note that this was no scholarly tome; it was a popular book, illustrated with scurrilous cartoons and loaded with typically prejudiced comments like this:

> DOGS know that life is . . . Ruff, ruff!
> CATS don't think of life, only of themselves. That's why they say
> . . . ME-ow.

These lines have, of course, the familiar ring of feliphobia. But if I hadn't already told you where they came from, would you have guessed that they were written in an era that had no word for feliphobia? Of course not!

Moreover, what about the possibility that Americans back then really did have such a term but that petual orientation was such a sensitive topic that it was discreetly edited out of the reference works of the time? Scholars have dug up the terms "cat-lover" and "cat fancier," but there is no evidence that these terms meant anything like what we now mean by the term feliphilia. In fact, these phrases probably had an explicitly erotic connotation—referring to people who had sexual relations with their cats. Many people in the twentieth century did have strong aversions to sexual matters and coined all manner of terms to refer to their sexuality, but only indirectly, so it is not surprising that they would have refrained from defining these sexually embarrassing terms in their dictionaries. Sexual matters, believe it or not, were just about as taboo back then as petual matters are today.

The social constructionist replies: But that's exactly the point! Back then, they had "homosexuals," "heterosexuals," "dog-lovers," "cat fanciers"—all those sexually loaded terms! They made a big deal about that sort of thing, and they had a separate word for every kind of socially deviant act. We don't. It's all a social construction. If there really was anyone back then who could be called a feliphile, it must have had entirely different consequences for the person in question. Back then, being a feliphile was perfectly okay. Nowadays it can land you in jail. Back then, catnip was openly for sale in local "pet shops"; now mere possession of catnip can get you twenty years. No, to talk of "feliphilia" in a culture like that is to talk of the ridiculous.

The realist, again: No, *this* is the point! Back then they didn't have words for petual orientation. True enough. But that doesn't mean they didn't know about it; it just means they didn't make a big deal about

[3] Dizick and Bly 1985.

it. If they didn't know about it, they couldn't have written books like *Dogs Are Better than Cats,* right? Maybe they thought of the book as a joke, but joking about something means you know it's there to be joked about. Think of it this way. . . .

And here, dear reader, we will leave our two doggedly caterwauling debaters—because I expect by now that you've gotten the point.

INTERACTIONISM

The point is that both social constructionism and realism are correct in very important ways. It's not that something "in between" the two is correct; it's that both are true simultaneously. Moreover, they interact in a way that is fascinating and that deserves a name of its own: interactionism (see fig. 5.1).

This might seem obvious, but to some of the Debaters it's not. Another thing that's not obvious is that the Debate is *not* a replay of the infamous nature-nurture debate. Although social constructionists sometimes are more comfortable with nurture and realists with nature, this is a different debate. Social constructionists are not just people with a good point; they are *right*: the social construction of homosexuality in different societies adds a captivating and vital dimension that is more than just "part of the answer." Likewise, realists are not just people interested in reducing homosexuality to some essential oversimplification; they are *right*: the similarities linking homosexual behavior around the world and over time are as interesting as the differences are.

When it comes to the pure theories—pure social constructionism and pure realism—there are strong and weak forms. The *strong* forms say that a particular theory is the *only* one that's important; all the others can safely be ignored. The *weak* forms say the particular theory

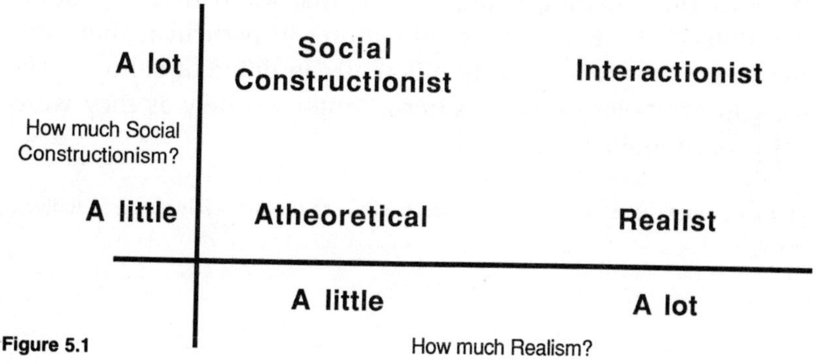

	A little	**A lot**
A lot	**Social Constructionist**	**Interactionist**
A little	**Atheoretical**	**Realist**

How much Social Constructionism?

How much Realism?

Figure 5.1

is just *one of several* theories that are important. Obviously, only one strong form at a time can be true; they are mutually incompatible. But the weak forms are not. As I just suggested, I think that weak forms of both the social-constructionist and realist theories are correct.

But interactionism goes further. Interactionism says not only that both factors are important but also that the two factors interact in a way that is more than the sum of their parts. Interactionism says that in order to understand the effect of one factor, you need to know how the other factor is operating—and you need to know that in detail.

Here's a simple example of interaction. Your genes affect your skin color. Also, being in the sun affects your skin color—a statement that happens to be true no matter what your race and genetic background. *How much* effect being in the sun has on your skin color depends on your genes; *that's* the interaction. Some people are too dark skinned to tan very much. Some light-skinned people burn rather than tan. And some people tan deeply and quickly. So in order to predict a person's final skin color, you need to know (1) their genetic makeup, (2) their environment, *and* (3) how the two interact.

In theory, someone could even have genes that make their skin *lighter* after exposure to the sun. After all, sunlight bleaches out lots of pigments used in printing and painting, so why not skin pigments? In such a hypothetical person, you'd need to be especially careful to focus on the interaction rather than just the sum of independent factors.

So let's pretend for a moment that we don't know the importance of interaction in sexual orientation and look at the argument for each side.

WHY "HOMOSEXUALITY" IS A SOCIAL CONSTRUCTION

There is a lot of evidence suggesting that homosexuality is a social construction. The most important piece is that the pattern of homosexuality differs a lot from culture to culture; in particular, that "the same" acts are construed entirely differently in different cultures. Let me give you examples of three patterns, approximately as they were set out by anthropologist Gilbert Herdt.[4]

---

[4]Herdt set out these three patterns in a speech given at the Kinsey Institute at Indiana University in 1986.

Age-Biased Homosexuality

One of the commonest forms homosexuality takes in other societies is the *age-biased* form, such as in ancient Greece.[5] In this pattern, sexual relationships conventionally or ideally take place between two partners rather different in age, experience, or power. Often, this is as true of heterosexual relationships as it is of homosexual ones. Different terms—usually translated as *lover* and *beloved*—are used to describe the two people participating in the partnership, and different things are expected of the two according to which role they are playing. In ancient Greece, for example, the lover was expected to be erotically aroused or obsessed by the beloved, to give him[6] gifts, to educate him (explicitly or by example), and to be persistent (but not too pushy) when the beloved was reticent. The beloved was expected to respond to the attentions paid to him by the lover, but not necessarily in kind—at least, not in public.

This pattern seems strange by modern standards in several respects. For example, if you were someone's beloved in ancient Greece, you could be someone else's lover at the same time. Parents would be concerned about the status of their son's lover and of the propriety of the relationship—not about whether their sons should be taking lovers in the first place—and they assumed as a matter of course that the lovers would be male. Sometimes there were specific rules about what kinds of gifts a lover should give to his beloved as tokens of having reached particular stages in their relationship. Rooster or hares, for example, show up often on Greek vase paintings as courtship gifts from lovers to beloveds. There were also, at times, ceremonies of commitment that were at least as meaningful as heterosexual ones and that were described using the same terms used for heterosexual marriage.

Homosexuality in ancient Greece was so well integrated into the social structure that it is impossible to understand the culture without learning about homosexuality in detail. It is true that there were no words for the generic "homosexual" and "heterosexual" as we now

---

[5] Classical scholars know that the term "ancient Greece" covers a staggering variety of cultural patterns, not all of them approving of this form of homosexuality. (See, for example, the discussion in Boswell 1980 and Dover 1978.) So my discussions of ancient Greece in this book should be taken only to apply to particular Greek city-states (especially Athens) at particular times in their histories.

[6] As is common in classical sources, males are far more often described than females—especially in detail. I will therefore use the male terms in this discussion, since it is not clear whether women's homosexual relationships were mirror images of the men's or if they were quite different. That they existed is clear from Sappho's poetry, of course.

use them, but the Greeks had an extensive erotic vocabulary. There *were* words for several specific sexual acts that would clearly be called "homosexual" in today's terms and for particular kinds of people who nowadays would be considered particular kinds of homosexual.[7]

Many Greek vases show quite explicit sexual interactions—or earlier stages of courtship—between older and younger males at various ages. These vases are some of the most valuable bits of information we have about Greek culture and are displayed in many museums around the world (although some of the more prudish museums don't display the obviously sexual ones or turn an offending scene against the wall, especially if another picture on the vase is more discreet by modern standards). Photographs of these scenes are now available in several books.[8]

In sum, Greek culture socially constructed homosexuality in a way totally different from the way ours does. They took it in stride, they put it on their artwork, and their literature is permeated with its influences. For people raised in modern Western culture, it is so hard to deal with these facts that they have been denied rather than understood.[9] After all, understanding them would be a bit like trying to make sense of Alice's Wonderland.

Inversion Homosexuality

A second common pattern for homosexuality is the *inversion* pattern, in which at least one of the participants in homosexual activity has officially taken up the role of the opposite sex. Or so it seems to the eyes of Western observers; as we'll see, their real status was far more complicated. According to a recent book by University of Southern California anthropologist Walter Williams, who has probably done more fieldwork with living berdaches (defined below) than any other anthropologist, many tribes regarded these people differently.[10]

---

[7] Some of these facts are not well known because the more obviously homosexual passages in the classics were mistranslated or left untranslated in the English versions available to those who do not read Greek. Sensibilities were so tender on this topic just a few decades ago that the Loeb Classics editions—with the original language on the left-hand pages and the English translation on the right—rendered "the good stuff" not into English but into Latin. Good stuff in the Latin originals was left untranslated or translated into Italian.

[8] For example, Dover 1978 and Boardman 1974 and 1975.

[9] The final chapter in Dover 1978 is an evenhanded discussion of why so many modern scholars have had trouble dealing with these issues.

[10] Williams 1986, p. 1. Williams and I have independently reached many similar conclusions about the berdache. His book appeared just as the final versions of this chapter were being prepared. I am delighted to report that he has documented, in far better detail than I could possibly have done alone, most of the major points I make here.

How many genders are there? To a modern Anglo-American, nothing might seem more definite than the answer that there are two: men and women. But not all societies around the world agree. . . . The commonly accepted notion of "the opposite sex," based on anatomy, is itself an artifact of our society's rigid sex roles.

The name anthropologists use for members of this third sex is *berdache*. What particular roles berdaches play depend upon the roles their society allows them to play.

Among men in American Indian and Eskimo tribes, for example, berdaches often are (or were) *shamans*—healers or medicine men— who acquired their magic powers while dressing as women.[11] One of the best-investigated cases occurred among the Chukchee Eskimo in Siberia.[12] Among the Chukchee, there were three kinds of shaman, differing according to the strength of their powers, for which men were required to wear some sort of female clothing. The least powerful shamans wore women's clothes only every now and then—at the commands of the spirits or perhaps when they became ill. (Supposedly, this was to confuse an evil spirit and get it to think it was living in the wrong kind of body.) More powerful shamans dressed as women for longer stretches of time—days or weeks, perhaps. There are hints that these shamans did so sometimes after losing a spouse or after encountering some other difficulty. And the most powerful shamans were completely sexually transformed: they wore women's clothes all the time, did women's work, and married men. Usually these people became shamans after they had a vision telling them to do so; the vision came to them during a *vision quest,* which was a period of time spent away from the tribe, fasting, and usually in a state that Western psychologists would call sensory deprivation.[13]

[11] Cases of females taking the role of males were known but are very little described, so I will again use male pronouns in my account. The most comprehensive recent account of the male berdache in modern Indian tribes is the book by Williams (1986), who reserves the term for genetic males only, using *amazons* for women taking up men's roles. A detailed (but psychoanalytic) description of both female-to-male and male-to-female individuals is provided by Devereux 1937, reprinted in Devereux 1963.

[12] The best account is by Waldemar Bogoras 1904 (pp. 448–457); I have summarized the pattern in much less detail in my Ph.D. thesis (Weinrich 1976). Note that anthropologists consider Siberian cultures to be different from American ones in many important respects. However, humans first came to the Americas by way of a land bridge (now flooded by the Bering Strait), expanding first into North America and then into South America. So it should not be surprising that there would be similarities among the cultures of both Americas and Siberia.

[13] I once had the impression that a vision quest involved a physical journey, with the person involved in the quest traveling through the forests away from the tribe. But Williams

Among American Indians, Williams noted that "shamans are not necessarily berdaches, but because of their spiritual connection, berdaches in many cultures are often considered to be powerful shamans."[14] Parents typically wanted to know which choice sons would make so that they could raise them appropriately. In some tribes, parents figured this out by putting the son through a specific test: they would put symbols of masculinity and femininity (women's weaving versus a bow and arrow, say) outside a tent while the boy was sleeping inside, then set the tent on fire. The boy, awakening in terror, would flee. On his way out, supposedly he would grab one article or the other—thus symbolizing a masculine or feminine choice.[15]

The status of berdaches varied from tribe to tribe, but many tribes gave them a place of honor and power. In some tribes, only the most intelligent and promising children found themselves encouraged to take the berdache's path. In other tribes, there are hints that people with particular problems were more likely to pursue the role. Conversations with berdaches surviving today suggest that these men had sexual relations with many of the men in the tribe—perhaps while on hunting or war expeditions, perhaps when other taboos prevented the men from having sexual relations with their wives, or perhaps just when the two men felt like it. Often the nonberdache men were (and still are) quite open in their sexual approaches toward—indeed, competition for—the berdaches.[16] Again, these facts are disorienting to Western observers.

Perhaps the most important aspect of berdachism was its spiritual side, similar in a way to the decision to join a religious order today. It was the gods that told you to take up the role, the spirits who told you to cross-dress. The spiritual aspects are so important, in fact, that Williams covers them first in his book about the berdache. On the other hand, although it was the spirits who commanded you to transform yourself, it was you who took the time to seek their advice, and it was you who actually walked over, picked up the clothing, and put it on. Accordingly, both choices made by your society and choices made by you were important in the role.

(1986, pp. 27–30) describes his own vision quest among the Lakota, and the journey is mental, not geographic—although the spot where it takes place is away from the settlement.

[14] Williams 1986, p. 35.

[15] A version recounted by Williams (1986, p. 24) among the Yuman placed the symbols inside an enclosure, made of brush, constructed especially for the test. Nor was the boy asleep.

[16] Williams 1986 is especially detailed on these points.

Role-Playing Homosexuality

A third pattern of homosexuality in other cultures is a variation on the inversion pattern: no one officially takes up the role of the other sex, but in any particular interaction one person takes a "receptive" role and the other an "active" role ("insertee" and "insertor," respectively, when penetration is involved). But neither participant pretends to be a member of the other sex.

This is the pattern[17] that exists in modern urban Mexico, according to the detailed descriptions by University of California anthropologist Joseph Carrier.[18] The insertor role is perceived as more masculine and hence more valued, so most Mexican homosexual men present themselves in this role. However, many of these men change their preferred role over time, or at least add aspects of the other role to their repertoire.

A significant aspect of the behavior of those who change, however, is that they usually do not play both sex roles with the same partner. They *rank* prospective partners as to whether they are more masculine or more effeminate than themselves. If thought more masculine, the prospective partner is generally rated active sexually; if more effeminate, passive sexually.[19]

This flexibility to the contrary notwithstanding, the cultural insistence that one or the other role be presented and played is very strong in Mexico. For example, travel features directed at American gay men (who, as explained in chapter 2, often "play" both "roles" with the same person) warn them that in Mexico (and several other countries) Americans are valued by native homosexuals because the Americans are willing to play the insertee role more often than the native homosexuals are. The message is: as a guest, be accommodating—but remember, you'll probably be asked to accommodate the same way each time. Americans may find that the acts they perform at home seem to have an eerily unreal interpretation abroad.

Conclusion

This last example of culture clash makes the social-constructionist point very well. What homosexuality "is" in a given culture is crucially de-

---

[17] Again, among men, because Carrier happened to study only men.
[18] See, for example, Carrier 1971 and 1976.
[19] Carrier 1976, pp. 120–121.

pendent on the way that culture constructs its categories of sexual acts. To the typical Mexican homosexual described by Carrier, an American willing to be inserted into has declared himself to "be" the insertee and to play a particular role, but the American may think nothing of the sort. In fact, gay Americans feel, when they look into "gay life" in other countries, that people that seem familiar act strangely. Presumably, foreign gays visiting the United States feel the same way. Seen in this light, definitions of "homosexuality" like the one I presented in chapter 2 seem culturally shortsighted.

Likewise, my very ability to refer to "the other sex" throughout this book presumes that there is only one other sex to refer to in any given context. If there is a third or a fourth sex, then I really ought to revise my definitions in chapter 2 to reflect this point of view.

Examples like these are what Mary McIntosh, a British sociologist who was the first proponent of the social-constructionist viewpoint in sexual-preference matters, had in mind when she wrote:

> The current conceptualization of homosexuality as a [medical] condition is a false one, resulting from ethnocentric bias. Homosexuality should be seen rather as a social role.[20]

Notice that McIntosh endorses the strong social-constructionist model: she uses the word "rather" to indicate not only that social constructionism is correct but also that realism is wrong. McIntosh's views are widely admired, and her paper on homosexuality and social constructionism is probably the most widely cited one in the field. But her views are incomplete, as I will now show.

WHY "HOMOSEXUALITY" IS ESSENTIALLY REAL

There is also a lot of evidence suggesting that homosexuality is a real[21] category—even in the examples I gave you in the previous section. In particular, there are cross-cultural similarities between them and the situations of corresponding groups in modern societies that are hard to explain if social customs are the only factors involved. These similarities are admittedly more striking in some cases than in others, but they exist in each case.

---

[20] McIntosh 1968.

[21] "Realist" is the term applied to this school of thought by Boswell 1982. The term the social constructionists use is "essentialist"; they criticize realists for assuming an essence in homosexuality that crosses cultural boundaries and for reducing complicated phenomena to simplistic equations.

The *age-biased* form of homosexuality survives today but—with the exception of homosexual rape—is the most frowned-upon type of homosexuality in the United States.[22] Of course, this role comes in heterosexual as well as homosexual varieties, but the belief that it is characteristic of homosexual men forms part of the American stereotype of homosexuality. (I'll have more to say about this stereotype in a later chapter.) Scientists single out this "type" of homosexual when they coin terms (for the older partners) such as "pedophile," "hebephile," and "ephebephile," depending on the age group the older partners find attractive. The validity (scientific "reality," if you will) of the categories these terms describe can be scientifically validated using penile plethysmography (of the sort explained in chapter 8). Likewise, many of the participants in these acts see themselves as particular types of people and use words to describe these types themselves. For example, the term used by men involved in such relationships is "boy-lover." Scientists lack a term for the younger partners (unless they are adults, in which case their partners are much older and the term is "gerontophile"). As far as I know, boys involved in relationships with older men do not have a term for themselves.

The terminologies can make some fine distinctions. Some boy-lovers do not consider themselves homosexual and tend to seek out boys they consider to be ordinarily boyish. These boys often grow up to lead conventionally heterosexual lives.[23] Other boy-lovers do consider themselves homosexual and often seek as sex partners teenagers who already identify themselves as gay (while understanding that this age preference sets them apart from other kinds of homosexuals). Homosexuals, for their part, also make distinctions, albeit not always the same ones; boy-love organizations are permitted to march in some gay-pride marches but are excluded from others. Yet boy-lovers and homosexuals alike see their emotions reflected in the more accurate modern translations of the Greek classics.

All this suggests that there is an underlying reality in the categorizations of same-sex love that has outlasted the cultural changes of the past two thousand years. There did seem to be "men who loved boys" in ancient Greece as well as "men who loved girls." And nowadays there do seem to be "men who love men," "men who love boys," "men who love women," and "men who love girls."

The *inversion* model of homosexuality is also alive and kicking today. First and foremost, it survives in the stereotype of homosexual

[22] Other Western cultures—including many Western European nations—do not frown upon age bias quite as much.

[23] Two examples are given in Money and Weinrich 1983.

men as effeminate and homosexual women as mannish. There is a grain of truth in this stereotype, too, but mostly in the childhoods of lesbians and homosexual men—the childhood gender nonconformity discussed in chapter 2—and in the results of some masculinity-femininity questionnaires I'll describe in a later chapter.

But more convincing than this stereotype is that the inversion pattern gives some of the spookiest examples of cross-cultural similarity I know. "Bitchiness"—being bad-tempered, complaining frequently— is one of these, even though some people might consider it a trivial trait. Let me review the evidence on this (during which you should keep in mind that heterosexual transvestites have no such reputation).

Drag queens are widely viewed as bitchy in the U.S., and apparently also in all Western societies. Moreover, drag-queen-like behavior is not difficult to find in non-Western cultures, and bitchiness shows up in most if not all of them.

The *hijras*—a Hindu caste in India consisting of males who dress as females—are one example. Hijras leave their families in their teen years, run away to a group of adult hijras living in a large city, and eventually may undergo a castration operation that finalizes their status in the caste. They entertain at weddings and other festivals, sometimes uninvited, but they always expect to get paid. If they are not, they have a habit of lifting their skirts in their disgust to show what they (no longer) have underneath.[24] Hijras are as a rule bitchy and insistent, and have been known to demand (rather than politely request) donations of used women's clothes from Indian women who are well off.[25]

Chukchee berdaches even have an argument that *requires* them to be bitchy or bossy.[26] The Chukchee berdache, married to an ordinary male, had a spirit who, according to Bogoras, "is supposed to be the real head of the family, and to communicate his orders by means of his transformed [berdache] wife. The human husband, of course, has to execute these orders faithfully under fear of prompt punishment."

[24] A rule of the sect, believe it or not, forbids hijras to wear underwear, so this display is one that fathers of the bride presumably wish to avoid.

[25] The best modern account of hijras is Nanda 1984. The skirt-lifting and underwear details are not mentioned in this paper; they come from a speech Nanda gave at a conference I attended. The dress-demanding incident was told to me by an American woman who had been a foreign exchange student in India.

[26] Williams 1986, p. 254, reminded me of this quotation, which is taken from Bogoras 1904, pp. 452–454. Incidentally, in his brief discussion of *castrati* (men castrated before puberty, in order to keep their soprano voices), Williams (1986, p. 261) notes that they became "the prima donnas of the high culture of their time"—and we all know how bossy prima donnas are.

Just about every drag queen I know would kill to have *that* weapon in her arsenal.

And then there are some American Indian berdaches who insist in the strongest possible terms that they really *are* women in a physiological sense. If they are doubted, they will scratch their thighs to simulate menstruation, claim to "get pregnant" and insist the baby was stillborn. These carryings-on fool no one but are engaged in dead seriously, sometimes literally so. One American Indian man had jokingly questioned whether a berdache was really a woman; that berdache then "picked up a club and for one or two weeks tried to assault the man whenever he saw him."[27]

This suspiciously strong insistence that role-inverted males be treated as physiologically real women is not limited to berdaches. There are some black drag queens in the United States who claim they can get pregnant and proceed a few months later to deliver a so-called blood baby (described as stillborn, just as in the berdache example).[28] And, as I described in chapter 2, there are male-to-female transsexuals who insist that their surgeons perform uterus-transplantation operations to make them capable of bearing children.

In striking contrast, heterosexual transvestites are rarely or never described as bitchy. I am not aware of any such description of them in scientific papers, and the ones I have met I would not call bitchy. In preparing this chapter, I asked a heterosexual transvestite I know about this. Significantly, she not only had an answer; the question had already occurred to her, because she had obviously thought about her answer. She pointed out that when transvestites want to act forcefully, vindictively, or pushily, they can do so in their masculine persona—and she added that many of them do.[29]

This is, then, another example of a generalization I made in chapter 2: that drag queens combine masculine and feminine qualities in a single androgynous personality, whereas transvestites prefer to express these two facets by way of two separate personalities.

What about the possibility that bitchiness is simply learned as part of the drag queen (or hijra, or whatever) role? That's conceivable but unconvincing. Why would so many culturally diverse groups have the same trait? Moreover, there are indications that bitchiness shows up long before the drag queens themselves know they're supposed to be bitchy. For example, sissy boys typically have a "bossy" personality

[27] Devereux 1937, pp. 510–513, reprinted as Devereux 1963.
[28] See Money and Hosta 1968.
[29] I thank Ariadne Kane for her suggestions and insight on this topic.

that could easily be viewed as the childhood antecedent of adult bitchiness.[30] Sissy boys are disliked by their peers not merely because they're sissy; typically, they also boss kids around in a way that is resented by their playmates.

Aside from bitchiness and envy of women's roles, there are other similarities between various gender-mixing institutions and the gender-inversion pattern of homosexuality in our own culture. In nearly every case, cultures with the inversion pattern of homosexuality believe that the signs of inversion show up in childhood or, at the very latest, in the teen years. (Recall that hijras usually join hijra groups at that age.) The inversion is not just of sexual acts but also of gender role. That is, it's not just that these males enjoy being penetrated rather than penetrating but, rather, that they enjoy taking up weaving, child rearing, or some other aspect of the other sex's *gender* role not specifically involving sexual relations. And the inversion is usually lifelong, or at the very least viewed as being long-term, with entry into the status being beyond the control of the individuals in question.

Another remarkable similarity—related to the gender-role inversion itself—is that drag queens around the world use feminine terms and pronouns to refer to each other, even when the gender crossing is incomplete.[31] But when females take up the roles of males, it is scarcely ever mentioned whether they are referred to as "he"—in fact, I cannot recall any instances in which they are.[32] Some feminine homosexual men use "she" or "her" when talking about other homosexual men, but I have never heard of lesbian women referring to each other as "he" or "him."

The *role-playing* model of homosexuality is also eerily echoed in other accounts. Walter Williams, again, reported:

> A Hupa berdache says of his partners, "As far as it was publicly known, he [the nonberdache] was the man. But in bed there was an exchange of roles. They have to keep an image as masculine, so they always ask me not to tell anybody."[33]

[30] Green 1974 is the now-classic reference on sissy boys, and it was Green who pointed out the bossy trait—without seeing the cross-cultural parallel or suggesting (as far as I know) that this bossiness develops into adult bitchiness.

[31] Examples here are too numerous to cite in their entirety. Whitam and Mathy 1986 give examples from the United States, Guatemala, Brazil, and the Philippines. Two examples from American Indians are on pp. 52–53 and 62 of Williams 1986. In my experience, American drag queens frequently or always refer to each other as "she," whether the queen in question is dressed as a woman or not.

[32] Nor, in a conversation, was Walter Williams able to recall any anthropological account of masculine women being referred to as "he."

[33] Williams 1986, p. 97.

Many other openly gay men have tracked down berdaches and found that they nowadays identify themselves as gay.[34]

Even the "third-sex" status of the berdache may be overstated. Here is what anthropologist Elsie Clews Parsons had to say about the Zuñi berdache way back in 1916. She was trying to figure out whether the berdaches *(la'mana)* in that tribe were "really" considered male or female by the other members of the tribe. After she made a number of observations about a *la'mana's* position in dances and rituals, she admitted to herself that she was confused and turned to the question of burial:

> When prepared for burial the corpse of a la'mana is dressed in the usual woman's outfit, with one exception, under the woman's skirt a pair of trousers are put on. "And on which side of the graveyard will he be buried?" I asked, with eagerness of heart if not of voice, for here at last was a test of the sex status of the la'mana. "On the south side, the men's side, of course. *Kwash lu itse teame* (Is this man not)?" And my old friend smiled the peculiarly gentle smile he reserved for my particularly unintelligent questions.[35]

Notice that this final question—"Is this man not?"—embodies a realist point of view.

So although there are few if any gay bars in Chukchee Siberia and few if any American fathers of the bride who permit drag queens to sing and dance at the wedding reception, there are nevertheless some aspects of the gender transpositions that appear cross-culturally far more often than would be expected by chance.

If this is so, then why hasn't it been observed by previous workers? Sue-Ellen Jacobs, an anthropologist at the University of Washington, suggested that different members of the Tewa tribe gave anthropologists different answers. The village elders gave one definition, but

> Going on accounts given by others, the characterizations of *quethos* [Tewa berdaches] begin to look more like characterizations of contemporary gay males, particularly.[36]

Indeed, if anthropologists don't know contemporary gay males, how can they be expected to recognize similarities to them?

[34] For one example from the earliest days of gay liberation, see Waltrip 1965.
[35] See Parsons 1916.
[36] Jacobs 1983, p. 460.

Examples like these are what Arizona sociologist Fred Whitam had in mind when he studied the inversion form of homosexuality in several countries (specifically the United States, Guatemala, Brazil, and the Philippines). He found many similarities, among them the very important one that children typically are not socialized into becoming homosexuals.

> While a role, as it is ordinarily understood, may be ascribed or achieved, children are neither socialized into the "homosexual role" nor do they rationally choose it. . . . Homosexuality is neither a [medical] "condition" nor a role but rather a sexual orientation and no useful theoretical purpose is served by regarding it as role behavior.[37]

Notice that Whitam, too, endorses a strong model—the realist one—in the phrase beginning "no useful theoretical purpose . . ."

AN INTERACTIONIST APPROACH

Hiding among these examples, of course, is evidence that both realist and social-constructionist approaches are required if we want to understand sexual orientation fully. Below is an excerpt from a story written by Plato; it shows that even though the ancient Greeks did not attach moral significance to homosexuality as opposed to heterosexuality, they still seemed to understand the distinction between the two.

The situation is a dinner party at which each guest gives a speech on love. It is assumed as a matter of course by all participants that they will talk of the love of males by males. One guest—Aristophanes —describes the mythical origins of what can only be described as preferential homosexuality. The Aristophanes character says that there were at first three sexes—male, female, and hermaphrodite. Every human had two faces, four arms and four legs, two sets of genitalia—double the usual number of everything. They were so powerful they attacked the gods, and of course the gods struck back: Zeus sent his thunderbolts to chop each of them in half. Here was the result:

> Each of us when separated is but the indenture [half] of a man,
> . . . like a flat fish, and he is always looking for his other half.
> Men who are a section of that double nature which was once

[37] The quotation is from Whitam 1977. Other works are Whitam 1980 and 1983. Whitam and Mathy 1986 is the most detailed.

called Androgynous are lascivious [for women] . . . : the women who are a section of the [former] woman don't care for men, but have female attachments. . . . But the men who are a section of the [ancient] male follow the male. . . . And when one of them finds his other half, . . . the pair are lost in an amazement of love and friendship and intimacy, and one will not be out of the other's sight, as I may say, even for a moment.[38]

One colleague of mine, reading between the lines in other works, tells me that the real Aristophanes was probably interested in women (in modern terms, "was heterosexual")—and was widely known as such. If so, then his character's stirring defense of homosexual love in "The Symposium" would have been interpreted as a bit of dry humor. Another colleague believes the entire story was intended by Plato to be taken as a joke. Neither suggestion changes the bottom line: that in ancient Greece one could talk and write about homosexuality and heterosexuality lightheartedly, *at the same time as* one talked as if they were unchangeable sexual orientations.

This conclusion shows how a realist factor interacts with a social-constructionist factor in a way equal to more than just the sum of the parts. Yes, ancient Greece clearly had a social construction of "homosexuality" that is very different from the one we have today. But yes, even ancient Greeks realized that people could have a lifelong trait that meant they would search for lovers among one sex only. In order to understand the sociology, you need the realistic "given," and in order to understand the biology, you need the socially constructed "given."

Moreover, ancient Greece was not as committed to the age-biased ideal as it may seem. Some documents imply that because of appearance or personality a particular person would be a beloved his entire life, while another would be a lover throughout his. Some of the famous lover/beloveds of the time were of the same age, and some couples were so well reciprocally bonded to each other that their friends never could figure out which of the two was "the lover" and which "the beloved." Indeed, recall the story told by Aristophanes above, which explained why each man seeks his "other half" erotically. There's an aspect to this story that I have never seen discussed. If indeed people search for a life partner because they were split off from the partner physically, then it follows that both partners must be the same age. Yet Greek literature records an ideal that the partners be quite

[38] Jowett 1973.

different in age. I don't know what to make of this; nor does any classicist with whom I've discussed it.[39]

The berdache-burial matter among the Zuñi is also more complicated than a purely realist point of view would admit. True, the berdache was buried among the men. But the phrase "Is this man not?" is ambiguous; it suggests that the informant viewed the berdache as both essentially male (as shown by the burial on the men's side) *and* essentially a mixture of the male and female sexes (as shown by the burial clothing). Tellingly, Parsons included a footnote to the word *"lu,"* explaining that "personal pronouns showing sex are lacking in Zuñi"—which is presumably why she translated *"lu"* as "this" instead of "he" or "she." It's our Westerner dualism, remember, that insists that a particular Zuñi would have only one point of view on the matter.

Jacobs likewise demonstrated how we have to get rid of our Western dualism to understand these other cultures; she asked her informants

> if women are ever *quetho*s. The answer was no. Then I asked if men were the only ones who were *quetho*s. Again, the answer was no. In trying to force a categorization of *quetho*s as women or men (or female or male), I only exasperated my Tewa friends. . . .[40]

And Williams himself pointed out:

> If those [American Indian] languages are intentionally vague on this matter [whether berdaches are a third gender or a mixture of male and female], perhaps we should not split hairs. Man-woman, halfman-halfwoman, notman-notwoman—all convey the same idea.[41]

The late anthropologist Margaret Mead was interested in the light anthropology could shed on gender roles, and her work is often cited to demonstrate that human sex differences have cultural roots. Few people know she studied the berdache, however, and fewer still have run across the following passage:

[39] John Boswell, the noted Yale historian, however, suggested in a recent conversation that this aspect of the story told by Aristophanes means just what it appears to mean: that male-male relationships without significant age differences were taken in stride by the ancient Greeks.

[40] Jacobs 1983, p. 460.

[41] Williams 1986, p. 83.

During our stay in the field [among the Omaha Indians], we were visited by a male friend who had been living an avowed homo-erotic life in Japan, who was not a transvestite but who had a complete repertoire of homosexual postures. Within an hour of his arrival, the single berdache in the tribe turned up and tried to make contact with him.[42]

I'm not exactly sure what Mead meant by the phrase "homosexual postures," but the point is that this berdache clearly recognized a kin-ship with, and perhaps also a sexual attraction to, the visitor. Indeed, according to Williams, "All of the berdaches I have interviewed even-tually specified their sexual activities with men, but only after I had gained their confidence."[43]

This instant recognition is one that many gay people say they have when they recognize homosexuality in others—sometimes even be-fore admitting that they have homosexual desires. Compare Mead's story with the following passage from the autobiography of Robert Bauman, the conservative ex-congressperson from Maryland who lost his seat when his attraction to men became public in 1980. Bauman was nineteen or twenty when, one evening about dusk, a young sailor in navy whites approached him.

I cannot to this day explain what happened next. Something oc-curred between this young sailor and me, some undefined under-standing we both accepted. Without words, we knew what was going to happen. . . . It was a couple of hours later before I let him out of the car at the entrance to the Baltimore-Washington Parkway.[44]

It is very difficult to explain things like this purely with social con-structionism. The existence of such desires, and the fact that they can be acted upon with no explicit recognition of their meaning, strongly suggests that some underlying substrate is coming to the fore.

Children learn that "playing doctor" is a way of taking off clothes and examining each other's bodies; they don't need anyone to teach them that they enjoy playing doctor. I suspect that they'd invent something like playing doctor even if no one socialized them into its quasi-acceptability. Likewise, people like Bauman *act* as if they know

---

[42] Mead 1961, p. 1452.
[43] Williams 1986, p. 105.
[44] See Bauman 1986a or 1986b.

exactly what they want to do even when they and their society con-
spire to keep them from thinking about it consciously.

Yet whatever that substrate may consist of, it is clearly not enough
to explain the full range of variation from the berdache's bitchiness to
sex between congressmen and sailors. The social constructions through
which the substrates are interpreted are amazing in and of themselves
and become positively dizzying when you think out their interactions—just as dizzying as Alice's experiences in Wonderland were. On
the other hand, the substrates themselves must be pretty amazing in
order to survive repression by the powerful forces of culture and socialization.

In fact, when someone studies a culture in enough detail, *it turns
out again and again that the range of gender transpositions in the culture is
amazingly similar to the range in our own.* Even the barriers between
the three types of homosexuality (age-biased, inversion, and role-
playing) become fuzzy when you get to know individual people and
cultures well enough. Serena Nanda, professor of anthropology at John
Jay College of Criminal Justice, in studying the hijras, privately classified each one as "transsexual," "homosexual cross-dresser," and
"heterosexual transvestite," because these terms seemed to accurately
describe important variations in their personalities. Williams reports a
teenaged effeminate American Indian boy who ran away to a city and
was picked up by two Sioux Indian drag queens, who let him stay
with them and introduced him to the drag scene[45]—just as the hijras
do in their own way. In modern American drag pageants, participants
learn their best techniques from older and wiser drag queens who
have taken them under their wing after winning the pageants themselves in previous years. Many American Indian berdaches were highly
cross-gendered and insisted that they "really" were women (e.g., by
faking menstruation; see above)—just as many male-to-female transsexuals today insist that they are physical hermaphrodites even in the
absence of medical confirmation. These berdaches find their genitals
so inconsistent with their preferred sex role that they resist touching
their own erect penis and insist that their partners do the same[46] (i.e.,
refrain from touching the berdache's penis)—just as many transsexuals find their genitals repulsive, say that they do not touch them
when (and if) they masturbate, and insist that their sexual partners
likewise refrain from touching these parts of the body (the transsexual's body). On the other hand, other berdaches seemed perpetually
surrounded by teenaged males, with whom it was assumed they were

[45] Williams 1986, p. 213.
[46] Williams 1986, pp. 97–98, quoting Devereux.

having sexual relations,[47] while other berdaches report that they have always been attracted to men much older than themselves,[48] and yet others report behavior and attractions to boys and men their own age. Sexual relations or no, many berdaches adopt teenagers no longer willing or able to live with their biological parents[49]—and act, as the ancient Greeks did, as mentors and confidants to them. Some berdaches confined their cross-dressing to articles of women's *under*-clothing and seemed to have fetishistic attachments to such clothing and to women's jewelry,[50] which closely resembles the behavior of heterosexual transvestites.

Williams, who reported many of these instances, describes certain berdaches in terms that suggest that they resemble modern transsexuals. He has, apparently, independently discovered among modern working-class whites a category John Money calls "gynemimetic" and which I classify as a subtype of drag queen (a man who so effectively mimics a woman's behavior patterns that otherwise ordinary heterosexual men can be sexually attracted to him even when they know the gynemimetic is "really" a man). Since Williams approached the spectrum of the gender transpositions with a different set of assumptions than Money and I do, it is remarkable—and very important—that he nevertheless ended up with the same conclusion about the similarities between berdaches and the various gender transpositions as classified by Western scientists.[51]

And finally, consider a conservative culture like Saudi Arabia, where traditional women are still veiled, where no woman is ever left alone with a man not a close relative, and where what little homosexuality manages to escape severe suppression is supposedly satisfied with boys or with Western gay tourists willing to play a receptive role. But in such a society, there exist men quite like the openly gay men of the United States in all respects except their openness.

> I was more curious than ever about this man who challenged all the myths about sex with an Arab. . . . Once, in response to one

[47] Williams 1986, p. 100. See also the passage from Catlin that Williams quotes on pp. 107–108.

[48] Williams 1986, pp. 99–100. The largest age discrepancy he happens to report involved a relationship between a feminine boy of eight and a man over forty.

[49] Williams 1986, pp. 54–55 and passim.

[50] Williams 1986, p. 72, cites an example from Margaret Mead's work among the Omaha; on p. 73, a modern example from the same tribe.

[51] Since so many of these points depend on the book by Williams (1986), let me stress that his observations are widely confirmed by other observers. Note also that Williams does not endorse the concept of transsexualism (pp. 79–80), which makes his agreement on other points all the more striking. A gynemimetic is described on pp. 116–117 of Williams 1986.

of my personal questions, he shook his head disgustedly, grabbing my mustache and then his own. "You are a man. See? I am a man. See? No problem. We like fucking. That's all. OK?" But as he dropped me off a few minutes later, he said with the moon in his eyes, "Oh, Habibi, I will dream of us making love all night." And then he kissed me.[52]

Moreover, a formal berdachelike institution does exist in neighboring Oman.[53] The *xaniths*, as they're called, mix freely with women no matter what the rules of male-female contact would otherwise require. They wear an article of clothing called the *dishdasha*—typical for men, but they wrap it in a feminine way and dye it any of several pastel colors. (Ordinary men always wear white dishdashas.) Hairstyles and jewelry are (as a rule) intermediate between what would be considered ordinary for men and for women. So once again Arabic culture expresses the full range of homosexuality seen in the West: the cross-gendered, the age-biased, and the urban gay male buddy.

In short, *the better we know the cultures involved, the more the various gender-transposition patterns merge into and overlap each other.* Social constructionists say that's just the point—this incredible mishmash of gender patterns is organized by particular cultures into particular discrete categories: berdache versus nonberdache; ordinary homosexual versus drag queen versus transsexual versus ordinary heterosexual; hijra versus nonhijra. And they're right. The realists are also right; they argue that the similarity of this mishmash from culture to culture is very strong evidence that it is not constructed from culture alone.

CONCLUSIONS

There is more than one kind of homosexuality in the world. Most societies have most types and encourage them in different proportions. It is likely—as we will see in later chapters—that some of these types exist ultimately because of genetic factors that go at least as far back as our hunter-gatherer ancestors (which is where the human race spent most of its time evolving away from other primates). This means that we need to gather data on genetic factors in order to explain *why we are what we are.* But it is also clear that each society has its own way of socially constructing and emphasizing these types—constructions that can change and that have enormously important influences on individual people's lives. These behaviors are con-

[52] Traughber 1985, p. 36.
[53] Wikan 1982.

structed so drastically differently that people from one society trying to find themselves in another might just as well be looking for the Mad Hatter and the March Hare. These different constructions perhaps depend in part on the genetic distributions prevalent in a given society, but if so, they are certainly not completely determined by such distributions. In order to understand *why we love whom we love,* we need to know how society has constructed particular sexual classifications, because the effects of having particular genetic predispositions can be entirely different, depending on the social constructions of the society possessing those genes.

In short, genes and societies don't just add; they interact. Was it all right for me, back in chapter 2, to give definitions of transvestite, drag queen, transsexual, and homosexual—as if they constituted real categories? Yes. Was it culturally biased for me to give these definitions rather than others? Yes.

So: are the gender transpositions social constructions of particular societies, or are they essential realities transcending particular cultures? The answer, of course, is yes—which is obvious, once you've transcended your own Western dualism.[54]

If you are a native speaker of English, you don't really comprehend its complexities and limitations unless you know at least one foreign language. You cannot imagine how varied the English language can be until you seek out the languages that are most extremely unlike it. And, of course, these variations are due to cultural factors, not genetic ones.

But neither can you arrive at a complete understanding of language without understanding the uniquely human adaptation that language constitutes biologically. We speak because others around us speak, but we also speak because we have circuits built into our brains that seem designed to understand speech. Accordingly, as I construct my theory of the gender transpositions in the chapters that follow, I will have to pay close attention to the interaction between genetic predispositions and the society in which those predispositions have their effects. I will have to explain not only why we are what we are but also why we love whom we love. It's time to start constructing human sexual desire socially and biologically: in both heterosexual and homosexual varieties, for both females and males. That's the job of chapter 6.

---

[54]Once you've solved this problem, you can start dealing with the sound of one hand clapping.

6

LIMERENCE, LUST, AND BISEXUALITY: A NEW THEORY

"Many Lesbians didn't know they were Lesbians until their 20s or 30s," said [Lesbian sexologist] Loulan, "because they didn't know the feelings they were having about their best friends—wanting to stay over every night and talk—were *sexual* feelings. Gay men, on the other hand, *knew* they wanted to have sex with their best friends."
JoAnn Loulan, author of *Lesbian Sex,* quoted in the *Washington Blade,*
17 May 1985, p. 9.

"Yes, I'm still a lesbian, even though I love a man."
Harriet Lane, quoted in *The Advocate* (8 July 1986, p. 9, issue 450).

The idea that there are different sorts of sexual attraction is not new. The ancient Greeks, for example, had three words—*eros, philia,* and *agape*[1]—that they used for different kinds of attraction,

[1] However, Boswell 1980, pp. 46–48 suggests that distinctions among these three are difficult to make in practice.

and modern English has at least two—love and lust. But not many scientific theories pay attention to these different kinds of sexiness. In fact, sex-research books like Kinsey's are often criticized for talking only about sex, ignoring love.

Not this book! I have constructed a theory that puts the idea of at least two sexual attractions into a precise form.[2] I call it the "limerent and lusty" theory because it postulates the existence of two different sexual attractions: a "limerent" type and a "lusty" type (defined below). This theory explains parts of several of the puzzles introduced in chapter 3, namely:

- *The "how common?" puzzle:* How common is bisexuality?
- *The "what is bi about bisexuals?" puzzle:* In what respect are bisexual people bisexual? Is everybody bisexual?
- *The approval puzzle:* Why is homosexuality better accepted by and among women than among men?

Briefly, I'll sketch my theory's solutions to these puzzles, then plunge into the theory itself in detail.

Brief solution to the "how common?" puzzle: The limerent/lusty theory proposes that there are two different kinds of sexual attraction. Suppose that one of these two attractions figures into one definition of bisexuality and the other kind figures into another definition. If one attraction can be bisexual while another kind usually is not, then using one definition will lead to the conclusion that bisexuality is common, and using the other will lead to the conclusion that it is not.

Brief solution to the "what is bi about bisexuals?" puzzle: This puzzle is solved in different ways for the two sexes. Bisexuality in men happens most often when one kind of sexual attraction is mostly for men and another kind is mostly for women. Bisexuality in women happens most often when one of the two kinds of sexual attraction itself is an attraction for both sexes.

Brief solution to the "approval" puzzle: The limerent/lusty theory proposes that one kind of sexual attraction is usually easier for women to discover and the other easier for men to discover. If the heterosexuals in a survey judging homosexuals consider their own sexual attractions, it would be easier for them to understand a type of sexuality

---

[2]The theory described in this chapter arose from my thinking about the periodic-table model described in chapter 7, which in turn grew from an idea proposed by my colleague Richard Pillard. I doubt I would have thought out the present theory without the stimulus of the periodic-table theory. I would also probably not have worked out an important aspect of the theory had I not received a challenging letter from University of Wisconsin zoologist John Kirsch.

that has parallels in their own lives. (Heterosexual women are attracted to men, and so it is easier for them to understand how a man would be attracted to men. And vice versa for heterosexual men.) Moreover, if the sexual attraction most women experience is the kind more likely to focus on both sexes, then women will disapprove less of homosexuality in women than men disapprove of it in men.

Before I expand on these brief answers, let me explain why we need a new theory of sexual attraction in the first place.

OTHER THEORIES

Most psychological and social-psychological theories don't do a very good job of explaining the three puzzles above. Here, for example, is a theory proposed by a social psychologist:

> A hypothesis was derived . . . that heterosexual females would recall socialization experiences that channelled their erotic potential towards heterosexual role performance; whereas, in contrast, the Lesbians would recollect socialization experiences that alienated them from such psychosexual role behavior.[3]

This specific hypothesis came from the more general social-psychological one that everyone is bisexual, at least to begin with. It suggests that conditioning in childhood and adolescence (and perhaps also in adulthood) is responsible for causing people to prefer one sex or the other erotically. It is "significant others" who use "gestures, overt behavioral manifestations and role model performance"[4] who deflect sexual behavior toward homosexuality or toward heterosexuality.

Now this theory has a problem: male homosexuality is more disapproved of than lesbianism is. If male homosexuality is more disapproved, then it is less saliently role modeled, and this socialization theory suggests that male homosexuality would be rarer than lesbianism is. It is not, as I showed in chapter 3. Why not?

One answer is a simple generalization: *men are more likely to be sexually atypical than women are.* This seems to be true in a number of departments: from fetishism to exhibitionism to transvestism to transsexualism.[5] But this poses a problem in the study of bisexuality, be-

---

[3] Poole 1972, p. 56.
[4] Poole 1972, pp. 51–52.
[5] Some sexologists believe males do not outnumber females in every single one of these categories. But as a generalization it's true.

cause bisexuality of most types is more common in women than in men.

One popular solution to both these problems is a variation of the "everybody is bisexual" theory mentioned above. Assuming that all humans have natural attractions to both sexes, how would people react when they discover that society disapproves of the homosexual part of their desires? Female-female pairing is less disapproved of (women can live together with less suspicion than men can, for example), so women are more often able to fulfill the same-sex part of their bisexual desires. Therefore, it is argued, women less often need to label themselves homosexual in order to act on those desires. Males with feelings for other males, in contrast, know that acting on those feelings will be more heavily disapproved. So only the most highly motivated males (the "most homosexual" ones) do so. This explanation claims that social disapproval forces a choice on people with bisexual feelings if they are men more often than it does upon women and that it is this that creates the impression that homosexuality is more common among men than women but that bisexuality is more common among women than among men.

There may be some truth in this explanation, but there are many difficulties with it. The first problem is that the explanation is complicated—or, as we scientists put it, "not parsimonious." By itself, this objection isn't very strong; after all, some things really are complicated and require convoluted explanations. But it makes scientists suspicious because it suggests the reasoning is after the fact.

The second problem is that this explanation grew out of labeling theory, which suggests that a "deviant"[6] group has psychological problems *merely* because they are labeled as "deviant" by society at large. But labeling theory has been explicitly tested for homosexuality, and it didn't explain things very well; homosexuals living in societies that labeled homosexual acts as strongly "deviant" had about the same level of psychological problems as those living in societies that labeled them "deviant" much less extremely.[7]

A third problem is that many bisexuals say they are even more discriminated against than homosexuals are—that they are disliked by heterosexuals for their homosexual desires and by homosexuals for their heterosexual desires. If people really do dislike and distrust bisexuality that much, then socialization theory suggests that bisexuality should be less common than either heterosexuality or homosexuality.

---

[6] As these scholars called homosexuals.
[7] Weinberg and Williams 1974.

But some bisexuals say it's more common, and it certainly is so under some definitions.[8]

But the best rebuttal of this theory, I believe, comes from looking at the history of beliefs about how common homosexuality is. That female-female relations are less taboo is a fact that has been known for over a century. Until recently this fact was used to infer that lesbianism was much *more* common than male homosexuality. This belief was widespread in 1952:[9]

> The number of homosexuals in the population has always been a matter of dispute. The usual figures of 1 to 2% up to 8 or 10% . . . gives an enormous number in such a large country as the United States. . . . Moreover, this is only for males; the number would be much larger for lesbians.

After all, common sense supported this belief: anyone could see women embracing on the street, no one made much of a fuss about it, so of course it seemed there would be more of it. But the Kinsey researchers showed just the opposite: lesbianism is not more common than male homosexuality. Did this send everyone off in a frenzy looking for other disciplines that could explain the new fact other than social-psychologically? No; the older theories were simply reworked and became the people-are-homosexual-because-society-forces-them-to-choose theory.

As it happens, I do not think that the biological theories of the time were good ones, and I make it clear in another chapter that biologic and social-psychological models are not incompatible or "the opposite" of each other. I'm just suggesting that social psychology is not the only place to look for answers to these questions, and it's surprising that so many people believe that it ought to provide all the answers.

THE LIMERENT/LUSTY THEORY

None of the complaints I've just voiced above are fatal to the social-psychological view. Taken together, however, they do suggest that we should shop around, scientifically speaking.

In my humble opinion, the limerent/lusty theory is a good buy. I've tried to construct it as efficiently as possible. I begin with a minimum

---

[8] Klein 1978.

[9] The quotation is from Allen 1952, p. 237. For other examples, see Kinsey et al. 1953, pp. 475–476.

number of plainly stated hypotheses, then add a few principles of deduction. Then I let these principles loose upon the hypotheses; the results are deductions that match the facts as we now understand them.

As I've mentioned, I think the key to solving the puzzles lies in thinking about at least two different types of sexual attraction. C. A. Tripp, who was a consultant to Kinsey on homosexuality and is now a psychotherapist in private practice, was on the right track when he wrote that many bisexual men

> have developed a double [sexual] value system: They rate and choose their male and female partners by applying quite separate sets of criteria. . . . [Some of these men] point out that although they enjoy their contacts with both men and women, "you must understand, the two experiences are *entirely different.*"[10]

Tripp made a point now common in the bisexuality literature: sexual attraction to men and sexual attraction to women are not opposites and are not necessarily incompatible. I agree in part with this conclusion.[11] And in a second important passage, Tripp made a point about promiscuity and pair-bonding.

> Consider, for instance, the man who has had perhaps a hundred brief encounters, a number of short-range affairs, and one profound relationship which lasts for years or for the rest of his life. This combination of experiences is not at all unusual and it lends itself to three correct statements about the man: that he is highly promiscuous, that most of his relationships do not last, and that he clearly can and does maintain an important and substantial ongoing relationship.[12]

This passage suggests that desire for a long-term relationship and desire for short-term relationships are not opposites and are not necessarily incompatible. Either desire can present itself spontaneously as if it were an independent "impulse," and either might present itself only in reaction to certain stimuli as if it were a "response" (see definitions below). But if the two kinds of desire are distinct, a given person might be especially responsive to both of them, neither of them, or just one of them and less so the other.

[10]Tripp 1975, p. 95, italics in original. See also pp. 94–97 and chapter 8 of that book.

[11]Note how this is a two-dimensional point of view that says that homosexual and heterosexual responses are logically independent of each other and could be measured on different scales. This point of view will be strongly underscored in chapter 7.

[12]Tripp 1975, p. 160.

In the limerent/lusty theory, I connect these two insights with other ideas to form a general theory of sexual attraction. This theory begins independently of the periodic-table model described in chapter 7, but by the end of that chapter the two theories merge. The result is a powerful theory of sexual attraction that explains most of the features of sexual orientation in humans, including bisexuality.

DEFINITIONS

The first distinction is between *sexual impulses* and *sexual responses*—more generally, between an *impulse* and *response*.[13]

A *response* is a behavior that occurs after a stimulus, is reliably related to the stimulus, and makes sense in the light of the stimulus.

Individuals have a response if they perform it with some regularity after the appropriate stimulus has been provided.

An *impulse* is either (1) a mental state associated with seeking whatever brings out a particular behavior—that is, looking for opportunities to perform a response—or (2) a readiness to perform a behavior that occurs even without a particular stimulus.

Individuals have an impulse if they seek out opportunities to perform particular responses in the absence of a stimulus that would logically be expected to elicit them.

So both an impulse and a response are readinesses to perform particular behaviors. The difference is that a response occurs only under a particular set of circumstances logically related to the behavior, whereas an impulse reflects the readiness to perform the behavior even without a particular circumstance. Another way to put this is that the threshold for eliciting a behavior is high or specific for a response, but it is low, random, or nonexistent for an impulse.[14] When I want to refer to either an impulse or a response without specifying which, I

---

[13] In an early version of this theory, I used the term "drive" instead of "impulse." Some people believe the term "drive" is discredited. I agree it can be misused, but that's not a convincing reason in and of itself to drop it. But this dispute has nothing to do with the way I would *want* to use "drive," so I have decided to avoid getting distracted by something not central to my theory and use the word "impulse" instead. But some people have gotten confused by "impulse," too. The important distinction is between an attraction that arises from stimuli logically related to it and an attraction that seems to arise from no stimulus at all (not necessarily suddenly, however).

[14] In this view, then, responses and impulses are merely the ends of a continuum.

will use the term *attraction*: "attractions" is the general category to which impulses and responses both belong.

Here are some examples. Take a group of people and show them a sexually explicit film. With the right film, many of the penises of the men in this group will become erect, and many of the women's vaginas will lubricate (as I discussed in chapter 3). These reactions are those of sexual arousal and are understandable given the stimulus, so they are called sexual responses.

Now consider a group of people who simply want to see a film and are deciding which one to go see. Some of these people (even without consulting the film listings) may want to go see a sexually explicit film. Although this is not a strange reaction, aspects of it are not directly explainable in the light of the stimulus ("Let's go see a movie"). This kind of reaction is evidence of a sexual impulse—a readiness to engage in a sexually stimulating activity, even in the absence of overtly sexual stimuli. The earliest sexual dreams at puberty, typically, are examples of sexual impulses.

Now I'll describe two different kinds of sexual attraction: the "limerent" type and the "lusty" type.

Ladies and gentlemen, Ms. Cyndi Lauper—on limerence: [15]

> Lying in my bed
> I hear the clock tick
> And think of you
> Caught up in circles
> Confusion is nothing new.
> Flash 'back, warm nights
> Almost left behind
> Suitcase of memories
> Time after [time]. . .
>
> If you're lost you can look
> And you will find me
> Time after time
> If you fall I will catch you
> I will be waiting
> Time after time.[16]

[15] The term "limerence" was coined by Dorothy Tennov (in her 1979 book). On purpose, she chose it to have no root in any language.

[16] "Time After Time," by C. Lauper and R. Hyman. © 1983 Rella Music Co. and Dub Notes. All rights reserved. Used by permission.

Limerent sexual attractions eroticize the physical or personality traits of a particular Limerent Object.[17] That is, limerence is involved when someone "falls in love" with someone they have met or are getting to know and whose *particular* traits become erotic over a period of time. It is often inhibited when the Limerent Object is a new stimulus (viz., a stranger), although with some people this period of inhibition is short. Lauper's lyrics are limerent because they refer to memories of particular events in the life of a particular couple and idealize an enduring relationship.

And now, ladies and gentlemen, here is Julie Brown to tell us about *lusty* sexual attraction:

> When I need something to help me unwind
> I find a 6-foot baby with a one-track mind.
> Smart guys are nowhere, they make demands;
> Give me a moron with talented hands!
> I go barhopping, and they say "Last call!"—
> I start shopping for a Neanderthal.
>
> The bigger they come,
> The harder I fall
> In love, till we're done
> And they're out in the hall.
> I like 'em big and
> Stupid.
> I like 'em big and
> Real dumb.
> I like 'em big and
> Stupid.[18]

Lusty sexual attractions refer to the physical or personality traits of a particular *type* of person and are initially directed toward particular, previously unknown people who resemble that type. That is, *lust* is involved when a person "falls in lust" with someone with whom they are not previously acquainted soon after first seeing or meeting them. Lustiness is usually easier to recognize when the Lusty Object is a stranger and in some people is inhibited when the Lusty Object is

---

[17] See Tennov 1979, p. 33, for a justification for using the term "object" to apply to human beings.

[18] "I Like 'Em Big and Stupid." © 1984 Stymie Music, Inc. Used by permission. I thank Deryk Tejada for pointing out this song to me.

familiar (i.e., a friend). Brown's lyrics describe an attraction to particular physical and mental endowments.

It is extremely important to point out that both limerence and lustiness are *sexy*. Our society would prefer to believe that limerence is not very sexy: that it's warm romantic fuzzies, while lust is the "really" sexual attraction. Not so.[19] Likewise, I reject the (male-biased) notion that lust is "real" sexiness and limerence is "mere" love and the prudish notion that limerence is "good" sexiness and lust is "bad" sexiness.

Admittedly, sometimes lustiness turns to limerence with the passage of time, but in some people lustiness never becomes limerence. The crucial difference between the two is this: when you feel something is wrong with someone you're attracted to (call this person your "LO," since both "Limerent Object" and "Lusty Object" have the same abbreviation), what improvements come to mind? If your LO is brown-haired and at the moment you prefer blond, do you think of getting a different girlfriend? Do you ask her to dye her hair? If either one of these happens, then your LO is a lusty object: you want to change your human friend to better resemble your lusty type. If, on the other hand, you decide that brown hair looks pretty good, after all, or that you never really cared that much about hair color, anyway, then your LO is a limerent object: what is sexy to you changed as a result of your fixing upon the characteristics of your human friend. Likewise, if your LO picks his nose in public and you drop him quickly because filthy habits spoil your image of him, then you probably got rid of a Lusty Object. If on the other hand you worry that when he picks his nose no one else thinks he's cute, then he's a Limerent Object that your friends will be hinting you ought to drop.

In short, if your love is blind, then it's limerence. If your love is blond, then it's lust.

THE THREE HYPOTHESES

So much for the definitions; now it's time to deduce. Most of the facts about sexual orientation can be deduced from just three hypotheses of the limerent/lusty theory, presented below. I follow each hypothesis

[19]This point was clearly noted by Tennov 1979. Perper 1985, pp. 184–186, has made a similar point: women's sexuality—as represented by limerence—is public and approved, while men's sexuality—at least as represented by lust—is private and disapproved. This fact is reflected in song lyrics. I could have found hundreds if not thousands of songs illustrating limerence; I had a great deal of trouble finding any that clearly illustrated lust. And most popular songs are written by men!

with a discussion—an extended discussion in the case of the third and most controversial one.

The First Hypothesis

Limerence and lustiness are experienced by both sexes. There is, however, an average sex difference in the ease with which each can be elicited in a particular sex. In particular . . .

- Limerence is experienced by most women in our culture as an impulse, while lustiness, when it occurs, is experienced as a response, and . . .
- Lustiness is experienced by most men in our culture as an impulse, while limerence, when it occurs, is experienced as a response.

Of course the expectation of which kind of impulse or response is considered appropriate for which sex has cultural roots, and perhaps other roots, as well. (I'll get to this in a moment.)

This is the key hypothesis of the theory, and I have phrased it as gender-neutrally as I believe the evidence will permit. Both sexes are capable of responding in both ways. Men fantasize about falling in love, and they fall in love often.[20] When women are placed in sexually stimulating environments, they can and do respond with sexual arousal, to about the same extent as men do when placed in corresponding environments.[21] But there is an average sex difference in the ease with which these responses can be elicited in the two sexes and in the extent to which each sex actively seeks out such stimuli.

Here's an example of the sex difference in operation. Most men— of whatever persuasion—know ahead of time what turns them on sexually. In the language of chapter 3, they are *partial* to certain parts of the body or to certain types of people. Because these partialisms are part of lusty sexual arousal, they are at the center of men's sexual patterns. More women, on the other hand, do not know ahead of time what they are partial to; they are indeed partial, but these partialisms are not as central to their (limerent) sexual patterns. To discover these partialisms, they have to think about whether they have

[20] Friday 1980 is an entire book on men in love. See also Tennov 1979.

[21] I presented arguments to this effect in chapter 3. Evolutionary biologist Donald Symons (1979, pp. 170ff.) also has an excellent review of experiments supporting this position. If you doubt the existence of lusty sexual arousal in ordinary women, I recommend that you attend a burlesque show where men strip for women. Afterward, you will have no doubt that what you saw was lust.

them and what they are. Pat Califia, a California sexologist who writes the "Adviser" column for the national gay newspaper *The Advocate,* is herself a good example. A lesbian reader wrote Ms. Califia that gay men seem to know exactly which parts of the body turn them on but that she had never heard of such preferences among gay women—although she noticed that she had them herself. Califia responded, "Hmmm. This is a fascinating subject that could certainly use some more discussion," and said she would conduct an informal poll among her friends. "Now that I think about it," she continued, she noticed that she, too, had partialisms. But she could not remember seeing anything on the topic in the lesbian sex literature—to which she is a prominent contributor.[22]

To someone trying to understand female sexuality through the lens of male sexuality, this answer would be astonishing. A lesbian sexologist and author of women's erotica who has to *think* for a while to decide whether she has a "type"? Most men would think for about one millisecond before telling you what their type is! This example underscores the importance of not approaching female sexuality just from the point of view of a masculine model. Likewise, principles more prominent in women's sexuality—limerence, for example—can be applied to men's sexuality, but only with caution.

In sum, men know ahead of time that they have lusty impulses but typically have to *learn* that they have limerent responses. Women know ahead of time that they have limerent impulses but typically have to *learn* that they have lusty responses.

The Second Hypothesis

The definition of the limerent attraction states that it depends on friendship and familiarity. Accordingly, in some people the limerent attraction can be indifferent (or nearly so) to the sex or gender of the Limerent Object.

This hypothesis is unproved but very reasonable, as many people know they can be friends with both men and women. In these cases, limerent attractions can be bisexual, and the Limerent Object's genitalia and/or gender would be less important than his or her personality or character would be in eliciting limerence. However, there may be some people whose friendships occur among one sex alone; there is nothing preventing limerence in these people from being unisexual.

---

[22] In the past two years or so there has been a flood of sexually explicit erotica created by women for women. Lesbians and feminist heterosexuals finally decided it was time to stop complaining about erotica created by or for men and to show by example what they thought feminist erotica could be. Califia's column appeared in *The Advocate,* 8 July 1986, p. 90.

In contrast, lusty attractions are very unlikely to be bisexual because they key into a particular "type" of Lusty Object in which visual factors (and hence, usually, genitalia) are important. I formalize this belief below.

The Third Hypothesis

Most men and some women are capable of undergoing an eroticization/imprinting experience (defined below) before adulthood that imprints an image of the Lusty Object into the developing brain—an image that typically is discovered to be the sexually attractive object when the child's sexuality is turned on by hormonal changes in puberty or later life.

This third hypothesis is controversial because it sounds biologic, and it won't help very much to point out that some social scientists use similar language in purely cultural models.[23] In animals, eroticization/imprinting experiences are very well described, although species vary in their "imprintability."[24]

Just what is an eroticization/imprinting experience? It is an imprinting experience that causes a particular class of objects to be viewed as erotic or sexy. Well, then, what is an imprinting experience? It is an exposure to a particular stimulus that is latched on to by the viewer and used as a template in the future for recognizing important individuals or objects in the environment.

Here's an example. A newborn chick needs to know which thing in its environment is its mother because its mother is the thing it runs to when scared, that it peeps at when hungry, that it follows when she moves away. Experiments have shown that the chick will imprint upon any prominent thing moving in its environment during a particular period of time after hatching. Normally, of course, this *is* its mother, and the image of the mother is said to be imprinted into the chick's brain. After this moment in time (called the *critical period*) passes, the mother can be replaced by a colored paper cutout, by a human being, by a red paper circle, or whatever—all to no effect. The chick, imprinted upon the image of its mother, will only direct its attention to the mother herself—or to a very good imitation of her.

But if you replace the mother earlier—throughout the duration of the critical period—with a different hen, a human being (viz., the an-

---

[23] For example, Poole, whom I quoted near the beginning of this chapter, mentions "a critical learning phase" and "an indelible imprint" at the beginning of his article describing a social-psychological theory of lesbianism. See Poole 1972.

[24] For some good examples of imprintability, see Lorenz 1937, as corrected by Scott 1978, pp. 82–83. Alcock 1984, pp. 99–101, is a good introduction.

imal's keeper), or even a colored paper cutout, the chick will imprint upon that object instead and subsequently treat it as if it were its mother. For example, a chick imprinted upon a red paper circle will follow a red paper circle moving about the hatchery (under the control of an experimenter). It will, at least in many species, subsequently reject its actual mother if presented with the imprinted-upon object at the same time.

This can be an *eroticization*/imprinting process because sometimes the imprinted-upon object becomes the object at which courtship is directed after sexual maturity. That is, the chick grows up and then directs its courtship displays at red paper circles. This sexual imprinting is usually illustrated with examples from male animals, although some female animals imprint also, depending on the species and the circumstances.

This sexual aspect of imprinting is very well documented in certain species—with results viewed as comical (if you are a skeptic) or tragic (if you are a pessimist).

[Dr.] Portielje, of the Amsterdam Zoological Gardens, raised a male of the South American Bittern *(Tigrisoma)* who, when mature, courted human beings [because it had imprinted upon Portielje himself when young]. When a female was procured, he first refused to have anything to do with her but accepted her later when left alone with her for a considerable time. The birds then successfully reared a number of broods, but even then Portielje had to refrain from visiting the birds too often, because the male would, on the appearance of the former foster-father, instantly rush at the female, drive her roughly away from the nest and, turning to his keeper, perform the ceremony of nest-relief, inviting Portielje to step into the nest and incubate! What is very remarkable in all this is that while all the bird's instinctive reactions pertaining to reproduction had been repeatedly and successfully performed with the female and not once had been consummated with a human being for their object, they yet stayed irreversibly conditioned to the latter in preference to the biologically proper object.[25]

Needless to say, this kind of situation happens most often in zoos, and it presents a problem to zookeepers, who want their birds to produce offspring. Some of them, willing to do almost anything to get these creatures to breed, have literally moved in with them and started

[25] Lorenz 1937, p. 263.

imitating their mating rituals.[26] They help the animals build their nests and perform the species-typical mating gestures (like nest relief) required to stimulate reproduction.[27] There are those who would look askance at this heterosexual bestiality, wonder whether the birds in question have given informed consent for such procedures, and otherwise marvel at the lengths to which we are willing to go to promote heterosexuality in all its delightful forms. In the zookeepers' defense, however, I should point out that these efforts are especially important when the species in question is endangered. Just don't ask whether federal funds are supporting these programs, please.[28]

One cannot help but be struck by the apparent similarity between these facts and one found in human eroticism.

> The hormones of puberty mature the body and activate in the mind the erotic sexualism that is already programed therein. . . . Pubertal adolescents do not choose their erotic sexualism. They encounter it, as preformed in the mind. That does not preclude the possibility of one's having the personal, subjective experience (or illusion) of choosing or selecting among options. . . . The protruding shape of girls' nipples, for example, may . . . [enter] imperatively into his erotic fantasies. . . . This boy will classify himself as a "tit man," . . . [and] persuade himself that he prefers or selects breast imagery as an erotic turn-on, and even persuade himself that his preference is a voluntary choice, whereas in point of fact it is an option that was preprogramed into him without his informed consent, perhaps as early as the age of three, when he was still unweaned and suckling at his mother's nipples.[29]

If that sounds too biological to you, then listen to the words of famous anthropologist Margaret Mead:

> both male and female infants learn in infancy something about the mother's breasts which will be part of the adult pattern of foreplay . . .[30]

---

[26] With results viewed as comical, tragic, or heroic—depending on whether you are a skeptic, a pessimist, or me.

[27] McNulty 1983.

[28] Here is my fantasy version of forthcoming testimony before the Senate Appropriations Committee: "In response to your question, Senator Proxmire, yes, I *would* conclude that taxpayer dollars are far better spent encouraging heterosexual bestiality among zookeepers than in promoting unwed motherhood by way of cutbacks in sex-education programs."

[29] Money 1980, p. 37.

[30] Mead 1961, p. 1456.

Of course, animal examples cannot be used to *conclude* that such mechanisms *must* or even *probably* exist in humans.[31] But they can be used to *suggest* that it would not be surprising to find such mechanisms in humans, because the mechanism is widespread in the animal kingdom. Even if it does exist, it might exist in only one sex; in many animals, for example, sexual objects attractive to males are determined by imprinting, but those attractive to females are genetically preset.[32] In other species, the sexually attractive objects in adulthood are genetically preprogrammed for both sexes.[33] And there may be, for all I know, various environmental or genetic conditions that make such imprinting more likely in particular individuals.

But is there any *direct* evidence that human beings really do imprint sexually on things from their early environment? Yes, there is, but most of it comes from the clinic. After all, for ethical reasons we can't very well put our babies in incubators and have cutout red paper circles feeding them and cooing to them, can we?

Well, no, but luckily for science we *can* surround them with rubber sheets in the crib and rubber panties. (I hope it's clear I'm getting sarcastic here.) For better or for worse, we often raise our babies in very unnatural environments, evolutionarily speaking, and this constitutes experimentation of a sort. Such unplanned experiments have very suggestive results.

There are men, for example, who are primarily aroused by sheets of skin-hugging rubber in various ways; they're called "rubber fetishists" by scientists and "rubber freaks" by the general public. Some scientists claim (and I believe them) that as society's infant-rearing substances change, so do the fetishes that show up twenty to thirty years later in adults. So, not too long from now, we should see fewer rubber fetishists and more Pampers fetishists. In fact, just about any fetishist will be happy to tell you about the objects or substances he encountered in his childhood (or, less often, adolescence) upon which he became imprinted. (I say "he" because just about all fetishists are men.)

The problem is Are these recollections an effect of the adult fascination, or are they really part of the cause? That is, did fetishists really have more childhood contact with their fetish objects than nonfetishists did? Or do they just remember those experiences more because as

---

[31] Such an argument would be by way of phylogeny (evolutionary relatedness or descent), and the phylogenetic occurrence of such imprinting is clearly not continuous from group to group.

[32] Alcock 1984, pp. 99–100.

[33] Lorenz 1937.

adults they're more interested in them? Scientifically speaking, from just a few stories we can't say which is cause and which is effect. But sexologists such as John Money (quoted above) make it their business to collect such stories, and although they can't put a statistical-significance value on these data, their reports are convincing: some things are sexually arousing or compelling to people because they imprinted upon them long ago.

Money is in a unique position, having followed some of his patients from their birth or early treatment in Johns Hopkins Hospital through adulthood, with records of conversations with the parents and the child every couple of years. When a kid who underwent multiple surgeries for birth defects in early childhood comes back at age twenty and tells you she has fantasies of having her body pierced and cut in various ways, you sit up and take notice. (And, in Money's case, you start pointing out to pediatric units the damage caused by treatment of a physical problem with not enough attention paid to the psychological effects on the child.) Or, when a teenager comes to you with fantasies of cross-dressing accompanied by sexual arousal, you ask the parents to bring in their family photo album and see if they took any pictures of Johnny cross-dressing when he was much younger. There often *are* ways of independently confirming the imprinting stories told to so many psychotherapists over the years—not every time, of course, but often enough to convince.

And sometimes they can be confirmed in striking ways. Consider the case of Daniel Paul Schreber, one of Sigmund Freud's most famous nonpatients. Born in 1842 in the kingdom of Saxony (part of what is now Germany), Schreber led an apparently normal life as a judge until 1884, when for a few months he was treated in a mental hospital. In 1893, at age fifty-one, he fell ill with paranoia and was confined in a mental hospital for nine years. Toward the end of this period, he wrote a book explaining his weird fantasies, which Freud read years later and interpreted as classic examples of paranoid thinking. Schreber's book helped get him out of the hospital in 1902, but in 1907 he relapsed and was recommitted. He died in the hospital in 1911.[34]

Schreber's fantasies were extremely unusual. Sexologically, there are three important threads in his story:

[34] The chronology is from Niederland 1984, pp. 6–7. William Niederland is the psychoanalyst who discovered the relationship between the writings of Schreber and his father, and has doggedly followed up ever since. Schreber Jr.'s original book is Schreber 1903; an English translation is Schreber 1955/1903. A widely available paperback dealing with the Schreber story (incidentally concluding that Schreber's father's child-rearing practices were part and parcel of Nazism) is Schatzman 1973.

- Schreber believed that in order to save the world he had to be transformed into a woman, that such a transformation was indeed taking place, and that it must be exquisitely pleasurable to participate as a woman in the sex act.
- Schreber believed that masturbation was terribly damaging and was proud that he had not succumbed to the temptation to perform it.
- On *one* night within a week of his second admission to the psychiatric ward, he had half a dozen nocturnal emissions ("wet dreams").

In addition, there are two other important, nonsexological threads:

- In the mental hospital, Schreber repeatedly experienced a series of bizarre and painful "miracles," ranging from little "fleetingly-drawn men" opening and closing his eyes for him, which he had to wipe away with a sponge, to the dreaded "compression-of-the-chest miracle," which consisted of "the whole chest wall being compressed, so that the state of oppression caused by the lack of breath was transmitted to my whole body." Then there was the "head-compressing-machine," which "compressed my head as though in a vice *[sic]* by turning a kind of screw, causing my head temporarily to assume an elongated almost pear-shaped form."[35]
- Schreber's father, Dr. Daniel Gottlieb Moritz Schreber, was a world-famous orthopedist who wrote prolifically and crusaded for advanced child-rearing techniques—among them, various practices that nowadays would be regarded as sexually repressive and sadistic. Schreber Sr. recommended, for example, that infants have their eyebrows, eyelids, and eyes cleansed several times a day with little sponges soaked in cold water. He believed that posture in childhood was so important that he devised orthopedic restraints to ensure that children adopt the proper posture while sitting, standing, or sleeping. One of these devices, the *Geradhalter,* was fastened to a chair and consisted of a metal rod that came up from between the legs, joined a crossbar, and pressed firmly against the chest, making poor sitting posture impossible. A variation on this device had leather straps attached at the top that encircled and tightly bound the head in a posturally correct position. Schreber Sr.'s books rec-

[35] Niederland 1984, p. 76. These passages are from chapter XI, pp. 131–139 of the English translation. The sponge is mentioned on p. 138.

ommended that these and similar devices be used from the earliest ages possible and strongly implied that they had been used on his own children regularly.

Yet Schreber Jr. mentions no such devices or training techniques in his book and seems completely unaware that his psychiatric "miracles" had anything to do with the way his father raised him. How could he? Schreber Sr. was an internationally acclaimed authority on proper child-rearing techniques; organizations named after him survive in Europe to this day.

Need I say more? Yes, I do, and I will in a later chapter. For the moment, suffice it to say there are times when a single case will demonstrate a point: that human beings *can* (not necessarily *will*) psychologically and sexologically imprint upon objects and experiences that stand out in their childhood environments in some way and that they may utterly fail to recall those objects and experiences in adulthood. If they do recall them, however, it often is entirely true that they had these experiences more often than others who do not recall them (i.e., their memory of the "specialness" and frequency of those recollections is correct).

THE THREE HYPOTHESES, RESTATED

I will now restate and slightly extend the three hypotheses in the light of the above discussion, in reverse order, as follows:

• 3. *Your lusty sexual impulse (and probably also your lusty sexual response) is directed at a particular class of Lusty Objects that you have previously been imprinted upon. Your attraction to such an object begins with visual arousal at a distance.*

A logical consequence of this hypothesis is that lusty attraction is unlikely to be bisexual, since male and female roles, genitalia, and outward appearances are significantly different from each other—in every culture known to anthropology, not to mention in our own.

• 2. *The limerent attraction is directed not at a particular class of objects but at a particular kind of relationship with a Limerent Object— an eroticized particular friendship. Your attraction to such an object— a person—begins with getting acquainted with his or her particular characteristics, whether they be physical or mental.*

A logical consequence of this hypothesis is that the limerent attraction is capable of being bisexual, at least in some people—perhaps in most people.

> • 1. *Most women (at least in our culture and probably in many others) experience their "sex drive" as limerence, while most men experience their "sex drive" as lustiness. But both types of response exist in both sexes.*

For example, many men are aware of their attraction to visual erotica, but both men and women can be aroused by viewing it. Likewise, many women are aware of their attraction to romance novels,[36] but both women and men can be aroused by reading them.

BISEXUALITY IN MEN AND WOMEN: FOUR DEDUCTIONS

At last we can now get around to solving the puzzles that introduced this chapter. The key to understanding sexual orientation, I believe, is understanding precisely the nature of bisexuality—or more precisely, the nature of the bisexualit*ies* implicit in lust and limerence. In this section, I work out the implications of my three hypotheses for the theory of bisexuality, stopping just short of those implications that require application of the periodic-table theory of the gender transpositions covered in chapter 7.

The first deduction from the hypotheses is that

> • 1. *Bisexuality will be more common in women than in men,* although the bisexualities experienced in the two sexes are in general different.

Speaking in generalities, women experience their sexual attraction primarily as the limerent impulse, which can in its nature be bisexual. So a substantial number of women will notice bisexual tendencies in their (limerent) sexuality. Men in general, on the other hand, experience their sexual attraction as the lusty impulse, which in its nature is rarely bisexual. Hence, few men will notice bisexual tendencies in their (lusty) sexuality. Notice that when talking about their sexuality, women and men can end up talking past each other, because they refer implicitly to different frames of reference.

[36] Radway 1984.

127

The next two deductions originate in the two different types of bisexuality:

• 2. Many men who do have bisexual responses will find their heterosexual responses occurring in entirely different contexts (limerent contexts, say) from many or most of their homosexual ones (lusty contexts). Bisexual women, on the other hand, will often find their heterosexual responses occurring in nearly identical contexts as their homosexual ones (limerent contexts in both cases). So *many bisexual men will find their homosexual and heterosexual attractions to be entirely different, and many bisexual women will find the two to be very much the same.*

• 3. On average, *the sexes will differ in the extent to which heterosexuals are emotionally predisposed to understand and/or accept homosexuality among members of their own sex.*

Many heterosexual women who do not consider themselves bisexual will be able to understand why a woman might fall in love with a woman because they have women friends and can understand how someone might eroticize any friendship. But many heterosexual men with intense friendships with other men will find it incomprehensible that a man could be sexually aroused by another man, for in their own experience sexual arousal is not as closely connected with friendship. (Indeed, in some men sexual arousal is not connected with friendship at all.)

In the next deduction, I also address heterosexuals' acceptance of homosexuality, but this time among members of the opposite sex:

• 4. It should be easier for a heterosexual woman to understand (on the basis of her own experience) why a man might fall in love with a man than for a heterosexual man to do so, so *acceptance of male homosexuality ought to be higher among heterosexual women than among heterosexual men.* But it should be only somewhat easier for a heterosexual man to understand why a woman might be sexually aroused by a woman than for a heterosexual woman to do so, so *acceptance of female homosexuality ought to be only somewhat higher among heterosexual men than among heterosexual women.*

Empirical Evidence for the Four Deductions

These deductions are pretty well supported by the evidence.

In chapter 3, I've already given a lot of direct evidence for the first deduction.[37] Deduction 1 also strongly suggests that *lusty*-impulse bisexuality should be especially rare, because the lusty attraction depends on imprinting. The idea of an imprinting-dependent type of sexual impulse was suggested to me not only by the work of John Money and Margaret Mead (quoted above), but also by Kurt Freund, whose work is described in chapters 3 and 8. Freund defines a male bisexual as an adult man who is significantly sexually aroused by the sight of the nude body shape of sexually mature individuals of both sexes. Such a man would, under my definition, exhibit bisexuality in his lusty sexual impulse. Freund has conducted an extensive search for such men and has found none except those who are predominantly attracted sexually to very underage partners.[38] I take Freund's finding to be a confirmation that lusty-impulse bisexuality is rare.[39]

There is more evidence regarding deduction 1, admittedly indirect. Bisexuality is much more of a political issue in lesbian-liberation circles than male bisexuality is in gay-liberation circles.[40] The slogan "Any woman can be a Lesbian," for example, comes from one camp in this battle, the other claiming that women who sleep with men are problematic or politically incorrect. People arguing about this act as if they believed that the threat that a woman might leave a female lover for a man is one worth taking seriously.[41] In contrast, when bisexual men are controversial in the gay male community, it is far more often because they are widely disbelieved: supposedly, they have not come to terms with their own homosexuality. People argue about this act as if they believe that a bisexual man would be entirely homosexual if

[37] Survey data from the Kinsey statistics and the Hite report, for example.

[38] Freund 1974; Freund, Scher, Chan, and Ben-Aron 1982. My theory does not account for pedophilia, so I will ignore this complication. But note that the body types of underage males and females do not differ from each other as much as do the types of adult women and men.

[39] For some conflicting data, see McConaghy 1978. Both McConaghy and Freund measure bisexuality after showing subjects sexually explicit stimuli. But the stimuli are different: McConaghy uses films in which people disrobe, etc., whereas Freund shows slides of naked people standing still. This amounts to a (small) difference in their definitions of bisexuality—arousal to both naked male body shapes and naked female body shapes for Freund, versus arousal to men disrobing and women disrobing for McConaghy. Although these two definitions only differ a little bit, it is still not clear whether their results differ because of the definitions or because McConaghy has found the kind of person Freund says doesn't exist.

[40] Abbott and Love 1972, p. 153; Califia 1983.

[41] Schäfer 1976, p. 57.

he would only come to terms with his "real" feelings, by which I assume they mean his lusty feelings.

These two patterns make sense if the typical female debater understands female sexual responses as being based on friendship bonding (available from males as well as females), but the typical male debater understands male sexual response as being based on arousal to a particular type (which is much more available from one sex rather than the other).

Next, deduction 2. For men, evidence is sparse but very suggestive. I quoted Tripp (above), but most of the evidence I know is clinical. Minneapolis clinical psychologist Eli Coleman, for example, runs a therapy group for married bisexual men. It is not surprising that many of these men have affairs with men. What is surprising (to some people) is that *not one* of Coleman's patients had ever had an extramarital affair with a woman.[42] This strongly suggests that the heterosexual component these men have is very much unlike the heterosexual component typical heterosexual married men have. I suggest that these bisexual married men had a limerent attraction to their wives and lusty attractions (and perhaps also limerent attractions) to men. In contrast, many heterosexual married men do have lusty attractions to women other than their wives. I could certainly believe that some married bisexual men would refrain from extramarital affairs that were heterosexual because they were having more homosexual fantasies and thoughts. But it is difficult for me to believe that not a single one of thirty or so such men would do so if their attractions to women were like those of heterosexual men.

For women, the evidence is also sparse, but consistent with my theory. For example, one authority stated that "lesbians, like women generally, respond primarily to a combination of physical and psychic attributes, to a manner, a personality,"[43] and suggested that women's attractions to men and to women are similar.[44] It is also not difficult to find personal accounts in gay literature and the gay press of women who identify themselves as lesbian but who find themselves attracted to particular men (as in the quotation introducing this chapter).

---

[42] At least none had had such an affair at the time of the 4th World Congress of Sexology, held in Mexico City in 1979. At that congress, Coleman revealed, in answer to a question from the floor, that the bisexual men in his group had only homosexual extramarital affairs.

[43] Abbott and Love 1972, p. 101.

[44] On p. 140, Abbott and Love approvingly cite Stearn to the effect that some lesbians "acknowledged a liking for some males, but based their liking entirely on the individual's charm, wit, and intellect—not specifically masculine attributes." And on p. 145, they cite Shulman, who wrote that the sex of the love partner is relatively unimportant in female sexuality.

A more recent set of studies by Eli Coleman suggests that bisexual women and men enter marriage for quite different reasons. Bisexual men marry because they perceive a lack of intimacy in the homosexual world or hope marriage will help them overcome their homosexual feelings. Bisexual women mention, instead, family pressures and love for their husbands. Coleman also suggests that bisexual women enter marriage unaware of their homosexual responsiveness (and perhaps lack of heterosexual responsiveness).[45]

San Diego sex researcher Timothy Wolf recruited bisexual men *not* in psychotherapy and believes Coleman's findings do not apply to them.[46] Wolf found that 92 percent of the men in his sample listed "friendship of spouse" as first or second reason for marriage, 36 percent cited "children," and 24 percent "financial security." None gave religious reasons, social obligation, or family expectations. But notice that "friendship" was listed instead of "sexual attraction." Again, the heterosexual component of their bisexuality seems different from the heterosexuality of most heterosexual men.

Deductions 3 and 4 are closely connected, and so they tend to be tested by the same experiments. Here I have summarized the evidence in the introduction to the present chapter and in chapter 3. In most studies, heterosexual men are highly aroused by fantasies of lesbian lovemaking and (perhaps as a result) are more accepting of lesbians than they are of male homosexuals. On the other hand, heterosexual women are less disapproving of female homosexuality than heterosexual men are of male homosexuality. Future studies would do well to compare *arousal* and *approval* in the same sample and to compare attitudes toward homosexual *acts* and toward homosexual *persons*; these distinctions are relevant to my deductions.

In sum, my theory accounts for a wide variety of facts about the existence and expression of bisexuality and of attitudes directed toward homosexuality. At the end of chapter 7, I mesh the limerent/lusty theory with the "periodic-table" model of the gender transpositions and derive further conclusions about bisexuality.

DISCUSSION

Instead of attempting a summary here, I will conclude with some important qualifications.

The parallel between the lusty and the limerent attractions is the main reason I have allowed both "Limerent Object" and "Lusty Ob-

---

[45] See Coleman's article in Klein and Wolf 1985, p. 45.
[46] See Wolf's article in Klein and Wolf 1985.

ject" to have the same abbreviation (LO). Sometimes this can be confusing, but at other times it is essential, when one wants to refer to the object of someone's affections and one is not sure which type of affection is involved. Sorting out precisely which kind is involved is a useful exercise for anyone and is especially important clinically for people confused about their sexual attractions.[47]

Limerent and lusty attractions don't have to stay constant throughout life. In fact, it would not be surprising if the strength of lusty attractions in men lessens with age—just as erection does. If this is so, then in men the (absolute or relative) importance of limerence may *increase* with age. Nor do limerence and lust have to have a consistent relationship in women over the life span, although it is not clear from the theory alone what form any changes would take. These variations over the life span suggest that bisexuality would emerge at different times in men and in women—a suggestion I wish I had more space to explore.

Cultures and subcultures differ in the significance attached to various forms of sexual attraction, and these differences can complicate my deductions. For example, sometimes people have casual or recreational sex with friends or strangers, and it's likely that bisexuality in these situations can exist in both women and men.[48] So the existence of bisexuality in this kind of sex (even of the lusty variety) is not of the same significance as its existence would be in a situation where a recreational-sex ethic is absent or very uncommon.

Another point has to do with "choosing" sexual attractions. There are many women who state that they have "chosen" to be lesbian, for example—a statement that some other lesbians, some heterosexuals, and many gay men find difficult to understand based on their own experience. This emphasis on choice may be especially important for women, who for so many centuries have been given no choice at all in sexual matters or only the option to veto marital partners, not the option to choose them themselves.[49] But it may also be true—as embodied in the limerent/lusty theory—that this choice is related to the greater importance of eroticizing friendship in women's sexuality: you cannot choose who you are lustily aroused by, but to some extent you can choose your friends, and you can certainly choose *not* to be someone's friend.

[47] Minneapolis clinical psychologist John Gonsiorek and I plan to evaluate the limerent/lusty theory in the light of such people.

[48] A constructive criticism by San Francisco sexologist and psychotherapist Charles Moser got me thinking about this.

[49] John Kirsch suggested this point to me.

The particular ways in which social and biologic conditions interact are also important. Consider the male-to-female transsexuals who have some sexual attraction to women.[50] In a society that prescribes a rigid differentiation of male and female gender roles, these preoperative transsexuals might repress the heterosexual-attraction portion of their psyches and see themselves as men who want to become heterosexual women by way of a sex-change operation.[51] They might do this consciously after discovering that some doctors studying transsexualism consider sexual attraction toward women to be a disqualification for the sex-change operation. Or they might do this unconsciously and simply notice that the desire to become a woman is very strong—overlooking the sexual attraction to women or honestly believing that it will disappear as a result of the operation. In another kind of society—one that allows a role for women who love women—these people might be less likely to repress their sexual attraction to women and see themselves as people born male who want to have a sex-change operation and become lesbians.

As I discuss (for homosexuality) in chapter 5, socialization, learning, and culture are extremely important in the social construction of sexual realities, and these social constructions are in turn important in people's identities. The same so-called biological givens in an individual might have entirely different consequences in different societies. Even an entirely biologically driven model must acknowledge this, as these different outcomes can have enormously different consequences for reproductive success. So I would be perturbed if my model were taken as one that denigrated the importance of social factors.

But neither can biological factors safely be ignored by those modeling the social ones. The fact that many blond(e)s are blond because of environmental factors like hydrogen peroxide does not mean that strong socialization against blondness will prevent people from being "naturally" blond, although it certainly may affect the incidence of blondness in a particular population, and it might affect people's self-labeling choices (viz., "I'm a blond/e" instead of "I'm a Canadian").

In short, I do not view the roots of the gender transpositions as exclusively environmental; I see them as partly biological and not necessarily pathological. From time to time people have put forth the theory that transsexualism and/or cross-dressing are purely the result of our own culture's rigid gender roles—that transsexuals are just ho-

---

[50] The so-called heterosexual transsexuals, male-to-female lesbian transsexuals, or gynephilic transsexuals.
[51] Blanchard 1985.

mosexuals who cannot accept their homosexuality, for example.[52] The implication is that transsexualism will disappear as we move toward a society in which freedom of choice in gender-role matters is easier to accomplish. (Some would say the same thing about homosexuality.) To the contrary, I suspect that all the gender transpositions will survive in a liberalized environment—perhaps in less straitjacketed terms—and will grow to be better accepted and understood by society at large. The outrage that greeted Christine Jorgensen paved the way for the acceptance greeting Jan Morris, and now everyone seems to be humming Boy George's songs. Frankly, I do not expect any of these kinds of people to disappear until the human race itself does.

[52] For example: ". . . transsexuals are homosexuals who have internalized social sex-role structures"—Ross, Rogers, and McCulloch 1978, p. 324.

7

THE PERIODIC-
TABLE MODEL

Man delights not me; no, nor woman neither.
Hamlet, act I, scene 5, line 330.

As the French say, there are three sexes,—men, women, and clergy-
men.
Sydney Smith, quoted in chapter 9 of Holland 1855.

"If I were a g.g. [genetic girl], I'd be a lesbian. I'd like to live in a
world where there are *only* women."
Linda, a heterosexual transvestite, quoted in Yates-Rist 1983.

You remember chemistry, don't you? Probably the one thing you
remember from chemistry is the periodic table (see fig. 7.1). This
chart arranges the chemical elements in rows and columns according to their properties—what other elements they combine with,
their atomic weights, and so on.

There are three things about this table you should notice:

- The table is almost perfectly rectangular.
- Almost every spot in the table is filled.
- It is *not* the one you remember from school.

Actually, the third point depends on how old you are. The first
periodic table (fig. 7.1) is shown the way it looked when it was first

	H									
He	Li	Be	B	C	N	O	F			
Ne	Na	Mg	Al	Si	P	S	Cl			
Ar	K	Ca	Sc	Ti	V	Cr	Mn	Fe	Co	Ni
	Cu	Zn	Ga	Ge	As	Se	Br			
Kr	Rb	Sr	Y	Zr	Nb	Mo	Tc	Ru	Rh	Pd
	Ag	Cd	In	Sn	Sb	Te	I			
Xe	Cs	Ba	La*	Hf	Ta	W	Re	Re	Ir	Pt
	Au	Hg	Tl	Pb	Bi	Po	At			
	Fr	Ra	Act							

* Lanthanide series here   † Actinide series here

Figure 7.1

sketched out back in 1869, by Dmitri Mendeleev.[1] Call it *PT1*, for "Periodic Table 1."

If you took chemistry more recently, you've seen a different version of the periodic table (improved by Henry G. J. Moseley; see fig. 7.2). This modern version has been rearranged because we now know the fundamental laws of physics that created the regularities in the first place. For this book you don't need to know these laws. (They have to do with electrons and orbitals and quantum mechanics.) All you need to know is that they exist and that they are a little bit messy. That's why the modern, revised periodic table is not a perfect rectangle. Call this version *PT2*, for "Periodic Table 2."

In this chapter, I will begin to construct a periodic table for the gender transpositions described in chapter 2. Think of each gender transposition as an "element." The problem is to arrange them in a

H																	He
Li	Be											B	C	N	O	F	Ne
Na	Mg											Al	Si	P	S	Cl	Ar
K	Ca	Sc	Ti	V	Cr	Mn	Fe	Co	Ni	Cu	Zn	Ga	Ge	As	Se	Br	Kr
Rb	Sr	Y	Zr	Nb	Mo	Tc	Ru	Rh	Pd	Ag	Cd	In	Sn	Sb	Te	I	Xe
Cs	Ba	La*	Hf	Ta	W	Re	Os	Ir	Pt	Au	Hg	Tl	Pb	Bi	Po	At	Rn
Fr	Ra	Act															

* Lanthanide series here   † Actinide series here

Figure 7.2

[1] Actually, Mendeleev's very first table had some blank spots. It was his genius to notice them and then predict the properties of the undiscovered elements that he thought had to fill them. Mendeleev predicted three—now named gallium, scandium, and germanium.

rectangle in which each horizontal row has certain things in common and each vertical column has certain things in common. If the chart is successful, then other facts about the gender transpositions should literally fall into line when arranged the way the rectangle is.

In fact, if the chart is successful, there is probably some underlying reason *why* it succeeds. PT1 succeeded because there were things—electrons and orbitals, which Mendeleev didn't know about—that were the fundamental basis of the relationships among the elements. PT1 got chemists wondering about those fundamental causes. Once quantum mechanics was worked out, PT1 had to be replaced by PT2.

The task of this chapter is to construct a PT1 for the gender transpositions. Once we do that, I'll explain some guesses I have about why the arrangement works. The answer will take us toward a PT2.

But only partway. We'll get stuck halfway there, making some guesses about the underlying causes but not understanding them fully. So be it. If we don't know the mechanism, then we don't know the mechanism—yet that didn't stop Mendeleev, and it shouldn't stop us, from getting as far as we can.

THE PERIODIC TABLE

There are two ways to go about this. The way scientists normally go about explaining a theory is the way you build a house: from the ground up. Building from the ground up is the only correct way to actually do the construction. But to nonscientists it can be boring, because it takes so long to get to the results.

In this chapter I'm going to take a different view—the architect's, not the building contractor's—and show you the finished product. Walk on in, have a look around, and if you're interested, then we can talk about the details in a footnote.[2] Keep in mind that the architect is the one who tells the builder how to build the foundation in the first place, and the architect started out by thinking about the finished building. The foundation may be built first, but it's designed last.

The periodic-table model of the gender transpositions is actually built around two tables—one for each sex. I will call these two tables the *XX table* (for genetic females; fig. 7.3) and the *XY table* (for genetic males; fig. 7.4). In each case, I have arranged the gender transpositions for a particular sex in a neat, rectangular array. The result will be, I believe, the first time the gender transpositions have been *made sense of* in a fundamental, theoretical way. Better yet, they are made

[2] See Pillard and Weinrich 1987.

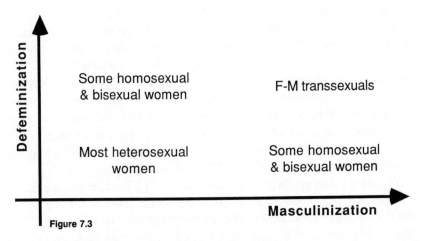

Figure 7.3

sense of in a way that suggests what underlying mechanisms might be at work. Just as with the original periodic table, this table may have to be revised and may become more irregular, once the underlying mechanisms are understood.

For the moment, don't worry about the labels "masculinization" and "defeminization" on the axes; those will be explained later. All you need to know is what's going on in the four corners of *both* graphs. This is provided by what I call the *underlying table* (fig. 7.5).

Just as with the first two graphs, the terms in this underlying table will be explained later. My next task is to point out the patterns that can be seen in the first two arrangements and to relate them to the underlying table. To do so, I must make and discuss some definitions.

MOUNTING AND MOUNT-RECEIVING

It turns out that *mounting* and *mount-receiving behaviors* are important ones in human sexual behavior—not to mention the periodic-table

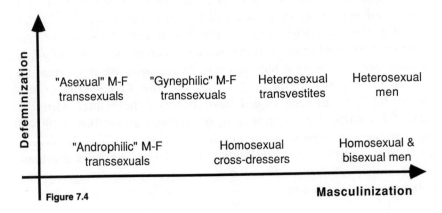

Figure 7.4

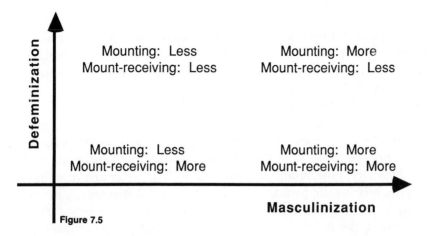

Figure 7.5

theory. These two words are defined in terms of the quintessential acts needed to conceive offspring—not just in humans but also in other mammals.

Sexual behavior in mammals is extremely varied. Add human variability into this and you get a staggering diversity of sexual patterns. But this variability is not entirely arbitrary. In particular, to conceive offspring, in any mammalian species certain acts are performed by the male, and other acts are performed by the female.

The term *quintessential masculine sexual behavior* means those acts a male must perform to become some offspring's father. In a word, that consists of *mounting*. Mounting behavior consists of the following sequence in the vast majority of mammal species, including humans:

- Becoming aroused (typically, achieving erection of the penis) by the sight or smell of another animal (typically, a female)
- Physically positioning oneself so that one's genitals (especially the penis) are placed near the body of the partner (typically, the female's genitals—specifically, the labia)
- Intromitting (typically a penis into a vagina)
- Repeated pelvic thrusting (typically, stimulating the penis inside the vagina), coordinated to some degree with the partner's thrusts
- Having an orgasm (typically, ejaculating semen into the vagina)

The term *quintessential feminine sexual behavior* means those acts a female must perform to become some offspring's mother. There are various words for these steps in different groups of mammals: *lordosis* in rats, a *present*[3] in nonhuman primates, and so on. For lack of a

[3]The accent is on the second syllable. A pre*sent*, in primate terms, is when an animal presents its rump to another animal, thus inviting that animal to mount it. A present can

term that applies to all mammals, I will use the term *mount-receiving* to describe both lordosis and presenting, along with analogous behaviors in other species (such as humans).[4] Mount-receiving behavior consists of the following sequence in the vast majority of mammal species, including humans:

- Emitting a signal (chemical or behavioral) that indicates one's sexual receptiveness, willingness to be mounted, or willingness to proceed to the next step of the courtship/coital sequence
- Physically positioning oneself for, and/or awaiting, the approach or mount performed by another animal (typically, a male) in response to the signal
- Arching the back or lifting the rump (to facilitate intromission, if it occurs)
- Pelvic thrusting, coordinated to some degree with the partner's thrusts
- Orgasm (sometimes), the function of which (if any) remains in dispute[5]

Now here's a political question: aren't these definitions sexist? Don't they imply that men must mount and intromit and that women must be mounted and passive?

The answer is no. There is nothing in these definitions that *requires* that mounting behavior be performed only by males and that mount-receiving behavior be performed only by females. Omit the parts in parentheses and you'll get definitions that are practically gender-neutral. Include the parentheses and you'll get ones that are much more stereotypical. In fact, some scientists would claim that my definitions do not embody the typical heterosexual sequence as much as they ought to.

---

be followed by sexual behavior but is also used to indicate submission. When it means the first and when it means the second is still discussed by primatologists.

[4] This was a difficult term to arrive at, and I welcome improvements; there is no general term for "the stereotypical feminine pattern in whatever mammal species we're talking about," as there is for "mounting" in males. I wanted to choose a term that described the typical feminine pattern accurately across species but did not imply passivity on the part of females. (John Money, in Money 1985, p. 124, suggests the term *quim* for the notion of "a vagina gripping a penis"—thus turning what is stereotypically regarded as a passive act into an active one.) I will describe in later chapters how the acts the female takes to become a mother—or, for that matter, to engage in any sexual activity—are far from passive. Even what I describe in this chapter as the quintessential sequence is begun by the female, not the male.

[5] If you are interested in this dispute, I recommend that you read Symons 1979 and review of it by Hrdy 1979. A new book by Daniel Rancour-LaFerriere has several chapters arguing that women's orgasms have an adaptive function (Rancour-LaFerriere 1985).

My definitions make it possible to describe animals of a particular sex performing several different sexual acts—even acts falling into different categories. A male might begin with typical masculine mounting behavior, then turn around and perform mount-receiving behavior in which *he* is mounted (by a female or by another male). Likewise, the definitions permit us to describe a female performing mount-receiving behavior, then turning around and mounting (a male or another female).

And perhaps most important of all, female and male need not perform the behavior quintessentially typical for their sex in the first place. In fact, the only thing that these behaviors are essential for is conception. Conception is biologically a very important event, so paying special attention to it is scientifically justified and not arbitrary. But this does not mean that other events are scientifically unimportant. And it certainly does not mean that there is something wrong with an individual who does something other than (or in addition to) his or her sex's quintessential role in conception.

This point of view is made even clearer when you understand the importance of polymorphism in modern evolutionary biology. *Polymorphism* exists when individuals vary in a trait that is biologically important. Most popular accounts of evolution overlook polymorphism and its importance. But polymorphism has been an important topic in evolutionary biology for at least the past fifty years,[6] because it often turns out that it is best for individuals in a species to be *different* from each other. For example, if you are in a species that tastes good to its predators and most of the members of your species are blue, it may be to your advantage to be green—because predators that have learned that the blue ones taste good may be slower to go after a green one. Here natural selection promotes not uniformity—everyone blue or everyone green—but variability: a species in which everyone is trying to look *un*like everyone else.

Natural selection can fine-tune the circumstances in which each sex performs mounting and mount-receiving behavior. That is, if it is sometimes advantageous for males to mount-receive and for females to mount, then Mother Nature will produce animals that can do so. But this doesn't mean Mother Nature will have to produce a species full of unisex androgynes. Instead, she could allow a general tendency for males to pursue mounting and for females to pursue mount-

---

[6] Students of Darwin know that he thought polymorphism was the very basis of evolutionary change. This point of view wasn't often stressed, however, until the new synthesis in evolutionary biology in the first half of the twentieth century. It has become even more important in the selectionist/neutralist debate of the past twenty years or so.

receiving, but set up predispositions or particular circumstances in which females enjoy mounting or males enjoy mount-receiving.

So let's say it's true—as I believe it is—that humans are a species in which variations in sex roles have been evolutionarily important in the past few tens of thousands of years. Let's say it's therefore true— as I believe it is—that there will be ever-changing circumstances in which it is advantageous for females to try to mount as well as to mount-receive and ever-changing circumstances in which it is advantageous for males to try to mount-receive as well as to mount. What kinds of mechanisms will Mother Nature use to actually put this variability—this sex-role polymorphism—into effect?

The answer is extremely important. Mathematical models in evolutionary biology show that *there is no uniform answer to this question*— at least no uniform answer that can be predicted from evolutionary theory alone. In particular, if you believe that there has been natural selection for sex-role polymorphism in humans, evolutionary theory can*not* predict which of the following ways this variability will actually come to occur:[7]

- The variability could evolve *between individuals*—that is, some people will be entirely typical in their sex roles, and other people will be atypical.
- The variability could evolve *within individuals*—that is, everyone will have the ability to behave typically or atypically, as circumstances dictate or predispose.
- *Both* of the above could hold true to some extent—in which case both in*ter*individual and in*tra*individual variability may occur.

These facts open the door, evolutionarily speaking, for the gender transpositions. If it is true that humans have been selected for sex-role polymorphism, then the mechanism producing this sex-role variability may well be subtle and varied—not only from culture to culture but also from individual to individual. There could be people whose role it is, for their entire lives, to behave differently from the roles quintessential for their sex. There may well be other people whose role it is, at various times in their lives, to act sometimes in concordance with and sometimes out of concordance with such roles, as circumstances change. There will probably also be people who conform to these reproductive roles in every conceivable way. And the theory of evolution by natural selection might be able to account for this variability

---

[7] See the discussion of *evolutionarily stable strategies* contained in Dawkins 1976.

in adaptive ways: to make sense of it rather than just to assume that the variations are "mistakes" or are random.

The periodic-table model of the gender transpositions classifies particular gender transpositions in terms of how its members adhere, or do not adhere, to the sex roles that quintessentially characterize their sex. I have defined those acts to be mounting and mount-receiving,[8] and that is why those acts appear in the so-called underlying table (fig. 7.5). We can now return to the tables themselves.

PATTERNS IN THE TABLES

It is time to discuss the actual patterns in the XX table, the XY table, and their relationship to the underlying table.

Patterns in the XX Table

Among genetic females, the correspondence between the XX table and the underlying table is simple. The underlying table provides four patterns—the four corners—that map onto four gender transpositions in women. Please note that although the four patterns are extremes—you might even call them caricatures—the underlying distribution of human beings really is continuous. Although any particular woman might find herself at *any* given point in the entire rectangle, she could measure her position, in some sense, by her distance from each of the four corners. It is people near the four corners that I will describe.

Down near the lower left-hand corner of the XX table are quintessentially heterosexual women. Compare this position with the underlying table, where you see the labels "mount-receiving behavior: more" and "mounting behavior: less." This means that quintessentially heterosexual women are thought to be very interested in mount-receiving and less interested in mounting. Note, however, that these traits for this group are *tautological*. That is, this statement contains nothing new or substantive, because I chose the characteristics of this corner by referring to what it was that typical heterosexuals quintessentially did. That typical heterosexual women turn out to quintessentially do these things is no surprise!

Next consider the upper right-hand corner, which is "female-to-male transsexuals" in the XX table. In the underlying table, this corresponds to the label "mount-receiving behavior: less" and "mounting

---

[8] Actually, they are a bit more complicated than this in the full version of the theory. But as a rough approximation—and for the purposes of a simple explanation—mounting and mount-receiving will do.

behavior: more." This means that the pattern of sexual desires of typical f–m transsexuals resembles the quintessential heterosexual male pattern. This, too, may seem to be a tautological assertion, but it is not. Transsexualism is defined according to what core gender identity a person has: these XX people feel they are men, fundamentally, not women. But mounting and mount-receiving are not part of core gender identity; they are part of sexual orientation or (arguably) part of social sex role. And so the prediction—that most f–m transsexuals are expected to enjoy mounting more and mount-receiving less—is *not* an automatic consequence of my definitions. It makes good sense, of course, but it is not tautological.

The women represented by the other two corners are both alike and different. They will be alike in being puzzled by what society says are the quintessential roles expected of women.[9] *Both upper-left-corner women and lower-right-corner women will be about equally attracted to the two quintessential possibilities.* That is, it will be a matter of relative indifference to them, in their sexual relationships, who plays "the woman's role" and who plays "the man's role" in bed. In fact, they might find it puzzling that other women (the women in the other two corners of the XX table?) seem to accept these roles.

But the women represented by these two corners are also expected to be different from each other in this gender-role disinterest—and in an important way, as indicated by the underlying table. Women in the lower-right corner would be about *equally interested* in the so-called masculine and feminine roles in sex, but women in the upper-left corner would be about *equally uninterested* in the two. That is, the lower right women would be relatively "sexy," and the upper-left women relatively "unsexy," in their intimate desires. (Sexy and unsexy, that is, with respect to mounting and mount-receiving; there are many other ways to be sexual.)

Research suggests that lesbians and bisexual women are those most likely to be experimenting with gender-role freedom in their sexual relationships (see chapter 6). For that reason I have placed them on the XX table in these corners. Reading between the lines, some lesbian writings suggest the existence of two groups that you might think of as "sexy lesbians" and "unsexy lesbians"—which, in the light of the limerent/lusty theory of chapter 6, might be renamed as "lusty lesbi-

---

[9] Perhaps it would be better to say that they would *act as if* they were less interested in or less accepting of such quintessential roles. These women need not be consciously aware of such feelings or ideas.

ans" and "unlusty lesbians."[10] In case it isn't obvious, I see the lusty lesbians in the lower-right corner and the unlusty ones in the upper left.

Patterns in the XY Table

This table is more complicated than the XX table, but it turns out that more patterns can be discerned in it. As with the XX table, the underlying table provides four extreme patterns—the four corners—that map onto four gender transpositions in men. And again, the four types are near the extremes of an underlying continuous distribution of human beings. A particular man might find himself at any given point in the entire rectangle, but it is the four corners that I will describe first. But remember that the other gender transpositions exist, too; they're just squeezed in at intermediate points, farther from some corners and closer to others.

Ordinary heterosexual men are placed in the upper right-hand corner—tautologically as a trivial consequence of the definitions, just as heterosexual women were automatically in the lower left-hand corner.

Ordinary homosexual men would find themselves mostly in the lower right-hand corner, that is, in the corner where there is a relatively high degree of interest both in mounting and in mount-receiving behavior. Recall from chapter 3 that in modern Western societies many homosexual men (at least in comparison to heterosexual men) do not pay much attention to making their role of "the man" or "the woman" in bed (if any) consistent with the roles they play out of bed (if any). This is exactly what is expected for men in this lower right-hand corner.

Homosexuality in other cultures is a more subtle proposition. First, the role-inversion pattern of homosexuality (the berdache and the hijra from chapter 5) is better described as homosexual cross-dressing or perhaps even transsexualism (see below). Accordingly, some of these gender-shifted people will be placed somewhere other than this corner (i.e., where some other gender transposition is).

Second, the age-structured pattern (common in ancient Greece, for example) belongs in the same corner in the following sense. Although at any given moment there are rules of thumb about who is supposed to insert and who is supposed to be inserted into (the older lover into the younger beloved, in this case), over the course of a lifetime any particular individual will play both roles. Some experts (Yale historian

---

[10] Recall that limerence is a trait thought to be easy to elicit in most women of whatever sexual orientation, so in that sense all lesbians are limerent lesbians.

John Boswell, for example) also claim that these rules of thumb were violated in practice far more often than is commonly realized. Recall also that it turned out that the sexual behavior even among berdaches was more variable than the simple prediction that it would always be mount-receiving.

And third, the pattern of homosexuality in which each homosexual is supposed to declare himself "butch" or "femme" can be more flexible in actual practice than superficial readings of the evidence would indicate. Recall from chapter 5 the example of gay life in modern urban Mexico, where it is generally the case that gay men prefer to play either the "insertor" or "insertee" role in sexual relations. Although this suggests that gender-role stereotyping in Mexico is much more severe than it is in the United States, remember that there are circumstances under which Mexican men change these sex-role preferences. A particular gay Mexican man may want to mount with one person and want to mount-receive with another. Only a superbutch or superfemme would do only one thing all the time.

These facts all suggest that roles in Mexico, among American Indians, and in ancient Greece may be quite varied—more like the typical American pattern than it might have seemed at first.

By the way, I do not want to leave you with the impression that Mexican and U.S. cultural patterns are extremely similar. The *behavior* is more similar than it first seems, but the *cultural rationale* for it is quite different. An anthropologist quite properly spends more time on the culture, while I, a behavioral biologist, spend more time on the behavior. In Mexico, it is impossible to be a gay man without devoting far more attention than gay men do in the United States to one's presentation as butch or femme.

The sexual patterns of transsexuals, too, are represented by their positions in the XY table. Recall from chapter 2 that many scientists believe male-to-female transsexuals to be asexual. This belief comes from case histories like this one: [11]

Mickey did not date in high school or college. At the age of 15 he saw a television program on transsexualism and felt that he had found what he wanted to be. After the program he masturbated for the first time. His masturbatory fantasy involved changing gender and living as a woman. His sexual history is quite limited, consisting of one contact with a male while in the original male role and one while in the female role. In both cases the

[11] Shore 1984.

other person initiated contact, with Mickey acting as a passive participant.

So m–f transsexuals do masturbate (every now and then) and do achieve orgasm by fantasizing about being female, so they are clearly not entirely asexual. *But they are asexual in terms of the sex acts used in the definitions of mounting and mount-receiving.* That is, asexual transsexuals are as a rule uninterested in both of these activities; when they perform them, it is usually upon the initiative of someone else. (In the language of chapter 6, for them these activities are responses, not impulses.) For that reason, I have placed them in the upper left-hand corner of the table.

But recall also from chapter 2 that some sexologists adopt a more subtle classification of transsexuals, dividing them into asexual, homosexual, and heterosexual types. It is, clearly, the asexual transsexuals that I have classified above. The m–f transsexuals who are attracted to men (whom some call ''homosexual'' and others call ''androphilic'') are in the lower left-hand corner of the XY table, in order to line them up with the ordinary homosexual (androphilic) men in the lower right. Finally, there are the m–f transsexuals who are attracted to women (whom some call ''heterosexual'' and others call ''gynephilic'' or ''lesbian''). I've squeezed them in between the asexual transsexuals and the heterosexual transvestites (see below).

A careful analysis of these types by Kurt Freund and his colleagues[12] suggests that these transsexuals fall into two major—and simpler— groups: those sexually attracted to men and those sexually attracted to women. Those attracted to men are the so-called classic transsexuals first described when transsexualism became widely known. Those attracted to women are a mixed bunch. Many experts now agree that it is difficult to distinguish among them (i.e., among asexual transsexuals, gynephilic transsexuals, and heterosexual transvestites). In fact, these transsexuals themselves sometimes say they aren't quite sure what to call themselves and have settled on the generic term *transpeople.* One heterosexual transvestite likewise told me that such specific terms are too restricting; he's known of people who have changed from one such group to another in their lives. He also prefers to use the term ''gender shift,'' because it implies that the movement can be reversed in some people. This consensus is reflected in the periodic-table theory by placing these three groups very close to each other, in the upper left.

[12] See Freund, Steiner, and Chan 1982.

We can place two additional gender transpositions on the XY graph. Heterosexual transvestites are, logically enough, placed between the ordinary heterosexual men and the transsexuals. These men are expected to be somewhat interested in mounting but just as uninterested in mount-receiving behavior as ordinary heterosexual men are. Homosexual cross-dressers (or "drag queens") are likewise placed halfway between ordinary homosexual men and the androphilic transsexuals. They are expected to be somewhat interested in mounting but just as interested in mount-receiving as typical homosexual men are.

Now we can move on to some fascinating patterns within the XY table. One of these is obvious: the three groups across the bottom are all sexually interested in men, and the four across the top are all sexually interested in women (with the possible exception of the asexual transsexuals). But another pattern is not obvious until you know a bit about the gender transpositions: there's an intriguing pattern in the top half of the table that has to do with lesbianism.

Lesbianism? In the XY table, the male table? Yes, indeed. Think back to the "pseudolesbian porn" puzzle of chapter 3. This puzzle points out how strange it is that ordinary heterosexual men would be sexually aroused by women making love to women. In the periodic-table theory, this piece of the map hooks up with a similar one about m–f transsexuals—more than a few of whom remain sexually attracted to women after the operation. These people, as women, sometimes *call themselves* lesbians.

Now recall (chapter 2) that some heterosexual transvestites enjoy wearing women's clothes while they have sex with their wives. A couple of things about this suddenly make sense in the light of the periodic-table model:

- Some of these men say they enjoy thinking of themselves and their wives as two lesbians making love.
- Some of their wives agree—that is, they also enjoy the lesbian fantasy, or come to accept it.

This pattern was documented in an interview by gay journalist Darrell Yates-Rist. Rist covered a week-long summer festival designed to give heterosexual transvestites a chance to cross-dress in a locale sympathetic to gender shifts. At one point he interviewed a wife (Marilyn) who had decided to stay married to her cross-dressing husband (Ben, whose femme personality is named Linda). Consider the following exchange:

[Linda said] "If I were a g.g. [genetic girl], I'd be a lesbian. I'd like to live in a world where there are *only* women."

. . . "Is Linda's lesbian fantasy . . . ? Do you and Linda . . . ?" I stumbled, nonplussed. "Does Linda come to bed?"

"That took a long time," Marilyn said. "I learned to accept Linda sometimes dressing in front of me at home. But I somehow realized that sooner or later she'd want to sleep with me. So I went to a porno shop and bought some magazines with women making love. I wasn't comfortable with it at all, but I kept looking at the pictures for weeks until it didn't upset me any more. I just kept wondering, 'How else can I hold on to Ben?' "[13]

Heterosexual transvestites are often thought to be male homosexuals. You should know by now that they are not. Yet some of them would like to be homosexuals, in a sense—*female* homosexuals—at least every now and then.

So there you have it: ordinary heterosexual men can be aroused by the fantasy of joining two women having sexual relations, heterosexual transvestites can be aroused by the idea of temporarily becoming one of the two women involved, and transsexual men can be aroused by the fantasy of permanently becoming one of the women having sex with a woman. Each of these three puzzling facts, like those in chapter 3, has, in one way or another, been remarked upon by sexologists. But only the periodic-table model, to my knowledge, locks the three puzzle pieces together. This pattern is one I myself did not notice until I arranged these three gender transpositions in the periodic table.

Finally, both the XY and XX tables display a pattern having to do with sex roles: how comfortable people are with the idea that there are (or ought to be) a "man's role" and a "woman's role" in courtship or in sexual relations. This is one of the great divides in human sexuality. Men and women who are comfortable with those roles question them only every now and then, if ever; those uncomfortable with the roles find them silly and confining. Projection is rampant. One of the commonest incorrect beliefs held about homosexual partnerships, for example, is the notion that one of them must play "the woman's" role and one "the man's." I have seen some of the nicest heterosexuals I know make this projection about gay couples—even heterosexuals who themselves are relatively gender-role-blind. But most homosexuals I know are quite irritated by this: the one who likes

---

[13] Yates-Rist 1983.

cooking more (or the one who hates it less) is the one who does most of the cooking, okay? The one that's more compulsive (or the one who hates hardware less) is the one who does the minor repairs, okay? Forget about what the cook or the handyperson does in bed, because you can't guess, and it usually doesn't matter.

On the other hand, many homosexuals are not aware *why* they find this projection so irritating or why it is so often made. To understand this fully, we need to learn about Philadelphia sexologist Timothy Perper's theory of courtship (see chapter 12), but we can make a start on it now, because the pattern is obvious in the XX and XY tables. Along what I'll call the *conformist diagonal,* from lower left to upper right, are the people to whom gender-role conformity seems normal and natural—or at the very least comprehensible, even if they themselves do not endorse it. (Masters and Johnson, for example, attack the notion that only the man is the "expert" in sexual relations.) Off this diagonal—in the upper-left and lower-right corners—are people for whom such conformity does not make sense.

What about those neither on nor entirely off the diagonal (gynephilic m–f transsexuals and heterosexual and homosexual cross-dressers)? Of course, they ought to be somewhere in between. In fact, along the top of the XY graph, the closer you get to the upper-right corner the more endorsement you see of gender roles. Heterosexual transvestites more or less endorse typical gender roles—they perform masculine roles when dressed as men and perform feminine roles when dressed as women. They often *wish* they could escape the male role, and they do so by cross-dressing. But gynephilic m–f transsexuals (and heterosexual transvestites) obviously have to play down such roles when they're thinking about having sex with women.

So the tables make sense. But in what sense does "making sense" make sense? So far, the periodic table consists of some tables, some definitions, and some patterns—nothing more. When I say that sex roles "make sense" for some groups and not for others, this boils down to nothing more than "There's no accounting for taste." Why make sense? Why not, as the Talking Heads suggest, *stop* making sense?

In order to answer this question, we have to consider some physiological facts. The axes of the periodic table are labeled "masculinization" and "defeminization," and it's time to explain why.

MASCULINIZATION AND DEFEMINIZATION

Masculinization and defeminization are two important processes involved in the development of the human body and brain. *Masculini-*

zation is the process by which the brain and body *gain* masculine characteristics, and *defeminization* is the process by which they *lose* feminine ones.

Sounds redundant, right? After all, the more masculine you are, the less feminine you are, right? So masculinization and defeminization must be the same thing, right?

Wrong, wrong, and wrong. Remember the lessons of chapter 1: masculinity and femininity are not opposites. Someone can score high on both masculinity *and* femininity; masculinity/femininity tests are two-dimensional, not one-dimensional. Admittedly, those were psychological lessons, and there is no guarantee that they would apply to physiology. But it turns out they do: *the parts of the body and the brain that differ by sex are usually two-dimensional,* just as the measures of masculinity and femininity are.

"Usually," not always, because it depends on which part of the body we're talking about. The internal genitalia are masculine and feminine along two dimensions; the external genitalia along one.

It sounds complicated, and complicated it can be. But the fundamental idea is not complicated; all you need to learn is a little sexual embryology.

The external genitalia consist, in the female, of the clitoris and the labia; in the male, of the penis and the scrotum.[14] As shown in table 7.1, the clitoris and the penis develop from the same embryological precursor: the genital tubercle. Likewise, the scrotum and the labia develop from the same precursor: the labioscrotal folds.

Table 7.1. Development of the Fetus

Ordinary Female	Fetus Hermaphrodite	Ordinary Male
Clitoris	Genital tubercle	Penis
Labia	Labioscrotal folds	Scrotum

So external genitalia differ only along one dimension. Every fetus starts, in some sense, as a *hermaphrodite*: with a genital tubercle and labioscrotal folds.[15] But most people are born as nonhermaphrodites: most men with a penis, most women with a clitoris. Hermaphrodites are born with something in between. *But no one is born with both a*

[14] I am omitting the gonads from this because testes end up outside the body cavity, while the ovaries are inside. Don't worry about this; it doesn't affect the point I'm making.

[15] The term *hermaphrodite* comes from the Greek names for a male god (Hermes) and a female goddess (Aphrodite). When lay people use it, it means someone with genitalia that cannot be unambiguously considered either male or female. Physicians distinguish between hermaphrodites and *pseudohermaphrodites*; the distinction is so arcane it isn't even worth explaining.

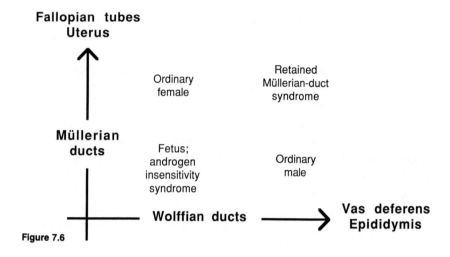

Figure 7.6

penis and a clitoris: you get a penis, a clitoris, or something in between. And no one who started with a genital tubercle is born with nothing at all where the genital tubercle had been. Likewise, one is born with either a scrotum, with labia, or with something in between—never both and never neither. That is, the external genitalia develop in a way that makes them *one-dimensional*—even when something goes wrong.

The situation is different for the internal genitalia (see fig. 7.6). Here male and female structures develop from two entirely different sets of structures laid down in the embryo. The *Wolffian* structures are the beginnings of the male internal ducts (the *vasa deferentia* and the *epididymes*).[16] The *Müllerian* structures are the beginnings of the female internal ducts (the *fallopian tubes* and the *uterus*).[17] That means that in theory it is possible for someone to be born with *both* female and male internal structures.

Possible, yes, and rare. But the point is, *it can happen,* because the internal genitalia develop *two-dimensionally.* Although most people are born with one structure fully developed and one withered away,[18] it is possible to be born with both (as in a condition called retained

[16] Here are the singulars and the plurals you never learned in school. Plural: epididymes; singular, *epididymis*—the duct attached to the surface of the testis that collects the sperm from it. Plural: vasa deferentia; singular, *vas deferens*—the duct that leads the sperm from the epididymis toward the penis. Plural, fallopian tubes; singular, *fallopian tube*—the duct that leads the ovum from the ovary to the uterus. Normal humans have no more than one *uterus*—the womb—that holds the fetus.

[17] Obviously, both kinds of ducts are named after their discoverers: Wolff and Müller.

[18] Actually, tiny remnants of the undeveloped structures remain—but they're even more useless than your appendix is.

Müllerian-duct syndrome) or with neither (as in androgen-insensitivity syndrome).

Now here's an important point: the first thing that happens in the development of the embryo is that both the feminine and the masculine structures are laid down. *So the fetus's first pattern is hermaphroditic.* What causes one set of structures to develop and the other to wither away?

The answer is sex hormones, but they work in a surprising way—a way that accounts for those two strange terms "masculinization" and "defeminization." Scientists have done experiments with animal fetuses: they can take out the fetal ovaries or fetal testes to deprive the fetus of sex hormones, and they can administer artificial sex hormones or sex-hormone-blocking drugs to affect the course of sexual differentiation. That means they can figure out how the genitalia develop—that is, they can work out the proximate causes[19] of genital development.

What happens to the fetus's internal genitalia if scientists remove all the sex hormones they can? The answer is very interesting and very important: the Wolffian and Müllerian ducts are laid down as usual, but then *the masculine ducts disintegrate, and the feminine ducts grow normally.* That is, even with no feminine sex hormones present— no estrogen, no progesterone—the Müllerian ducts will develop into normal fallopian tubes and a normal uterus.

This fundamental result is true for all mammals, including humans, and it is the basis for the following generalization: *the human fetus has a natural tendency to follow feminine pathways of development,* even in the absence of the so-called feminine sex hormones.[20]

How, then, do you deflect development from this feminine developmental pathway? You guessed it: *add* sex hormones. You can add them experimentally, by injecting them, or naturally, by letting the testes remain in place. In particular, if you add testosterone (the so-called male sex hormone), the masculine Wolffian ducts will *not* disintegrate and will instead develop normally into the vasa deferentia and the epididymes.[21]

---

[19] As opposed to the ultimate causes of genital development, which are evolutionary.

[20] This also happens to be true of the external genitalia: in the presence of no sex hormones, the genital tubercle develops into a normal clitoris, and the labioscrotal folds into normal labia.

[21] More precisely, "almost normally," because there's a subtlety involving the testes. In order to function properly, the epididymes and the vasa deferentia have to be hooked up, of course, to the testes. But if you're doing an experiment and the individual in question doesn't have testes—either because the individual has ovaries or because the testes have

But here's the kicker: if testosterone is the only thing you add, the Wolffian ducts are the only things that will be affected; the feminine ducts will develop *alongside* the masculine ones. The result will be someone with retained Müllerian-duct syndrome—a person with both masculine and feminine internal genital ducts.[22]

So what causes the Müllerian ducts to disintegrate in an ordinary male? The answer is, a second hormone—one that hasn't been completely analyzed yet. I'll call it *MIH*—for "Müllerian-Inhibiting Hormone."[23]

In a normal male fetus, the testes produce *both* testosterone and MIH. Testosterone causes the Wolffian ducts to develop, and MIH causes the Müllerian ducts to disintegrate. But MIH is chemically unrelated to testosterone and by itself has no effect at all on the Wolffian ducts. So here's another possible result in sexual differentiation: if a fetus has MIH that works normally but its testosterone doesn't work right, then *both* the masculine and the feminine ducts will disintegrate. One syndrome that this description applies to is called the *androgen-insensitivity syndrome.*[24] Androgen insensitives are born with no vasa deferentia, no epididymes, no uterus, and no fallopian tubes.

The bottom line is this. The fetus has two separate sets of internal ducts: a masculine set and a feminine set. It has two separate hormones that affect these two sets of ducts: testosterone and MIH. Testosterone is a *masculinizing hormone*—it makes the masculine ducts grow. MIH is a *defeminizing hormone*—it makes the feminine ducts go away. Female fetuses typically produce neither one of these hormones. Male fetuses typically produce both.

And now you can see why the two processes I've been referring to are called "masculinization" and "*de*feminization": because they are the two *physiologically separate* genitalia-differentiating processes ac-

been removed—then, of course, the ducts don't end up connected completely normally. There can also be problems in which the testes don't descend properly into the scrotum, which can prevent the normal connections with the epididymes.

[22] This kind of person looks like a boy on the outside and is usually raised as a boy. After all, he has XY chromosomes, testes, and a penis, and usually no one knows he also has a uterus. At puberty, the boy's uterus can start to menstruate; since it opens onto his urethra, he starts bleeding through his penis. This, of course, sends him to the doctor, who makes the diagnosis and schedules him for an operation. Often, unless the doctor wants to give a lecture about as long as this chapter, the boy is not told the names of the organs removed; he's just told he has some growths inside him that are bleeding and that need to be taken out.

[23] I understand, however, that a few research laboratories are hot on the trail of this hormone, which has been given several names: Müllerian-inhibiting substance (MIS), or anti-Müllerian hormone (AMH), for example.

[24] Androgen-insensitivity syndrome is one of the classic conditions described by sexologists John Money and Anke Ehrhardt in their 1972 book.

tively at work in humans (and other mammals). In every aspect, the internal genitals are a two-dimensional system, and so we need two terms to refer to the two dimensions.

But in this book we are discussing behavior more than genitals. So what about sexual behavior? What about the brain, the organ that literally embodies behavior? It is now time to ask how the brain supervises the sexuality we've been talking about.

SEXUALLY DIMORPHIC BEHAVIOR AND THE BRAIN

As I explained above, Mother Nature uses two different schemes for the development of the internal and the external genitalia: the external genitals vary one-dimensionally, and the internal genitals vary two-dimensionally.[25] Well, then, does the brain have sexually dimorphic parts? And if so, do they work in a one-dimensional or two-dimensional way?

The first answer is yes. You may not have learned this in school, but female and male brains do differ, on average, in several ways. How much they differ is a matter of perspective.

Forget brains for a moment; if you were a Martian coming down to study the anatomy of earth creatures, what would you think of the differences between men's and women's *bodies*? On the one hand, you might decide these differences are small and difficult to spot. To Martians, telling chimps from humans would be easy, but telling the difference between a man and a woman would be relatively difficult. On the other hand, you might decide that male/female differences are not difficult to spot at all. If you look down there between the legs, you can tell the difference, right?

It's the same with the brain. If you don't know much about it but take a casual peek inside some skulls, you'll have no trouble telling a chimp brain from a human brain, but you will have trouble telling a female brain from a male. However, if you know where to look, you'll have much less trouble. In fact, there are apparently a couple of gross anatomic differences between male and female brains and lots of differences visible under a microscope.[26]

[25] Now that you know about the importance of MIH, you can ask what effect it has on the external genitals. The answer is none. In the absence of sex hormones, the external genitals develop in the feminine direction. In the presence of testosterone (and its metabolic product, 5-alpha-dihydrotestosterone), they develop in the masculine direction. MIH apparently has no effect one way or the other.

[26] Refer to the following papers for more information: de Lacoste-Utamsing and Holloway 1982; Young, Goy, and Phoenix 1964; MacLusky and Naftolin 1981; McEwen 1981; and Swaab and Fliers 1985.

So now return to the question of how these sex differences in the brain develop. Do they develop one-dimensionally or two-dimensionally? We can't take either answer for granted, since the genitalia are known to develop both ways.

The answer is: two-dimensionally—at least most of the time, and possibly all the time. Experiments show that some sexually dimorphic behaviors are influenced by particular hormone treatments early in life. Certain structures and circuits in the brain are sexually dimorphic; once such sexual dimorphism is established, it does not change. In these experiments, it is possible to produce animals whose behavior shows *both* masculine and feminine aspects, *neither* masculine nor feminine aspects, or (of course) just one aspect and not the other.

Apparently these masculine and feminine aspects of behavior are laid down the way the internal genitalia are. That is, the first thing that happens is that precursors for both kinds of circuits are formed, but what happens next depends on hormones. It is fairly well demonstrated—even in humans—that in the presence of testosterone[27] the brain's capacity for certain masculine behaviors will develop. In particular, physical aggression, rough-and-tumble play, and mounting behavior have all been linked to prenatal testosterone. What is not as well demonstrated is what causes brain defeminization—that is, what causes the feminine capacities to disintegrate (or, by its absence, allows them to develop).

The answer apparently depends on the species and may well depend on environmental factors as well as genetic or biochemical ones.[28] In some species—rats, for example—testosterone causes not only masculinization but also defeminization.[29] No one knows if MIH (the hormone that causes defeminization in the internal genitalia) causes it in the brain of any species—although some indirect evidence suggests that it does not. (No one has tested this directly.)

According to some scientists, some species do not show defeminization of behavior at all! However, these researchers have adopted a restricted—but very precise—definition of defeminization. It boils down purely to lordosis (in rats) and presenting (in primates). In this defi-

[27] Or possibly related hormones, the androgens.

[28] If the truth be known, the influence of testosterone on the *masculine* behaviors is probably also moderated by environmental factors.

[29] However, even in rats, the *critical periods* for the two processes are different. That is, testosterone at one point in time causes masculinization and at a different time causes defeminization. This means that rats can experimentally be manipulated to produce individuals who are masculinized but not defeminized or defeminized but not masculinized.

nition, if males show lordosis or if males present, then the males have not defeminized—period.

I define masculinization and defeminization of behavior differently. By now, part of my definition should be obvious: masculinization involves an increase in mounting behavior, and defeminization involves less mount-receiving behavior. But I include more in the definition.

I include any other behaviors that differ on average between the sexes—if they can be shown to have a relationship to the quintessential roles of fathering and mothering offspring. So, for example, female mammals have *estrous* or *menstrual* cycles that are obviously related to their reproductive roles. Circuits that operate those cycles do exist in the brain, and in some species those circuits are clearly turned off in males. (In other species, including humans, it's not clear whether those circuits are actually turned off, not in use, or under the control of other parts of the body.) Such males, then, have been *defeminized* in their estrous-cycle circuits. Here's another example. In some species, females show a preference for sweet foods; this preference has been linked to the caloric requirements of motherhood. Males do not show such a preference, so by my definition these males have been defeminized with respect to sweetness preferences.

The details of what constitutes defeminization (or, for that matter, masculinization) in a given species are complicated. They are, moreover, changing every week as new results are announced from scientific experiments. So I will not stick my neck out too far in making specific predictions about just what they all mean.

But one point is especially important to make. The periodic-table model suggests that *variations in masculinization and defeminization of the brain—and possibly other parts of the body—are the underlying causes of the gender transpositions.* That is, they are the sexological equivalents of the electrons and orbitals that cause the patterns in the chemical periodic table. This is why I told you, at the beginning of this chapter, that I would only get partway from PT1 to PT2 in the periodic-table model of the gender transpositions; we have only begun to figure out what the underlying causes are.

But one general consequence for gender transposition theory is already clear. If the sexually dimorphic parts of the brain begin development the same way the genitalia do, by laying down *both* masculine and feminine structures (circuits, in this case), then everyone has had—as a fetus!—circuits that could permit both quintessentially masculine and quintessentially feminine behavior. Therefore, if there is an evolutionary advantage to having males retain the ability to perform some

quintessentially feminine acts or an advantage to having females retain the ability to perform some quintessentially masculine acts, then
*it will not be difficult for natural selection to produce animals that retain
such abilities*—because the raw material for such abilities has for millions of years existed in every mammal fetus without exception. All
that natural selection would have to do in a particular species is to
keep the circuits that would otherwise disintegrate from disintegrat-
ing. In fact, the scientists who believe that males in some species do
not defeminize in behavior are claiming that such circuit retention has
already happened in those species. Moreover, these scientists say that
primates, *including humans,* are nondefeminizing species. If they are
right, then there is all the more reason to expect that there can be
variations in human gender-role behavior that make sense in evolutionary terms. This is because it is not difficult to produce variations
in human gender-role behavior in evolution; Mother Nature only has
to fiddle a little with the development of some standard brain circuits
taken off the shelf.

In short, the gender transpositions in human beings are probably
not some weird fluke. On the contrary, there are strong theoretical
arguments and well-supported experiments that suggest that the variables underlying the gender transpositions have been changing in history and evolution for a very long time. This is not an ironclad disproof
of the notion that the gender transpositions are pathological, but it is
a very strong one.

CONCLUSIONS

This has been a long and complicated chapter. I will conclude by spec-
ulating about how the periodic-table theory can be meshed with the
limerent/lusty theory (chapter 6) in an intriguing way.

One way to do this is to say that lustiness goes along with masculinization and limerence with lack of defeminization. But we have to
be careful how we say this. If we aren't careful, we might hypothesize
that men wouldn't be limerent at all and women wouldn't be lusty at
all—and the main point of chapter 6 was to demolish stereotypes like
that. My solution is to hypothesize that masculinization does not turn
lustiness from off to on but rather turns it from a response into an
impulse. Likewise, I hypothesize that defeminization doesn't turn limerence from on to off but, rather, turns it from an impulse into a
response (see fig. 7.7).

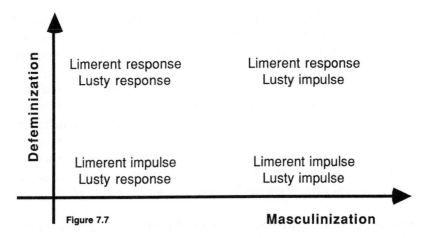

Figure 7.7   **Masculinization**

Now superimpose this chart on either the XX or XY periodic table.[30] You can then deduce the following:

- M–F transsexuals, whom I have described as asexual, might be better described as sexually responsive, not impulsive, in limerence and lust. That is, they can fall in love (limerence) and be aroused on the spur of the moment (lust), but mostly *in response* to external stimuli (such as other people's initiatives). They are therefore, in the periodic table, located at the spot where lust and limerence are responses, not impulses. Indeed, many of the written accounts of transsexuals' sexual arousal have prominent responsive or passive themes; think of the story about Mickey quoted above, for example.

- It is among gay men, the "sexy" lesbians, and bisexuals that the interplay—some would say conflict—between lust and limerence will be most extreme. It was in a book by New York psychotherapist C. A. Tripp where I recall first reading that a desire for enduring relationships and a desire for variety in relationships coexist in the same people.[31] Tripp was a gay man arguing from data gathered mostly from gay men, so it is reasonable to suppose that this coexistence can often be found in gay men. But there are plenty of literary sources that suggest the same thing—about both gay sexes. Sappho's poetry, for ex-

[30] Don't worry that the limerent/lusty chart has four elements and the XY table has seven. All the axes on all the charts can be expanded or contracted somewhat, because the theory is not yet precise enough to have units marked on them. That kind of precision will come with time.

[31] In fact, I quote passages from Tripp's book to this effect in chapter 6.

ample, was deeply romantic, but it also clearly described arousal at a distance. Walt Whitman, another homoerotic poet, spoke about chance meetings leading to brief sexual encounters, yet was also deeply concerned with the love of comrades. And I have already described (in chapter 6) the difficulties and delights some bisexuals face in understanding the various ways they are attracted to women and to men. This is not to imply that heterosexuals are unaware of the tension between limerence and lustiness. But in heterosexual sources this tension would be expected to be most evident in relations *between* the sexes and be less prominent within a single person's outlook.

I think, obviously, that there is a lot of evidence in support of these deductions, but I'm not going to go into them here. This is postgraduate theory, folks, and we have to stop somewhere, right?

Right. But then we'll start up again. Some of the evidence in favor of the periodic-table theory and the limerent/lusty theory can come only from actual observations, preferably quantitative observations, of human beings undergoing sexual arousal. There's a technique for doing that, and it wasn't even invented by Masters and Johnson. It's called plethysmography, and it's described in the next chapter. The periodic-table model has given us a sketch of the general lay of the land, and now it's time to call in the surveyors to make the maps.

8

PLETHYSMOGRAPHY

Home is heaven and orgies are vile
But I like an orgy, once in a while.
Ogden Nash

All right, class, sit down, fasten your seat belts, squirm and squiggle around in your chairs, and adjust your clothing, because this lecture's going to make you uncomfortable. It's about plethysmography: the direct measurement of sexual arousal.

That word is "plethysmography"—pronounced "pleth-iz-mahg'-raf-fee." Those of you who know Greek, I see, are already giggling, because you've figured out that the word is derived from two Greek roots meaning "fullness writing" or "engorgement recording." *Penile plethysmography* is the direct measurement of the volume of erections of the penis,[1] and *vaginal plethysmography* is the direct measurement of vaginal blood volume.[2]

That's all right, class; go ahead and squirm. That's why I warned you ahead of time.

A *penile plethysmograph* consists of a glass or metal instrument that looks like a bell jar (or, in another version, a tin tube) with an opening at the tip. The base is fitted with a converted condom or fingerstall that seals it against the base of the penis. The tip connects to a tube that leads to a polygraph[3] that measures the volume of the air be-

---

[1] Some of you may think the phrase "erections of the penis" is redundant. It's not; clitorises and nipples also have erections.

[2] For women, sometimes measures other than vaginal blood volume are used.

[3] A polygraph is not a "lie detector"; it is a device that records ("graphs") several ("poly") physiological measurements on a single strip of paper. A lie detector is a setup that *uses* a

tween the penis and the jar and squiggles a record of this volume onto a long strip of paper like that used for electrocardiograms.

A Czechoslovakian sexologist named Kurt Freund described penile plethysmography in a paper published in 1965, although he had invented it by 1957.[4] Freund left his native country in 1968. By that time he had demonstrated the scientific validity of his technique (which I'll discuss soon) and used it in diagnosing[5] sexual orientation among men worried by their sexual fantasies. Freund moved to Germany and then to Toronto, Canada, by which time he had stopped using the technique in therapy, concluding that sexual orientation could not be changed by his method.[6] He has since used the technique to establish an erotic taxonomy of male sexual response that has had an important influence in sexology.

Penile plethysmography is also used by Australian researchers Nathaniel McConaghy and Ronald Barr and by other workers in several Western countries.

There is another device that measures erections of the penis: the *penile strain gauge*. This device measures the penis's circumference, not its volume. It was invented soon after the plethysmograph by Edinburgh sexologist John Bancroft and his colleagues.[7] It is a thin rubber tube filled with mercury and capped with electrodes that send a weak current through the liquid metal. The strain gauge is slid around the penis. The wires from the electrodes go to a polygraph that squiggles out the resistance that the mercury presents to the electric current, which varies according to the cross section of the column of mercury. That cross section, in turn, is a function of the diameter of the penis: the thicker the penis, the thinner the mercury.

There are also *vaginal plethysmographs*; they take several forms.[8] The

---

polygraph to record physiological measures of interest to law enforcement. This usually does not include direct genital measurements—as far as I know.

[4] Freund, Sedláček, and Knob 1965. Please note that the name is spelled Freu*n*d, with an *n*, not Freud as in Sigmund—you don't want anyone accusing you of making an unfriendly little Freundian slip, now, do you? Ever since 1920, when a sexological institute in Prague was founded, Czechoslovakia has supported sex research a little bit more than they support the Catholic Church, free enterprise, and investigative reporting. That means it takes place and sometimes is of high quality, but it's not exactly common. The United States, on the other hand, supports sex research a bit *less* than it supports the Catholic Church, free enterprise, and investigative reporting. Curiously, the result is nearly the same: some good research but less than is needed. In each country, some sex-research projects are unexpectedly easy and others more difficult, but exactly which seems to be unpredictable.

[5] His term; just hold on.

[6] And probably not, for that matter, by any other techniques; see Freund 1977. Therapy is discussed later in this chapter.

[7] See Bancroft, Jones, and Pullan 1966.

[8] A complete review is in Hoon 1979.

most popular one was invented by a group of researchers at the State University of New York at Stony Brook—George Sintchak and James Geer—with bells and whistles added by other workers over the years.[9] This device is a small, transparent acrylic probe about ½ inch by 2 inches, hollowed out to make space for a tiny light source and photocell. The light bounces off the vaginal wall and reaches the photocell, which converts the light into an electrical signal. The amount of light bouncing back from the vaginal wall reflects—figuratively as well as literally—the amount of vaginal blood engorgement[10] and thus the amount of physiological sexual arousal. Because light, not volume, is what is directly detected, this device is often called a *photo*plethysmograph.

Comfy, everyone?

WHY BOTHER?

Before I describe the results of the studies that use plethysmography, I want to address an important question: why on earth is this technique needed in the first place?

Here's a brief quiz, class:

- Right now, I would say that my blood pressure is
  —so low I'm practically asleep.
  —higher than that but still pretty low because of the Valium.
  —about average; I feel pretty normal—normal for me, anyway.
  —higher than average, because all this sex talk upsets me.
  —I think you'd better call my physician.
- Right now the amount of adrenaline running through my body is
  —oh, I'd say, less than 3 nanograms per milliliter.
  —more than that, but less than 100,000 International Units.
  —about as much as was running through my blood while watching "Friday the Thirteenth—Part 47."
- Right now, my degree of erotic arousal is
  —chilly.
  —low.
  —lukewarm.

[9] Sintchak and Geer 1975.

[10] Actually, two aspects of vaginal blood volume can be measured: the total blood volume or the moment-to-moment increase in it—that is, the *velocity* of the increase. It would be too much to hope that there would not be different schools alleging which of these two is preferable under which circumstances and as to exactly how to calculate them from the raw data.

—high.

—sizzling.

Think how unhealthy it would be if we believed taking some-one's blood pressure was embarrassing. Why, we'd rarely take any-body's blood pressure. We'd worry about the motives of people who studied blood pressure. Whenever possible, we'd just *ask* people what they thought their blood pressure was rather than risk embarrassing them by actually taking it. We'd probably give blood pressure scien-tists some "Golden Fleece" awards, and someone would point out that taking someone's blood pressure amounted to treating the human body like a mechanical pump. How silly!

But sexual arousal can be measured just like any other physiologi-cal item can. And when it ought to be measured, put your embarrass-ment aside and get out the polygraph. If you prefer to answer a polite questionnaire about your body's responses of sexual arousal—or not to be asked at all—this is your right. But it is also uncomfortable to have your blood pressure taken. Although physiological measures are not the *only* way to study sexual arousal, there are times when they are needed.

For example, let's say you're a man or a woman having trouble getting an erection or lubricating when you want to. If you're sane, you ought to be willing to let the doctors find out whether your trou-ble has physiological roots.[11] The apparatus scientists use to investi-gate the physiology of lubrication and erection may seem bizarre if you're not acquainted with it, but it has noble purposes and is no weirder than breathalyzers or lie detectors.

But scientists *are* looked down upon for investigating sexual physi-ology. That means people working in labs that help women and men with sexual problems have had a history of ostracism ranging from snide comments in the media, through loss of tenure or licensure,[12] to arrest and imprisonment.

[11] Diabetes, for example, often causes impotence, and some workers now believe that as much as half of all impotence can be traced to physiological factors. The Masters and John-son group found that about 8 percent of all their male patients (not just those being treated for impotence) had abnormally high secretions of prolactin (a female hormone that men normally produce in tiny amounts)—not an enormous percentage but high enough to make it worth checking out, because too much prolactin would interfere with male sexual func-tioning.

[12] John B. Watson, the professor who introduced the term "behaviorism" to American psychologists, was one of these unfortunates. After his divorce got tangled up with the fact that he had been making physiological recordings of himself and his mistress making love (in his laboratory at Johns Hopkins to boot), he was forced to resign—and spent the rest of his life in advertising (see Magoun 1981). Not, I hasten to add, that there's anything wrong with advertising; why, one of my closest relatives was an advertiser.

These problems arise, of course, from the sex taboo, which I've covered in chapter 4. For the moment, let's talk about two nitty-gritty scientific questions. First, is the plethysmographic technique scientifically valid: that is, does it really measure what it claims to measure? And second: just what is sexual arousal, and thus what is it that plethysmography claims to measure?

IS PLETHYSMOGRAPHY SCIENTIFICALLY VALID?

Frankly, penile plethysmography is about as "face-valid" as one could imagine. After all, if I were to stand up here with an erect penis, I'd be sending you all a pretty obvious message. But for the scientific record, Freund and others have done studies that do demonstrate what might seem to be obvious:

- Heterosexual men's penises grow in volume when the men they're attached to are shown pictures of naked women and do not grow in the presence of pictures of naked men.
- Homosexual men's penises grow in volume when the men they're attached to are shown pictures of naked men and do not grow in the presence of pictures of naked women.
- The penises of pedophiles (child-lovers) and exhibitionists (see below) grow when the men they're attached to are shown pictures of children and exhibiting, respectively. Once again, not surprising—but many scientists have tried and failed to find something physiological that indicates sexual orientation.
- These results are obtained by different investigators using different kinds of pictures (slides, movies, videotapes, etc.) and different versions of the apparatus. McConaghy, for example, uses a different kind of movie as the stimulus, a slightly different sort of plethysmograph, and a different statistical technique for analyzing the results than Freund does—but he reaches the same general conclusions.
- As with lie detectors, faking is moderately difficult. Sometimes you can conceal or prevent your arousal,[13] but it is more difficult to pretend to have a response that you do not ordinarily have. That is, in scientificese, false positives are less common than false negatives.

[13] For example, you might try sharply stepping on your toes as soon as you see the picture you want to cover up your reaction to. Freund himself points out that a man can frustrate the test by masturbating a few times beforehand. And he admits that it is difficult to decide on a person's classification if he is actively trying to mislead (see Freund, Chan, and Coulthard 1979).

- Sometimes plethysmography works when the subjects themselves don't think it will. The following experience is not uncommon. A volunteer warns Freund that he isn't turned on by sexy photographs, and after the session is over, the subject says, "See? I told you I wouldn't get turned on." Yet Freund chuckles all the way to the databank—because although the subject might not have had very large reactions, the reactions he did have were unambiguous. The plethysmograph, remember, measures *any* volume change, not just full erections.
- No penile reactions at all can be detected in response to so-called *control* or *neutral* stimuli—pictures of landscapes, for example, which one presumes are not sexually arousing (but see below).
- Although vaginal plethysmography has encountered more difficulties, most workers agree that it is at least a rough correlate of sexual arousal. For example, most vaginal plethysmograph readings correlate well with what women say is sexually arousing to them.[14]
- Under certain conditions, vaginal plethysmography can be as reliable as penile plethysmography is. Scientists finally seem to be agreeing on which measures and which conditions are the best ones.

There are some opponents of these techniques, however. Leaving aside those who attack the motives of the plethysmographers,[15] some people have technical reservations,[16] and I even worry about reliabil-

---

[14] As recorded, for example, in one experiment by the woman's positioning a lever along a scale from 1 to 10 during each stimulus.

[15] According to the editor of the *Journal of Homosexuality*, a professor of psychology at San Francisco State University, "Surely those few investigators who determine sexual orientation in males by clamping a phallometer onto their subjects' penises to detect (gleefully, one imagines) any engorgement that may occur . . . are viewing sexual orientation as only physical. They never ask their subjects anything about sexual orientation, extracting the 'truth' by surveillance" (De Cecco 1981, p. 65). But I do not detect glee in the reports or in conversations I have had with their authors. And it is a matter of record that no such investigator views sexual orientation as "only physical." Most if not all of these scientists do ask subjects about their sexual orientation and subjective sexual responses and caution readers not to assume the two are synonymous.

[16] For example, one pair of authors once wrote—before the technique became widely accepted—that penile plethysmography is unreliable because it cannot "indicate whether a change in penile volume is in response to the apparatus or to the experimental erotic stimulus materials" (Money and Athanasiou 1973, p. 133). This particular objection puzzles me. Some men may be turned on by the idea of having someone monitoring their arousal; someone else, by putting his penis into a device that constrains it. But if so, it seems unusual that they would show increased erections only to certain stimuli and not to others (the landscapes, for example, or the photos of people of the sex one is not attracted to). At the

ity and validity.[17] There is also the possibility that a repressive regime might use plethysmography in repressive ways[18]—although plethysmography has the disadvantage, if used in this fashion, of making it very clear to the testee what is being tested for. These complaints should not keep us from looking at the results that have been obtained so far.

The Controls

Now let's look at the *control* stimuli used in these experiments. Control stimuli are those that are thought to be neutral—sexually neutral, in this case. Plethysmographers include them to make sure that a subject's arousal is to the sexual nature of the stimulus and not to the apparatus or—we should be so lucky!—the research staff.[19]

Freund's neutral stimuli are pictures of landscapes—and that sounds pretty safe to me. But Ron Langevin, a Freund collaborator, has explained that these landscapes were carefully screened to make sure they have no especially pointy or unduly rounded topological features. After all, such things might be mistaken for phallic symbols or breast imagery.[20] How nice to know that scientists are aware of the importance of art criticism in the modern world!

How the neutral stimuli are used depends on the design of the experiment. In one case, subjects had to wait for sexual-arousal levels to return to a low baseline level before moving on to each succeeding stimulus. So in between the good stuff, subjects got to stare at a blank

---

very least, these hypothetical plethysmographic exhibitionists seem to fall into homosexual and heterosexual categories, and this suggests that their penile volume changes are not merely in response to the apparatus.

[17] I do not know, for example, of any plethysmographic work that checks over a period of time to see if sexual orientation remains constant—except for the long-term follow-up studies of behavior therapy, which suggest that it does. See below.

[18] As a general rule, when it comes to repressive regimes and what they would do with Skinner's behaviorism or Wilson's sociobiology, I prefer to spend my time preventing the regime from taking power instead of arguing against a theory based on the way imaginative dictators might misuse it. Such misuse is tragic, but ironically the misuse usually has nothing whatsoever to do with the intellectual substance of the theory. I suppose it may be true that a repressive regime that believes in a genetic theory would repress by murder and a repressive regime that believes in an environmentalistic theory would repress by torture. I think our goal should be to avoid the repression in the first place.

[19] Skeptics would claim that what experimenters choose as neutral stimuli reveals the experimenters' beliefs about sexual response and may even invalidate the experiment if they are poorly chosen. This is a danger in any scientific experiment. But for the most part this criticism fails. It is, after all, a hypothesis you can test plethysmographically; if you believe a particular control stimulus is arousing rather than neutral, then find another that is less so.

[20] Langevin reports on a large number of plethysmographic studies in Langevin 1983.

screen for a while. But sometimes "a while" wasn't long enough, and then they got to read a political biography aloud until the erection went back down.[21]

In another study, subjects got to watch videos.[22] The lucky ones got to watch the good stuff—the videos depicting human beings—and went back, no doubt, to tell their roommates about this experiment they really ought to volunteer for. The control subjects, on the other hand, merely got to watch a video of a square moving across the screen that, they were told, *would be moving in an erotic way*. (Little did the lucky subjects know the problems their reputation suffered after the controls innocently started spreading the word about their roommates' weird tastes in rectangles!) This control video, of course, was included to be sure that their anticipations of *humans* moving across the screen in an erotic way did not unduly influence the results.

Another control was a videotaped lecture on oceanography by an octogenarian professor.[23] Mind you, departmental politics are a touchy issue, and this is not a study the plethysmographers should wave under the noses of the Marine Sciences Department. Methodologically, this videotape probably should not be used, either, if your subject pool or your grant's site-visit committee includes gerontophiles visiting from the coast. And you probably shouldn't tell Kurt Freund about it, either; he'll be an octogenarian himself in a few years, albeit a spry one.

But my personal, all-time favorite control stimulus is this one:[24]

The nonerotic film was an 8-min[ute] black and white film entitled "The Crusades" which depicted scenes of battles and court life during the time of the Crusades. The film was selected because of its nonsexual and generally boring content.

Frankly, I'd worry (just a bit) about whether this study got any subjects who had Joan of Arc fantasies (the subjects were women), but I'll take the authors' word that they did not. There are times, I guess, when landscapes are hard to beat.

Every now and then, however, there's a study where the controls really are a problem. One study used slides of flowers, for example. Alas, plenty of people have sexual associations to flowers,[25] and this

---

[21] Gillan 1976, cited in Hoon 1979, p. 20.

[22] Kabash et al. 1976, cited in Hoon 1979, p. 14.

[23] Hoon, Wincze, and Hoon 1976, cited in Hoon 1979, p. 14.

[24] Geer, Morokoff, and Greenwood 1974, p. 561, cited in Hoon 1979, p. 18.

[25] Not me! I swear! I'm not even a botanist! The study in question was Hamrick 1974, cited in Hoon 1979, p. 12.

doesn't even have anything to do with the fact that flowers are the sexual parts of plants!

More bothersome was a segment criticized—and probably justifiably so—in an otherwise excellent study comparing female with male sexual arousal patterns:

> I wonder, in fact, whether a male investigator would have been as likely as [Julia] Heiman [1975] to consider a conversation between a young man and woman [about the merits of two college majors] to be a "control" tape at all.[26]

So what can I say? Plethysmographers' experiments aren't always perfect. But determining what is and is not an erotic stimulus is really no more difficult than determining what is and is not an aggressive stimulus. I'm not suggesting that either one is a snap, but both tasks can be carried out by experimenters sensitive to the issues involved and willing to let others try replicating their experiments.

JUST WHAT IS SEXUAL AROUSAL?

Now the second methodological problem. I've described the devices that measure sexual arousal, but I haven't said what sexual arousal is in the first place, physiologically speaking. We need to know before we can be sure that these devices do what sexologists say they do.

This is one of the oldest sexological questions, and I'm happy to report that we now have some answers. Sexual arousal consists of the vasocongestion of the body's blood vessels, particularly in the genital and pelvic areas. *Vasocongestion* means blood pooling—in many places in your body, mind you, but especially in the erectile tissues of your penis or clitoris, nipples, earlobes, and nose, and in the capillaries down there in your pelvis. (*Capillaries* are the tiny blood vessels connecting the arteries to the veins.) *Pooling* means that more blood is going into those capillaries than is coming out of them. At the same time, musculoskeletal tension is building up, especially in the back, the face, the hands, and the feet—that is, your muscles get tense, your toes start to twitch, and your face becomes strained.

Unscientifically speaking, you're getting hot and bothered. Because blood is warm, you're getting hot, and because you're getting (vaso)congested, you're getting bothered.

Orgasm happens when this vasocongestion and sexual tension are

[26] Symons 1979, p. 173.

suddenly released: your blood vessels dilate all at once, your muscles relax, and you emit a grunt or two. Two Danish medical films document these signs and symptoms in clinical detail.[27] If your local library does not have these films available for loan, local organizations can obtain them elsewhere.[28]

So vasocongestion of the penis produces erection; more vasocongestion means more blood pooled in the penis, which means a bigger penis, which is exactly what Freund's plethysmograph measures. Vasocongestion in a woman means more blood pooled in the pelvic area, which means the reflectivity of the wall of the vagina is changed, which is what Sintchak and Geer's photoplethysmograph measures. As you can see, the penile plethysmograph has better face validity; exactly how vasocongestion changes the color of the vaginal wall isn't well understood.[29]

THE RESEARCH

It is now time to move from the classroom to the lab. By now I hope I have established that plethysmography is a legitimate technique in scientific sex research. What, then, have all us sexologists been doing with these tools? The research I'll describe mostly has to do with the gender transpositions. It falls into three categories: therapy, taxonomy, and theory.

Therapy

Freund was the pioneer here. Early in his career he began using behavior modification—a bit disreputably by modern standards—to "cure" people who had been "diagnosed" with particular sexual "deviations."[30] In Czechoslovakia he had homosexual men coming to his clinic to be cured, as he would have in any Western society. If he was like most behavior modifiers, he would have thought that behavior-

---

[27] See "Physiological responses of the sexually stimulated female in the laboratory" and "Physiological responses of the sexually stimulated male in the laboratory," both films by Dr. Gorm Wagner at the Institute of Medical Physiology, Copenhagen University.

[28] They are available only to educational and scientific groups from Multi-Focus, 333 West 52nd Street, New York, NY 10019.

[29] James Geer, personal communication.

[30] Just about every reputable scientific group—including psychiatrists, psychologists, social workers, and sociologists—now agrees that homosexuality is not properly classified as a "disease" in need of "cure." Hence, the quotation marks. (Only the psycho*analytic* society is a holdout; even today no analytic training institute will accept as a student a man or woman who is openly homosexual.) However, it gets tedious to keep up with those quotes, so henceforth I drop them.

modification therapy was more scientific than other forms of therapy—its techniques were more scientific, and it could generate objectively verifiable data to document that a particular technique really worked. In any event, Freund was one of the first sexologists to use various versions of aversion therapy—in particular, emetic therapy[31]—to treat homosexual men.[32]

Perhaps as a result of this behavioristic background, Freund wondered how he could demonstrate objectively what a homosexual was. In some circles, for example, the term "homosexual" is used in a variety of contexts, and Freund discovered that some people doubted that "homosexuals" were merely people sexually aroused by their own sex.[33] He came up with the plethysmograph to test these doubts and then tried using it to assess whether his patients were really cured.[34] Here is what he found:

Almost 20 years ago I started a therapeutic experiment [as a result of which his homosexual patients got married]. . . . Virtually not one "cure" remained a cure. The patients had become able to enjoy sexual intercourse with females . . . though much less than with males, but there was no true, lasting change in sexual preference. . . . Many patients admitted this only much later than they themselves had clearly noted this fact.[35]

In short, just as a good scientist is supposed to, Freund gathered data about his patients and their progress. When it turned out the data didn't show he had succeeded in curing anyone, he changed his mind. He stopped doing this therapy in 1960 or 1961.

Remarkably, several other behavior therapists have followed suit. For example, Gerald Davison served a term as president of the American Association for the Advancement of Behavior Therapy. He was known as the originator of "Playboy therapy" for homosexual men, which used not stomach upset but positive rewards to help them discover heterosexuality's delights. Now if you are a skeptic who believes

[31] In emetic therapy, the patient is given a drug that upsets his stomach at about the same time as he is presented with the stimulus that he is trying to become unattracted to—a photograph of a naked man, say, for a homosexual patient.
[32] Only men are mentioned in this section—for two reasons. First, Freund himself has used his technique only on men. Second, for reasons that the therapists, at least, don't understand, nearly all lesbians have had the good sense to stay away from clinics that try to change sexual orientation.
[33] Kurt Freund, personal communication.
[34] I infer—but do not know first hand—that Freund might have been attracted to plethysmography for this reason as well as the more theoretical one.
[35] Freund 1977, p. 238.

that scientific neutrality and objectivity are mere myths, then Davison would be one of the last people on the face of the earth you would expect to give a speech renouncing an interest in his own creation. But that's exactly what he did, in a now-famous speech delivered as his presidential farewell address.[36]

Interestingly, he didn't say in his speech that behavior therapy for homosexuals didn't work (although it is reasonable to infer that he believes this); he said it would be unethical to use it in a society that tried so hard, and so unjustly, to keep the lid on its members' homosexual attractions. Others challenged him in various ways,[37] but the net result is that far fewer behaviorists will try to cure homosexuals nowadays.

There are some men who describe themselves as former homosexuals, and one has written his autobiography. But as one reviewer sympathetic to the possibility of cure wrote, that particular author's "erotic response . . . to other men is [still] present, although he will not yield to it, and hopes that as his marriage develops, it will diminish."[38]

Australian researcher Nathaniel McConaghy is another behavior therapist who agrees that homosexuals are not helped by trying to change their sexual orientation—and who concluded this because of his own plethysmographic work.[39] McConaghy stated—and Freund agrees[40]—that nonbehavioristic methods probably worked no better than their behavioristic methods did.

For completeness, I must mention that the question of exactly what can be achieved in "cures" for homosexuals is not completely settled. Masters and Johnson, for example, believe that some people can "convert" or "revert" from homosexuality to heterosexuality after two weeks of sex therapy at their clinic in St. Louis. This conclusion has not been greeted warmly by many, to put it mildly, since Masters and Johnson admit that their documentation of these cases is incomplete[41] and that success is critically dependent on patient-selection criteria that they have not divulged.[42]

[36] Davison 1976. This paper has been reprinted in several places.

[37] See, for example, Freund 1977, Binder 1977, or the rebuttals published at the same time as Davison's speech in the Journal of Consulting and Clinical Psychology.

[38] Sagarin 1973, describing the autobiography of "William Aaron," published in 1972.

[39] He stated this particularly strongly on p. 563 of McConaghy 1976.

[40] Freund 1977.

[41] See Masters and Johnson 1979, p. 409. The subsequent book in which they promised to describe these results has not appeared as of 1986. Although Schwartz and Masters 1984 contains more detail about some aspects of their program, it is insufficient on this point.

[42] Masters and Johnson 1979, p. 340. They claim that divulging these criteria would allow homosexuals insufficiently motivated to change to appear to be more highly motivated than

Taxonomy

Therapy for homosexuals seems to be of most interest to the general public, but plethysmography is far more interesting theoretically. But there's a problem: good theory requires a good taxonomy—and most people think taxonomy is boring. Luckily, we're dealing with sex, and that means our taxonomy will be livelier than taxonomies usually are.[43]

A *taxonomy* is a system of classification; it's the system you use to name the things you're studying. Laypeople are usually bored by taxonomy, because it reminds them of having to memorize twenty-seven kinds of vertebrates or twelve varieties of quartz. But taxonomy is vital, for it is always related to a theory—a theory that lays out the basis for classifying things that particular way. The definitions of the gender transpositions in chapter 2 were based on a taxonomy that didn't get explicitly examined until chapters 5 and 6. And I didn't even require you to memorize the two categories of cross-dressers or the four kinds of male heterosexuality!

One important taxonomic question was discussed in chapter 5: are the various gender transpositions real traits that have some enduring essence across time or across cultures, or are they social constructions specific to a particular society at a particular time? Plethysmography has been used in support of the first position, by establishing an *erotic taxonomy* of sexual response in men.

Once again, Freund was the pioneer. Freund says that men, sexually speaking, fall into particular categories based on their plethysmographic responses. If you like a challenge, twist your tongue around these:[44]

- *Gynephiles* (ordinary heterosexual men) are erotically most aroused by the body shape (see below) of adult women.
- *Androphiles* (ordinary homosexual men) are erotically most aroused by the body shape of adult men.
- *Ephebephiles* are erotically most aroused by the body shape of youths, approximately seventeen to twenty-three.
- *Hebephiles* are erotically most aroused by the body shape of sex-

they are. Schwartz and Masters 1984 gave more statistics but did not provide more information about the selection criteria.

[43] But alas (again), the taxonomic discussion will involve only men. For reasons I don't entirely understand, penile plethysmographers tend to study quite different questions than vaginal plethysmographers do. And in particular, vaginal plethysmographers have not adopted a taxonomic approach.

[44] Although I obviously support Freund's terms, there are times when I wish that Freund (and John Money) would remember that anything more than a mouthful is wasted.

ually mature teenagers; they can be homosexual or hetero-sexual.[45]

- *Heterosexual pedophiles* are erotically most aroused by the body shape of sexually immature girls.
- *Homosexual pedophiles* are erotically most aroused by the body shape of sexually immature boys.

There are, in addition, a few more categories—some to be described below.

Freund's taxonomy was inspired by *ethology,*[46] the study of animal behavior from two biologic points of view: what behavior tells us about the evolutionary descent of a species and how physiological mechanisms cause a behavior proximately.

Freund's ethological approach was to use *releasing stimuli* (even though Freund doesn't mention the term) in his experiments. A *releaser,* or a *releasing stimulus,* is one that reliably—almost automatically—produces a certain response in a particular kind of animal.[47] (In the bad old days, this might have been called an "instinct," but this term has become so vague that it is now discredited. Ethologists are quick to insist that the behavior released by a releasing stimulus is *not* an instinct—because even the seemingly most automatic responses are influenced in their development by environmental factors.) For example, when a herring-gull chick sees the red spot on a parent's bill, it pecks at it. Ethologists say the red spot "releases" the pecking and the pecking in turn "releases" the parent's response (in this case, regurgitation of food). Freund's work embodies the assumption that *visual images of naked bodies serve as releasers for erection*—although what kind of naked body elicits this response in what kind of man presumably depends on imprinting experiences of the sort described in chapter 6.

Freund's stimuli are usually slides—pictures of naked people stand-

---

[45] In some papers, Freund talks of "heterohebes" and "homohebes"—men who prefer female and male teenagers, respectively.

[46] Kurt Freund, personal conversation.

[47] An *innate* releasing stimulus is one that is so automatic it requires nothing but proper nutrition to evoke it. The definition can be broadened slightly to include responses that are not quite automatic, in which case I drop the term "innate." Most examples of releasing stimuli are those that emerge very early in life (and thus are very unlikely to be due to learning); under the broadened definition, we need not be restricted to that time frame. It is very likely that erection in males constitutes a response to a releasing stimulus according to this broader definition. After all, despite the most strenuous efforts on the part of society to keep them from arising, erections (and eventually, ejaculations) occur spontaneously and without advance conscious wishes in the overwhelming majority of physiologically normal boys.

ing, arms at rest, smiling at the camera. These photos show no sexy leer, no suggestive gestures, no devices, no clothing: just naked people smiling. Even when Freund uses movies as stimuli, they are just movies of naked people smiling while walking toward the camera. Once again, there is nothing other than the smile and the nakedness to indicate sexiness. He chooses his stimuli in a way that makes their value as releasers as clear as possible.[48]

It is reasonable to suppose that homosexual and heterosexual men differ in which stimuli will release their sexual arousal. But until Freund, no one really proved this scientifically. Rather, people just assumed it, observed it without proper scientific controls, or didn't believe it to begin with.[49]

As you'll see, Freund's experiments are a good example of the relationship between a good taxonomy and a good theory. Are there significant numbers of people who are sexually aroused by a forest with especially bushy firs, perhaps, or by an especially curvaceous butte? The answer apparently is no. But if there were, then maybe "landscapophiles" really do exist, and Freund would have to get some new neutral slides. Are there significant numbers of men who are aroused by photos of nude amputees? In this case, the answer apparently is yes, and the term *apotemnophilia* was coined by John Money to describe them. Are there significant numbers of men who are aroused by photos of nude people with blond hair, regardless of whether they are nude male blonds or nude female blondes? Yale historian John Boswell implied the answer is yes,[50] but Freund and I would be more cautious. If Boswell is right, we are permitted to coin a term like "blondophilia," but if he's wrong, we may not.[51]

[48] Freund would be the first to admit that this is an incomplete view of sexual arousal, and I would be the second. But we have to start somewhere. Trying to break a behavior down by studying one of its components is one way to begin, just as stepping back to look at the big picture is another.

[49] Actually, as I mentioned above, Freund began thinking plethysmographically when he noticed that colleagues in Czechoslovakia didn't seem to believe that a homosexual man was merely someone who was sexually aroused by other men. Although this seems obvious to some people today, in fact, it is not obvious. Indeed, Schwartz and Masters 1984 seem to take a different approach, and in a sense Freund's definition goes to the very heart of the realist/social constructionist debate of chapter 5.

[50] Boswell 1980, p. 42, footnote 3.

[51] Of course, some would argue that "blondophilia" is a term we should not be permitted to coin under any circumstances, on linguistic grounds alone. As an aside, keeping in mind the fact that Boswell himself is fair-haired, his interest in the existence of blondophilia could be yet another instance of the blond heeding the blond.

Research Results and Theory

Research using plethysmography has been some of the most interesting in all of sexology. Luckily, it has been much more evenly distributed between women and men than the other work reported in this chapter. But as I mentioned above, the questions asked about women are usually not the same as those asked about men. Partly this is because it is not possible to compare directly the readings from a vaginal plethysmograph with those from a penile plethysmograph. Nevertheless, some comparisons can and have been made, especially in two areas.

First, work on the effects of alcohol on sexual arousal have been done with careful replications in both sexes. Second, there is work that helps solve the "sexual arousal" puzzle of chapter 3—that women find explicit erotica to be sexually arousing even though they sometimes don't act as if it is as arousing to them. I will discuss these two areas first.

Alcohol and Sex

Boy, were you drunk last night! And the things that you did! The question is Did you do those things because of, or in spite of, the alcohol?

The answer is It depends on whether you're male or female—and perhaps on what effect you *expected* alcohol to have—at least according to the Alcohol Behavior Research Laboratory at Rutgers University.[52] This group's experiments are models of scientific design, with controls for what seems like every conceivable confounding possibility.

In these studies, for example, subjects were given various doses of alcoholic drinks, ranging from no alcohol at all to enough to get you pleasantly high (but not drunk). Sometimes subjects were purposely deceived (along with the graduate student conducting the session) as to exactly how much alcohol was in the drink. Sometimes they were told that the drink would probably make them more aroused, sometimes that it would make them less aroused. They were then shown erotic films, and their sexual arousal was measured with a strain gauge or photoplethysmograph.

The results are invariably fascinating. In one pair of experiments, both men and women had *lower* levels of sexual arousal the *more* alcohol the drink contained, which confirms the medical view of al-

---

[52] The studies are Briddell and Wilson 1976 and the three Wilson and Lawson papers.

cohol as a central nervous system depressant. But being deceived as to the true alcohol content of the drink, or being led to expect different things as the result of the drink, had no measurable effects. In a second pair of experiments, the subjects were manipulated not about whether they could expect alcohol to increase or decrease their arousal but about whether their drink had alcohol in it at all. Here it turned out the manipulation had an effect in men but not in women. That is, the women had lower levels of arousal when their drink really did contain alcohol. But the men's arousal depended *not at all* on the actual alcohol in their drinks but on whether they *thought* the drink would affect their arousal. In sum, then, women's arousal was affected *only* by the alcohol, but the men's arousal could be affected by what they thought its effects would be.

The Erotica Puzzle

This puzzle, you'll recall, is that women buy and/or use sexually explicit visual materials (magazines, videos, etc.) less often than men do, although when they are exposed to such materials they are aroused not much differently than men are. Luckily, just what it is that women and men find sexually arousing has been the subject of a large number of plethysmographic studies. But as far as I know, only one investigator, Julia Heiman, actually used the same stimuli for both sexes (in her doctoral thesis at the State University of New York at Stony Brook). After discussing her results, I will move on to studies of group-sex stimuli and their relationship to "homosexual" and "heterosexual" stimuli. (I put those words in quotation marks because, as you will see, there is some dispute as to just how homosexual and heterosexual these stimuli were.)

Heiman used four kinds of stories as stimuli in her experiments: those that were romantic but not sexually explicit, those that were explicit but not romantic, those that were both, and those that were neither.[53] Each of these four kinds itself had four subtypes, according to whether the man or the woman initiated the sexual encounter and according to whether the language of the story described the woman's or the man's reactions and physical appearance.

Heiman's subjects were thirty-nine male and fifty-nine female college students. While their genital responses were recorded (the women's by photoplethysmography and the men's by strain gauge), each

---

[53] Recall that it was these "control" stories—about a college man and woman discussing the relative merits of anthropology over premed as a major—that were questioned as valid controls devoid of sexual content. Nevertheless, I believe Heiman's fundamental results are valid.

of them listened to four stories: all of the same kind but differing according to subtype.[54] For example, a particular subject might have listened to four stories that were erotic but not romantic; these four stories would differ according to which person initiated the eroticism and according to whose reactions were described.

The results were just like the studies summarized in chapter 3: male and female arousal patterns were about the same. Or, as Heiman put it, "explicit sex, not romance, is what turns people on—women as well as men."[55] Erotic and erotic-romantic stories were most arousing for both sexes (and equally so), and the purely romantic stories were not significantly more arousing than the control stories.[56] Interestingly, all the men knew exactly when they were physiologically aroused, but many of the women did not—especially during the romantic stories.

There was also a consistent pattern with the subtypes of the stories. For *both* sexes, the most arousing subtype was the one in which the woman initiated the sexual activity and in which the woman's reactions were described. The second most arousing type was the one in which the man initiated it and the woman's reactions were described. Heiman concluded that "the description of the woman's body and her sexual response is apparently an important ingredient in the erotic script for men and women alike."[57]

These conclusions are entirely consistent with what Sigusch and Schmidt found in their West German college students (described in chapter 3). They are also consistent with my limerent/lusty theory (chapter 6).

Notice that Heiman found some departures from the stereotypical patterns *supposed* to be true for heterosexuals, in that she found a women-initiated, female-centered story to be most arousing for women (not to mention men). How can we explain this? Heiman said she was "fascinated" by this. In a sense, this reflects the bisexuality puzzle of chapter 3: this is one of the ways in which more women are bisex-

---

[54] Actually, these numbers are those reported in Heiman 1975, an article in *Psychology Today*. Two years later, she published her results more formally in a scientific journal (Heiman 1977); the numbers of subjects had increased to seventy-seven women and forty-two men, and two additional experimental groups had been added beyond the four described here.

[55] Heiman 1975, p. 92.

[56] However, a substantial minority of the men found the control stories arousing, up until the point at which they realized that explicitly sexual activity was not going to take place in them. This was the complaint raised by University of California evolutionary biologist Donald Symons.

[57] Heiman 1975, p. 93.

ual than men. Other studies of sexual arousal get hung up in precisely this area, and it is to those that I will now turn.

Group Sex

When the stimuli presented in plethysmography experiments depart from the 100 percent heterosexual, unusual results are sometimes obtained. One of the first groups of researchers to use vaginal plethysmography found, for example, that five of the six women in their sample were more highly aroused by a group-sex scene than they were by any other stimulus in the experiment! But the women's *written* ratings of their sexual arousal didn't rate the group-sex scene arousing at all.

This, of course, has two interpretations: (1) the women "really" were aroused, but they censored their verbal accounts (consciously or unconsciously); (2) they "really" were not aroused but verbally stated arousal and physiological arousal are just two different things. Alas, there were only six women in this study, so how representative their results are is hard to judge. Let's throw caution to the winds and try to interpret it, anyway; the logic will turn out to be important.

A scene of group sex is, after all, one in which several men and several women are interacting sexually. Were these women aroused most by the large number of men, by the large number of women, by the large amount of heterosexuality, or by some other aspect of the film?

The "pseudolesbian porn" puzzle of chapter 3 is closely related to this one. Heterosexual men are often aroused by images of two women having sexual relations. Is this true because (possibility 1) the men project themselves into the picture (fantasizing that there are not one but two women who need a man)? Or are the men simply aroused (possibility 2) by images of naked women (one woman is arousing, two are even more arousing)?

The key to these puzzles, I believe, has been discovered by David Sakheim and David Barlow (and colleagues) at the State University of New York at Albany. These researchers recruited a sample of eight homosexual and eight heterosexual men, then showed them some sexually explicit films, slides, and audiotapes with varying content (heterosexual, homosexual male, and lesbian).[58] During this time, subjects moved a lever back and forth to report how sexually aroused they were feeling. At the same time, a penile strain gauge was sending its own report of sexual arousal.

[58] Obviously not a large sample but adequate for certain problems if properly matched and tested. The study is Sakheim, Barlow, Beck, and Abrahamson 1985.

The SUNY/Albany researchers reported a remarkable pattern of arousal in these men. Not surprisingly, the homosexual men were most aroused by the man-with-man stimuli, next most aroused by the man-with-woman stimuli, and least by the woman-with-woman stimuli. Likewise, the heterosexual men were least aroused by men with men. But the big surprise was how stimulating the woman-with-woman stimuli were: *they were the most arousing stimuli for the heterosexual men!* (This was true for both the strain-gauge and self-report measures of sexual arousal.) These researchers found they could classify twelve of the sixteen subjects correctly as to sexual orientation by knowing whether they were aroused more by the male/male film or the male/female one.[59] But their success rate rose to fifteen out of sixteen when they substituted scores on the female/female film for scores on the heterosexual one. That means that arousal to female/female stimuli is a *better* indicator of heterosexuality (for men) than heterosexual stimuli are.[60]

Now admittedly this study used a small sample, but the percentages are still impressive. (Several other studies have come up with data not too different from this one, although they missed the comparison with the lesbian stimuli.) To explain these findings with possibility 1, you'd have to go pretty far afield. How many teenaged boys do you know who are socialized to be *more* interested in lesbians than in heterosexual women?

Possibility 2 does better; it makes sense of the Albany group's data with just one extra observation. Consider this: homosexual men are interested in men, period. So a picture with two naked men in it is highly arousing, a picture with one man in it is less arousing, and a picture with no men in it is boring. What if homosexual men and heterosexual men are, quite simply, mirror images of each other—that is, that homosexual men respond to stimuli containing men and that heterosexual men respond to stimuli containing women? Then we would expect heterosexual men to find a stimulus with two women in it highly arousing, a stimulus with one woman in it less arousing,

---

[59]They used a *discriminant function analysis,* which is a statistical guessing game: you give the computer the data on sexual orientation and sexual arousal, and it constructs a mathematical formula that tries to predict one variable on the basis of another. In this case, the function would try to predict sexual orientation on the basis of the arousal scores.

[60]This conclusion was backed up by a second kind of analysis: a *stepwise multiple regression* in which data concerning the lesbian film entered the mathematical regression formula first, followed by the data pertaining to the male homosexual film. This means that these two measurements, in that order, were statistically the most important in "guessing" the sexual orientation of the subjects—the first one in the heterosexual direction, of course, and the second in the homosexual direction.

and a stimulus with no women in it boring. *That's what the Albany group found,* and that's what I think is the best solution to the pseudolesbian porn puzzle.

Other researchers didn't initially reach the same conclusion because they were using what turned out to be a misleading analogy. By labeling the releasing stimuli as "heterosexual" or "homosexual," they hypothesized that the most arousing stimulus for heterosexual men would be the "most heterosexual" one, whereas in fact it turned out to be the "most female" one. For homosexual men, in contrast, the "most homosexual" stimuli were also the "most male" ones. Experiments that didn't include female-female stimuli thus had a subtle asymmetry—an asymmetry you'd miss if you hadn't studied the homosexual men in the first place.

This suggestion has an important consequence: it implies that Freund's use of photographs *as if they were* ethological releasers is more powerful and more correct than it might at first have seemed. A releaser is by definition a stimulus that operates almost automatically: [61] the herring-gull parent gets its spot pecked at, and it opens its mouth. The heterosexual man sees a naked woman, and his penis gets bigger. The herring-gull parent gets its spot pecked at several times, and it opens its mouth more quickly or more often; the heterosexual man sees several naked women, and his penis gets even bigger, or gets big quicker or more often. The Albany studies have, in a sense, confirmed that pictures of naked bodies are releasers for sexual arousal—in men.

This raises an obvious question: are women aroused by the sight of two (or more) naked men doing sexual things? The experiment that revealed that women were aroused by group-sex scenes also included a male-male scene, and both the plethysmographic recording and the women's own verbal accounts suggested that they were *not* aroused by it. But I wonder.

I raised the same question after speaking at a gynecology grand rounds at a local hospital.[62] Most of the fellows (young physicians, fresh from their residencies) at the speech were women, and one of them telephoned me excitedly a week later. She had conducted an informal poll among eight of her fellow female fellows, and seven of the eight reported to her that they thought that they would indeed be aroused by watching a film of two or more men having sex with other men. Now given the data on the low levels of agreement between

---

[61] This does not imply that it is genetically transmitted or that it cannot change.

[62] "Grand rounds" is the term used in hospitals and medical schools to describe the weekly seminars given by local experts and attended by the professors, interns, and residents in a particular medical specialty.

plethysmographic recordings and self-reports of sexual arousal, not to mention the small sample size, this poll is more enticing than definitive. But it does suggest that experiments on larger samples—and especially samples from more diverse groups—need to be undertaken.

Also yet to be studied scientifically is the kind of woman known as a "fag hag" or "fruit fly." (These are slang terms for heterosexual women who enjoy spending time with gay men.[63]) Some believe that these women "really" have lesbian fantasies but haven't yet decided to act upon them, others that they are women too homely to be attractive to heterosexual men. Or perhaps gay men are the preferred escorts of women who want male companionship without the threat, fear, or worry about sexual approaches. I know of no formal studies of the matter, but I frankly wonder if they are truly heterosexual women who know they would like to join a gay male couple making love. That is, what if they are the female equivalent of the heterosexual men aroused by pseudolesbian porn?

Ah, the excitement of research on the frontiers of sexual science!

Bisexuality

As I mentioned in chapter 3, plethysmography has been used to investigate bisexuality. Freund, for example, wanted to know what kinds of bisexuality exist in adult men. He defined a bisexual arousal pattern as one in which there are clear penile reactions to slides of both naked men and naked women—not necessarily exactly equal responses, just any significant responses at all. That is, he defined bisexuality in reference to body shape, the criterion used in his other definitions.

Freund recruited samples of heterosexual and homosexual men from the Toronto area, brought them to his laboratory, and showed them his typical slides.[64] As I described in chapter 3, the homosexual men were most aroused by slides of naked adult men, next most by male pubescents, next by the older boys, and least by the younger boys. In fact, for the homosexual men the slides of the younger children were no more arousing than the control landscapes. A nearly perfect mirror image prevailed among the heterosexual group, who on average were most aroused by slides of naked adult women, next by female pubescents, next by the older girls, and least by the younger girls—which were, for these men, just a little bit more arousing than the control landscapes (but statistically significantly so).

---

[63] A lot of people are unhappy with these terms, including many people who use them. May I impishly propose "homophilphiliac" for formality and "queen queen" in the vernacular?

[64] Freund 1974.

Notice that Freund's general patterns for homosexual and hetero-sexual men did not show any hint of bisexuality: either adult men or women were most arousing, and as the slides moved away from that extreme, the arousal value decreased. There wasn't anyone aroused by masculine and feminine body shapes to roughly equal degrees. In fact, Freund has conducted a search for men bisexual according to his body-shape definition and claims that he can't find any.[65] I have merely stated that bisexuality is less common among men than it is among women; Freund says, in effect, that I haven't gone far enough, be-cause he can't find it among men at all!

Actually, that's not quite true. Using his strict definition, Freund has found bisexual responses in a few carefully restricted groups of men—these three:

- Homosexual hebephiles—men who are most aroused by male teenagers—can be weakly bisexual. When they are shown pic-tures of naked *adults,* their arousal sometimes is about equal for both men and women.
- Some masochistic men who enjoy being humiliated in sexual encounters don't care much whether it's a man or a woman doing the humiliating and thus might be called bisexual masochists.
- Some pedophiles are aroused by both boys and girls. That is, there are not only homosexual and heterosexual pedophiles but also bisexual pedophiles.

But remember, Freund's definition uses pictures specifically de-signed to mimic ethological releasers. He calls the arousal that results arousal to "body shape." In my opinion, he is implicitly confining his definition of bisexuality to bisexual *lustiness* (as defined in chapter 6). Limerence might be different, as might lusty definitions a bit broader than Freund's.

In fact, Freund is aware of other definitions of the term "bisexual" and admits that many *homosexual* men *are* bisexual in a particular sense: they can be aroused by listening to stories during which they are told to fantasize themselves in the role of the male character who takes steps toward having sex with a woman. (But this is not what he would mean by "body-shape bisexuality.") Homosexual men in one experi-ment read, and were read, fifteen-second story fragments that illus-

---

[65] Freund 1974, p. 39.

trated four stages of flirting—from meeting to sexual intercourse.[66] The first stage involved, as Freund put it, "location of a suitable prospective partner." The second went on to "pretactile interaction" but involved no touching or only slight touching. The third proceeded to "tactile interaction" and the fourth to sexual intercourse. Freund found that compared with control stories,[67] the first two kinds of story were not sexually arousing to the homosexual men but the last two kinds were (at least to a moderate extent). Notice that a story is more likely to suggest a romantic—dare I say limerent?—context than a single photograph or short film clip is. And so the bisexuality that showed up in this experiment may be different from the bisexuality that would be indicated by Freund's ethological (releaser-based) approach.

So here we have a particularly good example of how taxonomy affects theory and vice versa. Freund does not include bisexuals in his taxonomy (perhaps he would call them *gynandrophiles*) because he does not find that any exist using his plethysmographic technique and "body shape" definition. The bisexuality he does find among men (teenlovers, child-lovers, and masochists) is not the sort to warm the hearts of bisexual liberationists. They, of course, use more inclusive definitions of sexual orientation, for example, the definition that one is bisexual if one has had sexual relations with both men and women. But even Freund admits the existence of this kind of bisexuality; he even demonstrated the existence of a particular type of bisexuality in his stories experiment: what we might call "body-touch" bisexuality, as opposed to the "body-shape" bisexuality.

To be frank, I am not entirely convinced by Freund's data; I would like to see his studies replicated by other scientists. But the strength of his point of view is that it makes important distinctions and thereby *makes sense* of an otherwise confusing jumble of behaviors. The key to making sense of the jumble is taxonomy: it is his definitions that embody the distinctions his experiments show are important.

"Cures"

Freund believes, by the way, that it is this "body-touch" bisexuality in body-shape homosexual men that was elicited by his "cures" back in Czechoslovakia. His failure made him doubt other people's cures,

---

[66] Freund, Langevin, Chamberlayne, Deosoran, and Zajac 1974. These men were "prearoused" to a particular level of erection by viewing slides of naked men; then these slides were replaced by the text of a story.

[67] These control stories were, according to Freund, descriptions of "neutral situations." Perhaps they were stories about men encountering new and attractive landscapes.

and that in turn made him doubt the reasons people gave for why their cures worked—including the reasons people gave for homosexual men becoming homosexual in the first place.

One popular psychoanalytic notion is that homosexual men are homosexual because they fear women: in particular, that they have an actually phobic response to the female genitals.[68] This has never been a strong argument. One researcher[69] wrote quite rightly that no one likes something positively because they dislike an alternative: you don't love tomatoes because you hate spinach. But Freund put some scientific teeth into this by extending his plethysmographic technique in the following way.

He recruited a sample of homosexual men, then showed them slides of naked men until their penises reached a certain degree of erection. Then he switched over to any of several other pictures: naked women, close-ups of women's genitalia, people with disfiguring skin conditions, and landscapes. When shown the disfiguring skin conditions, these men clearly showed aversion: their erections were lost in a hurry. But when the slides were switched to landscapes, then the men exhibited no sign of aversion; they lost their erections, but only slowly, over a period of time. Well, what about the slides of naked women or of female genitalia? Here the response of the penises was just like it was for the landscapes: a slow loss of erection indicating lack of interest, not out-and-out aversion. Homosexual men's penises acted as if the men didn't find the feminine stimuli disgusting, just uninteresting.

The men themselves reported a bit differently. The genital close-ups, especially, were *consciously* rated by the homosexual men, in written ratings, as more disgusting (in comparison to landscapes). Once again, you might conclude that Freund's technique measures something completely different from conscious arousal, or you might think it shows that gay men don't know very well what turns them off. Since heterosexual men are, like gay men, often consciously turned off by pictures of the sex they're not interested in, Freund's aversion experiments suggest that the theory of heterosexual aversion in homosexual men itself results from projection on the part of heterosexual therapists.[70]

---

[68] With a definition like this, you can begin to imagine why someone would doubt that a homosexual was "merely" someone whose penis became erect at the sight of a naked man.

[69] Tripp 1975.

[70] Projection is the presumption that others share one's own point of view, motivations, weaknesses, and so on—especially when there is little or no evidence that those other people actually do share those factors. It seems that psychologists love to accuse other people of projection all the time.

Child Molestation

Projection may also bring to bear on the experiments Freund performed dealing with heterosexual men's arousal to different body parts (summarized in chapter 3). Recall here the plethysmographic evidence that ordinary heterosexual men are a little bit aroused by pictures of naked little girls—even very young little girls. Do some of these men go around accusing ordinary homosexual men of being aroused by little boys and conclude that it would be dangerous for ordinary homosexual men to teach young children in school? I doubt that the accusers would allow themselves to be tested by Freund, but their homophobic reactions suggest projection.

In a subsequent study, Freund focused exclusively on the stimuli that released sexual arousal in nondeviant heterosexual men. This time the men were shown pictures not of complete people but close-ups of body parts. As you'll recall from chapter 3, plethysmographic results showed that adolescent males' buttocks aroused the *heterosexual* men a little more than landscapes. Again, the amount of arousal to this stimulus shown was not high. But it was there.[71]

CONFLICTS BETWEEN PLETHYSMOGRAPHY AND SELF-REPORTS

By now it should be clear that self-reports of sexual arousal can conflict with plethysmographic measurements. As it happens, I have overemphasized this disagreement. In many of the studies mentioned above, people's self-reports correspond quite well with their plethysmographic recordings; it just hasn't been important to the ideas I've been trying to get across to point out the agreement when it exists.

But the disagreements are frequent enough that they need further discussion. Which is more accurate—plethysmography or self-report? Here's an analogy that can help us decide.

Clocks

Think of clocks. Which is more accurate: an hourglass or an atomic clock? An hourglass "keeps time" by showing how long it takes for grains of sand to fall through a small hole. An atomic clock "keeps time" by showing how long it takes certain atomic particles to vibrate. These two methods of "keeping time" are really quite different; atomic-

---

[71] Hmm. . . . Does this mean it may be time for mandatory plethysmographic testing of everyone opposed to gay rights laws?

particle vibrations have nothing to do with grains of sand falling through a hole. But we believe that both devices measure the "same thing"—"time"—because they correlate with each other: if one grain of sand drops after 143 zillion vibrations, then a second grain of sand will drop after about another 143 zillion vibrations.

But we also know that an atomic clock is "more accurate" than an hourglass. Why? What if people say that as far as they're concerned hourglass time is "real" time and atomic time is something else entirely? They are welcome to their opinion, but why do we feel there is something inaccurate about such a preference?

The answer comes from looking at more than one of each kind of clock. Make a bunch of hourglasses, all designed to measure the same interval. Turn them all over at once and measure how much they disagree *with the other hourglasses*. Then make a bunch of atomic clocks, all tuned to the same vibration. Set them going all at once and measure how much they disagree *with the other atomic clocks*. You will discover that the disagreement among atomic clocks is much smaller than the disagreement among hourglasses no matter how hard you try to make your hourglasses identical. Moreover, the atomic clocks agree with each other about the inaccuracies of a particular hourglass to about the same extent they agree with each other about "time"; they all indicate that a particular hourglass took about 143 zillion vibrations to drop the first grain of sand and about 156 zillion vibrations to drop the second. But the hourglasses disagree among each other far more when they are used to estimate inaccuracies in the atomic clocks.

Atomic time and hourglass time are *not* "the same thing." But they are close enough for scientists to decide, as a convention, that they will consider them both approximations to "the same thing"—namely, "true time," which is imperfectly measured by both kinds of device. Because atomic clocks present a simpler, more consistent, and less variable picture of the world than hourglasses do, they are adopted by scientists as the "better" measure of true time.

Likewise, you are welcome to be interested only in self-reported sexual arousal, only in plethysmographically recorded sexual arousal, or in both. But since the two measurements correlate fairly well with each other under most circumstances, we have to consider the possibility that both reflect what we might call "true sexual arousal" (albeit imperfectly in both cases). The measurement that is more internally consistent—that shows the world in a simpler (but not *over*simplified!) way—is the one that, for the moment, should be accepted as the "better" approximation to true sexual arousal. But keep in mind that even if we do accept one particular measure, that does not mean the other one is uninteresting on its own terms. And the existence of a discrepancy between the two is probably significant.

A Disagreement

With this discussion about accuracy in mind, let me describe one experiment in which the disagreement between self-reported sexual arousal and plethysmographically recorded arousal was especially important.

I have mentioned that it is sometimes difficult to make the distinction between heterosexual transvestites, asexual transsexuals, gynephilic transsexuals, and androphilic transsexuals. I have also mentioned that some male-to-female transsexuals are thought (or known) to have told surgeons and psychiatrists that they are not attracted to women in order to receive permission to undergo sex-reassignment surgery. One of the categories these transsexuals are afraid of being put into by the doctors is the heterosexual-transvestite category, because some people approving transsexual surgery believe that heterosexual fetishistic arousal to women's clothes ought to disqualify men from the operation. It is in such instances that the power to classify amounts to the power to control.

Some of Freund's colleagues in Toronto, headed by psychologist Ray Blanchard, have investigated how to make this distinction plethysmographically—although they are careful to note that they do not allow it to influence their decision about surgery.[72] Subjects in the study were thirty-seven men, who said, on questionnaires, that they were sexually attracted to women and that they felt like a woman when dressed as a woman (and perhaps also at other times; see below). Blanchard divided them into four groups according to their responses to a question asking about sexual arousal when cross-dressed (during the past year):

- Those who *always* were sexually aroused while cross-dressed
- Those who were sexually aroused while cross-dressed at least half the time but not always
- Those who were sexually aroused while cross-dressed but less than half the time
- Those who never were sexually aroused while cross-dressed

[72] Blanchard, Racansky, and Steiner 1986. These authors explicitly reject the belief that these taxonomic classifications should affect decisions to perform transsexual operations; they decide for surgery on other grounds.

Additionally, there was a control group composed of those who had never cross-dressed, period.

These groups of men then listened to stories read by an actress describing various activities, one of which was a cross-dressing story involving no explicit sexuality or romantic fantasies, and another story that was neutral (no cross-dressing and no sex).[73] However, each story was narrated in the second person, putting the subject into the story himself: for example, "The full skirt of your burgundy gown is made of yards of swirling chiffon." Penile reactions were recorded plethysmographically.

As expected, the control group was not aroused by the cross-dressing story significantly more than it was by the neutral story. Likewise, the neutral story was the least arousing of the various stories for all groups. But each of the groups admitting cross-dressing had significantly higher penile responses to the cross-dressing story than to the neutral story—even the group that claimed that they were *never* aroused by cross-dressing.

How can we account for this discrepancy? One possibility was that the supposedly never aroused group was lying (or that some of its members, at least, were lying). Blanchard himself, however, thinks this is not the best answer, because if such a liar didn't want someone to know he was aroused by cross-dressing, he would have found it easy to refuse to take the test.

A second possibility is that the never aroused group was simply unaware of its own arousal. Plethysmography can detect fairly small volume changes; if the subjects think the verbal question about arousal when cross-dressed refers to full erections, it is not difficult to see how someone might believe they are "never aroused" but still have their penis respond somewhat to a cross-dressing story. Remember Freund being told by subjects that testing them plethysmographically was a waste of time because "pictures don't turn me on"? The same thing may be going on here.

Blanchard's third possibility (which can coexist with the second) is that the arousal used to be stronger in previous years but has died down. After all, any particular lusty stimulus sooner or later loses its arousal value; a familiar face is less lustily arousing than a new face is. And, after all, the questionnaire only asked about the past year.

Now let me explain why Blanchard and his colleagues conducted this experiment in the first place. They wanted to find out if cross-dressing in heterosexuals is *always* associated with fetishism: that is,

---

[73] Some erotically explicit stories, unrelated to the question here, were also read to them.

do *all* heterosexual cross-dressers get some fetishistic arousal from wearing women's clothes, at least at some point in their lives? If so, do some *completely* lose that fetishistic arousal when they get old enough? He concludes from his experiment that the answers are yes and no, respectively. Although Blanchard does not explicitly endorse the notion, it is reasonable to conclude from his experiment that the plethysmographic measure more accurately reflects true sexual arousal because it simplifies the resulting explanation. If heterosexual cross-dressing and fetishism are *always* connected (according to plethysmography), then there is just one clear-cut fact to explain with a scientific theory. If the two are not always connected (according to self-reports), then there is a jumble of confusing facts to explain with a scientific theory. Accordingly, it is scientifically "better" to use the plethysmographic measure as the principal one taxonomically.

THE SOCIAL CONSEQUENCES OF CLASSIFICATION

The problem is—and for all I know, Blanchard and his colleagues are in complete agreement—that we live in a society that stigmatizes people with sexual proclivities unlike those of the majority. It is legitimate for sexologists to classify people sexologically, but in the larger society people are classified sexually only when that society wants to put those people down. It's not considered polite to talk about what you do in bed. So if society classifies you according to what your penis wants to do in bed, then you're being stigmatized.

There's a solution to this dilemma; think back to the berdaches among American Indians (see chapter 5). Indians believe that berdaches are men with particular *spiritual* virtues; that is, a certain spirituality is the quintessential aspect of berdachism for the Indians themselves. Western sexologists then come riding into town full of questions. They report that all the berdaches they meet say they are sexually attracted to men. This is an important fact, because many nonberdaches are not sexually attracted to men. The sexologists may be excused if they fail to investigate the spiritual aspects because those are aspects that they find uninteresting.

But they may not be excused if they act as if the sexological aspects are the only important ones:[74]

Some folks have fun with those anthropologists, telling them wild stories, playing games with them. The game works like this:

[74]Lame Deer and Erdoes 1972, p. 150.

Anthropologist: "How's your sex life?"
Indian: "Fine. How is yours?"

The same is true of transvestites. One I know says that a *gender shift* rather than a sexual fetish is the most important aspect of transvestism to the heterosexual cross-dressers he knows. He places a lot of emphasis on the spiritual feelings involved in cross-dressing and dislikes the term "transvestite" because it strikes him as too clinical. Yet he does not deny the empirical association between transvestism and sexual arousal by women's clothing. Show him a picture of a naked "she-male" (someone with breasts and a penis) and he will in all probability become sexually aroused. But far more important to him, subjectively, are the nonsexual feelings (relaxation, satisfaction, happiness, relief, etc.) he gets when he puts on women's clothes. These feelings relate to his personal expression of the masculine and feminine aspects of his personality—a personality that includes a sexual component, of course, but which is scarcely limited to it.

ANOTHER TAXONOMY FROM FREUND

Intriguingly, Kurt Freund himself pointed this fact out to the scientific community in a fascinating way. Freund, like Blanchard, was trying to figure out a way to distinguish the various types of transsexual, and he and his associates hit upon a simple question that would help draw this distinction.[75] A man "is" a transsexual when he feels enough "like a woman" to seek a sex-reassignment operation. Just when, Freund asked, does such a man feel "like a woman"?

Some men only feel like women when they are dressed as women. For example, heterosexual transvestites feel like women when dressed as women but feel like men at other times. (In the language of my cross-dressing friend, they have experienced a gender shift that causes them to express their feminine spirit by cross-dressing.) Other men feel like women all the time, *even when they are naked*, but have been aroused by cross-dressing at some point in their lives. (These people, says my friend, have gender shifted much further.) So-called borderline transsexuals only feel like women from time to time. (These are in the process of gender shifting.) An important scientific/taxonomic point is that *all these kinds of people described so far are gynephilic*—that is, they are sexually aroused by women.

There is, however, a final category of man who feels like a woman.

[75] Some of Freund's colleagues in these ideas are, not surprisingly, the same as some of Blanchard's: the paper reporting this classification is Freund, Steiner, and Chan 1982.

Someone of this type always feels like a woman (and has for over one year) *and* has never been aroused by cross-dressing. Interestingly, Freund found that *these transsexuals are all androphilic* (sexually attracted to men).

Obviously, this is taxonomy again. In theory, there could exist men who are gynephilic, feel like women all the time, *and* have never been aroused by cross-dressing. Freund didn't find any; neither did Blanchard. What's interesting about Freund's involvement is that plethysmography was *not* used to construct the taxonomy this time! Freund's assessments of homosexual and heterosexual interest were done using questionnaires. (It was Blanchard that used the plethysmograph in another study.) Accordingly, the taxonomy established by using self-reports has validated the taxonomy established using plethysmography; both taxonomies are "simpler" if one believes that people can be unaware of aspects of what is "truly" sexually arousing for them.

CONCLUSIONS

It really can make sense to say things like this:

- She was really turned on by group sex but didn't know it until her husband took her to a swingers' party.
- Heterosexual cross-dressers always have some sexual arousal to the fantasy of wearing women's clothes even if they're not consciously aware of it.
- He really was gay ever since puberty but wouldn't admit it to himself until he fell in love with his roommate in college.
- Some lesbian women don't know that their feelings for their friends are really sexual feelings.
- Some gay men may say that they are turned off by women's bodies, but in fact the aversion is only in their heads.

All these are statements that can be proved—or disproved—using plethysmography. Without plethysmography, they would be much harder to assess and sometimes even nonsensical to ask.

Throughout this book I discuss people called "homosexual," "bisexual," "transsexual," and so on. Are these categories figments of my imagination? Plethysmographic experiments suggest the answer is no. Can the existence of these categories be independently confirmed? Yes. Are these the only categories that are valid? No. Are they the most important categories? That depends. If these categories validly exist, does that mean they are genetic? No. Does it mean that these terms will be used in an unbiased fashion by society at large? Clearly not—and Freund's experiments strike me as especially useful here, for they suggest why certain distortions occur and why certain others do not.

Plethysmography underscores the conclusions in chapter 5. The existence of heterosexual and homosexual categories is not entirely a social creation; it is to some extent a consequence of the way things are in any human society. But the elevation of homosexual and heterosexual categories into all-important and all-consuming stereotypes *is* a social creation, with both social and scientific consequences.

If categories like "transvestite" and "homosexual" do have demonstrable validity, then we are allowed to theorize about how they came about in human societies. Of course, the fact that these transposed transpositions are stigmatized by society at large explains some of the interest in them, but we sexologists are allowed to be interested in spite of this bias. After all, psychologists are interested in introverts and extroverts, and neither personality trait seems to be particularly oppressed in this age of outgoing talk-show hosts and reclusive computer-programming geniuses. Yes, a scientist interested in the size of Jewish noses is suspicious, but a scientist interested in the genetics of Jewish migrations is not (although both scientists may have their research used by anti-Semites).

Accordingly, it's time to look at the stratigraphy and geology of the sexual landscape. What metamorphoses do its features undergo? What layers are laid down over the course of a lifetime? To answer these questions, it's time to take some core samples and look at family history.

9

FAMILIES OF ORIGIN: SISSIES, TOMBOYS, BROTHERS, SISTERS

The first thing we do, let's kill all the lawyers.
Henry VI, act III, scene 3, line 86.

One day a professor of English made the mistake of asking me about my current research project. He had to listen as I described the hypothesis, the wording of the advertisement recruiting subjects, the procedures to prevent bias in interviewing and data collection, the rules for admitting people to the subject pool, the way I was kept "blind" about certain things until the end of the experiment—and the results. This took about fifteen minutes. After I was done, he breathed a sigh and said, "Boy, I'm glad I don't have to handle all that in literary criticism." And I hadn't even mentioned what we have to do when we write a grant proposal.

Good science is hard work. Sometimes it's fun work, but when we're trying to impress people with our methodological butchness, we don't mention that part. Instead, we just complain about how difficult it is, how self-sacrificing we are, and how certain we are that the scientific method leads to truth.

But even scientists are ambivalent about the scientific method. The methodological controls required by the scientific method—those landscapes in plethysmography, for example—are like lawyers, and does anybody really like lawyers?

Push ordinary citizens into a corner and they'll admit that they really do need courts, laws, and lawyers. Push scientists into a corner and we'll admit that we really do need controls and statistics. But frankly we long for a world in which we don't need any of that stuff. It's a waste of money to pay control groups to watch erotic rectangles and to pay lawyers to gather depositions, right? First thing we do, let's drop all those controls.

As the enormous howl rises from the referees on the editorial board, let me now take back my words. Methodology is important. *Very* important. But you can't understand how important it is until you see its benefits, and you can't see its benefits until you see it in action.

The purpose of this chapter is to tell you more about the origins of the gender transpositions by way of two research projects—both of which happen to be excellent examples of the scientific method. Luckily, both projects are interesting in and of themselves; that'll make the methodological parts less tedious. Better yet, both reached surprising conclusions that they might not have reached had they been conducted more sloppily. That doesn't always happen with good methodology, but when it does, it makes the extra effort especially worthwhile.

The first project is Richard Green's study of sissy boys and tomboy girls. These studies ask what happens to boys and girls who do not show the play patterns typical for most boys and girls in our culture. Do they turn out homosexual? Transsexual? Transvestite? Heterosexual? The second is Richard Pillard's study of homosexuality in families. Pillard's work asks whether homosexuality is distributed randomly across families or if it has a statistically detectable tendency to concentrate in certain families and not in others.

WHAT HAPPENS WHEN SISSIES AND TOMBOYS GROW UP?

Raising children has never been easy. Supposedly, raising a boy is tougher than raising a girl—although there are many parents nowadays who, to minimize sexism, would never admit it. But what's a poor parent to do when confronted by a son who wants to own a purse?

In the olden days, I suppose, the parents would freak. Johnny would be told he couldn't have a purse under any circumstances, and if he got one himself, it would be confiscated. Maybe the same thing would happen in the newer days, too. Although modern parents might know better than to socialize Johnny so forcefully, still I imagine they'd try to get him to change his mind. Johnny, why do you want a purse? 'Cause they're neat. Why are they neat? 'Cause you can carry stuff in them. How about a briefcase? Briefcases aren't neat. But you can carry stuff in them; women carry stuff in purses, men carry stuff in briefcases. I dunno; I just want a purse. Very well, a briefcase it is, then.

But the moment Johnny picks up his Eddie Bauer ripstop nylon yuppie briefcase, it's with a limp wrist—and as he carries it around the house, he's handling it *like* a purse. You never thought such body language was possible with a briefcase, but here is a walking rebuttal.[1]

And then what do you do when you discover—let's say you're Johnny's mommy—that someone's rearranged your high-heeled shoes a bit? That your makeup isn't put back in the drawer quite the way you usually leave it? That your dresses seem slightly askew on the hanger? That there are pencil drawings of beautiful ladies in evening gowns hidden in the den? Assuming for the sake of argument that your husband doesn't have lesbian fantasies, what's a poor mother to do?

Well, you might talk to your family doctor. Back in the mid-1960s some child psychologists and psychiatrists began to get interested in so-called *sissy boys*,[2] each of whom have at least one of the following traits (almost always more than one):

- Stating that he wants to be a girl or really is a girl or that he wants his genitals to change from a boy's to a girl's

---

[1] This anecdote is loosely based on a real case in the sample of sissy boys described below.

[2] Various other terms have been used: "feminine boys," "effeminate boys," "gender-disturbed boys," "feminoid boys," and "pretranssexual boys," for example. Each has its own disadvantages—especially the last, which presumes an outcome that may not often occur.

- Stating that he will grow up to be a woman or that his genitals will grow into women's genitals
- Being intensely preoccupied with cultural icons of femininity (such as Cher, Mae West, or even Lucille Ball)
- Dressing in women's clothes (high heels, dresses, etc.), or—if prevented from doing so—pretending that other objects are women's clothes (e.g., a nightshirt worn as a dress)
- Being intensely interested in hairstyles (especially women's), or—if discouraged from doing so—pretending that other objects are long hair (e.g., a towel wrapped around the head)
- Having an intense desire to participate in girls' games and activities or strongly preferring to play with girls

In short, sissies are not just boys raised by nonsexist parents, nor are they boys who prefer hitting the books to hitting home runs. They are boys with a distinctive and disturbing[3] attraction to everything that's feminine (except, apparently, childbearing)[4] according to cultural stereotypes of what is feminine in a particular culture. That is, it's not that sissies the world around are interested in beehive hairdos; it's that they are interested in beehive hairdos if that's how women in their community wear their hair. Boys will be boys, it seems, unless they want to be girls—at which point they'll make even Dr. Spock a bit nervous.

There are also *tomboys*: girls each of whom have more than one of the following traits:

- Stating that she wants to be a boy or really is a boy—not merely that it would be nice to be a boy because boys are better off—or stating that she wants her genitals to change from a girl's to a boy's
- Stating that she will grow up to be a man or that her genitals will grow into a man's genitals
- Dressing in boy's or men's clothes (blue jeans, dress shirts, sports uniforms, etc.) with extreme persistence or never being willing to wear more stereotypically feminine clothes
- Having an intense desire to participate in boys' games and activities or strongly preferring to play with boys

[3] Disturbing, that is, to grown-ups and other children; not disturbing to the sissies themselves.

[4] Evolutionarily, this is important, but explaining why goes beyond the scope of this chapter.

The criteria for sissies and tomboys are not quite mirror images of each other. That's because sissies usually disturb grown-ups, but tomboys rarely do. A girl acting like boys are supposed to act is more socially acceptable than a boy acting like girls are supposed to act. And so sissies are taken by their parents to see psychotherapists more often than tomboys are. These facts mirror several others about social acceptance of the gender transpositions. Recall from chapter 3 that among adults, lesbianism is more socially acceptable than male homosexuality is. Recall from chapter 6 that adult gay men visit psychotherapists more than lesbians do.

The result of all this in science is that money to study sissies and male homosexuals is granted earlier and in larger quantities than money to study tomboys and lesbians. Although there are studies under way both of sissies and of tomboys, the tomboy studies have not progressed as far as the sissy studies have. I will summarize both kinds of evidence, but be forewarned that, for all the reasons above, sissies will be more prominently discussed.

Sissies

People studying sissies fall into two categories: therapists[5] and researchers.[6] The therapists observed what every playground watcher knows: that sissies are teased, sometimes mercilessly, on the battlefields of boyhood, and that this can make them unhappy. At the very least, they wanted to help the boys reduce their unhappiness, so some tried to help the boys stop acting sissy. But they quickly found that these efforts only caused the sissy behavior to go underground.[7]

Young children, of course, are unselfconscious; if they are sissy boys, they act sissy without thinking much about it. As they get older, they become aware that parents' and peers' reactions are negative. Therapy

[5] Of course, the therapists who publish their results thereby became therapist-researchers, so the distinction is a bit academic. Their research subjects were patients, referred to them one by one over a period of years or decades.

[6] Apparently the first reports were Zuger 1966 and Bakwin 1968 (see also Zuger 1978). Zuger was the first to establish that the incidence of sissy behavior in boys in general really is very low (Zuger and Taylor 1969); this is an important methodological point that has been confirmed in more recent studies (Zucker, Bradley, Corter, Doering, and Finegan 1980). Lebovitz 1972 apparently studied a population of boys who were *especially* gender disturbed; three of his fifteen subjects have had transsexual operations, which has not occurred in any of the other study populations, although one of Zuger's ex-patients has prepared for the operation. But it was Green and Money who started the ball rolling that resulted in Green's sissy-boy and tomboy-girl study—the largest so far. A report on a new sample appeared just as this book was going to press (Davenport 1986).

[7] Richard Green has some heartbreaking examples of this; see Green 1974.

seemed to speed up the sissies' awareness that grown-ups didn't approve of their behavior any more than their peers did.

The therapists were interested in reducing the boys' unhappiness; the researchers were interested in studying the boys' adulthoods. Researchers suspected that sissies grew up to be homosexual, transvestite, or perhaps transsexual, but they weren't sure. When gay men were asked about their childhoods, anywhere from 40 percent to 70 percent described sissy patterns to varying degrees. Drag queens and transvestites reported a lot of cross-dressing in childhood. And almost 100 percent of male-to-female transsexuals said they had been sissies and had wanted to be girls and to grow up to be women for as long as they could remember.

But these reports were *retrospective*: adults recalled their childhoods, and no one knew for sure if this reflected childhood realities. In fact, there were scientists who worried that these results were merely distortions; they wondered whether adult heterosexual men would be more likely to cover up or forget about childhood gender nonconformity than others would. And there were some transsexuals who made the researchers suspicious; they would refuse to let their parents come in to be interviewed (perhaps because they might contradict stories about their childhoods?), or they later admitted that they did not have as sissy a childhood as they had said they had (in order for their childhoods to appear the way the therapist thought they ought to appear?).

So *prospective* studies were designed: sissies were found, their parents contacted, and the family recruited for a study that would last for years. The largest and the most meticulous of these was conducted by Dr. Richard Green (then at the State University of New York at Stony Brook, now at the University of California at Los Angeles). Sissy boys were recruited from referrals in response to a letter that was mass-mailed to schools and mental-health professionals. Each of these families was matched with a control family, including a boy whose family matched the sissy's family on socioeconomic status and other variables, and the boys themselves matched on age, sex of siblings, and position in the sibling order. These controls were recruited from newspaper advertisements, and they were accepted for the study strictly on the basis of how well they could match one of the other families' socioeconomic status and so on. In particular, a control boy's family was *not* evaluated for sissiness until after they were accepted into the control group. Accordingly, the control group is probably very close to an unbiased sample of families of the sort likely to volunteer for psychological studies and not biased against sissiness.

The boys and their parents were invited to Green's research labs, where they were tested and interviewed in dozens of ways. The most sensitive evaluation was the parents' responses to questions about their sons' boyish or girlish behaviors—because, of course, this would establish how old a supposedly sissy boy was when he started acting sissy (and, if so, exactly how sissy), and because in the control group it would establish the level of sissiness in the population at large. So in order to ensure neutrality, the interviews were tape-recorded, transcribed, separated by topic, and then given to two raters who actually established the level of sissiness. These raters were kept "blind"—that is, they did not know from which source the boys they were dealing with were recruited—so that they could make a completely unbiased assessment of sissiness.

Green published the first complete report on these boys—110 of them in the two groups combined—back in 1976. In that paper, and in other papers and speeches he delivered at about the same time, he seemed to believe that he would probably find many homosexuals, some heterosexuals, and perhaps a few transvestites and transsexuals once the sissy boys grew up.

Green also published two major follow-up papers: one in 1979 and one in 1985. The contrast between the two is striking.

In the follow-up study published in 1979, when most of the boys were in early to mid-adolescence, everything seemed as Green expected for these boys (taking into account the fact that many of them had not yet started having sexual relations). One teenager was already a drag queen, one "genuinely bisexual," and several had varying degrees of homosexual experience and/or fantasy. But Green also rated several of the boys as heterosexual. In short, he thought the sample had a wide variety of sexual orientations. Since he had data on how these boys had acted in childhood, he concluded that he would probably eventually be able to figure out which childhood behaviors predicted adult homosexuality, bisexuality, or heterosexuality—and possibly even transsexualism or transvestism.

At about that time, I attended a conference at which Green reported these results to scientists. I knew some people thought it was too soon to tell whether certain of Green's boys were heterosexual; after all, nearly all homosexuals go through a stage in which they do their best to pretend, even to themselves, that they are heterosexual. How, I asked during the question period after the talk, could Green be *sure* that his preheterosexual boys really were heterosexual?

Green replied that if a boy said he had heterosexual fantasies or experiences, then this would be followed up by further questioning.

He and his assistants, he said, were experienced interviewers who could probe to verify whether the boy's self-reports were accurate or were merely self-deceit. He added that he had no reason to doubt the boy's reports.

About the same time, John Money and Anthony Russo, at Johns Hopkins, published another report following up sissy boys.[8] This study had a much smaller sample—eleven in all, and no control group—but was begun much earlier, so the boys had reached much older ages (twenty-three to twenty-nine). *All* of the boys located for follow-up in this study—nine of the eleven—came to call themselves gay.[9] And since the other two in this study were simply untraceable, not necessarily heterosexual, it was quite conceivable that the percentage of homosexuality in these grown-up sissy boys was 100 percent.

Now that is a striking finding; it is rare that any study of childhood development finds a 100 percent correlation of anything in childhood with anything in adulthood, much less something as highly charged as sexual orientation. So Green's study, being larger and methodologically more complete, had to be carefully watched.

In 1985, Green published his latest follow-up, for which he was able to contact forty-four of the former sissies and thirty-four of the controls. The results showed a very important change: already thirty of the former sissies (just over two-thirds of those followed up) had experienced bisexual or homosexual fantasies or behavior. This was far higher than Green had detected at his first follow-up. Two other facts were striking. First, without exception, *all* the former sissies then rated as heterosexual[10] were under twenty years old. Since the prime ages for gay men to come out are eighteen to twenty-five, this is a telling fact; the percentage of homosexuality in Green's sample may yet approach 100 percent. Second, without exception, *none* of the control boys was bisexual or homosexual. In fact, the controls were a remarkably heterosexual bunch; none of them was rated by Green as even incidentally homosexual in behavior, and only two had even the most fleeting homosexual fantasies.[11]

These findings are remarkable, and that's putting it mildly. Although just about everyone guessed that many of the boys would grow up to be gay, the high percentage of homosexuals in the group sur-

---

[8] Money and Russo 1979.

[9] One of the nine had for a while thought he might be transsexual, tried living as a woman, and abandoned the attempt after six months.

[10] For this discussion, I define "heterosexual" to mean a rating of 0 or 1 on the Kinsey scale of sexual orientation: 0 being "exclusively heterosexual" and 1 being almost exclusively so, with only incidental homosexual experience or fantasy.

[11] Those two were rated Kinsey 1 in fantasy; the others were all Kinsey 0 in fantasy.

prised many people—including Green himself, if we presume to infer his reaction from the contrast with his earlier report.

What about transvestites? Green found none—so far. This suggests that heterosexual transvestites were not sissy boys in childhood. Or if they were, they were sissy in a way that kept them from being recruited for studies like Green's. That is, they would have to be a different, less detectable kind of sissy. In fact, preliminary results from a study reported by Kenneth Zucker, of the Clarke Institute of Psychiatry in Toronto, suggest that heterosexual transvestites only start doing girlish things (cross-dressing, in this case) in substantial numbers at puberty. As a general rule, boys found cross-dressing in early childhood usually turn out to be homosexual (possibly drag queens); boys *first* discovered cross-dressing in adolescence often turn out to be transvestites. This fits in, by the way, with retrospective reports; as adults, heterosexual transvestites recall childhood cross-dressing but few if any other sissy behaviors.

What about transsexuals? It turns out that Green's study can't tell us much about them. That's because transsexuals are so rare in the population that we'd need to study at least five hundred sissy boys in order to discover even one who turned out transsexual![12] So male-to-female transsexuals might or might not have been sissies as boys.

Given these results, why did Green hang on as long as he did to the idea that some sissy boys would probably turn out heterosexual? The answer, I think, is obvious once you assume something about Richard Green's view of childhood sissiness.

Green's 1985 results were also reported first at a scientific conference that I attended, and I once again had a chance to question him from the floor. This time, I mentioned the two-dimensional masculinity and femininity questionnaires like the Bem scale,[13] with which Green and the audience were familiar. What if we made a similar *two*-dimensional distinction among three groups of boys?

- 1. Boys who are *overtly masculine*—that is, are interested in the things stereotypical boys are supposed to be interested in— toys like trucks, games like baseball.
- 2. Boys who are *overtly feminine*—that is, are interested in the things stereotypical girls are supposed to be interested in— toys like dolls, games like hopscotch.

[12] The mathematics behind this conclusion are worked out in Weinrich 1985.

[13] Recall the distinction between questionnaires scored in a one-dimensional way that assume that more masculinity means less femininity and vice versa, and those two-dimensional scales (like the Bem scale) that do not; see chapter 1.

- 3. Boys who are merely *nonmasculine*—that is, neither of the above; they are interested in things acceptable for either sex— toys like doctor kits, games like Monopoly.

I said that his study, taken with the others, strongly suggested that most of the overtly feminine 2 boys grow up homosexual or bisexual. But what about the nonmasculine 3 boys? What do they grow up to be? Green replied, with a wry grin, that some of them grow up to be sex researchers who study what happens to sissy boys!

And suddenly his reports all make sense. All you need to do is combine categories 2 and 3. Assume that a lot of 3s end up hetero-sexual. If you were expecting such boys to show up (along with the 2s) in a sample of sissies, then you would expect some of your sample composed of 2s and 3s to turn out heterosexual. But what Green ac-tually got in his sissy sample, I believe, was 2s, and controls who were mostly 1s. The nonmasculine 3s are, after all, occasionally teased by being called sissies but are probably not sissy enough to get referred to a doctor.

My point is that Green's evidence suggests that 1s usually turn out heterosexual, 2s usually homosexual or bisexual, and 3s some of each. This pattern is displayed in figure 9.1 below (which adds a couple of reasonable but unproved guesses about how one becomes a transsex-ual or cross-dresser).

Before I go on, I have to make one extremely important point. It is, after all, a stereotype in our culture that homosexual men are effemi-nate. Putting aside the scientific merits of a study like Green's, what are the philosophical consequences of conducting such a study? Why did a proposal to study sissies get submitted in the first place, and why was it selected for government funding?

These questions have important scientific aspects, too. If associa-tions between male homosexuality and femininity are studied and as-sociations between male homosexuality and masculinity are not, then it's going to be easy to discover ways in which gay men are feminine and difficult to discover the ways they are masculine. So let me spend some time rounding out the picture.

First, the boys who are sissies typically lose much of that femininity in adulthood. It was this pattern—childhood sissiness turning into adult homosexuality—that I was referring to in chapter 2 when I described how gender nonconformity for most gay men is a memory, not an actuality. It is a fond memory for many of them and a painful one for others, but not one that insistently intrudes upon the adult men's own behavior.

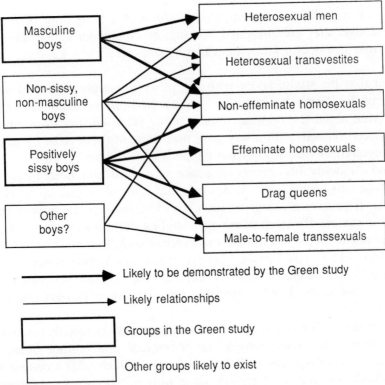

Figure 9.1

But there are plenty of gay men who were not sissies as boys. The retrospective studies suggest that most of them were nonmasculine boys,[14] but there are exceptions who seem to have been entirely typical boys. Green's study suggests that few of the typically masculine boys grow up gay.

But this may be an underestimate, because the age at which someone becomes aware of his homosexuality is related to his degree of femininity. If you are a sissy and if you've been called "faggot," "queer," and similar things in childhood, it won't come as a surprise if you start having homosexual feelings. Coming out will be a relatively small step, because people have been assuming that you'll be sexually different all along. You may like the idea or you may not, but at least you're used to it being applied to you.

[14]This is, actually, a previously unpublished idea and is probably a bit controversial. The retrospective studies use slightly different definitions of childhood sissiness. Typically, when *overtly feminine* behaviors are the only ones included in the definition, the percentage of gay men who recall being girlish ranges from a large minority to a moderate majority—let's say 40–60 percent. When *nonmasculine* behaviors are included in the definition—typically, disinterest in or dislike of rough sports—then the percentages shoot up toward 90 percent or more. In my opinion, studies of sissy boys are still subject to the criticism that they do not adopt a two-dimensional view of childhood masculinity and femininity.

If, on the other hand, you're merely a nonmasculine boy, you may have been teased, but the sexually related epithets would have been less frequent or absent. When you start noticing homosexual feelings, it may take you longer to come to terms with them. You know you're *not* like that effeminate faggot over there, and so you may conclude you can't be gay.

And if, on the third hand, you are a boy interested in all the stereotypical pursuits of boyhood, when your homosexual feelings begin, you may be extremely reluctant to admit to yourself what they are. Not only are you not like that faggot over there; you've never felt even remotely like him. In fact, you've never felt different from other males at all. It will probably take you many years to come out, if you ever do.

The causes of this socially determined trend may or may not be exclusively social. It is likely not only that gay sissies come to terms with being gay earlier than nonsissy gays but also that they genuinely do experience homosexual feelings earlier than the nonsissies do.[15] If so, then the younger the age group of a homosexual sample, the more likely it is that sissies will be disproportionately represented in it. Green's subjects were no older than twenty-five, and most were about twenty or twenty-one. By that age, the majority of sissies know they're gay, but many of the prehomosexual, nonmasculine boys and gender-typical boys do not.[16] If so, then Green will have documented that homosexual feelings develop, when they develop, at different rates in different kinds of boys.

Tomboys

Now let's move on to the tomboys. As I've already mentioned, tomboyishness doesn't bother grown-ups as much; it only becomes a problem if it is too extreme. What constitutes "extreme," of course, is

[15] Green, for example, reported some instances in which sissy boys behaved toward their fathers or other adult men in ways he interpreted as seductive. Seduction of or by the father is a theme prominent in one strand of the gay male world. One can, for example, buy T-shirts that say, "Even daddies need daddies," and gay novelist Edmund White has written that he feels sorry for gay men who have never wanted to seduce their fathers. Perhaps the heterosexual equivalent would be a boy who wants a girl just like the girl that married dear old dad.

[16] Remember those two control boys whose fantasies were rated as Kinsey 1s? It would not surprise me if they turn out to be homosexual or bisexual—but in a few years. I would expect two to four of the control boys to end up homosexual. Indeed, as this book goes to press, newspaper accounts of Green's most recent report on his boys (Green 1987) state that one of the control boys is bisexual.

not well-defined—but one of the purposes of the tomboy study is to figure out how to define it better.

The received wisdom on tomboys is as follows:[17]

- They are more common than sissies.
- Their behavior is not considered as deviant as sissiness is.[18]
- The vast majority grow up to be ordinary heterosexual women, some grow up to be lesbians, and a very small number become female-to-male (f–m) transsexuals (probably those who are in that vague way "extremely" tomboyish).

Green and his colleagues made the first report on the tomboys in 1982, too recently for formal follow-ups to have been published.[19] This sample began with ninety-nine girls (tomboys and controls). Green's colleague Katherine Williams, now at the University of Maryland, is in charge of this phase of the study. So at the moment, we know little or nothing, really, about how tomboys turn out. But we do know about their childhoods—and there are already some interesting differences apparent between them and the sissy boys.

The sissies, you'll recall, were recruited by a mass mailing to schools and psychotherapists. The tomboys were recruited through simple newspaper ads asking for families who had a tomboy daughter. This route was taken because tomboys were thought to be more common and because these researchers doubted tomboys would be taken in for therapy. Control families were matched in the usual way, but this time the controls had to have a daughter of the same age who was *not* a tomboy (rather than trying to recruit a control sample with an average number of tomboys in it). Again, this presumably resulted from the fact that tomboys are thought to be less deviant; in order to highlight differences, then, it would make sense to choose two groups that were specifically as different as possible on the gender-role variables.

One interesting difference between the tomboys and the sissies has to do with their cross-dressing. Both groups of children preferred, more often than their corresponding control groups, to wear clothes considered typical of the other sex. When the kinds of clothing were listed for the boys, the list included "high-heeled shoes, outer garments,

---

[17] A good review is Williams, Green, and Goodman 1979.

[18] In fact, there is evidence that boyhood sissiness is often associated with other behavioral problems having nothing to do with masculinity-femininity issues. See Sreenivasan 1985 and Coates and Person 1985.

[19] Green, Williams, and Goodman 1982.

undergarments, and accessories." When genuine articles were un-available, they were improvised from other materials.[20] The list of boys' clothes worn by tomboys, on the other hand, included only boys' shoes and boys' outer garments, and "only 29 percent of the mothers re-port ever seeing their [tomboy] daughters improvising masculine clothing."[21]

The observation about improvisation may well reflect, as the au-thors note, that there are plenty of clothes for girls that imitate boys' styles. But I see other factors operating in the other instances. Tom-boys often say that they prefer the clothes they do because they are functional; if you want to climb a tree or play baseball, as so many tomboys do, it's difficult to do so while wearing a dress or girlish shoes. But something other than mere practicality seems to be in-volved in the sissies' preferences for girls' *under*clothes and accessories. If you need to carry things, a briefcase will do quite well.

One interesting finding is that the mothers of the tomboys more often reported having been tomboys as girls themselves. The authors point out quite rightly that this may be due to socialization, but they also mention the possibility that genetics may be involved. I'll come back to this finding in the second half of this chapter.

As I mentioned, no follow-ups have been published yet on these tomboys. But Green did once undertake[22] a very preliminary study of four tomboys from an entirely different sample, with striking results. In 1979, these four tomboys were mid-teenage or young adult. One had become "conventionally feminine" and "very interested in dating boys." Two were still acting like tomboys; one of these had not had sexual relations with anyone, and the other had just "discovered boys." And the fourth? She was living as a man, taking androgens to in-crease her masculine appearance, and had had her uterus removed— that is, she was on the road taken by female-to-male transsexuals.

Now even this tiny sample is remarkable. If m–f transsexuals are so rare that we cannot expect even one to show up in a random sample of hundreds of sissy boys, if f–m transsexuals are no more common than m–f transsexuals (see chapter 3), and if tomboys commonly grow up to be heterosexual, then it is remarkable to find even one transsex-ual in a sample as small as four tomboys. Of course, flukes are possi-ble, but you may be overlooking an important piece of data if you call this a fluke and forget about it. It is very suspicious.

My favorite suggestion at this hazy stage is that there really is a

---

[20] Williams, Green, and Goodman 1979, p. 111.
[21] Williams, Green, and Goodman, 1979, pp. 114–115.
[22] In collaboration with John Money.

difference between ordinary tomboys and extreme tomboys and that this minisample of four was weighted toward the extreme tomboys. If so, then all bets are off concerning how many transsexuals one could expect to find because we don't know what proportion of ordinary tomboys would happen to get included in such a weighted sample. It will, nevertheless, be extremely interesting if this unexpected finding is replicated in the larger tomboy sample now being followed up.

In the larger sample, there were as of mid-1986 no girls as insistently masculine as the transsexual mentioned above. Katherine Williams, the associate of Green's responsible for the follow-up, told me that most of the behavioral differences between the tomboys and nontomboys seemed to disappear when the girls entered the junior high school years. There were few if any tomboy/nontomboy differences on career plans, motherhood plans, dating, and so on. The tomboys continued to be more physically active than the nontomboys and seemed less interested in makeup. Perhaps they are a bit delayed in their dating and romantic attachments, too, although the analyses needed to be certain of this haven't been done yet. Whether all this is a temporary nod in the direction of teenage conformity or longer-lasting evidence that being a tomboy really is "just a stage" for some girls remains to be seen. Stay tuned!

Discussion

Green's studies have had two principal effects. First, it has made it extremely difficult—in my opinion, impossible—to claim that sissy and nonsissy boys grow up to be homosexual men in roughly equal proportions. Here the effect has been minor; most people knew this before Green's study, and now the recalcitrant ones have to agree. But second, the result was unexpectedly uniform: most of the sissies have become homosexual or bisexual if you followed them up long enough, and very few of the nonsissies have (so far). This means that Green's sample selection procedures found a group of boys who turned out to be fairly uniform (as these things go) in sexual orientation.

The uniformity is increasing; Green's 1985 report suggested that two-thirds of the sissy boys had become homosexual or bisexual; advance newspaper reports of Green's 1987 book state that this proportion is approximately three-fourths. The fact that Money and Russo hit upon a similarly uniform group of sissies, in their mid-twenties at follow-up, suggests that this was not a fluke. In fact, there's an interesting facet of the Money and Russo study: how some of the subjects were tracked down. After ordinary follow-up procedures were exhausted, some additional subjects could be located by asking members of the gay community if their whereabouts were known. Most of the subjects grew up in Baltimore, a town with low rates of migration to other cities, so often it was not difficult to find gay people who had gone to the same high school, say, as the subjects and who knew where they were. Of course, in a large-scale study willing to settle for tracking down only a fraction of the original subjects, taking this step would have been methodologically inadmissible, especially given the fact that there was no control group. This is because looking for subjects by way of the gay community is obviously biased in the direction of finding subjects who are gay. But the strategy is acceptable *if* it results in the recruitment of a sufficiently high percentage of the original subjects—and nine of eleven is indeed sufficiently high. In the worst possible case, those two untrackable subjects should be counted as heterosexual, but even then the percentage of homosexuality cannot be less than 81 percent in this sample.

The sissy-boy studies with less uniform results had younger samples and less well understood selection procedures. Perhaps, like the pilot study of the four tomboys, they happened to recruit a sample of *extreme* sissies. Admittedly, this is a hypothesis, not something that can be strictly deduced from the data, but I think it's a good one.

All this suggests that there is a well-established correlation between childhood gender nonconformity and adult homosexuality, although the correlation is not perfect. This may not seem like much, but in fact it is an important finding for the science of child development.

What, after all, are people studying child development trying to do? They are trying to find factors in childhood—be they factors of personality or factors in the environment—that correlate with, or "predict," adult personality.[23] Of course, it is easy to find straightforward correlations—that extroverted children become extroverted adults, say—but these are intellectually not very exciting. In child-development research, you hit the jackpot when you find a correlation that is surprising: a correlation that isn't "the same thing" in childhood as in adulthood.

---

[23] Or at least they were up until a few years ago, according to Emory University anthropology department chairman Melvin Konner. In a recent conversation (9 August 1986), he explained to me that most developmental psychologists have abandoned attempts to find strong correlations between childhood and adult personality traits because the correlations seem so weak or uninteresting. As exceptions, he cited studies of criminality by Mednick, and of timidity. Methodologically, the best studies are those conducted on monkeys by Harry Harlow. But those took place using evolutionarily extremely unnatural environments (wire-mesh mother surrogates and so on) falling far outside the range of modern child-rearing practices and therefore are relevant only to certain cases of extreme child abuse.

Green's correlation is one of these. Recall from chapter 2 that gender role and sexual orientation are not synonyms; just because you want to take the role of the other sex does not imply that you want to have sex with a member of your own sex. Accordingly, it is not a trivial fact that *gender role in childhood* turns out to correlate with *sexual orientation in adulthood*. The trivial correlations would be that sissy boys become transsexual or transvestite in adulthood—not homosexual— or that boys who perform homosexual acts in childhood turn out to perform homosexual acts in adulthood. Instead, in sissy boys we see a *metamorphosis* from an atypical gender role to an atypical gender identity.

Other than this sissy-boy finding, there is little research from child development that correlates childhood factors with adult personality nontrivially.[24] So Green and the other sexologists who have worked on sissy boys have succeeded where developmental psychologists have so far failed: by coming up with *interesting* correlations.

There is a lesson in this. If child developmentalists had been more willing to study *sexual* parameters, they could have come up with Green's result long ago—but they weren't, so they didn't. There are and have been, in addition, several prospective medical studies of human development, some of which have followed their subjects for several decades. (Typically, they are trying to show connections between childhood or young-adult factors and medical problems among the middle-aged or elderly.) Any one of them could have, had they wished to, hired competent sexologists to ask questions about sexual orientation, gender role, and gender identity. And then they, too, could have gotten results like Green's long before Green did. That they did not is a result of the sex taboo, and developmental psychology has been the poorer for it.

In short, your tax dollars have been spent paying for studies that find weak or obvious correlations, if any, between childhood characteristics and adult personality. This money has not been wasted, but it could have been spent even more effectively. Instead, the studies that would have found large and interesting nontrivial correlations have been discouraged—because the correlations would have dealt with sex, and sex is too hot to handle. Of course, I can understand why

[24] The only exception I can think of is the research on childhood stress done by the Whitings (see, e.g., Whiting and Whiting 1975). The Whitings claim that childhood stress leads to increased vigor in adulthood in several unexpected ways. However, their findings were based on cross-cultural anthropology, not carefully controlled follow-up studies like Green's. So they probably apply more directly to differences between cultures instead of to differences between individuals within the same culture.

many investigators in these long-term studies didn't include sexological hypotheses in their original grant proposals, some of which began decades ago. I probably would have done the same thing at the time. But now that there are well-established, well-funded, and highly prestigious studies, why don't these researchers find the courage to hire a few people and make up for lost time and lost hypotheses?

DOES HOMOSEXUALITY RUN IN FAMILIES?

At first glance, it may seem absurd that homosexuality might run in families. How could that be?

Think first of environment. Most homosexual children come from heterosexual parents (or, at the very least, bisexual parents), so most children would be expected to be heterosexual. A mechanism that caused homosexuality to run in families for environmental reasons would be a very unusual one, for it would be one in which "like" working with "like" results in "unlike." "Being Catholic" or "speaking French" runs in families because Catholic or French-speaking parents socialize their children to be Catholic or to speak French. But an environmental factor that causes heterosexual parents to have homosexual children would be quite different from these.

Now think genetics. It seems that any gene that predisposes people to prefer sex with their own sex rather than with the other sex would die out pretty quickly (see chapter 13 for theories that rebut this). Blond parents having blond children makes for more blonds in the next generation. But a mechanism that caused homosexuality to run in families for genetic reasons would be a very unusual one, for it would run the risk of dying out the very first time it popped up.

But in study after study, whether originally planned this way or in analyses run after the fact, homosexuality *does* seem to run in families. This is as true of studies over fifty years ago in Western Europe as it is in the Kinsey Institute's study of homosexuality conducted about 1970.[25]

The problem is that none of these studies was methodologically very good—at least regarding the runs-in-families question. For example, table 9.1 shows some results from that Kinsey Institute study just mentioned.[26]

[25] Pillard, Poumadere, and Carretta have summarized the data from some of these studies in their 1981 paper.

[26] The data are from the "San Francisco Study," so called because that is where the interviews were conducted; see Bell, Weinberg, and Hammersmith 1981a. I thank S. K. Hammersmith for permission to publish these data.

TABLE 9.1. PROPORTION OF HOMOSEXUAL SIBLINGS

	male respondents (%)	*female respondents (%)*
among homosexual respondents	11	12
among heterosexual respondents	4	0

These differences—11 percent versus 4 percent, and 12 percent versus 0 percent—are statistically significant, and a good example of how runs-in-families data often turn up even when the study was not designed to address this specific question. But pleased as I am with this study, I must admit it has problems.

I was able to reconstruct some of this study's raw data from its statistical appendix. The heterosexual women reported what seemed to me to be far too few homosexual siblings: a total of 2. Only two heterosexual women—from a sample of hundreds—each reported a single homosexual or bisexual sibling.[27] This suggests that some people must have had homosexual brothers or sisters and not told the Kinsey interviewers about them—perhaps because they didn't want to or because they didn't know about them. Either way, we don't know for sure that the homosexuals have more homosexual siblings in this sample because the results for heterosexuals appear to be unreliable. (As it turned out, they may have been completely reliable, after all—as I will point out later in this chapter.)

For reasons such as this, Dr. Richard Pillard, a psychiatrist at the Boston University School of Medicine, decided a better study was necessary to resolve the issue. He obtained a small grant, which I later joined, to study homosexuality in families. We conducted two studies: the first of 101 male subjects, the second of 86 women.[28]

The Male Study

Subjects were recruited for this study through newspaper ads:

RESEARCH SUBJECTS NEEDED

We want to interview subjects about their personality, sexual behavior, and mental abilities. You must be male, age 25–35, unmarried, and in good health. Time required: about 5 hours. Payment: $25.

[27] Even more unlikely, both those two siblings were rated as Kinsey 2s—on the heterosexual side of bisexual. That is, these hundreds of women reported not even one sibling who was completely homosexual, or even fifty-fifty bisexual!

[28] The reasons why our female sample is smaller are complicated. Simply put, government-grant proposals are awarded a priority score, and Pillard's proposal to study 100 women received a lower score than his proposal to study 100 men. In case you haven't noticed yet, science is a social endeavor as well as a scientific one.

212

Notice that the ads did not say anything about sexual orientation. We specified that subjects be currently unmarried in order to increase the percentage of homosexuals responding to the ad[29] but otherwise never hinted that sexual orientation was a specific focus of our study. We required subjects be at least twenty-five years old, since eighteen to twenty-five are the prime coming-out years. The upper limit of thirty-five was specified to assure that subjects were all from approximately the same generation. When they telephoned, subjects were also told they had to have at least one sibling age twenty or over.

Those qualifying and still interested came to the laboratory for interviews, questionnaires, and tests. The sex-history interview—which of course revealed whether the subject was heterosexual or homosexual—was conducted at the end of the day in order to avoid biasing the questions and tests beforehand. There were two interviewers; in the few (less than five) cases where the subject was personally known by one interviewer, he was interviewed by the other. Since we were interested in more than the runs-in-families question, most of the materials were not obviously related to sex, although subjects had been told (in the ad, over the phone, and again in a consent form signed at the beginning of the session) that sexual questions would be among those asked.

In a personal interview before the sex-history interview, we asked subjects several questions about their brothers and sisters aged twenty or over, their mother, their father, and their more distant relatives (aunts, uncles, cousins). Two of these questions asked about the marital status and sexual orientation of these relatives. If a subject told us someone was homosexual or bisexual, we asked how he knew, and rated the answer conservatively. For example, if someone said he knew Susan was homosexual because she had said so and had taken him dancing in a gay bar, we rated Susan "probably homosexual"— "probably," rather than "known," because our information was secondhand (from the subject), not direct (from Susan herself). If he said he thought Paul was homosexual because Paul had never had a girlfriend and he had seen him in junior high school hugging another boy, we rated Paul "possibly homosexual." Others we did not apply

[29] Estimating from the Kinsey statistics, Pillard thought about 15 percent of the ad respondents would be homosexual. We actually got about 12 percent, so we have no reason to believe that our sample was far from the norms established by Kinsey. Once we got the appropriate number of heterosexual subjects—about fifty—from this ad (placed in general-audience Boston newspapers), we placed the ad again in a gay community newspaper. This filled up the rest of the fifty or so slots planned for homosexual subjects. There were, incidentally, some heterosexuals who responded to the ad in the gay paper—because that ad, too, did not specify any particular sexual orientation.

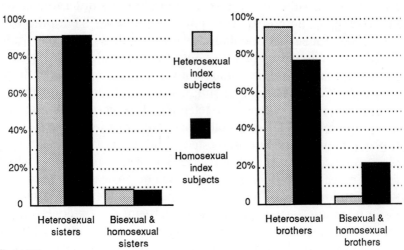

Sisters of male index subjects   Brothers of male index subjects

Heterosexual index subjects

Homosexual index subjects

Figure 9.2

a label to, since if someone was thought to be heterosexual, we did not ask how the subject knew this to be true.

The results were striking (see fig. 9.2).

Let's start with the men's sisters. First, a definition: we called the men recruited through the ad *index subjects* in order to distinguish them from the *sibling subjects* who were their brothers and sisters. It turns out (see fig. 9.2, *left*) that the heterosexual and homosexual index subjects did not significantly differ in the percentage of homosexual or bisexual *sisters* they reported having. On the other hand, the homosexual index men reported far *more* homosexual or bisexual *brothers* than the heterosexual index men did (see Fig. 9.2, *right*).

Among second- and third-degree relatives (aunts, uncles, cousins—not shown in the charts) the homosexual men also reported a lot more homosexual relatives than the heterosexual men did. But this was only among *male* relatives. The homosexual index subjects knew of a total of twelve male relatives who were homosexual (not counting brothers), the heterosexuals knew of none; but both homosexual and heterosexual subjects knew two such homosexual female relatives.

Now how many of your gay aunts, uncles, or cousins have come out to you? If you're heterosexual, probably not very many; there would be little reason for them to do so. If you're homosexual, on the other hand, you or they might have thought of the possibility and decided to give coming out a try. This argument suggests that these particular figures—the twelve versus the zero—might just be the result of birds of a feather finding each other, not of the birds actually being more common. But this explanation is questionable because on the female side there was no difference in the number of female relatives (two versus two). To make the argument fit, you'd have to modify it to say that homosexuals are likely to be curious about, and come out to, only their homosexual relatives of the same sex.

The figures for brothers and sisters show a similar pattern, but it's harder to explain them away in this fashion. First, homosexuals of each sex are very interested to learn of homosexuality in their siblings—even siblings of the other sex. We would expect the homosexual subjects to report more homosexual brothers *and* more homosexual sisters if the only factor operating were this desire to find gay siblings.

That's a good argument, but it's not a perfect one, so we undertook the next phase of the study: contacting the brothers and sisters themselves. After securing permission from the index subjects, we wrote a letter to each of the brother and sister subjects who were aged twenty or over.

I myself was in charge of this sibling recruitment and was kept "blind" as to the sexual orientation of each index subject *and* to the supposed sexual orientation of each sibling. This was to avoid my being prejudiced—consciously or unconsciously—in how persistent my recruitment was. If a sibling didn't return the card in the solicitation letter, for example, how quickly would I send off a follow-up letter? If the letter was unforwardable, how much effort would I expend trying to track the person down? If the letter was forwarded to San Francisco or another city with a high known homosexual population, would I be more or less likely to keep after the sibling to get the questionnaires? If I had an idea as to whether the person's information would support a particular hypothesis, I might let these little details influence the outcome even if I didn't intend to.

Luckily, an additional fact gave me some protection. Let's say there was some detail that might have led me to suspect that index subject *X* was homosexual. If I still didn't know what he said his siblings' sexual orientations were, results would remain unbiased; I just had to be careful not to go near the files that would give me telltale information about the siblings. Likewise, if I happened to guess that subject *Y*'s sister was heterosexual, any bias this might have caused would not affect the results as long as I was careful not to learn anything about *Y* himself. In sum, only knowing the sexual orientation of *both* an index subject *and* his sibling(s) would cause a bias since only then could I have consciously or unconsciously recruited (say) the homosexual siblings of the homosexual index subjects or the heterosexual siblings of the heterosexual index subjects.

Depending on where they lived and how eager they were, siblings either (1) came in for an interview like their brother, (2) filled out two hours' worth of questionnaires that just happened to have a couple of questions about sexual orientation on them, (3) had their most crucial questionnaires filled out by me as I interviewed them over the phone, or (4) told us, in various ways, to get lost. As luck would have it, over 70 percent of the siblings did respond to our various requests, which is a very good response rate. (It was especially good considering that it was the index subjects, not the brothers and sisters, who had volunteered.) Once we got their responses all assembled, we had to change a few sexual orientation ratings—but only a few. (We did not make any distinction, however, between "probable" and "possible," because the information was coming directly from the siblings themselves.) Figure 9.3 shows the revised numbers.

As you can see, there were no major surprises: homosexual and heterosexual index subjects still had roughly equal percentages of lesbian and bisexual sisters, but the homosexual men had far more homosexual brothers—*according to the brothers' own reports.* As far as we know, our study is the first to actually contact the siblings to see if what the index subjects had said about them was true. That these charts are indeed very similar to the first set of charts shows that such information probably was true.

Well, when the initial reports were wrong, how were they wrong? Table 9.2 lists what the index subjects had told us, cross-referenced by what the brothers and sisters themselves subsequently told us:

TABLE 9.2. COMPARISON OF REPORTS OF SEXUAL ORIENTATION

Index brothers said sibling was:	Siblings themselves said they were:		
	heterosexual	*bisexual*	*homosexual*
probably heterosexual	146	**6**	0
probably bisexual	0	2	0
probably homosexual	0	0	12
possibly bisexual	0	1	0
possibly homosexual	**8**	1	0

There were only two categories in which the index brothers made nontrivial mistakes about their siblings (highlighted table 9.2).

First, there were six siblings who told us they were bisexual but

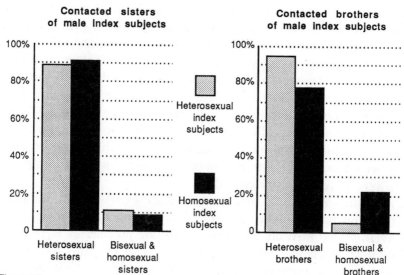

Figure 9.3

who had been described as heterosexual by the index subjects. It is conceivable that some of these six were really homosexual but worried to tell strangers (us) that this was so. But these six were *evenly reported* (three and three) by homosexual and heterosexual index subjects. So there is no evidence here that heterosexual index subjects were worse at reporting truly homosexual siblings than homosexual index subjects were.

Some people think this conclusion is impossibly optimistic because it implies that homosexuals aren't much better than heterosexuals in detecting homosexuality in their siblings. We don't think it's too optimistic, for the following reasons. First, the age requirements in our study meant that most of the index subjects and their siblings were fully grown men and women. We agree that homosexuals probably are better at spotting homosexuality among their siblings but that the main component of this ability is the ability to spot them *earlier* than most other family members do. Grown-ups know quite a bit about their brothers and sisters and—at least in the generation we studied—are pretty confident they know important things like their sexual orientation. Second, in families with more than two children, we had an additional check: *all* the subjects were asked about the sexual orientation of *all* their siblings. If Joe told us David was homosexual, Susan usually told us, too. Finally, there probably were some extremely closeted homosexuals hidden somewhere in our samples that we never became aware of. The point is, there is no evidence we could detect in our sample that these closeted homosexuals or bisexuals were hiding most of the time in the families of the heterosexual index subjects. If they were that closeted, they probably were concealing their feelings from their homosexual brothers as well as their heterosexual brothers.

Second, there were also eight siblings who told us they were heterosexual but who were described by the index subjects as possibly homosexual—when we specifically asked the index subjects to speculate as to who in their family *might* be gay. There was a moderate trend (not quite statistically significant) for it to be the homosexual subjects who made these incorrect attributions, but this happened only when we encouraged them, and even then these incorrect ratings do not affect our results reported earlier.

So in sum we are quite sure that the homosexual men in our sample really do have a higher percentage of homosexual brothers than the heterosexual men do. Since our recruiting procedures were scrupulously arranged to avoid bias with respect to the runs-in-families hypothesis, this suggests that the same may be true for men in general.

Before we can conclude this, however, we must consider whether our sample was biased in a way that would make our conclusion untrue. Basically, there is only one way this could happen.[30] Suppose that there are basically two kinds of families when it comes to sexual orientation: *open families* and *closed families*. In open families, everyone knows everyone else's sexual orientation; in closed families, only the homosexual members know this about each other. Assume that members of open families are also more likely to tell scientists (like us) the truth about their sexual orientations. And assume that homosexuality doesn't really run in either kind of family.

Now if we only had open families in our study and if homosexuality doesn't run in families, we would *not* have found what we did; we would have found no tendency for homosexuality to concentrate in the families of the homosexual volunteers. But if we had enough closed families, the homosexual index subjects would have told us—accurately—about their homosexual siblings, while the heterosexual volunteers would have underestimated the true proportion of their homosexual siblings. Even contacting the brothers and sisters wouldn't help, because presumably the closed families are closed not only to other family members but also to outsiders like us. And that pattern is consistent with what we saw.

Consistent, that is, up to a point. The open families/closed families

[30] There are other, more complicated ways that we address and reject in the scientific paper that reported these results. See Pillard and Weinrich 1986.

hypothesis implies that the homosexual index subjects from closed families would tell us a percentage of homosexuality in their siblings that is approximately *equal to the population average,* but the heterosexual index subjects from such families would tell us a percentage that is *less than the average.* But this is not what we found. Between 20 and 25 percent of the brothers of the homosexual men in our sample are also homosexual, and that's far above the most liberal estimates of the percentage of homosexuals in the general population. The 4 percent homosexuality found among the brothers of the heterosexual men, in contrast, approximates the estimate of the general population.[31]

There is one other possible way to explain away our data. We have, after all, only done the study once; perhaps there was some fluke of sampling that caused an unusually high number of homosexual men with homosexual brothers to volunteer. We don't know, frankly, what such a fluke would consist of, and statistical methodology automatically takes account of the sample size in the tests used to decide if particular percentage differences are statistically significant. (Ours are.) But it's a possibility we have to keep in mind.

But this, too, probably does not account for our results. First, remember all those earlier studies that found homosexuality running in families before ours did; their samples came from backgrounds quite different from subjects in our sample. Second, we have on occasion delivered speeches to gay audiences about work having nothing to do with this study—sometimes even before we began this study!—and conducted an informal poll of the audience. Typically, we would ask for a show of hands: first, of all the gay members of the audience with brothers (any kind), then of all those with gay brothers. The results are percentages roughly equal to what we found in the formal study: about one-fifth to one-fourth of the brothers of gay men are gay. So we believe the finding is a robust one and was not merely a fluke from one particular sample.

Still skeptical? You can try this out, too, the next time you lecture to a gay group.

---

[31] Some readers familiar with the often-quoted statistic that 10 percent of the population is homosexual may challenge this. But if the figure really is 10 percent in the world at large and it really does run in families, then it must *concentrate* in particular families. In that case we would expect a figure of more than 10 percent in the families of homosexual men but less than 10 percent in the families of heterosexual men. This is just what we found. So this criticism is not as troublesome as it might at first seem. The 4 percent figure is also a reasonable estimate, we believe, of those exclusively homosexual enough to say so in a survey, whereas the 10 percent figure would include a substantial proportion of extremely closeted homosexuals.

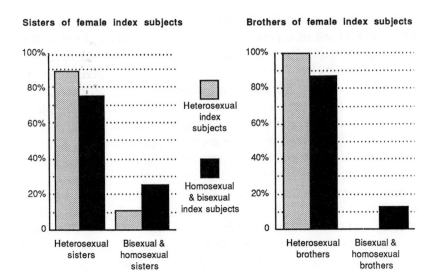

Sisters of female index subjects   Brothers of female index subjects

Figure 9.4

The Female Study

The next obvious question is Does female homosexuality run in families? This question is especially interesting in the light of the male study, which found that homosexual men do *not* have more homosexual sisters than heterosexual men do.

We recruited eighty-six index women and ran them through the same kinds of interviews and tests that the men went through. What they told us about their sisters and brothers is shown in figure 9.4.

In a finding that mirrored the 101 men, the lesbian and bisexual women reported more lesbian and bisexual sisters than the heterosexual women did. But there was a surprise: they *also* reported more homosexual and bisexual brothers! (And in an embarrassing finding that echoed the Kinsey Institute study, our sample of heterosexual women reported no bisexual or homosexual brothers at all.[32]) We have not, alas, finished analyzing all the data from the women's siblings themselves, so I will not present any data about whether the index women were accurate in their perception of their family members' sexual orientations.

Now *these* are interesting findings, since they seem to both support and contradict what we found with the male index subjects. They support the male data, for they suggest that female homosexuality runs in families, too. But they contradict the male data, because *if homosex-*

---

[32] Our total sample was, of course, quite a bit smaller than the Kinsey Institute's, and so random fluctuations could account for our result more easily than it could for theirs. But the experience is still chastening.

ual women have more homosexual brothers, then homosexual men should have more homosexual sisters—but we didn't find that to be the case in the study of the 101 men.

So what are we to do? The answer: think very carefully about the possible explanations, then use statistics. There are two possible explanations for our conflict:

- Male homosexuality runs in families, and female homosexuality runs in families, but *the factors causing them to run in families are completely separate.* In this case, our finding that homosexual/bisexual women have more homosexual/bisexual brothers than heterosexual women do is an accident. If the heterosexual women turn out in reality to have even two homosexual brothers—where we found none—the difference we found will become statistically *in*significant. That is, we can no longer say with reasonable certainty that our sample was fluke-free when it comes to homosexual brothers.

- One factor (or set of factors) causes male homosexuality to run in families and is very prominent; a separate factor (or set) causes female homosexuality to run in families and is somewhat weaker. But a *third* factor (or set of factors) can cause *both to run in families at once*—and it is this third factor that we are seeing when the homosexual/bisexual women report more homosexual/bisexual brothers. If this third factor is only about as strong as the all-female factor, it can get lost as statistical background noise in the male study, but in the female study it would stand out about as much as the all-female factor did. In this case, our finding among the 101 men—that homosexual men have no more homosexual sisters than heterosexual men do—is an accident.[33]

Which of these two possibilities is more likely to be correct? It turns out that number 2 is more likely, but only mildly so. Statistical tests suggest that the higher percentage of homosexual brothers of the homosexual female index subjects is probably not a fluke and that the absence of a higher percentage of homosexual sisters of the homosexual male index subjects might well be a fluke. But this is not a strong chain of logic. To be sure, we really should do the study with larger samples.

[33]In fact, those of you who looked carefully at the charts will have noticed that the homosexual men in our sample reported *fewer* homosexual sisters than the heterosexual men did. True enough, but the difference was not statistically significant.

Discussion

So once again, careful attention to specific methodology has gotten us somewhere we didn't expect to be. Given the various small studies over the years, it really didn't surprise us that male homosexuality turned out to run in families. However, no one really knew what to expect in the female study, and it was certainly unexpected to have homosexuality run, so to speak, "from females to males" but not "from males to females." We also really had no idea how readily the homosexual and bisexual sisters and brothers of the index subjects would admit their sexual orientations to us.

CONCLUSIONS AND CAUTION

This chapter has been pretty heavy on methodology. That's because methodology is important in science, including sexual science. It's high time we put a stop to the rumor that sexology is a fringe science using fringe techniques, careless of methodological details, and hence a waste of money and intellectual resources. I've gone to such lengths to explain the methodological details in this chapter and the previous one because I believe sexology now has some excellent examples of "hard science" to show the world.[34]

Of course, sexology is an underfunded science, and methodological precision can be expensive. (In some sexological studies, for example, we need not one but *two* control groups, each as large as the experimental group being investigated; this is because there are two factors that might explain the results, which have to be controlled for separately.) Any new field goes through a phase when budget constraints and the unfamiliarity of new questions makes the work look sloppy in retrospect. And after all, spending money on methodological precision means not spending it on something more interesting. If we didn't have to recruit and interview the control samples, we could have done the study for less money or spent it on twice as many "real" subjects, which would have gotten us more interesting conclusions per dollar spent. Methodological precision is sometimes boringly predictable, unimaginative, and uncreative. And worst of all, it can give those who have it unsufferable conceit—a "my methodology is holier than thine" attitude—which is particularly insufferable in the light of the fact that tomorrow we will find that today's methodology was inadequate.

[34]That's also why, incidentally, I've decided to keep the tone of this chapter more scientifically straightforward and less literary.

But hidden in the examples I've been giving you are cases in which careful methodology had benefits other than the merely methodological. In the previous chapter, for example, having landscapes as controls helped establish the existence of fairly subtle levels of sexual arousal. In the case of the sissy boys, the unexpectedly uniformly high levels of adult homosexuality allow scientists to propose more daringly deterministic theories of sexual orientation development. (These I'll describe in a later chapter.) In the case of homosexuality among brothers and sisters, careful methodological controls enabled us to discover some remarkable patterns that will help us discuss different subtypes of homosexuality.

The notion that good methodologists sometimes aren't very creative is only partly true. They do what philosopher of science Thomas Kuhn called normal science—which includes boring, predictable, grind-it-out science—but the notion that the only really important stuff is revolutionary science is incorrect. I hope we know by now that there's more than one path to the truth.

Nevertheless, some scientists will be taken aback by the notion that *non*scientists have something to teach them scientifically. I think they do—and that's the topic of the next chapter. It's time to throw methodological caution to the winds and to seek out that part of the sexual landscape where the other of the two cultures resides.

10

SOFT SCIENCE, HARD KNOCKS: WHEN SEX AND VIOLENCE MIX

"Love Hurts"
Title of song sung by Gram Parsons

So far in this book I've acted as if all's right with the world, by and large. Sex is spectacular, sexology is fascinating, and most things are enjoyable. Only every now and then have I hinted at the darker side of all this: that sex is dangerous, that conflict is inevitable, that love is hell. But we all know this darker side exists, and it's time to talk about it. On our tour of the sexual landscape we can't pretend that the only things to see are the scenic vistas. It's time to explore Puzzle 10: Why do sex and violence become intertwined?

To do this we'll need to use so-called soft science, which relies on intuition, hunches, off-the-wall ideas, and daring hypotheses. First I'll explain how I woke up to the virtues of soft science by way of a fellow named Paul Robinson. Then I'll give an example of how sexologist John Money puts soft science to work in his scary but inspiring work on child abuse. Finally, as a laboratory exercise, we'll use these techniques to piece together the personality of a tragic, crazy fellow named Daniel Paul Schreber.

PAUL ROBINSON: SCIENCE AS FICTION

I was an impressionable and proud graduate student finishing off my thesis. I'd read the *Male* and *Female* Kinsey volumes[1] about two years before and later ran across a reference to a book by a Stanford intellectual historian that analyzed them. I got a copy of the book, Paul Robinson's *The Modernization of Sex*,[2] and plunged in.

I was surprised. Here was a man who'd read every word Kinsey wrote, just as I had, and yet he was telling me all this fascinating stuff about Kinsey I hadn't noticed. Especially surprising was that he was absolutely right. And this was coming from a historian, not a scientist.

It's a good thing I hadn't read the reviews first, which pointed out the technique Robinson used to analyze Kinsey; it wouldn't have pleased my baby scientific sensibilities a bit to find out what it was. Robinson analyzed these works *as if they were fiction*, not science, and that came dangerously close to—pardon my French—literary criticism.

Are you crazy? You can't treat conclusions as if they are the product of a scientist's imagination; they're the product of the real world. *Data!* Yes, I'll admit Kinsey's point of view influenced what he decided to investigate and the framework he used to interpret his results. But analyze his results as if he had imagined every digit? Ridiculous! That's what all that methodology was supposed to protect you against.

An author of fiction has complete control over his or her emphases, plot, "data" on human behavior, etc. And so a literary critic pays attention to details such as the number of pages devoted to particular topics, how conventional those topics are, what terms the author coins and uses, and so on. Scientists, in contrast, are supposed to have all these things flow from their data. But Robinson proved me wrong on this point. For example, he found that Kinsey split up the stages of sex acts in a way different from the way society said they ought to be divided, and thought his data told him to do so.

What Robinson had done, in essence, was to pretend that every-

---

[1] *Sexual Behavior in the Human Male* and *Sexual Behavior in the Human Female* were the first two books published by the Kinsey Institute (then called the Institute for Sex Research), founded by Indiana University biologist and pioneer sexologist Alfred Kinsey. They were published in 1948 and 1953, respectively.
[2] Harper and Row, New York, 1976.

thing written by Kinsey (and three other sexologists) had been a *creation* of their predispositions, prejudices, blind spots, and genius. He gave little attention to the idea that Kinsey's emphases had flowed from his data. And yet nearly everything Robinson said about Kinsey was true. Even in the cases where he'd missed a fact, it almost didn't matter; he was sensitive to other details—literary ones—that brought him to the correct conclusions. Having read these books as if they were fiction, he ended up with fact.

For example, he discussed one of the most frequent criticisms of Kinsey's work—that it "merely" counted orgasms, omitting all that was unique, interesting, and human about human sexuality—in a way that I could finally understand it. Kinsey did indeed count orgasms—when the frequency of a person's orgasms was added up, it constituted what Kinsey termed his or her "total outlet"—but at first this struck me as one reasonable scientific choice among many. People's total outlets told you something about them, but Kinsey's most important conclusions, I thought, were based not on total outlet but rather on far more elaborate patterns in his data within which total outlet was a relatively insignificant factor. And Kinsey certainly didn't omit all the other interesting aspects as his critics had claimed. So I had thought the critics were just plain wrong.

But Robinson pointed out how Kinsey's framework implicitly demoted heterosexual intercourse in general, and marital intercourse in particular, by dividing total outlet into six categories (masturbation, orgasms during sleep, heterosexual petting, heterosexual intercourse, homosexual contacts, and animal contacts), each placed on the same footing, literarily speaking.[3]

> What for centuries had been honored simply as "the sexual act" here found itself tucked away unceremoniously in slot number four, and its socially acceptable form, marital intercourse, was even more rudely confined to a single chapter toward the back of the book, where it received about one-third the attention devoted to homosexual relations.

This suddenly made sense of Kinsey's critics even though those critics themselves seemed just as far off base as before. I couldn't remember any who had made this aspect of their criticism explicit—they couldn't have without making their own biases obvious—but Robinson in a single sentence explained them all for me. Moreover, he ac-

[3] Robinson 1976, p. 58.

curately went on to explain how the concept of total outlet, which I would have been willing to defend until the death of sexology, was really quite weak. Kinsey would never seem the same to me.

Upon rereading this passage recently, on the other hand, I noticed a funny thing: Kinsey counted orgasms, and Robinson counted pages. Using Robinson's technique on Robinson, I saw that he drew a conclusion by *counting the pages* devoted by Kinsey to particular forms of outlet. That's literary criticism, of a sort, and it would have struck my graduate-student self as insufferable arrogance. Now it strikes me as ironic, for Robinson hit the nail on the head nevertheless. Kinsey's scheme did demote conventional heterosexual acts, and in this case counting pages is a valid, if very rough, estimate of the extent to which he did so.

As I said, even when Robinson was wrong, he was right.

Obviously, all this made an impression on me. I haven't quite dropped the navel for the novel, sex for *Rex*, the limerent for the limerick, nudes for moods, the short paper for the short story, or even Freund for Freud. And I still refuse, on principle, to read *The New York Review of Books*. But let's just say I think I'd do better on the SAT Verbal the next time around.

Suddenly I was faced with a proven fact: this nonscientist—this *historian*—had reached the right conclusions in *my* specialty, and he hadn't even used my methods. And he'd succeeded often enough that I couldn't even say he just got lucky. No, there had to be something valid about *his* methods. And so I decided it was time to start checking them out.

The results might be called *soft science,* or—if you prefer—the *hard humanities*. I don't know how to describe these methods except by example. The basic principle, expressed from the point of view of my scientific training, is to construct *a theory that makes sense* from "soft" data such as stories, free-form interviews, observations of behavior, and so on. The ground is always shifting underneath you when you do this; reaching a conclusion using soft science is trickier than using hard science. But that doesn't mean it's less valid. It may take longer, of course, to prove that you're right. But sometimes it gets you to the truth much more quickly, or, more importantly, it tells you what's right so you know it's worth going back and proving it—the hard way. And sometimes it's the only way to go.

JOHN MONEY: HYPOTHESES TO TAKE YOUR BREATH AWAY

Johns Hopkins Medical School sexologist John Money is a master of the daring hypothesis: the shot in the dark that, when you turn on the lights, turns out to have been on target. He hasn't always been right, but every time he is, it's enough to take your breath away. Shooting in the dark? Yes, I'll admit that, from time to time. But shooting blind? Never.

In order to understand his work, you have to understand that he has a theory of human behavior *that works*. He keeps plugging away at the things he's interested in—gathering data, asking questions—until everything makes sense—and that's as precise as I can be. Sometimes he has had to revise his theory in the light of new data—that's where the historians of science start furiously taking notes—but his theory is a good theory, and it has had to be revised only rarely.

You've been gradually introduced to Money's work throughout this book. He coined the term "gender transposition," for example, and lectures often on the sex taboo. He was one of the first to evaluate transsexuals for sex-reassignment surgery and one of the first to follow up sissy boys.

And you've been introduced to Money's theory—part of it, anyway—right from the start. For if I had to summarize his theory in a single sentence, it would be this: sex is so spectacular that it must be woven into the fabric of any theory of the behavior of sexually reproducing organisms on this planet. It presumes that sex is involved in everything, or almost everything, that's important. His theory is far more than a sexual one, but it places particular emphasis on eroticism and everything connected with it. In John Money's universe nearly everything really *is* connected with eroticism. One reason I'm a sexologist is that I'm convinced that his universe, my universe, and your universe are all the same.

Psychosocial Dwarfism

The part of Money's work I will focus on is not a pleasant one. But it is an important topic, and it shows off how he mixes his interest in extremes and special cases with basic human decency. The topic is child abuse—especially those cases of children who stop growing as a result.

Stop growing? Yes. Every week, Money looks over a list of patients scheduled for the Johns Hopkins Hospital's Pediatric Endocrine clinic.

228

This clinic sees children from a large area of Maryland and Washington, D.C., who have hormonal problems complicated enough to be handled by a teaching hospital like Hopkins. It is through this stream of patients that Money became familiar with a syndrome called *psychosocial dwarfism.*[4]

Ordinary dwarfism—or *short stature*—has dozens if not hundreds of causes. Psychosocial dwarfism used to be a completely mysterious disease, but now it's much less so. What happens is that Susie just stops growing, and she soon falls behind in the normal growth curves for children—way behind. It can happen at any age, but we're talking, in the most extreme cases, of a sixteen-year-old boy with the height of an eight-year-old or an eight-year-old girl with the height of a two-year-old. (For you statisticians, that's three or more standard deviations below the mean for age.) Eventually people start to notice that Susie isn't getting any taller, and the family takes her to their local doctor.[5] Tests are done, and nothing turns up. Eventually Susie and her family get referred to an endocrinologist who knows about the syndrome—perhaps the people at Hopkins—and more tests are done. One of the tests is to send the family over for a chat with Dr. Money.

Susie's condition is called "dwarfism," of course, because Susie is no longer growing. It's called "psychosocial" because the cause is something in Susie's psychological or social environment. The cure is for Susie to move out: into a relative's home, a foster home, or even the pediatric ward of a hospital. If the diagnosis is correct, normal amounts of tender loving care are administered, and Susie starts growing again. The change is visible within two weeks. The diagnosis is conclusively established if Susie returns to her home and stops growing again. This cause and cure seem magical—almost ridiculously so. But there are thousands, if not tens of thousands, of children whose lack of growth fits this pattern precisely.

Money and his colleagues established, as did other endocrine centers, that the psychosocial factor in Susie's environment that causes her to stop growing often is child abuse. But no one knows for sure if this is *always* the cause.[6]

[4]The syndrome has a half-dozen or so other names given to it at other research centers.

[5]In the most extreme cases, however, the child is never even brought to a doctor. This was true, for example, of the two cases just mentioned.

[6]In fact, I was involved in treating a girl for whom child abuse was never conclusively established. I interviewed members of her family who admitted punishing her, but their descriptions of the punishment did not seem harsh or any more severe than that meted out to other children in the family who were growing just fine. Of course, it is possible that these reports were untrue. But it is also possible that some children are more sensitive to punishment than others are, so that what is "normal" punishment in a family, with no effects on growth in one child, may be too much for another's endocrinological system.

The endocrinological mechanism is only partly understood. Apparently the torture such children undergo cause the hypothalamus and pituitary (two glands buried deep inside the brain) to stop secreting growth hormone, the master hormone in charge of turning growth on and off in children.[7] Victims can develop *pain agnosia*—a deadening of normal pain reflexes—to the point where they no longer flinch when the nurse inserts a needle to draw a blood sample. This suggests that in torture the brain secretes endorphins (the so-called natural opiates) that dull the pain of the beatings. Probably these substances have a relationship to growth hormone that is not yet understood.

In any event, there are, alas, plenty of documented cases in which the child that stopped growing is the child who was locked in the closet for weeks on end, is the one burned with cigarettes by his mother and stepfather, or is the one who landed on her head when her mother threw her across the room. Or is the child who suffered all three. In these cases, psychosocial dwarfism is termed *abuse dwarfism.*

Several teams have described such children and shown how removing them from the environment of the abuse allows growth to resume. Money has shown how the child's IQ, severely depressed during the abuse, rebounds just as quickly as his or her height—sometimes all the way back to normal. (He documented, in one case, an IQ rebound of eighty-three points.) But Money's unique contribution, I think, is his sexological analysis of why certain parents would do this to the kid in the first place.

After all, parents love their children, right? It just doesn't make sense that they would slowly torture them to death, right? What impulses could possibly be strong enough to overcome the loving, tender bond between parent and child?

The answer is sex. Or part of the answer, anyway. Money's daring hypothesis is that some of the parents in abuse dwarfism are engaging in a sadomasochistic partnership in which the child is the nonconsensual victim. Although in a published report[8] he scrupulously avoided asserting that the six parents he described there were sadomasochistically involved, the likelihood that they were oozes out from between the lines: he gives the two premises of a syllogism and lets readers reach the conclusion.

Money was put onto this track by the story he heard from a young man who had been abused for years (perhaps as long as a decade),

---

[7] There are other hormonal abnormalities caused by the syndrome: see Money, Annecillo, and Hutchison 1985, p. 38.

[8] Money and Werlwas 1982.

was rescued at age sixteen, and in the course of fifteen years of follow-up told Dr. Money his family's story. That man said

> that his stepmother, with her husband's collusion, had required him to stand in one corner of their bedroom and watch her in copulation and fellation of her husband. The boy claimed, in addition, that his stepmother also had forced him into sexual activity, unspecified as to type, with the family dog, a German shepherd.[9]

Money and his colleague, June Werlwas Hutchison, spent the next several years working on how to detect abusing families and get the kids safely out of them. They noticed a suspicious pattern in these families when they brought up sex in their interview: it was *always* normal. Well, not normally normal, but "normal" was just about the only word they could get out of the parents by way of description—along with in-depth answers like "yes," "nope," and "everything's fine."

That's not normal. And here I have to pull rank.

You may have the impression that when Money and his assistants come round to talk to you about your sex life, you would be reluctant to say much. After all, that stuff is so private—so personal. You don't tell strangers your income; how can we expect you to tell us how often you had sex with your spouse last week?

Of course all that *is* private and personal, but sex-history interviewers from coast to coast and everywhere in between know that it typically is not difficult to get people talking about their sex lives. That's what we're trained to do, and usually we do it well. You need privacy for the interview itself, you need the assurance that we will keep your confidences confidential, the words giving those assurances must be backed up in every detail by our behavior,[10] and you need to work into the most sensitive questions gradually. And then, it turns out, you'll tell us just about anything. In fact, sometimes we can prove mathematically that you really *did* tell us, accurately, how many times you had sex with your spouse last week.[11]

[9] Money and Werlwas 1982, p. 58.

[10] For example, when your ex-boyfriend calls us up and asks for your address or phone number, he'd better not get it no matter what story he gives us. Same thing, for that matter, with your *current* boyfriend.

[11] We can prove it because frequency of intercourse is related to the average length of time it takes a wife to get pregnant, according to a complicated formula that even very few sexologists know. Just this approach was taken in Westoff 1974. Of course, it doesn't demonstrate that any *particular* couple is telling the truth; just that on average a particular *group* of couples is.

In contrast, the six parents—whose children were confirmed victims of abuse dwarfism—were paragons of alleged normality. Did these parents say they had sex with each other once or twice a week? No, they said they were "normal." Did they say they sometimes fantasized about having sex with someone other than their spouse but had never actually done so? "Look, I don't know what normal is, but you'd better believe we're normal, lady, and you'd better write that down." Did the husband sometimes lose his erection, then get it back again a little later in the evening? Well, he was—gosh—like other husbands, I guess. And that was "normal."

Money put his skepticism of this kind on nonanswer into two tables in a paper he wrote about these parents. Those two tables are riddled with question marks. A footnote says the question mark means "evasive."

By the time he wrote that paper, Money had heard another story— a story from a day-camp counselor who had indirectly observed, after the fact, signs of abuse in a boy who had attended his camp.[12] This observer was instrumental in bringing the case to the attention of the child-abuse authorities, who were able to coordinate a strategy that managed, finally, to stop the abuse.

The abusers were the boy's parents (who were not any of the six parents mentioned so far).[13] Here the counselor recounts a typical incident:

[The boy's mother] found a cigarette butt in the bathroom. The next thing I heard was her calling [the father] upstairs, and it amazed me how he seemed to know, just by the way she called him. He picked up his police belt . . . and went upstairs. She was not a witness to the beating [which followed]. They had sex again that night. Earlier in the day he had been told, no sex. So when she found that cigarette butt, he capitalized on it.

Let me fill in what's unsaid here. The boy presumably had been smoking—which was against the rules. The mother found the evidence, and called the father upstairs to punish the boy, using a special tone of voice. The father acted as if he knew what that tone meant and as if he knew what his reward would be for doing what his wife wanted. She, it seemed, would have sex with her husband only after he had beaten one or both of their sons. Perhaps she was erotically turned on by the idea of beating a boy (their daughter was never

[12] This story is also recounted in the Money and Werlwas 1982 paper.
[13] Incidentally, there was no psychosocial dwarfism in this family—just abuse.

beaten) but wasn't able to do the beating herself. Perhaps she thought sex was such a filthy thing she could only bear to do it after her husband had done a particularly filthy thing himself first. Perhaps he was erotically turned on by beating his son but needed an excuse, which his wife provided. Perhaps he wasn't but found by trial and error that the only way his wife would have sex with him was after he had beaten the boys. These possibilities are speculation; what was observed by the camp counselor was the boy's bruises (afterward) and the sequence of events on his visits to the home. Mind you, the sex the parents had after a beating was bang-the-wall-with-the-head-board sex, audible to the occupant of the bed in the den, which shared a wall with their bedroom.

It was what Money termed *sadomasochism by proxy*: the boys were unconsenting partners in their parents' sadomasochistic relationship. The parents had even developed specific blind spots to deal with their kink; the mother, for example, later claimed that she didn't like the fact that she had to have sex with her husband (which she didn't enjoy) in order to keep him from beating the boys. Just the opposite was the case!

A good example of Money's shot-in-the-dark skills is the way he transferred this information over to the cases of the three couples I started out describing. He does not describe any *direct* evidence connecting child abuse with sadomasochistic sexual goings-on in these three couples. But his report is highly suggestive; he clearly intends readers to see the connection between this obviously sadomasochistic story *not* involving dwarfism to the suspicious answers from the parents responsible for the confirmed dwarfism (see the original paper for more details). And alas, he's probably right. There is some risk for Money to suggest this, of course, because it is not an airtight sequence of observation and deduction. But it's one of the best tools we've got in a crazy, tragic situation.

First, it makes sense for pain in one context to be connected to pain in another.[14] Indeed, in the home of one of the three couples reported, there was grim equipment—whips, guns, etc.—on display and definite sadomasochistic aspects to the father's hobby. Put the pain together with the sex taboo and you get parents who know better than to talk about it to anyone.

Second, Money's explanation seems bizarre enough to explain why child welfare agencies haven't discovered it—at least not in as many cases as Money seems to suspect its operation. Caseworkers in those

---

[14]Especially sexually. For thoughts on how sex and pain might get wired together, see below.

agencies are not trained to deal with this kind of sexual phenomenon, and it's not clear they'd have the time to ferret it out even if they were.[15] As a result, when I see television programs on child abuse, I get this funny feeling in my stomach: I wonder if anyone's asked the abusing parents about that spectacular thing called sex.

Fairy-Tale Sadomasochism

Now let's move from soft science to hard humanities and look at these child-abuse stories as if they were literature. Wicked stepmothers? Abusive parents? A world in which everyone except the kid being beaten seems insane? Sounds like Cinderella—and the shot in the dark is to say that it *is* Cinderella. Indeed, Money hypothesizes that some of those who wrote these fairy tales were either themselves victims of child abuse or knew about it from direct observation.

The true origins of fairy tales are lost. We do know the originals are far more gory than Disney's versions; Cinderella's sisters, for example, were willing to cut off their toes and heels to fit their feet into that dainty glass slipper, and the Prince was dull enough to miss this until he noticed the blood on the ground on his way back to the castle! I think Money's hypothesis here deserves careful investigation. After all, if treating fact as fiction works more often than expected, we ought to see whether treating fiction as fact works, too.

Some of the stories Money elicits from his patients are so vivid and perversely interlocking that their case histories read like fiction. Indeed, people have noticed that if the stories were to be published as fiction they would be riveting—and they probably would get panned by the critics for being too unrealistic.[16]

To say that truth is stranger than fiction is a cliché. All I know is that truth is very strange. Patients who can't explain the cause of their problem directly give their therapists indirect hints that explain exactly what is wrong, and in doing so they sometimes construct symbolism that would make Hemingway and Ibsen proud. They express their

[15] This is not to suggest that such agencies are stupid; after all, for a variety of reasons they can't broadcast the details of their successes. But child batterers are remarkably good at fooling case workers; they manage to fool most people most of the time (including, I presume, Dr. Money himself every now and then).

[16] Money is aware of the possibility that his patients and clients may not tell (or remember) the truth. Accordingly, he takes special care to verify what can be verified, to be sure that what he's told isn't just caused, ultimately, by a hyperactive imagination working on fairy tales and horror movies as raw material. Although some of the stories are so horrible I wish they would turn out to be false, they rarely are.

plight in breathtakingly literary ways, and they don't even know they're doing it.

Recall the case of Daniel Paul Schreber (see chapter 6), who must have imprinted upon images and sensations derived from his father's child-rearing devices. His allegation that "rays" permeated his nerves and caused him unbearable torments is a striking image of his father's attempts to insinuate himself into his children's psyches. You don't have to be crazy to think of such images, of course, but if you've studied the life-styles of the intellectually rich and famous, you know that craziness helps.

Schreber had to start talking about "rays" and "soul murder" because his father and his society had put intensely self-contradictory ideas into his head. He felt he had to be unquestionably obedient to a father he shouldn't have obeyed. His father was famous—the author of books on child rearing so popular they went through edition after edition in several languages. How could such a famous man treat his children so wrong?

The self-contradictions that infest the sex taboo are of exactly the sort that can cause such problems. And so Money uses literary and religious imagery when he's explaining child abuse:

> Parents who abuse their child are, in effect, sacrificing their child. Whether they know it or not, they have assimilated the example of Abraham of old whose abusive knife got perilously close to sacrificing Isaac. It is the vengeance of a wrathful God that demands the sacrifice of one's own son. A wrath of such magnitude implies a sin of comparable magnitude. . . .
>
> Even when the sacrificial child survives, however, professionals and others are mystified as to the reason for the sacrifice. So also are the parents themselves. The sin that is being atoned for in the sacrifice of the child is either unspeakable, unspoken of, or logically disconnected from the child's suffering.

According to Money's colleague June Werlwas Hutchison, abusing parents routinely believe that they had no choice but to beat their child. The key to getting them to admit to the abuse, she says, is to empathize with them long enough to get them talking about how difficult it is to raise a problem child. "My goodness! What did you have to do to stop Susie from being such a bad girl?" "Why, I had to drag her all the way up the stairs by the hair is what I had to do."

This is a roundabout way of admitting to the abuse, but it is characteristic. The bottom line always is "I had to do it," "I had no choice," or "The baby made me do it." To put it bluntly, the baby was the devil, and the devil makes you do everything bad. Typically, one parent establishes the abuse, and the other goes along with it. That is, the two collude in establishing a *folie à deux*, psychiatrically speaking, in which the child's intractably bad behavior is the main delusion.

In each case of child abuse, Money finds a "sin" that is being atoned for. Sometimes the sin is committed by the mother, sometimes the father. A hard scientist would worry that if you looked hard enough, you could find a sin in everyone. Indeed you could, but not sins of this magnitude; they always have to do with sex, and they are always unspeakable. You'll see that the truth picks up where Faulkner's stories and *The Color Purple* leave off; the sin of incest is usually just the beginning. Read the details in his paper.

Well, what on earth could cause the abuse? The explanations so far are psychodynamic, proximate: they explain what's going through a parent's head, consciously or unconsciously, as they get out the strap— guilt, for example, about the child's conception by an unknown father, or the parent's own birth out of an incestuous relationship, perhaps. Left unanswered are other interesting questions. Here are two more ultimate ones:

- Why would a human being be constructed to beat up his or her children, anyway?
- What relationship might child abuse have to the sexuality of the children?

And here are two more proximate questions:

- How could someone get it into his or her head that a child is being naughty when in fact it isn't?
- Is there anything the child is doing that is somehow increasing its chances of getting beaten?

In brief, here are the answers:

- Animals destroy young under certain circumstances of resource scarcity or when it is not their own children they are destroying (the latter especially likely in males). Similar explanations only occasionally apply in humans, so maladaptive theories have to be looked into very seriously to explain human abuse.
- The relationship between being beaten up as a child sometimes

does, and sometimes does not, seem to be related to the child growing into an adult who is aroused by sadistic or masochistic sexual relationships. Money suspects it depends on the age at which the abuse occurs—with abuse at earlier ages, paradoxically, being associated with *less* sadomasochism once the child grows up.

- The unshakable conviction that one's child is being naughty or deserves punishment, whereas in fact it is not and does not (or the naughtiness is specifically provoked by the parent's behavior), can occur because of the way the brain is organized into semiautonomous subunits and integrated by a center of consciousness that is a clever, excellent rationalizer.
- It is tragically true that some children become, so to speak, "addicted" to abuse and act in a way as to ensure its continuance—essentially buying in to their parents' opinion that they deserve to be punished.

The bad news, then, is that physical child abuse is far more common than it ought to be; the good news is that in the grand scheme of things it's pretty rare. The best news of all—and it's not very cheery—is that we can start making some progress on these questions by taking a look at the story of Daniel Paul Schreber.

DANIEL PAUL SCHREBER: IMPRINTING RUN AMOK?

Schreber was, you'll recall from chapter 6, the German judge who, just before the turn of the century, started getting bizarre hallucinations and delusions that involved, among many symptoms, the conviction that he had to be transformed into a woman in order to save the world. He also experienced extremely painful "miracles" directed against his various organs by "rays" from God that penetrated those organs and his nervous system.

What was remarkable about these delusions is that Schreber wrote them down in a book. The book was read by Sigmund Freud, who used Schreber's story as a classic illustration of mental illness, even though they had never met. Schreber's father had been dead for decades when the son did his writing, but the delusions and the book are chock full of the father's influence nevertheless. Psychoanalyst William Niederland was the one who broke the code Schreber was writing in by going back and reading the father's own prolific writings on child rearing, exercise, and orthopedics.

The match between the two sets of writings is literally breathtaking, for some of the "miracles" that made the son feel unable to breathe in the mental hospital were remarkably similar to the effects his father's corrective apparatus for poor posture would have had upon him as a child. In chapter 6, I mentioned only a couple of striking similarities—the matter of the little sponges used to wash eyes, for example. There are dozens more recounted by Niederland and in the various books written about this remarkable family afterward.

These delusions sometimes took on an explicitly sexual character.

> After a few days the miraculous phenomena . . . were over; the sun assumed the shape which she has since then retained without interruption; the talk of the voices also turned again into a low whisper. I believe [that if] . . . the influx of God's pure rays had lasted unhindered, . . . my recovery would have had to follow, or perhaps even that I would have been unmanned and simultaneously impregnated.[17]

By "unmanned," of course, Schreber meant that he would be turned into a woman—a process that he believed occurred from time to time while he was hospitalized. He claimed, in particular, that sometimes his penis would retract inside his body, that anyone would agree that his chest seemed to have grown breasts, and so on.[18] Likewise, Schreber had no doubt that some of his nerves were feminine nerves and caused feminine reactions in him. Indeed, certain facts about human sexual response (Schreber used a German word translated as "voluptuousness") were known to him because of this.

> I am of course fully aware that the reaction of my own (female) nerves of voluptuousness does not in itself constitute proof for the very reason that it is exceptional for female nerves to be present in a male body as in my case.[19]

Does this sound familiar? If you thought of "a woman trapped in a man's body," you're not far from the truth. I strongly suspect that were Schreber alive today, he would consider himself a male-to-female transsexual. Indeed, one of the most often-quoted passages from Schreber's memoirs is the one in which he recalls "the idea that it really must be rather pleasant to be a woman succumbing to inter-

---

[17] Schreber 1955/1903, p. 126 (original p. 139).
[18] He discusses these transformations throughout his memoir, but especially in chapter 13.
[19] Schreber 1955/1903, p. 142 (original p. 166).

course."[20] And Niederland at one point agrees that Schreber would today be called a transsexual, although he began his work on Schreber before transsexual operations became widespread.

If you look back to my definition of "transsexual" in chapter 2, you'll notice that I do *not* define a transsexual as someone who is trapped in the body of the wrong sex but rather as someone *obsessed with the notion that they are such a person*. This fits Schreber perfectly. After all, he believed that the survival of the world depended on his transformation into a woman; it's hard to get more obsessed than that. Of course, what was probably really going on was very simple: some part of his psyche knew that he absolutely had to take up the role of a woman. It was some other part that rationalized this belief and came up with the notion that the world's survival depended on it.

Modern transsexuals are usually not as crazy as Schreber was, but some of them, when they first walk into a therapist's office, seem odd in ways that remind me of him. Getting them on the road toward the operation cuts down on the craziness quite a bit. Schreber went crazy at least in part, I believe, because his society had no way of dealing with his transsexual wishes. Indeed, his society believed (as did his father) that mere masturbation was a symptom and a cause of serious illness; imagine how he would feel if he, like some modern transsexuals, became sexually aroused by the thought of himself as a woman.

Some of the father's child-rearing discipline was specifically directed at preventing masturbation in childhood. And so when, immediately upon entering the hospital, Schreber had "perhaps half a dozen" nocturnal emissions in a single night, the effect on his psyche must have been threatening indeed.

Any antimasturbation devices the father may have used have not been discovered, but devices made (and patented!) by others living at the same time have been. They have the distinct flavor of sadomasochism and bondage: rings designed to spike the penis once it reaches a certain diameter, tight-fitting restraints designed to prevent a girl from touching herself sexually, and so on. Given that research has demonstrated that normal boys and men have several full erections each night in their sleep and that little girls often stimulate themselves sexually while riding hobbyhorses and the like, what would we expect the effect of such sexual repression to be?

Obviously, it could produce, via imprinting, an attraction for sadomasochism and/or bondage in adulthood—at least in some people.

---

[20] Schreber 1955/1903, p. 63; original p. 36.

Just which people is an empirical matter we cannot resolve in humans with any experiments that would be considered ethical. But we can get some insight into these matters by looking at some experiments in animals that were aimed at entirely different phenomena.

Animal S & M?

Animals (including humans) are not born blank slates. They are born with specific predispositions to behave in particular ways—at the very least, to do so in the earliest moments of life, before there has been time to learn the details of the world around them.[21] For example, baby chicks are born with a very strong tendency—desire, if you will—to follow large, slow-moving objects (especially those that cluck) such as their mother.

Ethologists and psychologists interested in imprinting and reinforcement have conducted experiments to see how this response to the mother figure could be modified by experiment. One pair of researchers used a standard reinforcer, electric shock, to see how a chick could be trained *not* to follow its mother.[22] So every time the chick approached its mother, they gave it a shock. They found, much to the consternation of people who want the connection between stimulus and response to be simple and consistent, that the more the chick was shocked, the *harder* it tried to get close to its mother. That is, instead of decreasing or eliminating the mother-following response, it seemed to reinforce it.

This finding can be interpreted by way of the following question: what does electric shock mean out there in evolution-land? After all, no chick has ever actually been electrically shocked in nature and lived to pass its response on to future generations. Well, it must be interpreted by the chick as a general kind of noxious stimulus, delivered by the external world—as if something snuck up from behind and hit it, say. What would the natural response of a chick be to being hit? Well, it would try to reach safety, which at this time of its life means finding its mother. Indeed, chicks at this age seem preprogrammed to seek their mothers whenever they are distressed. Accordingly, in an *artificial* situation, one whose contingencies had never before happened in the history of the chicken race, bizarre and self-defeating behaviors can occur—behaviors such as not decreasing or eliminating a behavior that causes oneself pain (as in the environment of this experiment). Mother Nature has simply not encountered these situa-

---

[21] A good introduction to this topic is provided by Gould and Marler 1987.
[22] Kovach and Hess 1963.

tions before and thus cannot be expected to have programmed chicks to respond to them in adaptive ways.

Recall from chapter 3 that mother-following imprinting can double, in adulthood, as sexual imprinting. As a sexologist, I therefore ask, Do chicks that participated in these (literally and figuratively) shocking experiments turn out to prefer courtship in which they are pecked or otherwise hurt by the hens or roosters courting them? That would make sense, wouldn't it? But no one knows.

In the chick-shocking experiment, the scientists discovered that the effect of the shock was variable in unpredictable ways. Usually, shock caused the chicks to try harder to reach their mother, but at certain ages it acted (as it would in adults) to keep the chicks away from her. This, too, is not surprising, since inconsistencies like this would be expected when the situation is one in which natural selection is spinning free of its usual controls. Moreover, the chick must mature: it must metamorphose from an organism that seems attracted to shock to one that seems repelled by it. We can use natural selection's logic to predict the behavior of a caterpillar and the behavior of the corresponding butterfly, but the behavior of the organism inside the cocoon? That's impossible. Likewise, the point at which the chick makes its metamorphic transition can be determined only from experiment, not theory.

Schreber and Sadomasochism

That leaves us in a very sticky situation when it comes to human beings, experimentally speaking. As I will now show, Schreber may well have been sexually abused as a child as well as physically abused by his father's devices and techniques. But if human children are at least as complicated as chicks are, we will not be able to infer that this *will* result in adult sadomasochism. For ethical reasons, the very best we will ever be able to do is soft science, getting our evidence from distressing case histories that will rarely, if ever again, be as well documented as Schreber's was.

We do know, beyond any reasonable doubt, that Schreber's father really did use the orthopedic devices he wrote about on his own children, Schreber included. We also know that the father was about as fanatically opposed to masturbation as many of his contemporaries were, because the father did write about efforts he made against masturbation in his children. Following the custom of the times, however, he only referred to these particular efforts indirectly. And finally, we know that some other people who ought to have known regarded the relationship between the father and the son as unusual, to say the least. For example, according to Niederland, a notation in Schreber's medical records at the hospital reads, as translated, "The father, founder of the Schreber gardens in Leipzig, suffered from compulsive manifes-·tations with murderous impulses"[23]—information Niederland believes could only have come from a relative, since the father was long dead. In the same vein, here is the second half of the *entire* text of chapter III from Schreber's book:

> I will first consider some events concerning *other members of my family*, which may possibly in some way be related to the presumed soul murder [committed against me]; these are all more or less mysterious, and can hardly be explained in the light of usual human experience.
> (The further content of this chapter is omitted as unfit for publication.)

Talk about a smoking gun! This omitted evidence, of course, does not in and of itself prove that Schreber's father tried to kill him or tried to have sex with him. But it obviously does suggest that some very strange things went on between the two. The psychiatric case history note makes the murderous part explicit, and the phrase "soul murder" used by Schreber is chillingly eloquent and evocative.

I know of no direct evidence that Schreber's father had sexual relations with him. But every psychoanalytically oriented author who has written about Schreber's fantasies has discussed the strong element of father seduction in them. In particular, those "rays" Schreber was obsessed with acted awfully suspiciously, manipulating Schreber in sexual as well as physical ways. Psychoanalysts equate "God" with "father" in Schreber's writings not only on general principles but also in accord with Niederland's discovery that Schreber's father himself did the same thing explicitly in his books. It was common in those times (and remains common enough today) to see the relationship between God and human beings as similar to that between a father and his family. You should obey your father without question when he tells you to do something the reason for which you do not understand, just as Abraham had to obey his God without question when He told him to sacrifice Isaac. There is abundant evidence that Schreber's nonsexual delusions directly arose from particular child-rearing practices that his father tried out on him. It is thus a reasonable infer-

---

[23] Niederland 1984, p. 58.

ence that when Schreber wrote about his delusion of being turned into a woman and impregnated by God Himself, Schreber's father probably did some things that Schreber as a boy would have interpreted as being treated as a woman sexually, or turned into one.

There is one more passage I wish to point out: this time from the same book in which the father recommended washing babies' eyes frequently with little sponges. Schreber's father once wrote that one of his children had, at the age of one and a half, come down with an illness—one that could be cured "only through the completely quiet submissiveness of the young patient. It succeeded," he wrote, "because the child had been accustomed from the beginning to the most absolute obedience toward me." [24]

I can't think of any illness that could possibly be cured simply—and only!—through "completely quiet submissiveness," much less one that affects one-year-olds. I'll never be able to prove that this "illness" was an abusive one inflicted upon one of the sons by Schreber's father, but I doubt I'll ever rule out the possibility, either. The "murderous impulses" mentioned in the psychiatric record would fit in perfectly here—and fit in with abuse of Schreber himself or his brother, or both. (Schreber's brother, incidentally, committed suicide in 1877, when Schreber was in his mid-thirties and the father had been dead for over fifteen years. Schreber himself also attempted suicide on a number of occasions.)

It "would fit"? Why? Because one of the likely consequences of a child's abuse—sexual, physical, or both—is a poor opinion of itself. After all, if your parents believe you deserve to be beaten—or to die—who are you to question their authority? Another possible consequence is the belief that one must suffer at the hands of those who love you. For if children are preprogrammed (rather as chicks are) to act as if their parents are a safe haven no matter how abusive they really are, then it would be completely understandable why they would connect love with abuse. The messages abusive parents teach their children would be these: "People who love you beat you up" and "People who don't beat you up can't possibly love you." Children are receptive to these messages because they are preprogrammed to act as if they believed that parents *always* love their children; if their parents beat them up, then beating must be a part of love. And if these kids grow up to have children of their own, it is easy to see how this message can get transmitted to the next generation, too.

This preprogramming may also be involved in a disturbing obser-

---

[24] Translation from Niederland 1984, p. 70.

vation, made by Money, about how abused children sometimes act in foster homes or hospital wards after they are rescued from their abusive environments. They are, in a word, difficult. According to Money, "This phase persists for several months, and possibly for as long as two years. It is marked by disputatiousness and noncompliance which exasperates other people and provokes their retaliation."[25] He illustrates these principles with the case of a boy who, unable to elicit the punishment he seemed to desire from his now unabusive caretakers, punished himself, anyway, by trying to commit suicide—and, in later years, by provoking members of a street gang to beat him up.

None of this, of course, justifies the parent's treatment of the child as "intractable"—indeed, it actually makes the treatment seem more horrible. But it renders the actions and justifications of the parent more comprehensible. Remember how abusing parents never directly admit to the abuse but sometimes can be induced to describe it as the justifiable result of the child's misbehavior? What they don't say is that if the misbehaving child is removed, another child often comes to be seen as the misbehaver. The parents insist, in effect, that *some* kid *somewhere* in their home is naughty and must be punished; if such a kid doesn't already exist, one will be found to take up the role.

I'd like to make one final comment on the effects of the antimasturbation attitudes so common in Schreber's time. Punishing a child's attempts at masturbation reminds me of punishing a chick for trying to reach its mother. Both are behaviors that are entirely natural and that are more preprogrammed than most behaviors are for the particular animals in question. It is not difficult to conclude that such punishment, if inflicted at the wrong times (and no one can know what such "wrong" times are), could have seriously deleterious effects in adulthood.

Childhood masturbation, whether or not it proceeds to orgasm, is in fact part of childhood sexual rehearsal play, a normal phase of child development that all primates (and probably all mammals) undergo. Experiments in primates show that if this sexual rehearsal play is interfered with, the result can be an adult who cannot or does not function sexually as well as other individuals who were permitted such play. (Indeed, the adults may not function sexually at all.) Children act as if they are preprogrammed to engage in sexually tinged games with other children at certain developmental stages in childhood. They can also, according to case histories recorded by Money and others, hook nonsexual stimuli into their patterns of sexual arousal if these

[25] Money, Annecillo, and Hutchison 1985, p. 36.

stimuli take place near in time or place to the sexual rehearsal play. (That's another way of saying that they can imprint upon them.) So, for example, exhibitionists often recall being interrupted while playing a genital show-and-tell type of game in childhood.

DISCUSSION

The phenomena of child abuse and sadomasochism demonstrate the unusual connections that can be formed when evolutionarily ordinary mechanisms operate in modern environments unlike those in which they evolved. Sexual rehearsal play goes on without interference in primates and usually without interference in hunter-gatherer bands. Child abuse is impossible in hunter-gatherers, among whom child rearing takes place in public and children can find nurturance from an extended family (not just their parents of birth).

The imprinting hypothesis presented in this chapter probably does not explain all sadomasochism, and of course consensual sadomasochism among adults would not be expected to result in child abuse. (In fact, if the couples studied by Money and Werlwas had been able to admit to their own sexual fantasies and work them out consensually with adults, I doubt that they would have had to involve their children in them.)

Some adults into consensual sadomasochism recall fantasies from their childhoods with a distinctly similar flavor, but many do not.[26] Experts are divided about whether this is cause and effect. One would expect, especially in males, for there to be some predisposition to connect sex and violence due to their association in our evolutionary past with intertribal warfare. But that connection should produce people interested in winning, i.e., in playing a dominant and/or sadistic role.

A childhood imprinting hypothesis explains, simply and directly, why most people involved in S & M are masochists (the last puzzle from chapter 3). After all, adults dominate children, not the reverse. If a child is going to imprint upon a sadomasochistic experience in childhood, it will more likely imprint upon its parent doing something sadistic to the kid than on the kid doing something sadistic to the adult. Accordingly, masochistic sexual fantasies in adulthood should be much more common than sadistic ones. They don't call the parent-child relationship a "bond" for nothing.

How might such a hypothesis be tested? In this chapter I've mentioned a few possibilities: discovering accounts like those of Schreber,

---

[26]Moser and Levitt 1987. A good general introduction to S & M is provided in Spengler 1977 and Breslow et al. 1985.

prospectively or retrospectively gathering case histories like those gathered by Money, and so on. Here's another. How would someone imprint, as a child, upon a *sadistic* role? I suspect it would usually happen with peers or younger children—not, for the reasons mentioned above, with parents. Accordingly, the sadistic fantasies in adulthood would probably have more to do with sadism performed upon peers or near-peers than with parent-child scenarios, and such case histories need to be gathered and scrutinized.

Another possible conclusion to be drawn from this chapter's evidence suggests how transsexualism comes about and why it is so rare. If Schreber was indeed a transsexual, we can guess he got that way as a result of his father seducing him and/or devaluing his role as a boy (by nearly killing him, beating him, etc.) so much that Schreber got the idea that becoming female would make him more acceptable to his father. This is, to say the least, a rare combination of circumstances, and it may just be that this is typical of transsexualism.

All this is soft-science logic. Some hard scientists may rail at the imprecision involved in it, but that's the nature of the beast. They may complain about a discipline like psychotherapy—and I admit that some of the psychoanalysts' interpretations are a bit hard to swallow—but they lose some valuable tools by doing so and cut themselves off from some very painful but rewarding and vital work.

Moreover, by staying away from soft science, they exclude themselves from a source of surprisingly powerful hypotheses. After all, the point of science is the discovery of *new* facts, and the newest facts are almost never widely accepted. And so hard scientists can all too easily serve as agents of the status quo—scientific bullies, in extreme cases, complaining that the case for this or the case for that is insufficient. But if hard science is good because it's logically straightforward and impossible to dismiss and soft science is bad because you can't guarantee it will be done well, who's got the higher-level skills: the successful hard scientist or the successful soft scientist?

Hard science is hard because it's hard to refute and it's hard to do. Soft science is easier to ridicule and easier to do poorly. But as the case of child abuse demonstrates, soft science can be far harder—not to mention far more important—to pursue well. It should be obvious from chapters 8 and 9 that I appreciate hard science and its methodological excellence. But everything has its place, and I get angry at scientists who describe the work being done along the lines of the current chapter as less valid, less believable, or less urgent. And I also find myself starting to get angry at scientists whose eyes roll toward the heavens when someone mentions history or—here I go again!—literary criticism.

In short, there are some questions in sexology that can be investigated only by soft science. As it happens, in this chapter I've illustrated this point mostly by using examples that people find unpleasant because they involve pain. But soft science can also help us understand topics in sexology in which the pain is confined to the heart, or is more than balanced out by the fun side of sex. What about the intrepid explorers venturing out into the lusher jungles dotting the sexual landscape? I see one couple heading toward a jungle called "Shangri-La." As you literary critics will recall, however, Shangri-La was (or is) in Tibet—not a country noted for vegetation. Indeed, the couple is approaching *The* Shangri-La, a bar I presume exists in New Jersey, and which has its palms in pots. Let's follow along.

11

COURTSHIP THEORY

"Since I am female it would be much easier for me to influence my date to have sex with me than for a male to influence a female. . . . I believe in the gentle approach—I would *not* pounce on him."

A twenty-one-year-old woman describing how she would let a date know she was interested in him sexually; Perper 1985, p. 136.

When two people are under the influence of the most violent, most insane, most delusive, and most transient of passions, they are required to swear that they will remain in that excited, abnormal, and exhausting condition continuously until death do them part.

Preface, *Getting Married*, George Bernard Shaw

You want monogamy? Go marry a swan!

Jack Nicholson's character in *Heartburn* (Paramount Pictures)

It was like watching two novices in a singles bar. Alex stared at Thalia until she turned and almost caught him looking at her. He glanced away immediately, and then she stared at him until his head began to turn toward her. . . . Finally, Alex managed to catch Thalia looking at him. He made the friendly eyes-narrowed, ears-back face and smacked his lips together rhythmically.

Barbara Smuts, "What are friends for?—Among East African baboons, friendship means companions, health, safety . . . and, sometimes, sex" *Natural History* 96(2):36–45 (February 1987).

Remember the first time you stared deeply into your lover's eyes? Their gaze was intense; their pupils bottomless. You could have gone on doing this for hours—in spite of the smoke, the loud music, the crowd. You lifted your glass, and so did she; you broke your gaze to do so, and your eyes locked back onto hers just a few moments later. Little did you know that over there in the corner of the bar were a mild-mannered Ph.D. named Tim and his girlfriend, Martha, who were watching you and writing it all down. As a matter of fact, they had just written down that the two of you were "in synch." That's what happens when you hang out too often in bars in New Jersey. Your mother warned you about that kind of place, didn't she? Wasn't that when she was telling you how she met your father?

The subject of this chapter is courtship—and what scientists have been figuring out about it. I'll describe two interlocking topics in *courtship theory*, which is the analysis of how humans (and animals) get together and get on with it. The first portion is theoretical (with practical sidelights) and comes from sociobiology. The second is practical (with theoretical sidelights) and comes from the remarkable human-ethology team of Timothy Perper and Martha Cornog (who are now not merely boyfriend and girlfriend but husband and wife).

The sociobiologists explain, from the ground up, the fundamental reasons why courtship exists in the first place—why its basic rules are the way they are. Biologist Tim Perper, in his book *Sex Signals: The Biology of Love*,[1] describes the next step up: what he saw during thousands of hours spent observing human courtship in singles bars, airport lounges, and anywhere else that someone might walk up and ask, "Do you come here often?" Fitted together, these two approaches make a compelling theory of human courtship. In the discussion, I will begin to apply these theories to understanding courtship in the other gender transpositions.

SOCIOBIOLOGY, SEXUAL SELECTION, AND MATE CHOICE

A fundamental theory of courtship is the *parental-investment-and-sexual-selection theory* developed by sociobiological pioneer Robert Trivers, now at the University of California at Santa Cruz. *Sexual selection* is a term that goes all the way back to Darwin; it means the evolution of sex differences by natural selection. Most laypeople, when they think of evolution, think of examples in which a trait benefits everyone in the species who has it. In this view, if you are an animal that gets preyed upon, progress in evolution means being able to run faster to get away from predators, say; or if you are an animal that preys on

[1] Perper 1985.

others, it means being able to run faster to catch more of them. But given two different sexes with two different reproductive strategies in producing offspring, natural selection can act differently in the two sexes. For example, one sex might develop a special color of skin or feathers that helps it do better reproductively than other members of its sex—and this special color may or may not be of any benefit to the other sex. It can even act to help an individual in a species reproduce better while hurting the reproduction of the species as a whole.[2]

Sexual selection is a classic use of *theory* in science. Trivers's theory is deductive. It is logical. It is deep. It is simple. It is beautiful. And it makes predictions that are so testable that there is now a small army of field biologists who check it out in the species they are particularly interested in.

Trivers's main hypothesis is that *parental investment* is a crucial variable to look at if you want to understand sexual selection. He defines parental investment with precision as "any investment by the parent in an individual offspring that increases the offspring's chance of surviving (and hence its reproductive success) at a cost of the parent's ability to invest in other offspring."[3]

Let me give an example. When a bird stuffs a worm it caught into a hatchling's mouth, that's parental investment (PI). Eating that worm increases that chick's chance of surviving, and if the parent hadn't fed the worm to that particular chick, it could have fed some other chick with it instead. Or it could have fed itself, which would have increased its own survival and thus its ability to invest in future chicks. So feeding the worm to the chick *is* PI, because (a) it helps the .offspring survive and (b) it prevents the parent from investing that worm in some other offspring.

The time the bird spends catching the worm is also considered PI, because (a) that time spent hunting will help the chick survive and (b) that time could have been spent helping some other chick survive.

Now for some examples of what is *not* PI. When a bird fights off another bird that's trying to interfere with its copulation, it is not PI, because no offspring has its survival increased as a result. It would be PI if the bird were fighting off a predator trying to eat an offspring. When a male elephant manufactures a huge quantity of sperm that it

---

[2] This refers to what is called the "group selection" controversy in biology, and explaining it is beyond the scope of this chapter. But beware: most modern biologists believe that nearly all traits that hurt the species but help the individual *spread* under the action of natural selection. That is, evolution usually benefits individuals, even at the expense of the species as a whole. If this goes against what you learned in high school biology, then so be it; a lot of what high schools teach about evolution is just plain wrong.

[3] Trivers 1972, p. 139.

uses in a single copulation, only an infinitesimal portion of that sperm is PI—the single sperm that actually fertilizes the egg. All the other sperm are "wasted" in the sense that they do not increase the survival of any offspring. But if the "wasted" sperm is absorbed by the female elephant's body in some way and used nutritionally, then it would be PI. (This happens in some species, but I don't think it happens in elephants.)

So every phrase in the definition of PI is significant. PI has to come from a *parent*. It has to benefit the *survival* of a *particular offspring*. And it has to *reduce the parent's ability to invest in other offspring*, even if only a little bit.

When people get confused about PI, it's usually *reproductive effort* they confuse it with. Reproductive effort is effort expended by an individual in reproduction. PI, obviously, is part of reproductive effort, but reproductive effort includes "wasted" sperm, fighting for the right to reproduce, and so on. That is, it includes the non-PI cases I mentioned above.

Now here's the key: *Trivers's theory says that it is parental investment, not reproductive effort, that is the key variable in sexual selection.* In particular, the key is the *relative* parental investment of the sexes in their offspring.

Accordingly, the theory divides species into two groups: those in which males and females invest very different amounts of PI in offspring and those in which the sexes invest about the same amount in offspring. It turns out that in the first kind of species the reproductive strategies of the sexes will be very different, and that means there will be a lot of sexual dimorphism, that is, differences between the physical characteristics of male and female. In the second kind of species, the sexes and their behavior will be much more alike (although not necessarily identical).

Species with Very *Un*equal Male and Female PI

If one sex's typical PI in offspring is much larger than the typical PI invested by the other sex, then the higher-investing sex becomes a limiting resource for the other, lower-investing sex. Some people find this obvious; others don't. If it's obvious to you, skip the explanation given below in the following two pages of indented material; if it's not obvious, then read on.

> Why is it that the higher-investing sex becomes a limiting resource for the lower-investing sex? The answer uses simple arithmetic, which I will exaggerate for clarity. Assume that you're an

animal of sex *A*—the sex that invests a lot in offspring—in a species in which having kids is expensive and in which you have kids over a period of time (unlike salmon, say), so that having a kid now means you'll have fewer kids in the future. This means you'd better not have too many kids right now, since it might cost you too much by way of reducing your future offspring.

So how many should you attempt to have now? Let's say that eight kids is too many: if you invest in as many as eight kids, you'll die of exhaustion. That is to say, if you have eight kids, there is a large hidden cost to you measured in terms of the kids that you'll *fail* to have in the future (because having so many knocked you out). Those future kids have to be subtracted from your total if you decide to have eight kids now in order to calculate a value for the *net* increase in reproductive success you expect given this particular reproductive decision.

There is a trade-off as you contemplate having fewer and fewer kids right now; if you have seven kids, you'll almost be knocked out, but you might survive to try reproducing again, so a smaller number of future kids will be subtracted from your current seven. At six kids, an even smaller number will be subtracted, and so on, with decreasing numbers of children all the way down to having no kids now, which presumably means you lose nothing in terms of future kids.

At some point below the killer maximum of eight, there will be a number of children to have now at which you'll have maximal *net* reproductive success: the point at which the difference between the kids you gain by having kids now and the future kids you lose by having kids now is the biggest it can be.[4] Let's assume that this number of kids for this example is four. All this discussion boils down to the following conclusion: if you're a member of a sex that invests a lot in offspring (so much that investing in just eight of them at once will kill you), then there is some optimal number of offspring for you to invest in—and that number is small.

Now assume that you're an animal of sex *B*—the sex that invests only a single, tiny sex cell in each offspring. This means your PI, by definition, is trivially small. Here, too, you could conceivably die of exhaustion from too much PI, but not until you have a billion kids, because your PI per offspring is so tiny. Just

---

[4]The biggest it can be for *you* at *this particular point* in your life, in *this particular condition of health*. What this number is would, of course, vary according to circumstances, but that doesn't affect the basic argument.

as with sex *A*, you will face a trade-off—a region in which decreasing your PI now will increase the number of kids you can have in the future—and there will be some point at which you will have a maximal *net* reproductive success when you balance the current increase in children against the future loss of children. But for you this point will be at a very high number: somewhere below a billion. Let's say it's at a half billion kids; here the difference between the kids you gain (a half billion) and the future kids you lose (by having that half billion now) is the biggest it can be.

All the logic so far, mind you, depends on the assumption that you are in control of every member of the species. If you want to have four kids, this theory assumes you can find enough other individuals to mate with you for those four kids. If you want to have half a billion kids, then you can find enough mates to have half a billion kids. Clearly, one of those two possibilities is a bit unrealistic, eh? In case the conclusion isn't quite obvious, let's continue with the step-by-step logic, from now on assuming that you are *not* in control of every other member of your species.

Consider yourself as sex *A*. How many sex partners do you need to maximize your reproductive success? Just one, thank you very much; you'll take four of those trivial PI units from that member of sex *B* and have your four kids. (More precisely, you'd need to keep having sex until you had your four kids; you might have just one partner to get those kids, or you might have several, depending on the particular species.) The point is, after you've had your four offspring, you don't want to risk having more—and most of the time that means you need only a few sex partners.

Now go back to being sex *B*. How many sex partners do *you* need to maximize your reproductive success? Well, at least 125 million of them; 125 million times four kids per partner makes half a billion, because you just can't force or persuade many of sex *A* to parent more than four of your kids. If you could find 125 million partners, though, that's the point at which your physiology gives you a headache at the very thought of sex.

The conclusion is this: the sex that invests more in offspring has its reproductive success limited by how much resource it can gather from the environment and turn into offspring, not by how many members of the other sex it can have sex with. But the sex that invests less in offspring has its reproductive success limited by how many of the other sex it can induce to mate with it.

Obviously, in the extreme example above, members of sex *B*—the sex that invests almost nothing in a given offspring—are usually never going to attain their maximum net reproductive success. That means they will spend a lot of reproductive effort not in parentally investing but in fighting or otherwise competing with other members of their own sex, all trying to gain access to members of the sex that invests more—sex *A*.

Now if you are the sort who believes that the kind of sociobiology I've just thrown at you is all pseudoscience, you're about to complain about the sexist manner in which I've given this example. Here I am, using biology to justify the status quo in humans, right? A status quo that says that women should stay at home and channel their reproductive effort into big packets of PI (i.e., those four kids) and that men should go out and do battle in the corporate jungle and do their best to have sex with as many women as they possibly can (125 million of them, in fact), thus spreading their trivial packets of PI around as much as possible, right?

Wrong—on two counts. First, PI theory predicts just the opposite—females competing for males—whenever males invest more in off-spring than females do. This does indeed happen in some species.[5] Second, Trivers makes it clear that although most mammals have a pattern of male and female PI that is pretty close to the extreme example given in the indented material above, humans do not. In humans, the relative amounts of PI by men and by women are *roughly equal*. Accordingly, the theory predicts an entirely different dynamic—and a much subtler one.

Species with Roughly *Equal* Male and Female PI

The extreme example I gave above does apply to humans, but only to the relatively few conceptions in which the father invests nothing more than a sperm cell to the baby's benefit and the mother invests everything else. But in fact, as a general rule, human babies need a lot of PI to be able to survive and reproduce. This means most babies don't do well unless they have a lot of PI from their father as well as from their mother. And that changes everything.[6]

[5] For example, in moorhens, males do most of the incubation of the eggs. The females compete for access to the fattest males, because fatter males can incubate eggs for the longest period of time. The heaviest females tended to win in this female-female competition, thus being able to lay the largest numbers of clutches of eggs in a given season. See Petrie 1983.

[6] You may have the impression that all those welfare mothers out there are a contradiction to this statement. They are not—at least, not obviously. Census figures show that although poor mothers do have more children than more wealthy mothers, a far higher proportion of their children die before reproducing, don't marry or try to have kids, or are

Trivers's theory says that when female and male invest about the same in each offspring, then there will be less sexual dimorphism—fewer differences between the physical characteristics of male and female—and the species will be more monogamous in its breeding pattern. Birds are a good example. Over 90 percent of bird species are monogamous,[7] and monogamous birds are the ones in which male and female are hardest to tell apart. The monogamous species are precisely the ones in which both the father *and* the mother invest a lot in offspring.

But this simply pushes the causation back one level: *why* do both sexes invest about the same amount in offspring in birds? Once we know that they do, we can infer, from Trivers's theory, that they will look rather alike and will be fairly monogamous. But what caused the cause?

To answer this question, you must understand the essence of being a bird. The answer is not part of Trivers's theory; it's a fact about the environment that birds have lived in for millions of years. This fact is the independent one that sets up the condition to which Trivers's theory applies. If this were not so, then we couldn't tell which was the chicken and which was the egg—whether equal PI leads to sexual monomorphism[8] and monogamy or whether sexual monomorphism and monogamy lead to equal PI.

To put it bluntly, birds have mastered the air. When threatened, they can go up to get away from the threat; they are not restricted to going sideways or down. This helps them avoid the things that animals confined to the ground have to put up with—earthbound predators, for example.

But there's a weak link in this strategy: having baby birds. The laws of aerodynamics set limits on how large and how small an animal can be, given its species' anatomy and so forth, in order to fly. Baby birds are too small to fly, and until they can, they are subject to all those problems on the ground. So it's very much in the interests of the

---

sterile when they do try. People who study birds likewise have to be careful to count not just the number of eggs laid but, rather, the number of eggs laid that hatch, grow up, successfully leave the nest, and survive to nest and mate. When all these extra factors are added in, the relative reproductive success of rich people and poor people, measured at one generation, is far more equal than the simple fertility measure of number of children ever born—the statistic that shows up in most census tables. In fact, it is probably the case that the very rich have the highest reproductive success. For more details, see my Ph.D. thesis (Weinrich 1976). For a recent update on the debate over fertility, social class, and IQ, see the paper by Vining 1986 and its associated comments.

[7] At least as monogamous as humans are, that is.

[8] Monomorphism is the opposite of dimorphism: dimorphism means two forms for the two sexes; monomorphism means one form (i.e., no differences).

parents to feed those little packets of reproductive success as much PI as they can, as quickly as they can, to get the packets airborne and out of danger. A male that does not invest enough in his offspring will see all of them die—and natural selection quickly removes the genes of such males from the population. In fact, one famous British ornithologist, David Lack, reported seeing a British robin trying to support two females at the same time. The male robin had paired with each of them, in neighboring territories, at slightly different times, so each was at a different stage in the sequence of courtship/nest building/mating/brooding/hatching/feeding/fledging. This double duty strained him so much he died, and both his broods perished. That's natural selection for monogamy.

So far, this argument about flying has been independent of the birds' social structure and independent of Trivers's theory. Given that baby birds need PI as fast as it can be provided, male birds and female birds will invest roughly alike: the maximum, or nearly the maximum, that a bird is capable of investing. This is the point at which Trivers's theory applies: it predicts that *both* sexes will compete with members of their own sex for access to resources and *both* sexes will compete with members of their own sex for access to the members of the other sex most capable of gathering resources. What's good for the goose will also turn out to be good for the gander.

That's not to say that sex differences in PI and courtship will entirely disappear (see below). But in comparison with other species, they will be small (even if, to individuals *within* a species, the sex differences that exist in that species might seem to be large). The differences that do exist will be subtle and more sensitive to individual variation. In these species, who competes with whom for access to what will depend on individual differences rather than on merely the genetic sex of the individual.

In fact, no single pattern characterizes every conception in the human species. There are some conceptions with high female PI and essentially no male PI. Far more common are conceptions in which male and female invest roughly equal amounts of PI in offspring. There can also be conceptions in which the male invests more PI in offspring than the female does—when the father is rich, for example, and passes a large inheritance on to his children.

In fact, we can make predictions, based on Trivers's theory, of *social class* biases in the patterns of parental investment. The theory says that the important independent variable is relative PI between males and females. If we understand that upper-level people have greater resources they can invest in PI than lower-level people do,[9] we can answer the following question: which group of people can invest the *most* PI in offspring?

In a society in which men have more power than women do, the answer is clear: *upper-level males.* And so, applying Trivers's PI theory, we should see women (of all social classes) competing with each other for access to upper-level males. Who can invest the second-highest amount of PI? Clearly, *upper-level females.* And so we should see middle- and lower-level men competing with each other for access to upper-level females. Who would be most willing to take a chance trying to raise a baby with only one parent's PI? I believe *lower-level females,* because they would be most likely to get stuck with this situation against their will. And who would be competing for access to them? *Lower-level males,* and perhaps other males, as well—if they can manage to gain the access and become fathers without having to contribute substantial PI, as well.

So notice that a very simple theory—Trivers's PI theory—already predicts very complicated consequences in human interactions; all we had to do was add social and sexual stratification into the set of hypotheses. The theory thus predicts a complex web of social relationships in which each sex competes for the other in an ever-changing set of circumstances. Subtle strategies abound, and I probably don't have to tell you about them. Some of the less subtle ones are getting pregnant in order to "catch" a man, discovering that you're really not in love with that woman after you've had sex with her, and so on. These and other strategies all make logical sense when seen in the light of Trivers's theory.

Logical sense, yes—but moral sense? No. It is very important to notice that Trivers's theory says *nothing* about morality, genetics, environment, learning, culture, or nature/nurture. That's because it's a theory in the real sense of the word: it is a statement about ultimate cause and effect, not proximate mechanism, and it describes what is, not what ought to be. These points are especially important in a world that has falsely equated sociobiological theories, like Trivers's, with "biological determinism" (which will also be discussed in chapter 12).[10]

---

[9] By *upper level* I mean people above the median socioeconomic status for a society; by *lower level* I mean those below the median. This distinction obviously only applies in a society in which these status differences exist. In a society that is relatively unstratified—many hunter-gatherer clans, perhaps—this analysis wouldn't work.

[10] Biological determinism is, loosely speaking, the notion that our genes determine our physical traits and our behavior in a gross and inflexible way. Sometimes it means something more specific than this: that *differences* in these things are caused by *differences* in genes.

Recall the definitions of "proximate" and "ultimate" causes in evolutionary biology (chapter 1). Trivers's theory is a theory of the *ultimate* cause of a particular behavior; it explains why a particular trait came to evolve. It is compatible with a wide variety of *proximate* mechanisms that could have evolved to embody that ultimate logic. Those mechanisms may include very substantial inputs from culture, learning, and everything else—not just physiology. And it is a theory that implies no particular ethical outlook, because it does not say that what exists is moral.

More precisely, it has moral consequences only for moralists silly enough to have tied their morality to biological tenets in the first place. If you say that what happens in nature is good, then of course scientific information about what happens in nature ought to affect what you say is good. In that loose sense, then, scientific findings have ethical consequences—but only for people who believe that what is natural is good. In fact, most of the people who say this act differently; they act as if they're constantly changing their mind about the proper relationship between the natural and the good. Do animals do something that they like? Then they call it natural. Do animals do something that they don't like? Then they call it animalistic. This fallacy is depressingly common, and it has pernicious consequences. But don't blame those consequences on the biologists who find out what happens in nature; blame them on the moralists who don't truly have the courage of their convictions.

Competition and Mate Selection

How, then, do animals actually perform this competition for members of the other sex?

Sometimes they threaten, and sometimes they fight. As two competitors approach a member of the other sex, first they display (in order to avoid needless battle, it is thought, if one will clearly emerge the winner). Sometimes this display escalates into a fight. The winner then proceeds to mate.

Whoa! Not so fast there! Another hurdle remains: after winning such a competition against a member of your own sex, will the "prize"

For example, people differ in skin color. Biological determinism of the second sort implies that some people have a particular skin color because their genes make their skins that color—no matter what the environment. Biological determinism of the first sort implies that some people have skins of a particular color because of the amount of time they've spent in the sun recently and that this relationship (but not the amount of time in the sun) is biologically determined. Obviously, for some traits both kinds of biological determinism are true. At other times, neither is, or only one is. It's an empirical matter, different for every trait.

be awarded? More precisely, will the prize *let* itself be awarded? What if the prize decides it would rather mate with the loser? Humans and animals are very good at avoiding sexual relations with individuals they don't want to have sex with. So most biologists suspect that it's not so much that the winner takes the prize but that the prize takes the winner.[11]

And so we find ourselves in the area of mate choice, proception, and courtship. *Courtship,* of course, is the series of steps and signals by which two individuals communicate and perhaps consummate their desires to have sexual relations. They scout each other out to make sure that each has what the other wants. *Proception* is the state first occupied by the initiator of courtship: it is the indication that one is ready to respond to an overtly sexual approach.[12] And *mate choice*— called *female choice* when it is females who are doing the choosing and *male choice* when males choose—is one of the most important concepts in courtship theory. If you are the sex that invests less in offspring (under a particular set of circumstances), then members of the other sex will compete for access to you; you decide which of those competitors you will actually mate with.

We have now followed Trivers's model to the point where we can see its explicit application to human beings. George Bernard Shaw was correct when he noticed that Man is not always the hunter, Woman the hunted; who is hunting and who is hunted depends on what the point of the hunt is. Marriage? Erica Jong's "zipless fuck"? Or something else? It also depends on the particular players of the game. Humans live in extremely diverse circumstances, and who is choosing, who is chosen, who (if anyone) is exploiting, and who (if anyone) is exploited are subtle and ever-changing questions. It's time to pack up our ethological gear and venture into the New Jersey singles scene to watch the not-so-primitive natives performing their mating rituals. It's a real jungle out there! Thank goodness we have a theory and a guide to lead the way.

COURTSHIP IN HUMANS

The species: *Homo sapiens*; subspecies, *heterosexualis*. The time: the late 1970s, early 1980s. The place: "the Marriott"—more formally, the

---

[11] Of course, rape happens in humans—and rapelike actions even occur in some animals. But in both cases rape is far rarer than sexual relations in which no force is used.

[12] Perper makes a distinction between *proception*, which either sex can do, and *proceptivity*, which only females can do (by definition). This distinction strikes me as arbitrary, so I will not use it in this book.

Main Brace Lounge at the Somerset, New Jersey, Marriott Hotel. Our native guide: Timothy Perper, Ph.D.,[13] at that time a biology professor at Rutgers University.

Our guide points out that cute blonde with the Ali McGraw nose who just walked into the bar. She stops just inside the front door and scans the joint. Her eyes alight momentarily upon us, our hearts leap—and then she scans on. She settles upon a fellow with salt-and-pepper hair in an impeccable but boring three-piece suit. Turning and nodding to her girlfriend, the two of them move in.

She's just made the first move—a *proceptive* move—in human courtship: namely, she put herself into physical proximity with the person she was interested in. Here's what happens next:

> When the two people are strangers, courtship begins as one person *approaches* or moves next to the potential partner. . . . [I]f the person approached does turn slightly, or look . . . , conversation opens. . . . As they talk, the two people now *turn* to face each other. . . . [T]urning . . . is usually slow and gradual—first the head is turned, then the shoulders and torso, and finally the whole body.
>
> Simultaneously, two other processes are starting. The first is *touching* [and gazing]. . . . The second process is even more remarkable: they start to move in *synchrony* with each other. . . . Full-body synchronization is striking. . . .[14]

Synchrony, remember, is the point that Perper saw you and your lover at at the beginning of this chapter.

Now if I were to tell you that these two humans are performing a mating dance as ritualized as that performed by, say, sage grouse, you'd object. "Animals are automatic," you might say; "they use their instincts. Humans think about things. They decide; they learn; they use their free will." Well, you're right; I've put words into your mouth that are, as far as they go, correct (especially if I forgive you for using the word "instinct"). What you might not realize is that humans also automatically use their "instincts" (see below). And animals decide, learn, and use their free will in courtship, too; if you don't know this already, you just haven't been out there in the field watching them as much as you've watched *Homo sapiens*.

In fact, all animal behaviorists (who watch animals for hundreds of

[13] Perper did most of this work while supported full-time by a grant from the Harry Frank Guggenheim Foundation, to which he directs deep gratitude.

[14] Reprinted with permission from *Sex Signals: The Biology of Love*, pp. 77–78, by Timothy Perper. © 1985 ISI Press, Philadelphia. All rights reserved.

hours in the field) come to appreciate their animals deeply. What look like bizarre and highly stereotyped, instinctive movements in animal courtship are in fact subtly varied in ways the animals are far better equipped to evaluate than we mere humans are. Everyone I know who has actually observed animals in the wild in this way agrees with the following law of nature, named after ornithologist William Drury, who first formalized it:

Drury's First Law of Animal Behavior:
The animal is assumed smart until proved dumb.

Translated, this means that if an animal does something, the several million years of research and development that went into shaping its behavior probably had some effects on it that make sense. For example, animal trainers know that their animals have intentions, think about things, and plan.[15] So when you explain an animal's behavior, first assume that the animal is doing something adaptive; only with very good evidence should you ever conclude that it is doing something maladaptive. Mind you, this is a working hypothesis, not a conclusion you jump to in every instance. Yes, animals do do maladaptive things from time to time, but this happens far less often than you might think.

Drury also formulated a law that applies to people who watch behavior:

Drury's Second Law of Animal Behavior:
The student of behavior is assumed dumb until proved smart.

That is, several million years of evolution have acted differently on student and animal. In spite of our species' highly advanced traits and achievements of intelligence, learning, socialization, culture, language, history, refinement, IBM compatibility, "The Love Boat" reruns, marching bands, and all-round common sense, there are still some things that other species do better than we do, and they still do some things that we don't understand. Members of lower species are sensitive to many cues that dialectical materialism, under-covers copulation, and even "Wild Kingdom" have not prepared us to be sensitive to. True, sometimes our understanding of the animal's situation is better than the animal's itself, but that is the exception, not the rule.

Here's an example of how to put these principles into operation in

---

[15] A particularly good description is in Hearne 1986.

the study of animal courtship. Someone I know who's watched birds courting on leks (see chapter 1) has a novel interpretation of what's going on there. Recall that the dominant male birds, who grab the best, central territories for themselves are surrounded by large numbers of less dominant, peripheral males. The dominant males gain the overwhelming majority of the copulations with the females, who visit for a few minutes, mate, and then fly off to build their nests and raise their young alone. (Such birds are in the small minority of bird species that are *not* monogamous, as predicted by PI theory, because males contribute no PI beyond their sperm.)

On a sage-grouse lek, most of the less dominant males get no copulations at all. Why, then, do those less dominant males go without food, fight for territories, subject themselves to the possibility of predation, and so on? Why bother doing all this if they don't get any reproductive payoff? Why not just stay off the lek and wait till they're bigger and more dominant?

My informant suspects that it's because they're watching the moves the dominant males make. They're watching *and learning* how to be sage-grouse smoothies as far as the females are concerned. How do you hold your head? Just how do you do that particular strut? When do you come on strong, and when do you let her come to you? And just what tone of voice should you use when you ask, "Do you nest in this neighborhood?"

One of Perper's most important observations is that there are aspects of human courtship that are just as stereotyped as those sage-grouse struttings—*and of which we are entirely unaware.* The language is the same at the Marriott in Somerset as it is at the Homestead in Highland Park. Anyone can observe these aspects; you just have to know what they are.

Hard to believe? Here's a noncourtship example that you can observe for yourself anytime you want to.[16] Talk to somebody. Or watch two other people talking. Then pay attention to their eyes and their mouths.

Among whites in the United States—and I don't know if this is true everywhere[17]—the eyes of the person talking roam about the room, occasionally alighting on the upper corners near the ceiling. They dart back to the listener's face every few seconds. The listener's eyes remain fixed on the speaker's eyes or mouth. When the speaker is ready to pause, his or her eyes alight on the listener's face, who then takes the hint, starts talking, and starts his or her own eyes roving.

[16]You can read about it in Duncan 1983 or Duncan and Fiske 1977.

[17]Indeed, Duncan 1983, p. 162, suggests that these patterns might not be universal.

This sequence of eye roaming and face watching is everywhere. You've never noticed it, now, have you? So go out and watch; you'll see it every time you look for it. Except when you don't—and when you don't, the exceptions will prove the rule.

For example, think of those bag ladies and bums who natter on so disturbingly. Their talk violates these rules of conversation—they'll talk to you while staring at you, for example, or they'll ask you a question. When you answer, their eyes aren't looking where you subconsciously expect them to be looking. Spooky! You may be consciously uncomfortable because you're talking to a bum, but the violation of these unknown rules adds to your discomfort.

Perper's research established similar sequences in the courtship of people. Everybody uses these sequences in this particular subculture, and nobody notices what they're doing—with only scattered exceptions. The initial proceptive approach, the touching, and the gazing are sometimes consciously understood, but the rotation of the body and the synchronization of gestures almost never are.

Isn't it amazing that it wasn't until recently that somebody watched humans the same way that humans have been watching robins, lions, and elephant seals? It turns out that humans and animals are a lot alike—not because humans are "lowered" to the level of animals by this watching but because animals are raised closer to the level of humans. Courtship has aspects that are obvious and straightforward, but it also has aspects that are deep and astonishing. And that's true in humans, sage grouse, elephants—you name it.

Drury's laws, in short, prescribe humility. We can use this humility to further our understanding *if* we think carefully about the animal's point of view and take aspects of the animal's world as evidence sometimes superior to the evidence of our own senses. We must also expect Drury's laws to apply when humans are watched: to suggest a little humility when we interpret other people's behavior. I hope I don't have to point out that the same is true of other cultures, other disciplines, other sexual orientations—other anythings. Human beings should be assumed smart until proven dumb, too.

Proceptivity and Female Choice

In spite of the great diversity of human mating arrangements—as predicted by PI theory—when it comes right down to sexual relations themselves, it's still the woman who's taking the bigger risk. This is one of the subtleties and variations worked out by Trivers himself in his parental-investment paper. The relative amounts of PI invested by the two sexes can *vary* over the space of investing in a single offspring. Perhaps the first investment is mostly made by sex A, and then sex B catches up and surpasses A. In this case, A would be more vulnerable to desertion early in the relationship and B later on. If the disproportion ever gets large at a given moment, then the rules for species with unequal relative PI come into play for those moments. In sea horses, for example, the female makes the larger initial investment (in eggs) but then hands them over to the male and takes off—leaving him with the rest of the investing to do.

In mammals, there is always an *initial* bias in relative PI: If a baby is conceived, then it is the female who will be forced to invest in it first (at least to the tune of nine months in humans), and it is during that time when she will be vulnerable to the loss of the male's PI by desertion. Mind you, once the baby is born into a world that does not depend on mother's milk to feed it, each parent runs the risk of being deserted, and the asymmetries in the relationship are much reduced. But by that time, courtship is over, too. So although in the grand scheme of things relations between the sexes in humans cannot be predicted on the basis of simple male/female categories, biology matters *when it comes to courtship*—which is, by custom if not by definition, precisely the time at which the woman's risk of being deserted is the largest in comparison to the man's.

So courtship in humans is a complicated affair. It typically *seems* to involve only a wary female and an eager male because at that stage the pair-bond has not been formed between the two, so the female is usually more at risk (for unwanted pregnancy) than the male is (for unwanted child support). But that is not to say that the female is globally passive or that the male is overall eager. Each sex faces its own risks *in the long-term game.*

Perper has documented proceptivity and female choice very clearly in humans. He has actually seen, hundreds of times, interactions, such as the one that began this chapter, in which proceptivity is very clear. And he has found that women are far more proceptive than men. In fact, he found that women as a rule know about proceptivity and that men do not. How scientists found this is a fascinating topic in itself.

The Courtship Sequence: Who Knows It Consciously?

Perper established, by direct observation, what the steps of courtship actually are. But who knows those steps consciously? Women? Men? Both? To answer these questions, Perper did a series of studies on courtship as understood by college students, following on the heels of, and in collaboration with, other workers.[18]

Typically, students in a class would be asked to describe in a one-paragraph essay what they would do in the following situation: they're on a second date with someone they like, and they are really turned on. What would they do to get the other person to have sex with them?[19]

The answers were surprising to someone who thinks men are in control of courtship and women are passive. What Perper saw women doing in the singles bars was exactly what, in the essay, they said they would do: they would act proceptively, by putting themselves in a situation where they would be noticed or which would elicit further responses from the man they were interested in. Indeed, over 85 percent of the women's responses were "highly and explicitly proceptive." This was true for the sexually conservative women as well as for the sexually liberal ones. Moreover, the women were, as a rule, pretty good at describing the later stages of courtship, too.

The men, on the other hand, seemed completely unaware of the proceptive steps taken by the women. Worse, many more of their answers were confused to the point of being unintelligible. Perper concluded, therefore, that many men of college age are confused by courtship; they seem to be living in a world in which things happen by chance, not because of anything they do themselves. Not surprising, actually, if you realize that as far as these men are concerned, they choose a particular woman to talk to because they see her and like her. Little did they know she had chosen them first and put herself where she would be seen by them. As far as the man was concerned, when he decided he wanted to strike up a conversation with a woman and pick her up, he used a "line" such as "Gosh, that's a nice pair of earrings." Little did he know that the line didn't really matter; what did matter was that the woman had decided that he was the one she was after. As far as the men were concerned, when they made the first obviously sexual approach—hand on breast, for example—sometimes it worked, and sometimes it didn't, and they didn't understand why. Little did they know that the woman had been con-

[18] Specifically, his collaborators were David Weis, then at Rutgers University, and Margot Crosbie, at the University of Windsor (in Canada). The courtship questions they used had been published by Naomi McCormick, who also contributed some responses from the study for which she had developed the questions.

[19] "Have sex" was defined as going only as far as they themselves wanted to go. For sexual conservatives, for example, this might mean deep kissing and some touching above the belt through the clothes. For sexual liberals, it might mean heavy petting or more.

trolling the courtship sequence up to that point and would have put herself into a position where it was easy for him to touch her breast if that was what she wanted.

I myself have done fieldwork and observed how heterosexual college men can be consciously unaware of the factors that lead to success or failure in courtship. The fieldwork was called "being a resident tutor in a Harvard dormitory," and it was informally conducted during my years as a graduate student.[20] The observation had to do with the fabled existence of the so-called Radcliffe bitch, Radcliffe College being the sister school to Harvard College (now merged under coeducation). The Radcliffe bitch was the woman that Harvard men—especially Harvard freshmen—thought they met in their classes, in their dining halls, and in the libraries. The Radcliffe bitch was seen as negative in all the ways that women from less exalted schools (or from back home) were seen as positive.

I think I understand the phenomenon of the Radcliffe bitch, and it has more to do with the men than with the women. The only assumption you need to make about the women is that they (like most women in our society) want to "date up" or "marry up" the ladder of socioeconomic status or date or marry on the same rung—or at the very least (perhaps especially so in this case) that they *don't* want to marry or date *down*.

Now think: a male high school senior about to go off to Harvard is in a pretty enviable positive vis-à-vis his competition. He's a senior and hence among the oldest in his school. If he's going to a public high school, the sex ratio is roughly fifty-fifty. And he's been accepted at **Harvard** and thus is probably among the smartest and most likely to succeed. When he calls a girl up for a date, he will on average be more successful with her than the average boy in his neighborhood is. And in all likelihood he'll get used to women responding to his social approaches in a relatively favorable way.

But in the space of those three short summer months between high school graduation and Freshman Week, he moves suddenly from the top of the heap to the bottom. He becomes the youngest at a school where the sex ratio is biased against males even in simple numerical terms. He is at **Harvard,** but so is all his competition. When he calls up a Radcliffe woman for a date, on average he will probably be less successful with her than he was with the average girl in his hometown. And in all likelihood it will never cross his mind that his new

[20] I thank the National Science Foundation for the predoctoral fellowship and the Society of Fellows, Harvard University, for the postdoctoral fellowship that supported me during these years of observations.

environment is the cause of his troubles. Instead, he'll blame it on the woman and call her a bitch. In short, he won't know what's really going on because he doesn't understand the early stages of courtship; all he knows is that he doesn't get dates the way he used to.

Let's return to the more general question of what men know and don't know about courtship. The men Perper saw in the singles bars responded to women's proceptive signals perfectly well. But the college men were writing essays that suggested they themselves were oblivious to it. Their descriptions, when they were coherent at all, often began directly with the overtly sexual, hand-on-breast part, ignoring the initial stages of the courtship altogether.[21]

It turned out that the men's and women's responses were neatly complementary. The proceptive parts were described precisely and accurately by the women but were skipped entirely or described vaguely and inaccurately by the men. The overtly sexual parts that followed were described in great detail by the men but far more fuzzily and indirectly by the women. The women understood the body-contact part better than the men knew the proceptive part, but neither sex was particularly brilliant in dealing with the other's area of supposed expertise.

Perper calls this a *romantic division of labor,* and demonstrating its existence and limitations is key if you want to understand *Homo sapiens heterosexualis* in this country. It dovetails rather nicely with what Masters and Johnson say about the cultural norm that dictates that men be the sexual experts and should know—*without having to ask, without having women tell them*—how to arouse a woman sexually. Masters and Johnson (see chapter 3) say that this is a destructive norm that prevents millions of married couples from attaining more satisfactory sexual relations. Lay sexologist Shere Hite's studies show that

[21] It is possible, of course, that the two kinds of men—college men and bar men—were different, the college men being inexperienced. But it is Perper's impression that the men in the bars were just as unaware as the college men were and that the college men could respond to the women's signals just as well as the bar men did. Naomi McCormick, a psychologist at the State University of New York, College at Plattsburgh, has observed behavior in college bars and demonstrated that college men do respond to women's proceptive signals without being consciously aware of them. And Monica Moore, a psychologist at the University of Missouri/St. Louis, has studied these signals ethologically. At a recent conference luncheon, she demonstrated some of those signals to us. There's the *head toss,* in which the woman tosses her head backward with a flip, a restrained version of the hair tossing that you see in shampoo ads on television. And there's the *primp* (shoulder-adjust version), where each hand goes up to its respective shoulder and sharply pulls out the fabric, as if to adjust the way the cloth falls on the shoulders, even if the fabric seems to need no adjustment. Odd the way these animals signal each other, eh? According to Moore, biologists find it odd, too. When she describes this work at animal-behavior conferences, she says, the audience acts uncomfortable. See Moore 1985.

many women expect men to know how to arouse them and that many men complain that their girlfriends never tell them what arouses them. And Perper has shown this norm operating in ordinary men and women in ordinary singles bars. For all I know, it may even operate in some of our finer university marching bands, among the men engaging in covert operations in foreign countries, and among the people working to reduce our federal deficit.

In sum, human courtship is as observable as animal courtship is. Trivers's PI theory explains why it is that females take the lead in courtship and why they have the power to choose which men they will have sexual relations with (except in rape). Perper's observations confirm that women do indeed take the lead in human courtship— and most of the time take the lead in escalating at each step of the courtship sequence (a process I haven't yet described but a very important one). Both men and women have the power to continue with each escalation or to decline it.

For example, recently Perper accompanied me to a restaurant bar in St. Louis where we watched couples sitting around the bar waiting for tables to become free. Directly across the bar from us sat a couple. The woman, Perper said, was attempting an escalation. They were very young: perhaps the office mail-room boy and a beginning secretary in the typing pool out on their first date. She was extremely proceptive; he was resistant. She was trying to escalate at almost every turn; he was declining. She leaned toward him at least thirty times in the half hour we watched, and he leaned backward (just a bit) nearly every time. She had turned to face him almost completely; he began by facing the bar directly (their shoulders thereby forming what Perper terms a "crossed T," which is a signal that the couple is not getting along well) and only toward the end turned somewhat in her direction. She touched him about a dozen times; at the end of the half hour she took his hand for a breathtakingly long ten seconds or so. We never saw him reach out to touch her. Over and over, the two of them were in what Perper called "countersynch"—they did things about as far *out* of synchronization with each other as is possible. In short, the two of them were not getting along, and when they got home, they would probably tell their friends that "that chemistry" just wasn't there.

In contrast, the couple at the corner of the bar, maybe five years older, were getting along just fine. Perper inferred that they were an established couple, probably sleeping with each other but not living with each other yet. Their shoulders were parallel from the start. They synchronized their movements: when she moved closer, so did he;

when he took a sip, so did she. At one point, each went to the restroom, one after the other, and the signals each had been broadcasting suddenly shut down as soon as the partner left: each turned directly toward the bar, stared into his or her drink or into the nothingness inside the bar's perimeter, and became almost immobile.

Learning the Courtship Sequence? Or Developing It?

No one knows how these courtship patterns are established. It's a puzzle itself; Perper estimates that over 90 percent of American males can actually *perform* the typical courtship sequence with a proceptive woman, but they couldn't *describe* it accurately to save their lives. So how does it come into being?

One possibility is that it is a human universal, with brain circuits ready to be whipped into shape with a little practice in the teenage years. There are some human behaviors like that: certain facial expressions, for example, or walking, just need practice to exercise the circuits involved in performing them.

This *automatic* theory is probably not correct for all of the parts of the courtship sequence Perper observed. Think of a conversation using the eyes-roaming-about-the-room body language I discussed above. This unconscious body language is probably not a cultural universal in all its aspects, and so it seems likely that Perper's sequence will turn out to be similarly variable. But frankly, no one has checked it out to be sure. If I had to make a guess, I suspect that the body alignment, touching, and movement-synchronization parts of the sequence are more universal than the details of proceptivity, although I expect females will be more proceptive than males are the world over. But this is only a guess.

The other extreme possibility is that the courtship sequence is entirely *learned.* If so, parts of it have to be learned, in men at least, completely unconsciously, since men are unaware of the early steps. That humans can do things with regularity (such as having conversations) and be completely unaware of their body-language signals is now well established. I think this extreme is unlikely to be completely correct, but again, nobody knows yet.

An intermediate possibility is that learning courtship signals is like learning language: there is a strong predisposition to learn something, but the vocabulary (so to speak) is different in every culture—even if the messages sent and received cover the same possibilities. (After all, I hope it goes without saying that not all cultures have singles bars and dates!) If so, then courtship will turn out to be a complicated web.

How could we investigate these questions? One answer, I believe, is to think about people for whom the standard courtship categories can't apply in their usual form. And so it's time to ask some questions about courtship in gender transpositions. Let's look, then, at the other subspecies of *Homo sapiens*.

COURTSHIP IN THE GENDER TRANSPOSITIONS

After all, in the gender transpositions—the transposed ones, that is, excluding ordinary heterosexuality—we do not reliably have one person who dances the man's steps and another who dances the woman's. *Regardless of which mechanism we suspect produced the courtship sequence*—learning, genetics, or some combination—in the gender transpositions we face fascinating courtship questions.

Let's say, for the sake of argument, that heterosexuals learn 100 percent of the courtship sequence in the junior high school years. That's when, you recall, rumors are flying about who's going out with whom, who thinks who's cute, whether so-and-so is still interested in so-and-so. Perhaps junior and senior high is the time teenagers are trying out their courtship skills, learning how to adjust them to the social situations they will face as adults. Girls would learn how to be proceptive toward boys. Boys would learn, unconsciously, how to respond to that proceptivity. Each sex would learn—at least in a preliminary way—how the typical member of the other sex reacts when you (a) come on strong, (b) send them a note in class, (c) tell your friends to tell them you think they're cute, (d) tell a lie to get rid of someone you're not interested in, and so on.

But what about the boys who are going to end up gay? The girls who will be lesbian? They are emphatically *not* learning in school how they can court and be courted by the people they find themselves attracted to. Given that some of the signals are unconscious, it may take them quite a while to realize that they're missing something—not just partners and prospects in the mating/dating game but also being taught the techniques for finding those partners and prospects.

The prehomosexual kids might learn their own sex's pattern but find it dull and unrewarding when they try to put it into practice with the sex their society expects them to. Or—especially because the kids who are most affected by childhood cross-gender behavior are the ones most likely to already know that they are gay—they will learn the other sex's pattern. Or, if they don't have overtly sexual feelings yet, they may learn neither pattern. And, for all I know, some may learn both patterns—although this seems unlikely unless the person is actively visiting the gay world.

On the other hand, let's say that the courtship sequence is 100 percent automatic. Then the awkwardness you see in junior high is the awkwardness of a developmental program getting its kinks ironed out: the birds awkwardly getting their flight feathers arranged right, their flying circuits exercised.[22] If this is the case, then young homosexuals will be developing their courtship skills, too, but will have nearly no one to practice them on in our culture.

Here, too, depending on the genetic theory you prefer, the homosexual kids might have the pattern of the same sex, the opposite sex, or both sexes built into them. After all, in most respects, homosexuals resemble their own sex's behavior patterns more than they do the other sex's. But in psychological tests they often score more in the cross-sex direction, especially in childhood, and perhaps this would be true for courtship psychology, too. The periodic-table model I presented in chapter 7 suggests that homosexuals might be equipped with both sets of responses, while transsexuals would be equipped with neither set. That is, if (as suggested in chapter 7) most homosexual men and some lesbian women are masculinized but not defeminized, then they could have the neural circuits activated for *both* sexes' courtship behaviors and responses. And if most male-to-female transsexuals and some lesbian women are defeminized but not masculinized, then they could find *neither* sex's courtship patterns easy to perform.

And finally, if courtship signals are neither automatic nor completely learned but rather something intermediate, then prehomosexual kids will find themselves needing to learn a language—the language of gay life—that no one around them is speaking. It's a language, moreover, that few people around them think needs to be taught. Again, if the periodic-table model is correct, prehomosexual kids may be trying to learn both languages, and male-to-female pretranssexuals may not be interested in learning either.

I don't know of anyone who is looking into these childhood questions, but I do know people working on closely related ones. Harlan Lane, a psychologist at Northeastern University in Boston, draws striking parallels between a homosexual child growing up with het-

---

[22] Flying in birds is a developmental process, not a learned one. Young birds *appear* to learn to fly, but in fact their flying skills develop on a fixed timetable. Birds kept in cages that permit them to exercise their wings but never to leave the ground are able to fly very well, from their first flappings, when they are released at the time their uncaged nestmates have finished "learning."

erosexual parents and a deaf child growing up with parents who can hear.[23] Lane believes that deaf children need to be put in contact with the deaf community as soon as possible so that they can develop their sign-language skills in as accepting and stimulating a context as possible. This is often beyond the comprehension of the parents, who want their children to speak the language they themselves do—spoken English—even if the kids have to do so imperfectly.

There are, likewise, heterosexual parents who cannot comprehend the language their homosexual children are speaking and who want their children to speak the same sexual language they do—namely, ordinary heterosexuality. In many societies, children have the freedom to choose with whom they will live (most American Indian tribes, for example; see Williams 1986). But this is not as a rule true in America nowadays, with the possible exception of foster care. Many social workers believe that when a child in foster care turns out to be gay, she or he can (or ought to) be placed in a foster home headed by a gay or bisexual parent (or parents), especially if they are having trouble finding heterosexual foster parents who can deal with the child. This is especially likely to be true with the more flamboyantly cross-gendered gay teenagers, whose body language and behavior is completely alien to that of most heterosexual parents. As a rule, the more cross-gendered the kid, the earlier he or she comes out as gay and the bigger (or at least longer-lasting) the problem is from the point of view of the foster-care system. A similar problem arises when the kids go to school; the gay high school you may have read about in New York City (the Harvey Milk School) handles this kind of kid, mostly.

When it comes to adults, there is a lot of anecdotal information about the gender transpositions that is relevant to courtship questions—which I will now discuss.

Courtship in Gay Men

If we start with the hypothesis that homosexual men are more like heterosexual men than they are like heterosexual women in courtship, then it's apparent that these men will face a courtship problem. Getting the sex under way will be no difficulty—unlike dancing, there's no problem if both partners take the lead—but how do you communicate the early stirrings if there's no one being proceptive?

Gay men start to address this problem by giving a name to its solution: *cruising*. Cruising is usually defined as the purposeful seeking

---

[23] See Lane 1984.

of sex partners among strangers, but I think that definition contains a distortion; you can cruise for a lover as well as for a one-night stand.

There are even guide books in the gay community—helpful hints for coming out, that sort of thing—that teach gay men how to cruise in so many words. *The Joy of Gay Sex*, for example, devotes 3½ pages to the topic, not counting a full-page illustration. A book called *Gay Spirit* devotes an entire chapter to describing the techniques of three different kinds of cruising.[24]

Both these books are fascinating to analyze from the point of view of Perper's theory. First, the very existence of "cruising lessons" suggests that some gay men, at least, need help with their proceptivity. But the description of one of *Gay Spirit*'s types of cruising only makes sense if its author believes many gay men need no such help at all. What the author describes, somewhat in jest, as the "Eyeball-to-Eyeball Contact or, Your Eyes Have Told Me So" type is described in only thirteen lines (out of a total of roughly eight pages) because "most of us are pretty good at this so I'm not going to dwell on it very much." Indeed, Perper reports in his book that he has met only a few men who understand and can describe the proceptive part of heterosexual courtship; it turns out almost all of these men are homosexual.

Both books' descriptions of "cruising" contain aspects of both the heterosexual woman's stereotypical role in courtship and the heterosexual man's. *Gay Spirit* says, for example, that in cruising the "crucial factors . . . are proximity to the gay you want, and wisdom and smoothness in your delivery of that first line, that all-important first line."[25] This is a perfect hybrid between what Perper describes as the woman's skill (proceptivity via proximity) and the man's misconception (the importance of the "line"). *Joy* is a similar hybrid. It clearly describes the proximity strategy of the proceptive phase and even hints at the turning to make the bodies parallel.

> Your interest mounts and so you move—not next to him, since that would make it awkward for him to turn to look at you—but rather to a position somewhat closer than you had been before.[26]

But then the book goes right into another discussion of "the line"!

In short, both these books describe cruising as a mixture of each half of the heterosexual division of labor in courtship. Both books implicitly suggest that cruising techniques not only come naturally to

[24] Silverstein and White 1977; Loovis 1974, chapter 10.
[25] Loovis 1974, p. 96.
[26] Silverstein and White 1977, p. 77.

gay men but also have to be learned. This observation is consistent with several theories of the development of courtship in my genes-versus-culture discussion above—alas for those of us who want our questions answered.

Courtship in Lesbians

If we start with the hypothesis that homosexual women are more like heterosexual women than they are like heterosexual men in courtship, then these women will face a problem. Getting the other woman's attention will pose little difficulty, but how do you get from physical closeness, ready for the partner to put her hand on your breast, to actual physical contact and genital sexuality? To use the dancing-class analogy again, there's no problem getting women to show up to take the lessons, but there is a problem if no one is then willing to take the lead.

Are lesbians proceptive? It's hard to say, judging from the written evidence. *The Joy of Lesbian Sex*,[27] for example, has no entry for "cruising" and no specific advice on how to attract a woman's attention. The entry for "eyes" states that "lesbian eyes seduce" and "lesbian eyes cruise"—but gives no details. The entry under "bars" is as close as the authors come to such specific advice: direct approaches ("a slap on her beautiful ass") are specifically frowned upon, as are "the grossly inappropriate habits of men" in making such moves. The only specific recommendation is to ask for a dance.[28] Interestingly, when Perper asked heterosexual women (in his questionnaires) how they would show an interest in a man, asking the man to dance turned up often in their answers.

This lack of advice suggests that lesbians' proceptive skills literally go without saying. After all, if girls in junior high school learn how to be proceptive with boys, it's easy to be proceptive with women after they grow up; asking a woman to dance isn't all that different from asking a man to. Remember, the approaches they learn are not, say, walking up to a boy and giving him a slap on his beautiful ass!

On the other hand, the whole purpose of *The Joy of Lesbian Sex* might be seen as being to help lesbians initiate explicitly sexual activity. Some lesbians do see this as a problem from time to time. Pat Califia, a lesbian sexologist in San Francisco who writes an advice column for a gay newsmagazine, has said she's frustrated by lesbians

---

[27] Sisley and Harris 1977.
[28] See the entry under "bars" and expanded upon under "dancing."

who seem to want all the sexual appetizers but none of the main course. It's as if, she says wryly, women's idea of a good time at lesbian music festivals consists of everyone joining hands, taking off their shirts, and dancing bare-breasted around the campfire—then falling asleep, exhausted, in each other's arms, before they have a chance to "do" anything![29]

Along the same lines, many gay and lesbian conferences seem to have at least one women-only workshop on lesbian sexuality and how to nurture it. In contrast, a proposal for a gay men's workshop to get them in touch with their sexual fantasies would probably be laughed off the program—although a workshop on how to maintain a long-term relationship would not.

The modern lesbian, if she has this problem, solves it by learning how to take the sexual initiative when it needs to be taken, thus overcoming her training and/or predisposition to play back in her lesbian life a message that was intended more for heterosexual women (and conventional ones at that). The less modern lesbian had a different solution: butch-femme role-playing.

I have already described (chapter 2) how poor the correlation is between the sex roles, if any, that lesbians play in bed and their apparent roles about the house. Such role-playing is passé among politically correct lesbians nowadays, but it is enjoying a resurgence among a few, urged on by some older lesbians who feel that these roles have been too quickly abandoned.[30] When such women are asked what butch and femme "really" boils down to, the answer is revealing: *the butch is the one who takes the initiative in moving to overt sexual activity.* The one who overtly begins sexual activity need not be the one who fixes the car, because fiddling with a carburetor need not be similar to fiddling with buttons on a blouse. These two tasks are connected only in the social structure of the male role in the West, not because the two types of fiddling somehow draw on similar skills.

In sum, then, different lesbians have different solutions to the puzzle of courtship. As women who love women, they can't count on a man being around to make the explicitly sexual moves. Depending on your point of view, that's either a curse or a blessing. If you see it as a blessing, you make those moves yourself, when appropriate, and hang out with others like yourself in this respect. If you see it as a curse, you decide whether you or your partner should be responsible for making those moves and call yourself "butch" or "femme" accordingly. And if you don't see it at all, then you have a different

---

[29] See Califia 1983 for an excellent analysis of roles in the lesbian community.
[30] Nestle 1983.

problem; you'll find yourself a lover, live with her for years, and start having sex with her just before you break up.

Courtship in Transsexuals and Cross-Dressers

I know of no evidence about the courtship of transsexuals, heterosexual transvestites, and drag queens. Reasoning from the periodic-table theory (chapter 7), I would not be surprised if female-to-male transsexuals were like typical heterosexual men in their courtship: a bit heavy on the sexual come-on and a bit weak on the proceptivity. Nor would I be surprised if male-to-female transsexuals were not good at either proceptive or overtly sexual signals. I suspect heterosexual transvestites would turn out to be like ordinary male heterosexuals in their courtship patterns, since, after all, they court ordinary heterosexual women. Moreover, their adoption of female clothing and roles, although motivated by an internal feeling of femininity, seems to be copied consciously from what they see in women. Since ordinary men don't know consciously about proceptive signals and since heterosexual transvestites are not trying to attract men, I doubt they would be proceptive. But I'm willing to be proved wrong.

Drag queens are a different story. The feminine and masculine aspects of their personalities are more integrated, as I explained in chapter 2 (whereas transvestites tend to segregate the two aspects into two separate personas). Indeed, the periodic-table model puts them only a short step away from heterosexual women. A certain kind of drag queen—whom John Money calls a *gynemimetic* (you can think of her as "a woman with a penis")—is a homosexual cross-dresser who enjoys being taken as a woman and usually takes hormones to grow breasts but does not want to be rid of her penis. Such a drag queen can often find herself a boyfriend who hadn't the foggiest notion he would be attracted to her until they met. And were you to meet and interview the boyfriend, you would probably find nothing out of the ordinary about him except the genitalia of his girlfriend.[31] In some

---

[31] For an intriguing interview with a gynemimetic and her gynemimetophilic boyfriend, see chapter 22 in Money 1986; see also Money and Lamacz 1984. Gynemimesis has been independently discovered by Walter Williams, the anthropologist who studied the berdache; see Williams 1986, pp. 116–117. Williams agrees that there may be nothing unusual about the boyfriend of the gynemimetic; these men respond to femininity in their partners, which the gynemimetics are very good at producing. In evolutionary terms, the gynemimetic can be termed a "parasite" of the ordinary attraction men feel for feminine women; they can give such men the femininity ordinary heterosexual women provide but with fewer of the sexual inhibitions that ordinarily come with the package—at a cost, of course, in reproductive success. In nature, successful parasites have to be better at doing what they're imitating than the real thing is; otherwise, they don't succeed as parasites. If this is true of gynemi-

cases, the boyfriend will express more sexual satisfaction with his gyne-mimetic girlfriend than with a former wife or heterosexual girl-friend. This suggests that gynemimetics can know what will please a man better than some women do. Is this because they can be more forward than is usually permitted in proceptivity? Probably so. It would be interesting to see if they are also more proceptive than men usually are. Sexologist Charles Moser, who teaches at the Institute for Advanced Study of Human Sexuality in San Francisco, has done field-work in drag queen bars (sometimes called transsexual bars) and suggests that the answer is yes.

Courtship and "Coming Out"—a Synthesis

Some homosexuals go through a promiscuous phase soon after coming out that they interpret as "catching up" on what heterosexuals were doing in high school. Courtship theory suggests that this promiscuity has another function, namely, that it helps them learn at least one, maybe two, sets of courtship signals and also how to apply them to other members of their sex.

Let's talk about dancing again, because it's a good analogy. A very large proportion of dances—everything from the Virginia Reel through square dancing to the fox-trot—were developed in heterosexual contexts and assume that the male and female partners should move in mirror images to each other or in complementary ways in some sense. For example, in the typical square dance, all the members of sex A get to twirl or be twirled by all the members of sex B, but the members of each sex never twirl each other. But if you are dancing with a member of your own sex, this either makes little sense or causes problems, and there are only a limited number of solutions:

- You can choose a dance in which the two of you do not mirror each other's movements, for example, noncontact disco dancing. This doesn't solve the problem; it merely avoids confronting it and deems it unimportant.
- You can adopt roles in which one partner performs the steps designed for their sex, the other those for the other sex. This works when two individuals have learned complementary steps but not when they both know the same ones.

---

metics, then we would expect their femininity to be very convincing—perhaps to be more feminine than average women typically are. Of course, "parasite"—a technical term in biology—is a poor term to use in this human case, where we are describing a truly consensual relationship, at least after the genitalia of the gynemimetic are revealed.

- Everyone can learn both patterns, and choose one role or the other on the spur of the moment, for the term of a particular dance. This works fine but can be confusing if you want your steps to be as automatic as possible.
- You can choose dances—the waltz instead of the fox-trot, for example—in which the steps are both mirror symmetrical *and* the same for both partners (albeit with a phase delay). This limits the dances that can be done but makes them nearly gender-neutral.

Each of these solutions corresponds to a solution to the problem of how to court one's own sex:

- You can find a way to court without using the ordinary signals. This is difficult, but sometimes it happens; take out a personals ad, say, or just walk up to people you find attractive and ask them to go home with you.
- You can declare yourself butch or femme and stick to it. This is, allegedly, the old-fashioned solution.
- You can learn both aspects and apply each as the mood strikes you. This is the most common modern solution; among lesbians, it used to be called being "kiki."
- You can restrict yourself to the parts of the courtship sequence that are not particularly sex-dimorphic: small talk, eye contact, synchronization, and so on. This is probably also a common modern solution, and it need not conflict with the previous strategy.

Each of these possibilities suggests that homosexuals just coming out have to master some unconscious techniques that heterosexuals face far less often in our society. There are, presumably, mix-ups that can occur when young homosexuals don't understand that certain behaviors constitute signals with meanings in courtship. The same mix-ups can occur, of course, with heterosexuals, but most heterosexuals have dealt with them at younger ages (think of the Harvard-boy/Radcliffe-bitch dilemma I discussed above). And with homosexuals there are apparently a larger number of miscommunications that can occur.

But if, once you come out successfully, you adopt the strategy of understanding both sides of courtship (consciously or unconsciously), you are arguably better equipped to handle courtship than most heterosexuals are. This is an elaboration of the explanation I constructed in chapter 4 for the "technique puzzle" discovered by Masters and Johnson. Homosexuals who learn more than just a butch or a femme role will have succeeded in seeing *something*, at least, from the point of view of both partners in a relationship—and that may help mutual understanding both in and out of bed.

DISCUSSION

So is the grass greener on the other side of the fence or on yours? Everyone has problems with courtship, and almost everyone finds some way to solve them.[32] But certain problems show up more often in certain gender transpositions than in others.

For example, if I were to caricature heterosexuality by making one of its common problems universal, I'd cite the finding of the Hite report and of Masters and Johnson. Marriage, I'd say, is that state of bliss in which the man is supposed to know everything about sex, hasn't been taught anything about it, never asks his wife what she wants, but wishes that she would tell him. The wife is supposed to know nothing about sex, is blissfully ignorant about it, never tells her husband what she wants, but wishes he would ask.

To caricature homosexual men in a corresponding way, they are men who have relatively little trouble asking for what they *want* sexually but don't know what they *need* in the long-term-love department. Sometimes they get it, but it's a struggle. Likewise, I'd caricature lesbians as women who know exactly how to bond but don't know what they need in the genital-sex department. Sometimes they get it, but it takes time and luck.

These pessimistic views result from focusing on the problems within each group. What conclusions could we draw if we focused on their strengths?

Let's play matchmaker and create some ideal pairings that capitalize on those strengths. Obviously, what a heterosexual man needs is a wife willing to be explicitly sexual; a butch lesbian should do just fine. And what a heterosexual woman needs is a husband sensitive to his partner's sexual desires; sounds to me like an effeminate gay man would be a perfect match. Homosexual women and men, on the other hand, should obviously get married to each other, since each is strong in the other one's weak spot.

Isn't the study of courtship fascinating?

This matchmaking exercise leads to an important suggestion: court-

---

[32] Even if you choose celibacy, you've got to deal with so-called particular friendships. I'll bet that the celibate get courted even if no genital sexuality is ever involved.

ship is not necessarily going to result in bliss. Heterosexual men and women, in particular, have different *reproductive strategies* that reflect the fact that they have different reproductive interests. If each kind of person is designed to carry out those strategies well, then bliss may have to be sacrificed at the altar. This conclusion will displease the romantics among my readership, but it will not surprise sociobiologists like Donald Symons[33] (nor crypto-sociobiologists like James Thurber), who argue that conflict and competition are inevitable concomitants of reproduction. This suggestion will be very important in the next two chapters.

Biology, Courtship, and the Social Sciences

The study of courtship has the potential not only to help us understand human sexuality but also to rectify certain antifemale biases in the social sciences. Perper claims that social-science theories of courtship have been male biased because they imply that women are passive objects of the power and courtship of men and antibiological because they imply that biology has little to say about courtship in humans. This is a strong and controversial statement, but Perper supported it well—for example, by pointing out that biologists have always been interested in female choice and proceptivity, in humans as well as in animals, and that few if any modern sociobiologists have ever assumed that females are sexually passive. (This is not to imply, of course, that sexism is absent in biology.) Perper believes, as I do, that the nature-nurture dichotomy is a false one, and the fact that so many social scientists still implicitly endorse it is unfortunate. Perper claims, in fact, that this division between nature and nurture mirrors the division of female versus male: social scientists assert, incorrectly, that nurture can win out over nature in all but the most extreme cases and that men win out over women in a similar proportion of cases. Perhaps not surprisingly, then, social scientists have studied nurture to the exclusion of nature and male power in courtship to the exclusion of female power.

Perper's courtship studies have also noted that while women's sexuality is public, positively reinforced, and referred to with simple, direct terms, men usually cannot refer to their sexuality publicly without negative reinforcement; even in private men often use terms that are indirect, sometimes cryptic. Marriages and bridal showers are public, legitimate affairs; the stag party is relatively private and shameful. *Sev-*

---

[33] See Symons 1979.

enteen magazine has an advice column on human sexuality that uses the right words for all the sex organs and sex acts; *Boys' Life* does not, and if it did, it would cause an uproar. Women's pornography—erotic romance—is sold openly in bookstores across the country; men's pornography is sold illicitly in shady outlets or in ordinary stores that worry about whether they will be boycotted for carrying it. Radio sexologist Dr. Ruth Westheimer is female and has mostly female callers; a male sexologist giving the same advice would be much more controversial.

In short, women may or may not have more power than men in the sexual sphere, but they are *not* passive—not by a long shot! This conclusion echoes that of chapters 3 and 6: that women can definitely be aroused by sexually explicit stimuli. Both these facts run against the grain of conventional wisdom in our culture these days, but both are consistent with—some would say predicted by—modern evolutionary theory. So let us see if we can use evolutionary theory to make some predictions about other sexological phenomena that seem counterintuitive. In particular, let's see how the gender transpositions might have evolved by natural selection.

12

HOMOSEXUALITY IN ANIMALS

In principle, subordinate males acted like estrous females. True to form, and incapable of absorbing this realization at once, I called these actions of the rams *aggressosexual* behavior, for to state that the male had evolved a homosexual society was emotionally beyond me. To conceive of those magnificent beasts as "queers"—Oh God!

Geist 1975, p. 98.

[Regarding *Crepidula fornicata,* the slipper limpet, which permanently stacks several small males on top of large females:] . . . lest you begin to suspect that the topmost males might be condemned to a life of obligate homosexuality by virtue of their separation from the first large female, fear not. The male's penis is longer by far than its entire body and can easily slip around a few males to reach the females.

Stephen Jay Gould (August 1983) Sex and size.
Natural History 92:24–27.

Homosexual behavior has never been the main choice, or even a customary minor part of the sexual pattern, of any mammal living in the free state. The occasional mounting of male animals by other males—apes in particular—is not true homosexuality but is in part playful and learning behavior in the immature, and in part a way of avoiding violent fighting between two males. The weaker one signifies submissiveness by "presenting" his rear, the stronger signifies dominance by mounting and making a few routine penile thrusts without intromission or ejaculation. . . . Biologically, moreover, homosexuality is abnormal in the sense that no children can be born of it. It is true, of course, that even contraception is abnormal in this sense, but the heterosexual couple using contraception has it within their power to be fertile or not, as they choose; and even when they choose not to, they

282

are still employing the neural, hormonal and muscular responses of sexuality in the fashion which evolution, with the goal of reproduction, cunningly designed to provide maximum reward.

Hunt 1974, p. 299.

The dedication to environmentalism [in psychology] is not over. . . . The discussion sometimes sounds like a commercial for the point of view that nothing is really built in, but is the product of experience.

Lockard 1971.

After 14 years of continuous conditioning and observation of thousands of animals, it is our reluctant conclusion that the behavior of any species cannot be adequately understood, predicted, or controlled without knowledge of its instinctive patterns, evolutionary history, and ecological niche.

Breland and Breland 1961.

A aaah, Jamaica! Island of sunshine! Land of rum! Birthplace of reggae and Jimmy Cliff! And hotbed of homosexuality in lizards! Homosexuality in lizards?

Well, yes—if you define the term "homosexuality" in a particular way. I'll get to that in a while. But if there's homosexuality in lizards, there must be heterosexuality in lizards, right?

Right; Jamaica is also a hotbed of heterosexuality in lizards. My Ph.D. thesis adviser, Robert Trivers, studied heterosexuality in a species of lizard there *(Anolis garmani)* for his own Ph.D. thesis. Along the way, he made an important sexological discovery. It's the purpose of this chapter to discuss homosexuality (on which there is the most evidence) and all the other gender transpositions as they occur in animals and to make comparisons with humans where appropriate.

But why bother with animals at all? Why go as far away as Jamaica in our travels across the sexual landscape? The answer is that animals constitute an excellent testing ground for theories of human sexuality. Do you claim that the human incest taboo results exclusively from culture and socialization? If so, you'll have trouble explaining how and why animals often go out of their way to avoid incestuous matings. Do you claim that human homosexuality evolved by natural selection? If so, and if the reason you postulate for its evolution also applies to animals, then you'd better be able to find animals behaving homosexually in similar circumstances.

Let me begin by discussing why Trivers was studying lizard heterosexuality. Orthodox evolutionist that he was, Trivers went to Jamaica to study reproductive success. Since heterosexual copulations in *Anolis garmani* take place in full view—on the trunks of trees, in fact—they were easy to count. And so this species seemed to be a good one in which to study reproductive success.

Here's how heterosexuality works in that species. When the lizards hatch, baby females and males are about the same size, but males grow faster. Females stop growing when they reach about 9 centimeters in length (3.5 inches), but males keep growing up to about 13 centimeters (5.2 inches). Adult females loosely defend small territories (home ranges, actually) in trees—several females per tree if the tree is large. The biggest males defend large territories consisting of an entire tree or a few trees located near each other. Small males—those still small enough to be female sized—often live inside the territory of a larger male, but once they grow large enough to be easily distinguished from females, they leave to stake out a tree of their own.

Heterosexual copulations take place at the initiative of the female, who only mates once a month—once for each egg she develops. When it's time for fertilization, she moves down onto the tree trunk in full view and adopts a distinctive posture. The resident male approaches her, then copulates with her for approximately twenty-five minutes.

Dedicated as he was to reproductive success in the interests of science, Trivers wanted (I presume) to observe every heterosexual lizard copulation in his study area. But of course there were limits to what he actually could observe; he couldn't be next to every tree trunk every minute of every day. And so he got scouts to find lizards copulating, snare them, and bring them to him for identification.

Interestingly enough, twice during Trivers's study the two lizards caught copulating were not male and female but male and male. Both times this happened, the male on top was the large territory holder for the tree he was found in, the male underneath was a small male already living within the larger male's territory, and intromission had been achieved. Trivers interpreted this to mean that by acting like a female, the smaller male may be getting the advantages of living in a tree near females: an occasional heterosexual copulation, perhaps, and access to the food in a particular territory, which may be associated with faster growth. Trivers wasn't sure the larger male knew the smaller individual was not female. It was as if, wrote Trivers, an "occasional buggery might be a small price to pay for the advantages of remaining within the large male's territory."[1]

[1] Trivers 1976, p. 266.

The first time a male-male pair was found, the two were copulating in an unusual spot: not on the tree trunk but on a small branch less than two inches thick, hidden among the leaves. A local naturalist had never seen this happening and told Trivers that this must have gone on because these two lizards, like humans, "maybe were ashamed" of what they were doing. Unfortunately for that hypothesis, the second male-male copulation took place right out there on the trunk.[2]

Now how can homosexuality be a decadent human trait if those lizards are doing it, too? Trivers found those male lizards copulating with other male lizards shamefully or shamelessly (as the case may be), oblivious to natural law. And doing it right out there in nature! What's going on here?

Well, maybe this lizard behavior wasn't *true* homosexuality. After all, the males on top were later seen copulating heterosexually. At the very worst, perhaps all we had here was bisexuality, or maybe even a simple case of mistaken identity. And anyway, why would this have anything to do with human homosexuality or the other gender transpositions? After all, a famous biology professor at Harvard (not Trivers, of course) says that it's ridiculous that people would think that they could understand humans by studying how monkeys go around (and I quote) "sitting on their asses"—and he's famous and at Harvard, so we ought to pay attention, right?

In this chapter and the next I'll use *sociobiology*—the study of human and animal behavior from the point of view of its evolution by natural selection—to answer questions about the gender transpositions. But first, since many people have misconceptions about sociobiology, I'll have to explain what sociobiologic models are and are not. Then I'll give more examples of gender-transposition behavior in animals. It turns out that these examples can help us explain the "technique puzzle" mentioned in chapter 3 in a different way than I hypothesized in chapter 4. In chapter 13, I'll describe more theoretical models sociobiologists can use to explain human homosexuality.

MISCONCEPTIONS

There are three misconceptions about sociobiology that I first want to clear up: the myth that it is biologically deterministic, the idea that it is just a series of generalizations and not a true theory, and the notion that it denies the importance of human learning and culture.

[2]The local naturalist would later become Trivers's mother-in-law, so I should point out that her remark was delivered with warm laughter.

Biological Determinism

Biological determinism is the idea that behavior is controlled by genes in a gross and inflexible way. For example, if one of a pair of identical twins is homosexual, a biologically deterministic theory would insist that the other twin be homosexual, too. It's the first thing some people think of when they hear of a biological theory. That's a shame, because it's been years, if not decades, since "biological" has meant "biologically deterministic."

Trivers's parental investment (PI) theory, which I described in chapter 11, is sometimes described as biologically deterministic. It's not. Most sociobiologists, Trivers included, think of behavior as the result of an adaptive *interaction* between the environment and genes that predispose people to do different things in different environments. So they're genuinely puzzled when this very reasonable position is seen as biological determinism. Here, for example, is the opinion of Peter Ellison, a sociobiological anthropologist at Harvard, writing in *Ethology and Sociobiology*.[3]

[Anthropologist F. Boas and his students] helped to reject . . . an incorrect application of evolutionary theory to human behavior, an application that equates "inherited" with "fixed" and "unresponsive to environmental differences." The modern [sociobiological] view suggests that what is inherited is more like a complex equation relating behavior to social and ecological conditions . . . [and which is] probably the common heritage of all members of the species. . . . This is in a conceptual sense very close to Boas' notion of "universal human nature."

Notice that Ellison, a sociobiologist writing for other sociobiologists, *takes it for granted* that today's biological theories are not deterministic, although those in Boas's time were. This is exactly what I was taught as a graduate student and exactly what I read in the writings of every sociobiologist whom I respect. Modern sociobiological theories are only as biologically deterministic as the data require them to be—and usually, that's not much.

[3] Ellison 1984, p. 69.

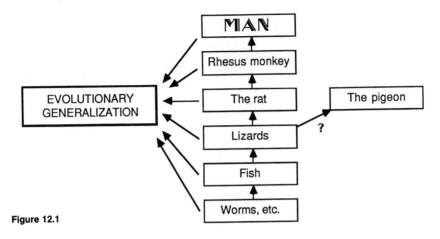

Figure 12.1

Evolutionary Theory: Not Just Generalizations

Some people think that evolution is hierarchical—that there is an evolutionary ladder, with slugs and worms and other slimy things down at the bottom and Man at the top (see fig. 12.1).[4]

In this view, it is *phylogeny*—evolutionary descent—that is used to make generalizations. Suppose you have a hypothesis: that males tend to have more sexual partners than females do. To test this phylogenetically, you would watch copulations in various groups of animals and hope you could find some generalization that applied in all the branches. Your first investigations would be at the bottom of the ladder; then you'd move to reptiles and amphibians, and so on up to Man.[5]

Let's say you succeeded in showing that in most of these groups of animals, males really did have more sex partners than females did. Your next step would be to look for a mechanism. You might try to show that exposure to testosterone develops brain circuits that cause an animal to enjoy novel sexual partners. If you found this mechanism operating in the so-called lower animals, you might cross your fingers and hope that it was true in Man, too. But the strategy boils down to the hope that Men will act like animals do because they and the animals had common ancestors.

Figure 12.1 presents this strategy as a caricature. It's got problems, because you can never be sure you've studied enough rungs of the ladder and because the application to humans depends on an extrap-

[4] I derived the chart from an argument appearing in Lockard 1971.

[5] You will recall that everyone was called Man back then, regardless of whether they were male or female. And Man is very special, so I've put him into the chart in a special typeface. The question mark on the chart refers to the fact that birds are a side branch on the evolutionary tree leading to Man, and so it's not clear what their role is in the study of human beings.

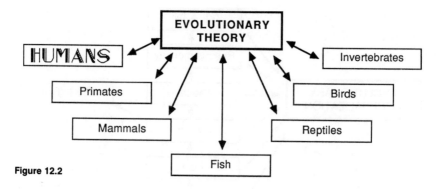

Figure 12.2

olation from the lower rungs of the ladder to the highest rung. Extrapolations are always risky.[6]

But sociobiologists are not as interested in phylogeny as they are in the *ultimate logic* of the behaviors under study. In sociobiology, there is no ladder of evolution and no need to depend only on species closely related to each other. Since it's the *logic* of the theory that is being tested, a theory can be applied to many species across the animal kingdom. A good theory explains why it makes sense for particular conditions of life to have particular evolutionary results. So distantly related species can be similar in some logical way that tests a critical component of the theory.

Notice that it is evolutionary theory that occupies the exalted position in figure 12.2.[7] Here, applying a theory to humans is not an extrapolation but an interpolation. In some sense, the human case is *surrounded* by various groups of animals that differ from humans in particular ways. Although interpolations can be wrong, they are usually more accurate than extrapolations are.

Trivers's PI theory (see chapter 11) uses logic in this second way. Females and males in a species invest various amounts in their offspring; the relative ratio of investment on the part of females as opposed to males determines much of that species' mating system. Nowhere does Trivers say that humans are the way they are because our close relatives—chimpanzees—sit on their asses (or do anything else) in a particular way. Instead, Trivers says that chimps and humans would be similar (or different) in their mating systems only if they had similar (or different) PI ratios.

---

[6] However, this point of view really is valid in medicine, in physiology, and wherever you care about the underlying mechanics of behavior. Diseases, for example, can follow phylogenetic lines, and so do some hormonal mechanisms. So I don't want to suggest that this view is always wrong; it's just wrong for our purposes.

[7] Since we Humans are still pretty special, I've kept the special typeface.

PI theory is gender-neutral. Although usually it is females that invest more in offspring than males, this is not always the case. In species in which females invest less than males, females should be the ones that have more sexual partners, and this seems to be so. In species in which males and females invest about the same—humans, for example, and most birds—the difference in number of partners is expected to be fairly small and to be subtly influenced by the environment.

As I discussed earlier, Trivers's theory says nothing about hormones or brains. A phylogenetic approach, remember, would have us chasing down testosterone or some other proximate cause. But sociobiologists don't care much about testosterone, because by itself it's not the ultimate cause of anything. God did not say, "Let there be testosterone and let it be the cause of things." Instead, Darwin said, "Let there be light thrown upon sexual selection," and testosterone was one of the resulting mechanisms. The logic, not the genetics, is what's being studied.

Learning, Culture, and All That Good Stuff

In order for the logic of a theory like Trivers's to work, you *do* need to understand the role of genetics—but only a little bit of genetics. In particular, you only need to conclude that behavior can be influenced by genes that predispose those behaviors, at least in a probabilistic sense over evolutionary time.

But what about socialization? What about culture? Don't they override genetic predispositions? After all, men are genetically predisposed to grow hair on their faces, but most American men override that predisposition every morning by performing an unnatural act called "shaving."

I don't have the space to give this point the attention it deserves. But I will point out studies that answer this question directly.[8] This point of view says that the laws of learning are *not* universal; they have patterns, and these patterns are exactly what one would expect from evolutionary theory.

Animals, including humans, are *predisposed* to do particular things in response to particular kinds of stimuli—sometimes very strongly predisposed:

---

[8] This school consists of the predisposition-in-learning work of people like John Garcia, Martin Seligman, Paul Rozin, and James Kalat. For a good summary, see Lockard 1971.

- It is easy to get pigeons to peck at a button that results in their getting food. But it is extremely difficult to get them to peck at a button in order to prevent themselves from getting electric shock.
- It is easy to teach cats to pull or push on something set up to open a door that is keeping them confined in a box. But it is extremely difficult to get them to lick themselves, if that is what is set up to open the door.
- It is easy to teach rats to avoid a stomach-upsetting X-ray dose by avoiding a certain *flavor* of food; it is nearly impossible to teach them to avoid the X ray by avoiding a certain *size or shape* of food.[9]
- If you try to teach rats to choose, when presented with a set of similar items, the item that differs from the others, they can't make the proper selection when the items are pictures. But they do just fine if you give them the same kind of puzzle where the odd-man-out item differs in odor. Humans can easily choose the odd man out when the choices are pictures, but they don't do at all well with odors.
- Horses and donkeys do a lot better than zebras do in most visual discriminations, but zebras do much better telling apart stripes of different widths.[10]
- As you'll recall from chapter 10, when newly hatched chicks are shocked every time they approach their mother, they try harder and harder to reach her instead of staying away to avoid the shock.[11]

All these predispositions make sense if you ask what functions these behaviors served in the evolutionary history of the species. Throughout their evolutionary history, pigeons have gotten food by pecking, but pecking has rarely if ever gotten them away from danger. Cats have never escaped from something by licking themselves; they have gotten out by manipulating objects in their environment. Rats are experts at avoiding poisons, for obvious reasons, but they connect the size or shape of food with its feel, not its taste. Stripes are a very important part of the visual environment of zebras but not of horses and donkeys. And any chick that permits a noxious stimulus to keep it from reaching its mother doesn't survive to pass on any genes predisposing it to do so.

[9] For these three studies, see Seligman 1970.
[10] For these two studies, see Kalat 1983.
[11] For details, see Kovach and Hess 1963.

We humans have our own set of evolutionary sensible predispositions. Four-month-old infants categorize colors according to the same wavelength boundaries adults use, and some of these boundaries are cross-cultural universals.[12] Humans have an extraordinarily strong predisposition to learn a language. Deaf children will start to create their own sign language if they are not taught one.[13] Immigrant children of parents speaking unrelated languages can construct a new language (a *creole* language) with predictable and universal linguistic properties—even though they and everyone else in their environment have neither heard nor spoken such a language.[14] Language learning goes through specific stages that are cross-cultural universals, even down to the details of what kinds of mistakes are made at what stages. Children learn the language of their environment and acquire the accent their neighbors speak—not the accent their parents speak. All this happens with no formal language training whatsoever; not even yuppies buy books telling them how to get their kids to *Start Speaking Sooner*.[15]

It turns out not only that behavior is genetically influenced in all species but that humans are apparently an ordinary mammalian species with respect to the rough percentage of our behavior that is genetically influenced, predisposed, or controlled. Admittedly, this hypothesis has not been tested as extensively as it has been in animals—it can't be—but tested it has been.[16] The best tests involve normal brothers and sisters adopted at birth into different families; there are also some good studies of men with abnormal chromosome conditions.[17] Both kinds of study demonstrate beyond any reasonable doubt that there are genetic influences in normal and abnormal human behavior.[18] In fact, I believe it is the case that whenever definitive studies such as these have been done, *some* genetic influences have always been found, although not always the ones that had been hypothesized

[12] Bornstein 1975; Bornstein, Kessen, and Weiskopf 1976.

[13] Goldin-Meadow and Mylander 1977; Goldin-Meadow and Feldman 1977.

[14] Bickerton 1983.

[15] The literature on biological predispositions in language is enormous. Here are some good starting points: Alcock 1984, pp. 101ff.; Chomsky 1976; Bickerton 1983.

[16] Wilson 1978 and Konner 1982 are good summaries of the evidence.

[17] A few of these studies are Kety et al. 1975, Mednick et al. 1984, Goodwin et al. 1973 and 1974, Schiavi et al. 1984, Witkin et al. 1976, and Bohman 1978.

[18] I say "any *reasonable* doubt" because of course there will always be some who arrange their beliefs to suit their predetermined conclusions. However, even a group as radically environmentalistic as the Sociobiology Study Group of Science for the People [Boston] finally admitted that the schizophrenia studies using children adopted at birth do indicate a genetic predisposition for schizophrenia. And so has left-wing population geneticist professor Richard Lewontin. (See Sociobiology Study Group 1977, p. 142, and Lewontin's comments on p. 3 of the *Harvard Gazette*, 16 January 1976.)

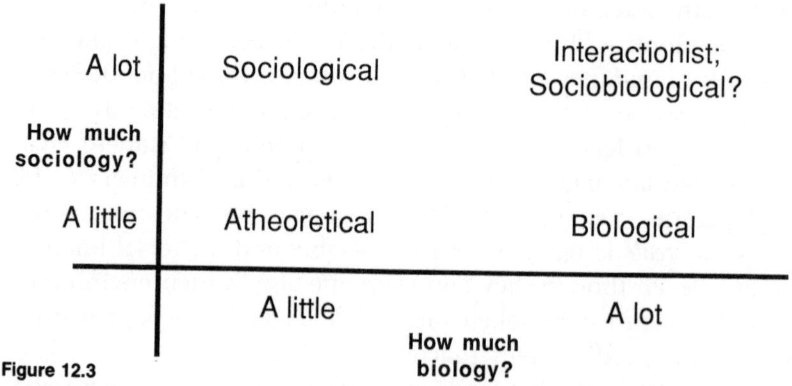

	Sociological	Interactionist; Sociobiological?

Figure 12.3

in advance. That is not always the case, however, for environmental factors; for example, one study of alcoholism running in families found evidence of a genetic factor, but no evidence of an environmental factor, in the familial component.[19]

Just like masculine and feminine, homosexual and heterosexual, I like to see nature and nurture—or biology and sociology—as a two-dimensional grid. Any given theory can be given a rating as to how biological it is and a separate rating as to how sociological it is. *More biology in a theory doesn't necessarily mean less sociology,* and vice versa. That means we can divide theories into four categories—biologically typed theories, sociologically typed theories, interdisciplinary or sociobiological theories, and atheoretical theories (see fig. 12.3).

Now some disciplines may enjoy pushing theories in a particular direction. Biologists may want to push theories farther along the biology axis; sociologists, along the sociology axis. That's fine; the result may be a well-rounded interdisciplinary theory. But some people act as if biology and sociology were opposites: as if a lot of biology in a theory means that there isn't any sociology in it or as if a theory with no sociology in it can't get some without first throwing out any biology it might already have. That's not so. The theories I present in this chapter and in the next are both biological and sociological in their assumptions.

So let's get on with them; you now have enough background to avoid falling into the most common traps faced by beginning biologists. In this chapter I'll discuss the gender transpositions in animals

[19]This study did *not* show that environment is unimportant in the development of alcoholism. What it showed was that when alcoholism runs in a family, "the thing that makes it run in families" is mostly or entirely genetic; if there is something environmental that "makes it run in families," that component is too small to be detected in the population studied. See Goodwin et al. 1974.

(especially homosexuality, upon which the most work has been done) and compare them to similar human behaviors. In chapter 13, I'll explain sociobiological models of the gender transpositions in humans.

HOMOSEXUALITY IN ANIMALS

Does it make any sense to talk about homosexuality in animals? Rather than give you the evidence first and the conclusions later, let me get right to the point: yes, it does *if* you believe it makes sense to talk about heterosexuality in animals. After all, animals and humans are alike in some ways, different in others. There is no animal species with a pattern of homosexuality that is *exactly* like the human pattern of homosexuality. But the same is true about heterosexuality. For almost any aspect of human sexuality, there is some animal species somewhere with a sexual pattern that resembles humans pretty closely in that aspect. Below I give a series of examples that show this for homosexuality.

But first some definitions. *Sexual relations* consist of all the acts by which two or more animals (including humans) arouse each other sexually. Acts in which one animal is aroused and the other is not are not sexual *relations*, strictly speaking, although they are in a loose sense. (Perhaps one could say that the one being aroused is involved in sexual relations but the unaroused one is not.) *Sexual intercourse* (or just plain *intercourse*) consists of sexual relations in which a penis or penis substitute is inserted into an orifice of the partner's body; it includes vaginal intercourse, oral intercourse, and anal intercourse. *Coitus*[20] consists of the act of sexual intercourse in which a penis is put into a vagina.

Now we can define homosexual behavior in animals unambiguously. *Homosexual behavior* is any act of sexual relations in which a female is aroused by a female or a male is aroused by a male. *Heterosexual behavior* is an act of sexual relations in which a female is aroused by a male and vice versa. These two terms, at least, are unambiguous. We could, if we wished, go on to define *homosexuality in animals* and *heterosexuality in animals* as everything having to do with the phenomenon of homosexual behavior and heterosexual behavior, respectively, in a given species. These last two terms are less precise, but

[20]This strictly limited usage of the term *coitus* is, I believe, its original meaning, although nowadays most dictionaries define it to be synonymous with "intercourse." But there is no point in having two words with exactly the same meaning. So according to my definition, "vaginal coitus" is redundant, and "anal coitus" and "oral coitus" are self-contradictory. "Coitus," by the way, has three syllables, and is pronounced COE-it-us. The process of performing coitus is called *coition* (coe-IH-shun), and the adjective is *coital* (COE-it-ull).

they are valid in a loose sense. Later I will come back to the question of just how valid they are.

A Dominance Pattern of Homosexual Behavior

A lot of the homosexual behavior seen in animals is related to dominance. So, not incidentally, is a lot of the heterosexual behavior. Mountain sheep, for example, have a reproductive pattern in which mounting for sexual intercourse is indistinguishable from mounting to show dominance.[21]

Many animals form a *dominance hierarchy*—a "pecking order" in which each animal in a group acts as if it knows who would defeat whom in a fight. In many mammals, individuals winning a dominance dispute display their new status by mounting the loser in a way that looks like sexual intercourse.

In mountain sheep, there is an important sense in which the dominance mount not only resembles sexual intercourse, but *is* sexual intercourse. That is, when two males fight and one wins, the winner gets an erection, mounts the loser, and thrusts away. (Intromission is an open question.) And when a male mounts a female during the rutting season, he gets an erection, mounts her, and thrusts away (with intromission if the female permits it).

Now some people have said that this kind of homosexual behavior—male mounting male—is not really sexual; it's *merely* dominance. Well, they are correct when they say it is dominance, but does that mean it's not sexual? Do you happen to know of anyone who enjoys taking control in a sexual interaction and gets sexually excited when she or he is able to do so? Do you happen to know of anyone who enjoys giving herself or himself to another person sexually and whose arousal is heightened by the knowledge that the other partner is, well, dominant?

Of course you do. But one of the reasons why people are reluctant to call mountain-sheep dominance mounts "sexual" is that they seem so extreme—so perfunctory and so apparently devoid of consent on the part of the mounted one (although that is, frankly, an open question). And to that extent, they're right.

The pattern of homosexual behavior seen in mountain sheep is similar to the pattern of human homosexual behavior seen in prisons. If I'm dominant over you, I mount you, and you don't have much choice in the matter. Of course, neither pattern is "the same" as the ordinary

---

[21] See, for example, Geist 1975.

pattern of homosexuality we're used to thinking of in humans. The point is, sex and dominance are not opposites; sexual intercourse *can* involve both at once.

And so it is that "mountain-sheep homosexuality" is rather similar to "mountain-sheep heterosexuality," imprecise though these terms may be. Mountain-sheep homosexuality is, however, different in that it does not proceed as often (or possibly ever) to ejaculation.

An Age-Biased Pattern

Now think back to the case of homosexual behavior in lizards that began this chapter. Believe it or not, it bears at least a moderate resemblance to the kind of homosexuality observed in ancient Greece and in many other societies: the age-biased pattern described in chapter 2.[22]

Recall that the age-biased pattern of homosexuality does not prevent heterosexual reproduction in adulthood. In fact, it can help a younger male get ahead in life, perhaps helping him to marry well by becoming successful and hence a more attractive husband. The older and younger men form an alliance, the bond being maintained in the ultimate sense by the benefits each partner gains from it and in the proximate sense by their being in love.

Now if a reputable sociobiologist believes—as one does—that subordinate males hang around a lek in order, in part, to learn how successful males court females and defend territories, then perhaps small male lizards hang around in the territories of large males not only to steal an occasional copulation from a neighboring female but also to learn how to court females and defend territories—and maintain alliances with dominant males in order to do so. It is not immediately clear what return benefit the larger male would gain from this strategy—the mere pleasure of sexual arousal being a big fat zero in terms of reproductive success—but several possibilities come to mind. Perhaps the younger one helps out from time to time in territory defense if threatened by other males. Or perhaps it would be too costly to kick the smaller one out; only when he became big enough to constitute a bigger threat would it be worth doing so. The possibility that the territory holder is just plain "fooled" and thinks the small male is a female is certainly a possibility, but one we should pursue at a later stage of analysis. Recall Drury's first law of animal behavior (chapter

---

[22] It was Paul Larson, a psychologist in Ohio, who suggested this crazy possibility to me. At first, I dismissed it out of hand, but the more I thought about it, the more sense it made. It may not be right, but it's a great hypothesis in the tradition of chapter 10.

11); we won't find adaptive explanations if we don't look for them.

And so it is that *"Anolis*-lizard homosexuality" is rather similar to *"Anolis*-lizard heterosexuality," imprecise though these terms may be. *Anolis*-lizard homosexuality may be different, however, in that it every now and then does not take place in the location (on the tree trunk) typically used in *Anolis*-lizard heterosexuality.

A Cross-Gender Pattern

There are several species in which individuals can obtain benefits usually not associated with members of their own sex by taking on the role of the other sex. Below I'll describe a case in insects; another (in fish) is described at the beginning of chapter 13.

University of New Mexico entomologist Randy Thornhill studies hanging flies, a species of insect that eats other insects. Flying around to catch their prey is very dangerous for these flies, because they can get caught in spiderwebs. Male-male competition results in males competing for access to females by offering them dead insects as an inducement to copulate—a *nuptial gift* that reduces the amount of dangerous flying that females otherwise would have to do. Typically, a male captures an insect, then hangs from a branch and emits a come-and-get-it scent (a *pheromone*). A female detects the scent, then zeroes in on the dead insect; she hangs nearby, holds on from the side opposite the male, and sucks the prey's body fluids while the male holds on to his side. Just before starting to consume the prey, however, the female performs a wing-drooping *invitational* pattern: an invitation to copulate. The male bends his genitalia around underneath, and if the prey is large enough, the female permits copulation for as long as the food lasts.[23]

But sometimes the individual performing the wing-drooping invitational pattern is not a female at all but is rather another male. In this case, the second male feeds for a bit but bends his genitalia *away* from the one that caught the prey.[24] Eventually, a fight ensues, and sometimes the interloper is the one who wins. He either consumes the insect himself or turns around and uses it himself to attract a female.

And so it is that "hanging-fly homosexuality" is rather similar to "hanging-fly heterosexuality," imprecise though these terms may be. Hanging-fly homosexuality is different, however, in that the individual performing the invitational pattern will not always become sex-

---

[23] At a certain maximum point—when further sperm transfer would fertilize no more eggs—the copulation stops. See Thornhill 1976, p. 533, and 1979.

[24] In order, I presume, to avoid buggery.

ually aroused. Indeed, if only one member in this case is sexually aroused, then this interaction if only partly homosexual. Or perhaps this interaction is better termed, on the part of the pirate male, "hanging-fly transvestism," because he is acting so as to be taken in the role of a female.[25]

Some Pair-Bonding Patterns

Perhaps the most obvious aspect of human homosexuality thought to differ from the homosexual behavior seen in animals is that of preference. Human homosexuals *prefer* sexual relations with a member of their own sex even when the other sex is available, and this does not seem to be so in the cases of animal homosexual behavior I've described so far—at least for some of the participants. So what about pair-bonds? Are there animals in which males or females are sexually aroused by members of their own sex and stay with a particular partner over a period of time, even in the presence of available members of the other sex?

The answer is yes, this is true in birds—the species in which heterosexual pair-bonds exist—and in primates, especially in the context of friendship (see below). I'll discuss the bird examples in this section.

Homosexual pair-bonds have been reported in birds for over a century. The reports are frequent,[26] and some of them describe entirely free-living individuals that had a choice between same- and opposite-sexed partners.[27] The most recent observations were carefully made

[25] Thornhill 1979 cites a definition of "transvestism," taken from Webster's, consistent with the use of the term in animals. His usage differs, however, from the more sexological one used in this book.

[26] The "father" of German ethology, Konrad Lorenz, has talked about male-male pair-bonds in his greylag geese for years (Desmond Morris, personal communication, March 1976; see also Evans 1974). A zoologist in Washington reported that two male geese (of different species: a Canada goose and a snow goose) pair-bonded back in 1968 in an artificially maintained breeding colony (Starkey 1972). A 1959 report mentioned female-female and male-male pairs in Canada geese confined in seminatural conditions (Collias and Jahn 1959). Craig 1909 mentioned how the behavior of doves, including their vocalizations, can in captivity cause a male to act like a female.

[27] In 1885, a bird-watcher in England, near Notts, reported that two swans built nests near his home but laid eggs in them so quickly that they must both have been female (Whitaker 1885). They stayed together for at least that breeding season, and one of them from time to time "performed the duty of the male." In 1923, in Renfrewshire, two male mute swans were observed to be pair-bonded and were photographed nesting together (Ritchie 1926). On occasions in 1938 and 1940, a Baltimore bird-watcher noticed two rock doves who each mounted the other and who each crouched to invite being mounted; this suggested that they were both male or both female. It was not obvious whether these two observations were of the same pair of birds or not (see Brackbill 1941). Homosexual courtship (not returned in kind) was observed in wild ostriches (which are not monogamous) in

and reported by behavioral biologists in the modern era. For example, in 1977, George and Molly Hunt, at the University of California at Irvine, reported female-female pairs in wild populations of Western gulls in southern California—pairings that lasted through the 1975 breeding season and, in seven of eight cases, lasting into the 1976 breeding season.[28] They followed this observation up with several subsequent studies.[29] It turned out that female-female pairs were rather common in wild populations of two other shorebird species: ring-billed gulls and California gulls.[30] Although the causes of all this homosexual behavior are still not well understood, one thing is clear: preferential homosexual behavior is indeed observed in natural, free-living populations of some animals.

And so it is that "avian homosexuality" is rather similar to "avian heterosexuality"—imprecise though these terms may be—because they both tend to involve pair-bonding. It is, however, different in that each partner sometimes adopts positions and performs acts that are not the same as those in the typical heterosexual sequence. Some birds, for example, perform the acts associated with both males and females, and in others both birds seemed to respond perfectly well to signals they normally send rather than those they normally receive.

Some Friendship Patterns

Homosexual behavior also shows up in contexts that are less exclusive than a pair-bonding pattern but more than just incidental interactions between acquaintances. For lack of a better term, I will call these contexts "friendship," and stress that they involve not just homosexual but also heterosexual relations.[31] Most of these examples involving homosexual relations take place in primates.

If you want to see some great drawings of what monkeys can do with each other sexually, check out the papers on stump-tailed ma-

---

South Africa in 1969 (see Sauer 1972). And a single female-female pair was observed in a group of zebra finches in an aviary in 1979 (see Burley 1981, and a criticism by Immelmann, Hailman, and Baylis 1982). Zebra finches are famous, by the way, for "pseudomale" and "pseudofemale" behavior; see Desmond Morris 1954 and 1955.

[28] You may have seen these so-called lesbian sea gulls in editorial cartoons and newspaper columns circa 1978 and 1979. I remember one cartoon in which Anita Bryant, then engaged in an effort to repeal a gay rights law in Dade County, Florida, was looking angrily up at a flock of gulls overhead, wiping something out of her eye.

[29] Hunt and Hunt 1977; Hunt 1980; Hunt et al. 1980, Wingfield et al. 1980a and 1980b.

[30] Ryder and Somppi 1979; Conover, Miller, and Hunt 1979.

[31] A recent book on friendship and sexuality in baboons (Smuts 1985) was written by University of Michigan primatologist Barbara Smuts. This book, I believe, justifies once and for all the use of the term "friendship" in animals.

caques.[32] These drawings will disabuse you forever of the notion that the only reports of homosexuality in monkeys are "really" just dominance mounts (admittedly common in primates) or are between animals that don't know what sex their partners are. One drawing (made from a photograph) shows two male monkeys bending over, rear end to rear end, so that *each* is presenting to the other![33] Moreover, each male is reaching between the legs of the other and manipulating the other's penis. (The same mutual presenting behavior has been described between males, and between females, in another monkey, bonnet macaques, in which it has never been seen in male-female couples.)[34] To put it mildly, this is clearly not a perfunctory dominance mount. Another drawing shows a small male climbing up the hindquarters of a large male, pulling the penis of the large male backward and sucking on it; good luck to you, too, if you try to interpret that one in dominance terms.

You might also want to observe the photographs and drawings of female homosexual behavior in rhesus monkeys, the favorite laboratory primate, studied by Jean Akers, a research associate with the Metropolitan Boston Zoos, and Clinton Conaway, then the director of a primate research laboratory in Puerto Rico (now retired). These female monkeys had homosexual relations not only in a position closely approximating the ordinary heterosexual one but also in about five other positions not usually seen in heterosexual interactions. The monkeys seemed to have favorite partners, and sexual behavior seemed to depend less on dominance status than on what stage the females were in the estrous cycle.[35] One female-female pair, for example, seemed to enjoy *ventral hugging,* in which the two hugged face-to-face and at the same time one of them rubbed her genitalia on her partner or on the ground.

> [Female] B1 usually initiated contact by badgering 4C. This included jumping up and down in front of her, pulling her tail, displacing her each time she sat down, and threatening her if she was with a male so they could resume contact. These females maintained a favorite corner of the cage for activity.[36]

[32] Chevalier-Skolnikoff 1974 and 1976.

[33] A *present,* as you'll recall from a previous chapter, is when one animal invites copulation with another by going over to it and presenting its rear end. It is often a signal of submission after losing a dominance fight, but it originated in sexual contexts.

[34] See Kaufman and Rosenblum 1966, p. 221.

[35] The mounter was usually in the follicular stage and the mountee in her ovulatory period. During the luteal phase, in contrast, such activity was low.

[36] Akers and Conaway 1979, p. 75.

In this case and in others, "females did show preference for each other over heterosexual mounting." Again, friendship was clearly involved in these relationships (as they also were in heterosexual interactions). Particular female pairs had various ways of soliciting sexual relations—"games," if you will.

In "hide and seek" the females took positions on either side of a tree and peeked at each other, moving slowly around the tree and keeping just outside each other's reach.

Other patterns were named "present and run," "follow the leader," "kiss and run," and—my favorite—"lipsmack and circle."[37]

Chevalier-Skolnikoff, Akers, and Conaway all saw behavior that strongly reminded them of orgasm in females. In the rhesus females, for example, several showed while mounting a pause "which resembled the male ejaculatory pause." Almost all of those mounted showed the "clutching reaction," reaching back with a hand to stimulate the mounter's genitalia, and usually turning the head around to look at her partner's face and lip smack. Some of the stump-tailed macaque females, too, showed a rigid-body pause that resembled orgasm.

There have been statements made that human females are the only animal females known to have orgasms. More rigorously, it's been stated that female orgasm had not been proved in any species other than humans. This is a good example of the pernicious "my methodology is holier than thine" attitude I complained about at the end of chapter 9. Some of these statements were made before any measurement devices were available that would permit the question to be settled conclusively. That means that no one should have denied orgasm in animal females; they really only ought to have said that the question was unsettled. And frankly, I think it would be fair to presume that female orgasm exists somewhere else in the animal kingdom; if we haven't proved it conclusively yet, then it's probably because of our own faults or oversights as investigators and not necessarily because it doesn't exist.[38] But can you imagine writing a grant proposal

---

[37] If all this talk of "games" strikes you as anthropomorphic, I urge you to look up the original paper, which is rigorously scientific. I have described the results informally, on purpose, to show you how similar acts would be described in humans. Remember that animals do play, that ethologists make entire reputations on being able to distinguish rigorously which acts constitute play and which do not, and so on.

[38] Remember Drury's second law of animal behavior: the student of behavior is assumed dumb until proved smart. In fact, the graveyard of the history of science is filled with the corpses of statements that took the form "Only humans do such-and-such" (only humans

asking some government agency for funds to study the question?[39]

Well, they can in the Netherlands. In fact, a research group in the Netherlands, joined by one American investigator, did such a study and published the results in *Science* in 1980. A group of six female stump-tailed macaques was observed in homosexual interactions of the sort described by Chevalier-Skolnikoff. One particular female seemed to have the highest frequency of behaviors (the round-mouthed face, etc.) that would signal ejaculation had they taken place in males. She was implanted with three battery-powered FM radio transmitters to send measurements of heartbeat and contractions of the uterus to an antenna (actually, the wire grid that constituted the cage). Then the experimenters placed her in the cage with the other five females and let nature take its course.

The implanted female seemed to have a favorite female partner, and on two occasions,

> the implanted female mounted her favorite partner and thrusted while continuously lip-smacking until the round-mouthed ejaculation face was displayed. . . .[40]

This female did indeed have an orgasm at precisely the time her face showed the round-mouthed expression, as judged from the recordings of the intense contractions of her uterus and sharp variations in her heartbeat. These are precisely the physiological events Masters and Johnson observe when women have orgasms.

Once that correlation was established, it could be presumed that other females had orgasms if they showed the same round-mouthed signs that this female consistently did. In heterosexual interactions, four females in a group of ten (caged with five males) showed the round-mouthed expression at least once. This happened in almost 20 percent of the heterosexual interactions, but there was a lot of variation; one female showed the round mouth almost 40 percent of the time.

So far, all the homosexual behavior in primates I've reported has

---

laugh; only humans plan; only humans kill members of their own species, etc.), and the only one that has proved true is that only humans use language. Frankly, given this empirical record, the burden of proof ought to be on those who state that animals don't do something, not on those who say they do.

[39] The very thought makes me shudder. After all, if the Kinsey and Hite statistics are to be believed, the committees judging such a proposal can be presumed to have many male members who don't even care if their wives have orgasms, not to mention whether female monkeys do.

[40] Goldfoot, Westerborg-van Loon, Groeneveld, and Slob 1980, p. 1478.

taken place in captivity, and it's not clear how relevant this is to natural selection in the wild. Akers and Conaway reported, for example, that their group of rhesus monkeys had adult males and females but only one infant, and they hinted, very indirectly, that had there been more infants, there might have been less female homosexual activity. However, any behavior that occurs in captivity is likely to occur in the wild—in a different context, perhaps, or at a very different frequency—and this indeed seems to be the case when we move on to reports of homosexual behavior in free-living animals.

For example, a group of investigators led by Cambridge (England) primatologist A. H. Harcourt has observed female-female sexual interactions in wild mountain gorillas. It was rare—ten occasions in 2,000 hours of observations of twenty animals—but it did happen. (How long, I wonder, would you have to watch twenty human beings before you saw two women having homosexual relations?) As in many captive primate colonies, most of the time the mounting seemed clearly related to the female's stage of the estrous cycle.[41] And in about one-third of the instances, the females interacted face-to-face rather than in the typical heterosexual position—again, just as in the captive colonies. Harcourt also observed some male-male homosexual behavior, although as of late 1980 its significance was obscure.[42]

Rhesus-monkey females have also been observed in homosexual interactions in the free-ranging troop living on Cayo Santiago Island, one of the classic study populations in primatology. Animal-behavior pioneer C. R. Carpenter helped establish the colony and then observed that

> Eight different females showed some type of homosexual behavior of varying degrees of strength. . . . The behavior varied from single and sporadic mountings in some cases to persisting association and repeated mounting series in the cases of [two pairs of females]. . . .[43]

Once again, this echoes reports of rhesus females pairing off in captivity.

Homosexual behavior among males has also been observed in wild-born monkeys. Oregon primatologist J. P. Hanby, more recently at the Serengeti Research Institute in Tanzania, reported male-male sexual

[41] See Harcourt, Stewart, and Fossey 1981; female-female behavior is also reported in Harcourt 1979, p. 255.

[42] Harcourt, letter of 11 November 1980.

[43] Carpenter 1942, p. 149.

mounting in Japanese macaques caught in Japan and brought to Oregon for observation. The monkeys captured had constituted a troop in Japan and had, of course, both male and female members. The different types of male-male mounts were too varied to generalize about except to say that not all the mounts were mere dominance mounts and not all of them could be considered purely sexual, either.[44] Hanby also noted that newly formed groups of monkeys always have high rates of sexual mounting, including homosexual mounting, and might have added that this is also true of newly *re*formed groups. In fact, the female Dutch monkeys mentioned above were separated and reunited regularly as part of the experimental procedures, and it wouldn't surprise me if this had been done specifically to elicit the highest frequency of sexual activities, because there are several reports of higher levels of homosexual relations in lab primates soon after groups are reunited.

Now I myself have observed, both in *Homo sapiens heterosexualis* and *Homo sapiens homosexualis,* that couples separated for periods of time often hop into each other's arms, and then into bed, as soon as possible after they are reunited. If I were a spoilsport, I would point out how methodologically holy I can be under the right circumstances. And I'd report that there is no evidence that this human "reuniting display" is truly sexual in nature; it may merely be caused by the artificial environment in which most humans choose to live. But I'm not that much of a spoilsport, and I accept these reports at face value.

There are more cases of male-male sexual behavior in the wild. Donald Sade, an anthropologist at Northwestern University, reported in his Ph.D. thesis the following observation of two male rhesus monkeys on Cayo Santiago.

Early in November [1965] EC copulated with IU. EC initiated the copulation, pushing IU from behind with both hands twice before IU stood up presenting. Then EC mounted and gave about five pelvic thrusts with anal penetration, followed by ejaculation, after only the single mounting.[45]

In a letter, Sade stressed that this behavior was rare, and that it was unlike heterosexual copulation in an important way. In primates, the pattern of mounting, thrusting, and ejaculation by the male varies sharply from species to species. Males often mount, dismount, and

---

[44] Hanby 1974.
[45] Sade 1966, p. 83. This interaction was mentioned briefly in Sade 1968, p. 27, but all the details were omitted.

remount a particular number of times (give or take a couple) before ejaculation occurs, the *particular* numbers and timing of the mounts, remounts, etc., being characteristic of the species. The case above took place, as it says, after only a single mounting, whereas heterosexual ejaculation in rhesus monkeys only happens after several mounts.

Carpenter, decades before, had also observed male-male interactions among the Cayo Santiago rhesus monkeys. He thought it may well have involved anal penetration, although he never saw ejaculation for certain and stated, like Sade, that the homosexual mounts were single mounts, not in series.[46]

By the way, these few reports are far from a complete list of the homosexual behavior of primates in the wild.[47]

And so it is that "primate homosexuality" is rather similar to "primate heterosexuality"—imprecise though these terms may be. Both types of behavior, for example, often include mounting and may sometimes be related to dominance and/or friendship. The two are, however, different in that the homosexual patterns usually include more inventive aspects or, in the case of females, higher rates of orgasm.

An "It Feels Good" Pattern

Manatees, sometimes called "sea cows," are mammals that live in the water off the shores of Florida. They look a bit like you'd expect sea cows to look: large, squishy, and peaceful, they eat vegetation and don't bother anyone except powerboat operators, who sometimes run over them accidentally. They were studied back in the 1960s by Daniel S. Hartman for his Ph.D. thesis at Cornell.[48]

Manatee heterosexuality depends a lot on hormones. When a female comes into heat, she is pursued by several males—"mobbed" might be a better word. When she finally accepts one for copulation, however, the result is idyllic by comparison: they begin copulating far beneath the surface of the water, with the female on top, and the male inserting from below. They rise to near the surface and then sink slowly as their bodies lose buoyancy.

Those other frustrated males, however, sometimes turn and have sexual relations with each other. Up to four males at a time were observed by Hartman engaging in various sexual activities with each other; there was usually erection and thrusting, and probably ejacu-

[46] Carpenter 1942.
[47] For further leads, consult Weinrich 1980a and 1982.
[48] See Hartman 1971 and 1979.

lation, too, although the water was too murky for him to be sure about the last possibility.[49] The most notable point is that the sexual activities between males were *always* quite unlike typical interactions between males and females: far more positions were used, and instead of being dead serious, the homosexual sexual activity seemed far more playful. It was almost certainly not dominance related; dominance fights were obvious in heterosexual courtship, as males butted against each other as they were trying to reach the female.

And so it is that "manatee homosexuality" is quite *un*like "manatee heterosexuality"; the former involves nearly orgylike assemblies of males mutually stimulating one another, but the latter involves only a single female, and often a reluctant one at that.

A DISTURBING GENERALIZATION

There is one thread running through nearly all these examples: the specific acts performed in male-male or female-female acts in animals are, *almost without exception,* a broader sample of possible sexual acts and/or positions than those typically observed in male-female encounters. What does this mean?

One possibility is that the animals are too stupid to know what they're doing in homosexual interactions. I suppose this is sometimes a remote possibility, but it's not likely. After all, you don't have to assume lizards are geniuses to conclude that a lizard that usually copulates on a tree trunk knows when it's copulating out in the foliage.[50] Even if it doesn't know it consciously, it has certainly been selected to act *as if* it does. And monkeys just aren't stupid according to any definition. The stupidity explanation violates Drury's first law of animal behavior, and should be discarded.

Another explanation is that there isn't any choice. By definition, a homosexual act cannot possibly be one in which a penis and a vagina interact. And so perhaps a wider variety of other acts take place in homosexual acts because none of them feels quite as good as coitus does.[51]

This might be true as far as it goes, but it doesn't go far enough. First and foremost, it doesn't reconcile with the cases where the animals themselves act as if they believe the homosexual acts feel bet-

[49] From notes of my conversation with Daniel Hartman on April 11, 1979.

[50] True, some juvenile sexuality in animals (and humans, too, for that matter) seems undirected and experimental, but even it quickly channels itself so that most of the interactions closely resemble the typical adult heterosexual pattern. So it's not as if the adults haven't had practice in what to do.

[51] See, in this connection, the quote from Hunt that introduces this chapter.

ter—as with those Dutch macaques, for example. And in some specific instances, this explanation clearly fails. In the case of the lizards, for example, the act involves a hemipenis and a cloaca in both heterosexual and homosexual cases, so it is unlikely that there is any difference in delight. Moreover, in one case—the foliage copulation—it was the *location* that was nonstandard, not the act, and that clearly was a variable not forced on the participants. Admittedly, the number of observations in this species is small, but that doesn't invalidate my suggestion.

Those Dutch macaques raise another question. Recall that Masters and Johnson found, in what I call the "technique puzzle," that the homosexuals in long-term relationships in their sample often had better technique than the married heterosexuals did. My main explanation, in chapter 4, was that the particular homosexuals volunteering for Masters and Johnson's study must have come to terms with the sex taboo in order to have been willing to come out as homosexuals and then to volunteer. But the heterosexuals need not have come to terms with the sex taboo in order to have gotten married (and perhaps not to have volunteered for the experiment). If having overcome the sex taboo helps one's sexual communication, then there would be a higher proportion of homosexual volunteers who had established better communication patterns with their partners.

I still think this is a good explanation, but it doesn't elucidate homosexual behavior with the macaque females or other animals. Animals don't seem to have a sex taboo, so how could we possibly explain why female-female relations in animals, too, sometimes seem more fulfilling than male-female ones (at least for some females)? Or how could we explain that a wider variety of acts are performed in homosexual relations in animals than are performed in heterosexual acts? Let's call this the "all-species" version of the technique puzzle.

Perhaps entirely different explanations apply to the all-species version of the technique puzzle and to the human version. But as a scientist I see that this is not parsimonious, and so it makes me suspicious. There is another explanation for such behavior, but you have to be a pretty hard-core sociobiologist to believe it. Let me give you the gist with the following silly story.

Remember the old TV show "The Millionaire"? Let's say a millionaire walks into the lives of you and your beloved and tells each of you the following. Every time the two of you make love, the millionaire will be there watching—waiting for one of you to have an orgasm. Each day, whoever has an orgasm first will be given $10,000 tax-free. He'll continue these acts of charity until he has given you two a total of one million dollars, then vanish from your lives forever.

Oh, by the way, he'll transmit this money by way of two Swiss bank accounts—one for you, one for your honey. This is to give each of you total freedom to do with your money whatever you please. It's fine if you want to share the money equally, but doing so has to be the free act of the person sharing it. If you want to keep every cent you've earned, that's fine, too, as far as he's concerned.

Well, congratulations: in 100 days (or less, if you work hard at it) you two could be a million dollars richer. But do you think that this reward system might add a little bit of conflict and tension to your sex life? Of course, couples might not worry if they have been together for a long time and trust each other in sexual and financial matters; they'd be licentious all the way to the bank, where they would even out the account balances every week. Or every hour.

But let's face it: a lot of couples would discover that sex play for high stakes spoils things. What if one of you built up a big balance and then took off? What if "the loser" had to plead with "the winner" to share the money? What if one of you always "won"–would sharing the money really help the "loser" feel better? What if you told the millionaire to get lost—but then he told you he'd spy on you and make the deposits, anyway?

As I've described it, this fantasy could be inflicted upon either heterosexuals or homosexuals. But if you're a hard-core sociobiologist, you'll see that in a sense it's inflicted upon heterosexuals by necessity. Sociobiologically, there's an enormous difference between homosexual and heterosexual copulations: heterosexual ones, under the right circumstances, can directly result in the biggest sociobiologic prize of all, reproductive success. Homosexual copulations can never do so directly. This is conventionally viewed as a disadvantage (some believe it demonstrates that homosexual acts are less "natural"), but the present argument turns the consequences around 180 degrees. Sociobiological views of heterosexual relations have a strongly competitive flavor: males and females competing on the sexual battlefield tooth, nail, and genital because their reproductive interests are so different, sociobiologically speaking.[52] If these views are correct, then we have to consider the possibility that conventional heterosexual sex turns out to be less fun not because it *has* to be—after all, heterosexuals are capable of performing precisely the acts that Masters and Johnson's homosexuals were so good at—but because the competitive nature of the interaction results in a less pleasing compromise in which sexual

---

[52]This is a prominent theme in the sexological writings of sociobiologists. Donald Symons, for example, claims that female and male reproductive strategies are almost completely opposed to each other (Symons 1979). See also footnote 53.

pleasure is not the only thing being maximized. Heterosexuals, in this view, can escape this trap only when the sex acts involved are the least likely to be reproductive[53]—a conclusion likely to give fits to those people who believe that only procreative sex is "natural" and permissible.

Which of these two explanations of the "technique puzzle" is correct? I haven't the slightest idea; for all I know, they may both be wrong. Keep in mind that the "millionaire" explanation is sociobiological and acquires its force because it focuses on reproductive success. In particular, there is no presumption that natural selection will maximize *your* pleasure, when that pleasure depends on acts by a genetically unrelated individual who is acting so as to maximize his or her own reproductive success.

CONCLUSIONS

I've spent a lot of space in this chapter on animals, and some readers may be wondering if it is relevant to our human behavior. I think so. In our society, it is easy to confuse what is "natural" with what "occurs in animals"—and things are a lot more complicated than that. In order to demonstrate the complications, I have had to give a lot of evidence. To keep it interesting, I have tried to spend the most time on our closest relatives, the primates. But it is important to demonstrate that homosexual behavior occurs across the animal kingdom.

That is, "homosexuality" exists in animals in roughly the same sense that "heterosexuality" does: in enormously varied circumstances. The *complete* pattern of human heterosexuality is not found in any other animal species (social-class differences in sexual behavior, pair-bonding, face-to-face copulation, hidden menstrual/estrous cycles, oral and anal intercourse, etc.), although any single aspect of human heterosexuality *can* be found in some animal species. The same statement can be made about human homosexuality. Earlier statements that "true" homosexuality does not exist in animals were premature; we just hadn't investigated enough animals yet.[54]

Even the fact that animals often show increased homosexual behav-

---

[53] Indeed, University of Chicago sociobiologist Daniel G. Freedman claims that reproductive competition in marriage between husband and wife doesn't decline until the production of new children is over (Freedman 1979).

[54] I do not mean to imply, by the way, that people who have stated otherwise ought to have known they were wrong or are stupid. Many of the cases I have cited in this chapter come from conversations and letters I have exchanged with scientists, and I cannot expect laypeople to be aware of them or to find them when they investigate. Nevertheless, I believe it is important to correct the record in detail.

ior in artificial conditions like captivity can be applied to the human case. After all, it's been several thousand years since most of us have lived in evolutionarily natural (i.e., hunter-gatherer) conditions. We shave hair that otherwise would trap odors emitted by scent glands, we shower to remove those secretions, and we deodorize to prevent further secretions—and then some of us have the nerve to claim that odors have no effects in human beings or that some forms of behavior should be forbidden because they are unnatural! It just doesn't make sense when we've stopped making scents.

Moreover, it turns out that homosexuality and the other gender transpositions exist in some so-called primitive human groups, too—groups that, apparently, are still living in the hunter-gatherer conditions in which humans evolved away from other primates. That suggests that some of these gender transpositions may not be so unnatural, after all; I don't think it is possible to explain them solely in terms of evolutionary pathology. The explanations we come up with may have to be geared specifically to the human case, but that just makes our job harder, not impossible. It's time to get theoretical again and see how natural selection *could* have produced an animal capable of not reproducing, even as it increases its genetic representation in future generations.

13

SOCIOBIOLOGY AND THE GENDER TRANSPOSITIONS

. . . five students—four of them men— . . . said that [college] President [Rev. Billy James] Hargis has had sexual relations with them.
. . . According to two of those present, Hargis, who has a wife, three
daughters and a son, admitted his guilt and blamed his behavior on
"genes and chromosomes."

Time magazine, 16 February 1976, p. 52.

The time has come to try to understand what formed the features
of our sexual landscape. Is this amphitheater a natural landform,
or could it have been constructed only with human help? How
many people are living on this side of the mountains and how many
across the great divide? How much fluidity is there in the features
themselves or in the migrations people undertake during their life-
times? And most of all, *why* are any particular answers the correct
ones?

I am, among other things, a sociobiologist, and so I'm happy to
remind you that sociobiology specializes in answering the "why"
question of human behavior. That's because sociobiology is, first and
foremost, interested in theories that have an adaptationist point of

view, and adaptation—or the lack thereof—answers the "why" question.

Sociobiologists ask, Do individuals exhibiting a particular behavior have a higher reproductive success when compared with individuals who do not? The answer usually is yes, if the behavior occurs in a natural environment. In an unnatural setting, such as the world we now find ourselves in, the answer is sometimes yes and sometimes no. So sociobiologists must ask whether a behavior would have been adaptive in the recent evolutionary past.

At first it seems paradoxical, but sociobiologists have applied this approach to homosexuality just as they did to heterosexuality. When the topic first arose in a sociobiological context, they viewed homosexuality as a fascinating set of behaviors deserving of the application of Drury's first law: that an animal (even a human animal) is assumed smart until proved dumb. At the time, the typical theory in psychology or sociology viewed homosexuality as a deviation from a normal developmental or socially reinforced path, and the logical question in the face of such a deviation is to ask what went wrong.[1] In contrast, sociobiologists first asked what went right. For years gay liberationists had demanded that heterosexuality be viewed with the same kinds of filters as homosexuality is, and with sociobiological theories their wish came true.

But not particularly because anyone planned it that way. Sociobiologists didn't have to be prodded by politics to take this approach; they had been prepared for it as evolutionary biologists. Variation is a central problem in evolution—it is at the heart of the creation of new species—and at least since Darwin it has not been regarded as abnormal in any way. Indeed, evolution is the process by which an undoubtedly abnormal event—a mutation—can be transformed by natural selection into something entirely normal. Indeed, sociobiologists deserve credit for following the traditions of their discipline in the direction of a theory that many people would be uncomfortable with—and for the most part for doing so without intellectual flinching.

Sociobiological theories of homosexuality have come a long way from those days, and in this chapter I'll tell you about them. Sociobiologists have also begun to apply the what-went-right approach to the other gender transpositions, and the results have been fascinating. Let's start with them.

---

[1] Only very recently have the social sciences developed theories in which homosexuality is viewed as a normal variation. I'm not enough of a philosopher of science to know if this what-went-wrong point of view is an inherent part of social science or if it is just the way social science happened to be in the 1960s and 1970s.

HETEROSEXUAL TRANSVESTISM

If animals don't wear clothes, how do they cross-dress? Obviously, in a strict sense they don't. But there are some instances in which animals do change their appearance—in fish, for example, the color of their scales—in ways that suggest a cross-sex appearance. Animals also have, very loosely speaking, "gender roles": acts that only females or only males seem to do, or that each does at very different frequencies, but which are not strictly speaking necessary for a particular sex to do in order to bear young or inseminate. (Obviously, this kind of "role" is not what most people mean by the term, that is, roles for men and women that are consciously recognized by the culture.) So if an animal can't "cross-dress," it can at least "cross-act"—that is, behave in a way that causes it to be taken as a member of the other sex.

Cross-acting is part of what was going on in those male hanging flies that wing-droop, as females do, in order to feed upon a male's prey (see chapter 12). It's closely related to so-called alternate reproductive strategies in a large number of species, for reasons that will become clear. So let me give you a couple of examples of those.

Biologists studying the behavior of a species are especially attentive to *displays,* which are acts performed by one individual designed[2] to be observed by another. Let me illustrate the point I'm about to make with a story.

I was at afternoon tea outside the home of a famous sociobiologist. Also at the tea were two well-regarded primatologists—a husband-and-wife team, who had brought their toddler along with them. At one point, the toddler, who was standing about five feet away from us, turned toward us and toddled in our direction. After two steps, he let out a loud "Ha!" and continued toddling. Our conversation continued as if nothing had happened. But in a minute or so the boy's father turned to him and said calmly, "All right, Jason, now what was that little display all about?"

An animal calling attention to itself is easily observed, usually, not only by other members of its species but also by the human biologists studying them. So the point is, behaviors related to displays are among the first things written about the species in journals and books. That's fine, but subtler aspects of behavior—things that would not be wise

---

[2] When manufacturers design lamps, there are human beings somewhere who consciously know what a lamp is supposed to do and how this particular design will let the lamp do it. In contrast, in evolutionary biology, the term "design" does not imply conscious intent on the part of the planner or that the animals designed their own displays. But natural selection causes the evolution of the *appearance* of design. For more details, see any book on the philosophy of Darwinism.

for an animal to communicate to others—are often overlooked until the biologists get to know their animals really well. *Alternate reproductive strategies in animals were often overlooked because they usually do not involve displays.* Accordingly, the displayed behavior can acquire the reputation for being the "normal" behavior, whereas a different strategy may be considered "alternate" even though it is extremely common. Below are examples of some of these subtler behaviors.[3]

Alternate Male Strategies in Frogs

Male frogs croak to attract females. Males defend their territories against other croaking males, and females seem to be attracted, as a general rule, to males with the loudest croaks. But in green tree frogs (and many other frogs, as well), there are also *noncalling* males. The noncallers hang around a particular calling male—presumably one calling especially loudly—then try to mate with the females approaching him. One experiment suggests that they may succeed as much as 40 percent of the time.[4]

Of course, the noncallers aren't displaying their behavior; if they were to do so, they would be quickly detected by the territory-holding male and chased out. So as I suggested above, these males tend to get reported upon later in the study of frogs.

Alternate Male Strategies in Elephant Seals

The elephant seal, as you may guess from the name, is a species of seal that grows very large. They weigh so much—up to hundreds of pounds per individual—that they never come up on land except during the breeding season or to moult. Out of the water, none of them eats a thing; milk for the babies, metabolic energy, and energy for the males to fight each other are all drawn from fat reserves alone. Male elephant seals compete viciously with each other for access to the hundreds of females in a particular breeding colony. The positive payoff for a winning male is the chance to inseminate scores of females during his tenure as king of the hill. The negative payoff is that competition is so stiff that a particular male often occupies this exalted position for less than one breeding season. Many of them are severely injured as they end their reign; some are even killed.

But elephant seals have alternate male strategies, too. As mother

---

[3] For an excellent review of the various alternate male strategies and the theories used to explain them, see Cade 1980.

[4] Perrill, Gerhardt, and Daniel 1978.

and pup return to the water after the breeding season ends, the mothers—still fertile—are mobbed by males too low in the dominance hierarchy to risk directly attacking the dominant male still on land above.[5] Again, although in any given season more males perform this underwater mobbing behavior than challenge the dominant male, underwater mobbing is far less often written about; it is not a display. And in this case, of course, it happens out of sight of landlocked human observers.

Alternate Male Strategies in Deer

Deer have antlers, right? Male deer, I mean? Well, yes, some people say they are supposed to have them. But among red deer, some males don't; they're called "hummels." Game wardens, knowing how prized antlers are by hunters, don't like males with this antlerless trait and try to get rid of them—so far, unsuccessfully.

A theoretical evolutionary biologist, Madhav Gadgil, has come up with a good explanation why the hummels persist. I call it the "big bucks" theory. He claims that antlers are energetically very expensive—like laying on fat for elephant-seal battles—and that a less costly alternate male strategy has evolved in equilibrium with the more costly one.

> This costly arms race comes to an end when those investing in weaponry [bucks with antlers] are just as well off as those which have totally opted out of such investment [hummels]. Such a mechanism could precisely equalize the selective advantages of the two alternatives.[6]

That is, when there are "too many" bucks with antlers around, more and more costly antlers are required to win a fight, so it is more advantageous to opt out of the battle and go after a lower reproductive success at lower cost. But when there are "too many" hummels around, then a deer can achieve a high reproductive success by growing some antlers and pushing a lot of hummels aside.[7] The result is

---

[5] The insemination produces an embryo that develops up to the blastocyst stage—a few dozen cells or so—and then lies dormant for months, until the females are on their way back to the breeding grounds during the next breeding season. So pups born in year Y were created by a fertilization that took place in year Y − 1.

[6] Gadgil 1972.

[7] Another way to put this is that if you are a deer that wants to maximize the return on your parental investment, you want the highest reproductive success per unit of investment. Natural selection effectively calculates this return for the antler/hummel options and keeps

an equilibrium in which, most of the time, about the same amount of reproductive success is obtained per unit investment in each of the two strategies.

Once again, because antlers are so spectacular and fights involving antlers are so spectacular, people have gotten the impression that male deer have antlers, period. Not always! We have to make a distinction between what is conspicuous and what is normal. Male deer with antlers and male deer without antlers both occur normally in this species; it is humans that impose the notion that one is the "norm" and the other an "alternate."

Alternate Male Strategies in Fish

A South American leaf fish also illustrates this point. Nonbreeding adults (of either sex) are colored dull brown, usually with scattered white and black spots. By the time females are ready to spawn, they have turned yellowish-pink or white, with some scattered, inconspicuous brown spots. Some males set up territories surrounding a nest or lair, and as they do so, they turn nearly black.

If you read the paper that discusses these colors,[8] you'll find the descriptive section placed near the beginning of the article and the color patterns themselves illustrated in a full-page drawing. But *males* in this species sometimes exhibit male-to-female color changes: they can change color to look more like females and apparently exploit the color change in an attempt to steal copulations. The fact that males can easily exhibit this "female" coloration is not mentioned at the point where the sexes' color patterns are first described; it is postponed until much later in the paper, and it is not illustrated with a drawing. Accordingly, the scientist who wrote these descriptions gave them to us with a distinct association with masculinity and femininity. That is, he didn't hide the fact that these so-called pseudofemales exist, but he did structure the paper to declare that there are adult "male" and "female" color patterns, whereas in fact the color patterns are more interestingly distributed between the sexes.

I am not accusing this author of bias or scientific inaccuracy. After all, he described the pseudofemale coloration and behavior in detail, which is not what would be expected if he really were embarrassed by this behavior or wanted to conceal it, consciously or subcon-

---

adjusting the investments made in each option until the returns are roughly equal. (It is a similar mechanism that keeps the sex ratio about fifty-fifty.) It's as if Mother Nature, hunting reproductive success instead of trophies, wants the biggest bang for her buck.

[8] Barlow 1967.

sciously. Moreover, he wrote and published the article in the first place, which some other people might not have done. What I do want to point out is that the pseudofemale fish in question are behaving in a way that, were they human, we might call "sneaky"; they are acting as if they were trying to steal a copulation from the territory-holding male, by "pretending" to be a female entering the same nest in which a real female has just laid her eggs (and which have not yet been fertilized by the black male). It is thus not in their self-interest to display in a way that would give the game away to the territory holder—and accordingly, the human observer is also apt to overlook what is really going on, at least at first. One of the reasons the human observer gets a little confused is that the fish themselves are acting, frankly, in a confusing way.

Here's another example. Several times this same biologist observed pseudofemales repelled by attacks from a territory-holding male. This suggested that territory holders were pretty good at defending their territories against intrusions by the pseudofemales. Only once did he see a pseudofemale actually inside the male's lair. Tellingly, *he didn't see it enter*; he only saw it inside after it had gotten in. Again, if the fish succeeds in fooling the territory holder, it may have to do so in a way that also fools a human observer.

Pseudofemale behavior has been observed in many other fish species, usually with variations that have their observers scratching their heads.[9] This puzzlement makes sense if the fish themselves are not being entirely up-front about what they are doing—if "sneakiness" in some real sense manages to cross the species boundary between fish and human.

Alternate Male Strategies: Conclusions

The bottom line is this: there is nothing sacred about the obvious, ordinary, clearly displayed behavior of males (and probably also females, although this has not been studied as much—but see Morris 1955). Males can and will display behavior that is less stereotypically or exclusively masculine if it is to their advantage to do so. On a separate dimension, they can and will display overtly feminine behavior if it is to their advantage to do so. Mother Nature has built sex roles into every sexually reproducing species, but many of these roles, even if they are stereotypical of one sex, are performed by individuals

---

[9]Van den Assem 1967 describes it in the three-spined stickleback, Morris 1952 in the ten-spined stickleback. See also Morris 1955 and 1970.

of either sex. Instincts in animals are not as automatic as people think they are, and we must be careful not to impose our Western sexual dichotomies onto an animal world that doesn't reflect them as we wish. This sounds simple, but in fact it can be difficult, because if sex is spectacular, then what animals allow to be observed will often be related to sex, and what is concealed may even more often be related to sex and may even be more interesting.

So if natural selection can allow animals to vary in how closely they follow particular masculine and feminine patterns in their species, perhaps there are ways humans can be naturally predisposed toward the various gender transpositions. Let's continue looking at each of them in turn.

TRANSSEXUALISM

Transsexualism tests the limits of the adaptationist approach typical of sociobiology. Because it is so rare—less than 1 in 10,000, and maybe as rare as 1 in 50,000—sociobiologists cannot assume that its frequency went from nothing up to even this tiny percentage by natural selection. That's because genes mutate at about that frequency, and regardless of whether the gene is dominant or recessive,[10] a trait that is caused solely by mutation, and which always causes the individual showing the trait to die before reproducing, shows up in a population at about this frequency due to mutation and recombination alone. Accordingly, population geneticists call this very low frequency a "mutational equilibrium." Bluntly put, any trait showing up at this level is so rare that it might be considered an evolutionary mistake.

This does not mean that transsexualism really *is* an evolutionary mistake, however. For example, it might have nothing to do with genetics. All it means is that if someone insists that it is, then sociobiologists have to shrug their shoulders and admit that this might be true. But if some trait has a frequency well above the mutational equilibrium, sociobiologists can presume that *something* adaptive is associated with any genes predisposing for the trait in some way. Exactly what or how is unspecified.

The only sociobiological theories of transsexualism I know assume that it is an extreme form of homosexuality. That is, these sociobiological models take nonreproduction as the biological question at issue and assume that transsexuals are, like homosexuals, less likely than heterosexuals to reproduce. Accordingly, I will not discuss transsex-

---

[10] In a book about sexology and genetics, we have to be careful not to confuse "dominant and recessive" with "dominant and submissive."

ualism in this chapter but move on to sociobiological models of homosexuality.

HOMOSEXUALITY

At least four different sociobiological models of homosexuality have been advanced by a total of seven different sociobiologists:

- Kin selection
- Everyone marries
- Imprinting
- Heterozygote advantage

I call these models "orthodox" because each tries to find a way in which homosexuality is evolutionarily adaptive—that is, orthodox with respect to the sociobiological working hypothesis that we should look for what's going right, not what's going wrong. There are, in addition, at least four less orthodox sociobiological models, proposed by five other sociobiologists and psychologists. These theories are less orthodox because they do not claim that homosexuality in humans is adaptive. I'll discuss the orthodox theories below, but I don't have enough space to describe more than one unorthodox one.[11]

Kin Selection

The most widely known theory is called the *kin-selection* theory; it was proposed independently by two sociobiologists and reported by a third.[12] Roughly speaking, kin selection is the notion that you have to consider not only your own children but also your relatives' children in order to understand the evolutionary effects of a given act. How this applies to homosexuality I'll explain in a moment; first I'll explain kin selection itself. This requires a heavy dose of sociobiological theory.

[11] The four unorthodox theories are as follows:
- A theory by sociobiologist Richard Alexander, of the University of Michigan, which is described in Ruse 1981.
- A theory by psychologists Gordon Gallup, Jr., and Susan Suarez, of the State University of New York at Albany; see Gallup and Suarez 1983.
- A theory sketched by sociobiologist Donald Symons of the University of California, in Symons 1979.
- Hutchinson's version of the heterozygote advantage model, which is the one that will be briefly explained later in this chapter; see Hutchinson 1959.

[12] The two sociobiologists were zoologists Herman Spieth and Robert Trivers, both now at the University of California; the reporter was Harvard's Edward O. Wilson. See Wilson 1975, p. 555.

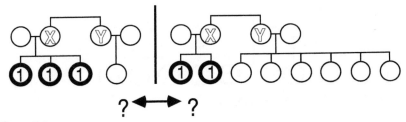

Figure 13.2

In figure 13.1, two family trees are diagrammed. *X* and *Y* are full siblings (brothers or sisters) and each has a family of his or her own. *X* is about to make a fateful choice: there is an act *X* could do that would change the number of children *X* and *Y* would have. The two possible outcomes (of doing or not doing the fateful act) are shown on each side of the heavy vertical bar.

On the left, in the absence of the fateful act, *X* has a reproductive success (RS) of 3, reflecting 3 children; on the right, *X* performs the fateful act, with a resulting RS of 2. If there were no such thing as kin selection, evolution would produce behavior that maximizes the number of offspring people have.[13] If *X*'s behavior has been molded by natural selection, what would *X* do in this case? Obviously, *X* would choose the (non-) act that resulted in the family on the left, because 3 is larger than 2. Any genes permitting or predisposing *X* to do this would be selected for and win out over any genes predisposing *X* to choose the right-hand possibility.

But kin selection says that natural selection takes account not only of direct descendants but also of *indirect* descendants. That is, we must pay attention not only to *X*'s children, but also to *Y*'s children, *even if we look at things only from X's point of view*, because *X* and *Y* are siblings. However, *Y*'s children are only half as closely related to *X* as *X*'s own children are, so from *X*'s point of view they are each counted as 1/2.

Figure 13.2 shows the same two family trees and the results of *X*'s doing or not doing that fateful act. But this time the fractional weights for nieces and nephews are written in. The *X* on the left has reproductive success (RS) of 3, reflecting 3 children, plus an additional half-child equivalent from *Y*'s child, if *X* does not perform the fateful act. This total is called *X*'s *inclusive fitness* (IF). *X*'s inclusive fitness is thus 3.5. But on the right, if *X* does perform the fateful act, *X* has RS of 2,

[13] Of course, as mentioned in chapter 12, the number of children is not the best measure of reproductive success, for children can die, be sterile, or decide not to reproduce. So whenever I show a family tree, think of it as showing not the number of children born but the number of children who survive to adulthood to reproduce, etc.

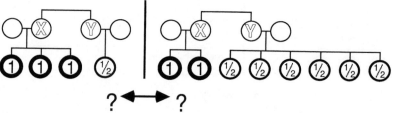

Figure 13.1

reflecting 2 children, plus 6 additional half children, for a total inclusive fitness of 5. With kin selection, since 5 is greater than 3.5, natural selection acts in favor of Xs who turn their family trees from the one on the left to the one on the right. Likewise, natural selection would act against Xs who turn their family trees from the one on the right to the one on the left.

It is easy to see the general principle. If X can do an act for a full sibling Y that decreases the number of children X can rear but increases the number of children Y can rear, X will be selected to do that act if the benefit to Y is 2 or more times as large as the cost to X. In the example above, the benefit to Y is 5, the cost to X is 1, and 5 is more than twice as large as 1 is.

An act that increases someone else's RS at a cost to your own RS is called a *reproductively altruistic* act. The theory of kin selection says that genes permitting, predisposing, or causing reproductively altruistic acts in their carriers can *in theory increase* under the action of natural selection if the reproductive altruists act reproductively altruistically enough to increase their relatives' RS by an amount sufficiently greater than the cost to their own.

A simple formula tells us how much greater. If the benefit to the recipient of the act is B, the cost to the altruist is C, and the degree of relatedness (see below) between the two of them is r, then if

$$B \times r > C$$

the act will be selected for. The number r is the degree of relatedness between the two individuals involved; it is always a number between 0 and 1. You can think of it as the probability that the recipient of the act shares the same gene as the person performing the act. In the example above, B was 5, C was 1, and r was 1/2. Since $5 \times 1/2 > 1$, the act was selected for.

A Human Example: Now it is time to apply the kin selection theory to homosexuality. In this theory, being homosexual is viewed as a reproductively altruistic "act." That is, Mother Nature could have conspired, through genes and environment, to make someone heterosexual and reproductive. Instead, someone turned out homosexual, and that reduces his or her reproductive success.[14] If there is something about homosexuality in a culture that causes the homosexual's relatives to increase their RS as a result, then genes permitting or predisposing people to homosexuality (and the resultant reproductive altruism) can spread under the action of natural selection.

Consider the cross-gender pattern of homosexuality so common in some other cultures (see chapter 2). We have already seen that there are animal species in which individuals of one sex perform acts human observers usually or typically associate with the other sex. In some species there is a lot of such behavior, and in others there is little or none. Sociobiologists ask, Why are humans the kind of species in which cross-gender behavior is moderately common instead of the kind of species in which this is out of the question? (Or, to phrase this another way, why are humans the kind of species in which the two sexes overlap a lot in the behaviors they perform rather than only a little?) Sociobiologists answer that it was probably reproductively advantageous for individuals to be able to gender-nonconform under the appropriate circumstances. In particular, it could conceivably have been advantageous, under a kin-selection model, to gender-nonconform even to the point that you reduced your own RS to zero.

Consider, for example, a so-called primitive society in which a *bride-price* is paid. In bride-price societies, marriage is expensive for the groom; he and his extended family pay a carefully negotiated and very substantial sum to the bride's family, which divides it among the various relatives according to specific rules.

But what about those particular families that are unlikely to be able to raise a bride-price? Or those particular sons who, through injury or whatever reason, are unlikely to be able to raise a family? Such a family might benefit from having a boy take up the role of a girl, because it would turn his marital liability into an asset. In the case of a poor family, the benefit to the extended family—the "*B*," if you will—of having a son "turn into" a daughter would be especially large. In the case of a weak or (pardon the expression) low-quality son, the

---

[14] Actually, whether homosexuality usually decreases RS is an empirical matter; it is certainly logical that homosexuals would have fewer children than heterosexuals, but it is not a logical necessity. In fact, the very few studies that did happen to collect data on RS in homosexuals show exactly what our hunches tell us: homosexuals do have fewer kids. This was true of the gay men in our sample of homosexuality running in families, for example (Pillard and Weinrich, unpublished data), and if anything, our sample was biased against such a finding, because we required *all* subjects to be unmarried—whether they were heterosexual or homosexual.

cost of his foregoing reproduction—the "C"—would be especially small. In either case, the probability that B would be greater than $r \times C$ for this particular son in this particular family would be especially high. Anything—genetic, cultural, or whatever—that favors sons wanting to act like daughters in situations like this would become more likely by natural selection.

Conclusions

In chapter 14, I will fit the above example in with the institution of the berdache among American Indians (described in chapter 2). It will be my contention, based on Walter Williams's excellent study of the berdache, that *a man taking up the role of a woman is one of the human species' alternate male reproductive strategies*—and likewise that a woman taking up a warrior role may be an alternate female reproductive strategy. That is, I will claim that there may well be four, not two, common gender roles available as reproductive strategies in humans: one for masculine men, one for feminine women, one for masculine women, and one for nonmasculine men.

But for the moment, let me focus on the bride-price example's strengths and weaknesses. Its main strength is theoretical; it explains how it *could* happen that a particular social system could set up selection pressures that would make it reproductively advantageous, through kin selection, for particular individuals to reduce or eliminate their reproduction. Now some people were taught that evolution maximizes reproduction at all costs, and so they have trouble accepting or understanding this kin-selection model. But that's not so; natural selection maximizes inclusive fitness, not reproductive success.[15] Another strength is that it is at least mildly quantitative: the values of bride-prices are numbers, after all, and perhaps one could see if these numbers respond to the reproductive value expected from marrying particular brides. Female brides make children *and* goods that help children survive; male brides only make the goods (see below).

Weaknesses of the bride-price model, however, are substantial. A primitive tribe would have to have had bride-prices for many, many generations in order for there to be any genetic evolution that takes their calculations into account, so it is unlikely that today we'd find anything other than rough greater-than/less-than predictions tested under the theory. That is, this bride-price theory may be quantitative,

---

[15] Remember that inclusive fitness was calculated in the numerical examples above. It's the total that takes into account not only your own children but also your relatives' children.

but it is only roughly, not precisely, so. Moreover, only certain societies have bride-prices, so it is not a universal theory. However, it ought to apply in societies that have had it long enough—and a point I will make in chapter 14 is that selection pressures for homosexuality, if any, have probably been very different in different societies.

Another weakness of the model as presented so far is that it only looks at the kin-selection pluses and minuses from the point of view of the cross-gender person himself. But this weakness is easy to address. When we look at the interaction from the point of view of the family that pays the bride-price in such a marriage, we can ask what they might get out of it, evolutionarily speaking. After all, it's not as if they're fooled that they're getting a "real" daughter-in-law; they know they're getting a male who *acts* like a daughter-in-law.

These societies are usually polygamous, and the cross-gender wives are typically the second or third wives of a man who already has some female wives. Theory predicts that the bride-price for such a wife would be lower than that for a female wife, since the husband is only getting one of the two things that wives are good for: work, these men say, but not children. So although the bride-price would be lower, it wouldn't be zero, and the cross-gender wife would still receive a bride-price that would be distributed among kin.

So in some societies, accepting a man in the social role of a woman might be consistent with kin selection for every person in the culture: for the berdache himself, for his family, and for the husband and his family. That doesn't mean that it always will be, of course.

There are other cases in which the $B \times r$ can be greater than C—situations that don't depend on the unfortunate-sounding notion of a low-quality son. Some jobs or roles in a society might have a very large payoff to relatives—a large B—but would require, for their best performance, that the person performing them not have the burden of raising children. In this case, if an exceptionally high quality child (son or daughter) were homosexual, it would make it easier for them to aim for such a role. If being a shaman were such a role, then this could explain the association between shamanism and homosexuality in many cultures—and that's a theory I'll explore in chapter 14 in a lot more detail.

EVERYONE MARRIES

The next sociobiological theory of homosexuality I call the everyone-marries theory, for it asks, What does "homosexuality" mean when parents arrange marriages, and/or when love is not presumed to be the basis of marriage?[16] In this case, it seems that sexual orientation would range not from heterosexual to homosexual but from heterosexual to bisexual.

In a society like this, homosexuality affects not so much whether you marry but the people with whom you would be attracted to sexually outside of marriage. If you're homosexual, you are tempted to have affairs with people of the same sex as yourself. If you're heterosexual, you are tempted to have affairs with people of the other sex.

Such societies are common enough outside the Western world and have been very common in the history of the human species. It is easy to lose track of this fact in our society, which idealizes monogamy and encourages romantic marriage. But even in our society not everyone is monogamous, and not everyone marries for limerence or lust. Although most parents in our society do not arrange marriages of their children, a few do, and more try to influence their children's choices of spouse; the everyone-marries theory would apply to them. Indeed, think of the colorful example of royalty. A crown prince might best be heterosexual enough to marry and pass on the throne but homosexual enough to avoid heterosexual extramarital entanglements. After all, a king who falls in love with a woman who isn't the queen might have to abdicate or, worse yet, find his family's reign abruptly terminated—and so there is the involvement of the family's fortunes that is essential to the kin-selection theory. Good breeding counts for a lot in those circles.

In many societies, people do not believe that you ought to be in love with the person you marry or that you have to be sexually attracted to your spouse. Sociobiologically, then, we have to ask whether limerence and lust, in their most violently impulsive forms, evolved mostly to motivate marital, or extramarital, bliss. I don't have space to discuss this in detail; all the present theory needs, however, is for these emotions to *sometimes* be involved in promoting extramarital liaisons.[17]

In this kind of society, homosexuals and heterosexuals differ in two important sociobiological ways. I'll mention them first and then explain their importance. First, homosexuals would be involved in fewer extramarital pregnancies, all other things being equal. And if universal-marriage societies treat illegitimacy harshly, then extramarital pregnancies are especially dangerous.

Second, homosexuals would probably be less unwilling to marry

[16] This theory is explained in detail in Weinrich 1987.

[17] Again, for more detail, see Weinrich 1987.

the partner their parents have chosen for them. Heterosexuals, after all, might fall in love with someone other than the person their parents want them to marry, and this can cause a lot of conflict. But homosexuals would not expect to marry someone they're in love with, and so they ought to be more willing to go along with the choice their parents have arranged.

It turns out that both these suggestions have the *same* consequence in sociobiological theory: they imply that *homosexuals, in comparison with heterosexuals, will behave in a way that sociobiological theory classifies as more "reproductively altruistic"*—just as in the ordinary kin-selection theory, with one difference discussed below.

To explain this, I have to get mathematical again. Trivers proposed, in a classic paper, that there is a fundamental sociobiological reason why parents and offspring are in conflict: the reproductive interests of parents would be better served if offspring would act more altruistically toward their siblings and family than the offspring themselves would find in their own best self-interests. He demonstrated this by a simple algebraic argument, which I do not have space to work out for you.[18]

Trivers demonstrated, as a result of this argument, that some subtle, surprising acts get involved in parent-offspring conflict. It turns out that one of those subtly altruistic acts is being willing to marry the spouse your parents desire for you rather than the one that would maximize your own genetic interests. Another is, perhaps, refraining from extramarital reproduction when it is available. These are precisely two traits we would expect homosexuals to have in a society in which everyone marries.

So in this theory homosexuality remains a reproductively altruistic trait, to which we can apply a kin-selection explanation. But the degree of the altruism is smaller than in the cross-gender version; that is, the homosexual reproductive altruist's decrease in RS (the cost C) is small rather than large. That makes it easier to satisfy the $B \times r > C$ inequality.

This theory, by the way, explains the older/younger type of homosexuality described in chapter 5 better than the cross-gender model.

[18] If you are interested in the details, consult Trivers 1974. You can get the gist, however, by looking back at the two illustrations of the family tree of X and Y. The calculations were made from X's point of view; if they were made from Y's, it would turn out that Y would prefer the right-hand situation even if the reproductive benefit to Y were a lot less. So there could arise situations in which Y would prefer X to do an act that X would not be selected to do. The parents of X and Y would be in between; in some cases with intermediate amounts of benefit to Y, X would be selected against doing the acts, but Y and the parents would be selected to try to get X to do the act.

First, cross-gendering need play no part in this theory, and we saw that cross-gendering need not be involved in the older/younger type. And second, if you are very cross-gendered, you may not be able to get married and reproduce! So these two theories are likely to apply to two different kinds of people.

Imprinting

A third sociobiological model was proposed by Nobel Prize-winning German ethologist Konrad Lorenz. This theory begins with a simple ethological observation: in captivity, it is easy to imprint male greylag geese (Lorenz's favorite experimental bird) so that they will, as adults, court other males, not females.[19] Given the observations cited in chapter 12 that male-male and female-female pairs have been observed in many bird species in the wild, this is a possibility that has to be taken seriously for any species capable of pair-bonding—which includes humans.

It is so far, however, an ethological theory, not a sociobiological one. Ethology, remember, is more interested in proximate mechanisms; sociobiology, in ultimate evolutionary logic. In an interview, however, Lorenz connected his imprinting idea with a plausible explanation as to why natural selection could select in favor of such a mechanism.[20] In short, he linked ethology with sociobiology and proximate cause with ultimate cause.

The idea is this. Believe it or not, in many birds that pair-bond and nest near one another, eggs and chicks have to be protected from cannibalism by the adults in neighboring territories.[21] Lorenz reasoned that if males are better at defending chicks than females are (and they are in many bird species), then a male-male pair would be better at defending them than a male-female pair would be. By what mechanism might a male-male pair-bond be produced? Why, by males having imprinted upon males as sexual partners; in adulthood, they would choose—"prefer," if you will—male partners over female partners when given a choice.

How would such a pair ever lay any eggs? Well of course the males themselves could not lay any, but as they each directed their typically masculine courtship performances toward the other, an unattached

---

[19] See Lorenz 1966/1963, pp. 195–200.

[20] Evans 1974.

[21] Cannibalism of chicks may seem to be a bizarre possibility, but if you've seen films of herring gulls gobbling down neighboring chicks—swallowing them whole, in fact—you take it seriously.

female in the vicinity might be stimulated by them and insert herself in between the two males somehow and be inseminated by one of them. She would lay her fertilized egg in the nest and then take off, returning in subsequent days every time she's ready to lay another egg. Probably about half the eggs in the nest would be fathered by one of the paired males and about half by the other. Indeed, Lorenz claimed that the relationship would sometimes become "triangular," with two males and one female participating in courtship simultaneously.

Here comes the sociobiological part. What would be the reproductive success of these males? Each would be rearing offspring that are his own about 50 percent of the time. If the threat of cannibalism from neighbors were very high and if the success of a male-male pair in preventing cannibalism was also high, then perhaps on average a male-male pair could raise more than twice as many chicks successfully as a male-female pair could. If so, and if there were not a predictable and strong bias as to which of the two males got to fertilize particular eggs,[22] then forming such male-male pairs could be completely consistent with evolutionary theory. Better yet, you wouldn't require kin selection in the explanation.[23]

And here's the coda of Lorenz's remarkable theory. He asserted in his interview that there was a species of bird in Iceland that showed exactly this pattern of male-male or triangular bonds in the wild!

Alas, the theory may not hold up. I wrote to the naturalist who Lorenz said conducted the study that found the male-male bonds. He wrote back that Lorenz was wrong; he had not sexed his birds (males and females are difficult to tell apart without capturing them) and thus he just didn't know whether his pairs were male-male pairs or male-female ones.[24] The possibility is intriguing—those California gulls were forming female-female pairs, mind you, long before anyone discovered them—but it is at the moment unproved. Moreover, his colleague later wrote me that there weren't any such "triangularly" bonded birds in this population, either.[25]

---

[22] That is, the probability of paternity really was about fifty-fifty. If it were a lot different from that—say, eighty-twenty—then one of the two males would be getting the short end of the stick. Then, the greater the disparity was, the more selection there would be for him to desert the nest.

[23] Mind you, if kin selection *were* operating—if the two males were brothers, say, rather than unrelated—than the r factor of 2 (twice as many chicks raised) would be reduced to 1.5, making it easier for the trait to spread.

[24] Letter from Peter Scott, January 24, 1975.

[25] Letter from G. V. T. Matthews, August 8, 1978 (Scott was abroad). I wrote Lorenz himself a letter (February 2, 1976) trying to resolve this discrepancy; I did not receive a reply, perhaps (as my colleagues suggested) because he was too busy. In his defense, I

However, aspects of Lorenz's theory are very attractive in their possible explanation of human homosexuality. As I mentioned in chapter 5, I believe that "lusty" sexual attractions in humans depend on a process that resembles imprinting, and I described the striking evidence that such a phenomenon actually is at work in both typical and atypical sexual preferences. Of all the theories of animal homosexuality—whether sociobiological or not—only the imprinting hypothesis really models well the notion of "preference" or "orientation." Surprisingly, this phenomenon has almost never been cited as even a remote parallel by people who study human homosexuality.[26] As you'll see in the next chapter, I think this is an unfortunate oversight.

Heterozygote Advantage

The final sociobiological theory is one proposed by zoologist John Kirsch, of the University of Wisconsin, and botanist James Rodman, of the National Science Foundation (both at Yale at the time it was first published). This theory picks up where a previous theory left off: a theory that involves something called hetero*zygote* advantage.[27]

A *zygote* is a fertilized egg. Recall that the nucleus of nearly every normal human cell has forty-six chromosomes, which come in twenty-three pairs. One set of twenty-three is in each sperm, and another set of twenty-three is in each egg. On the chromosomes are *genes*—roughly speaking, short stretches of DNA that code for the structure of proteins needed for life. Each gene occupies a particular spot on a particular chromosome. Since chromosomes come in pairs, so do genes; each gene is matched with another gene at the same spot (called a *locus*) on the paired chromosome. A person is called *homozygous* at a particular locus if he or she has two copies of the same gene at that locus. People are *heterozygous* at a given locus if they have copies of two different versions of the genes at that locus.

The simplest version of the Kirsch and Rodman theory first hypothesizes that there is a gene that, in a homozygous (double-dose) state, makes it likely that the person carrying those genes will be heterosex-

---

should point out that perhaps in the heat of the interview Lorenz simply got the species or the particular population wrong.

[26] I'll admit that I am guilty here myself. In half of my Ph.D. thesis, I discussed many models of human homosexuality in sociobiology and in the animal world, and this is one that I scarcely mentioned, although I did cite Lorenz's interview. See Weinrich 1976, part II.

[27] See Kirsch and Rodman 1982. The previous theory was proposed by G. Evelyn Hutchinson—now a grand old man of evolutionary biology, who also taught at Yale. See Hutchinson 1959.

ual. Then it hypothesizes that there is an alternate gene that, when homozygous, makes it likely that the person carrying those genes will be homosexual. But when people get one copy of each gene—one predisposing toward heterosexuality and the other toward homosexuality—then the theory hypothesizes that they will be bisexual. The key assumption is this: that the people with the highest reproductive success are *bi*sexuals who are hetero*zygous* for a gene supposed to influence sexual orientation.

Let us pause for a moment to show that this last assumption could make sense. Think, for example, of the Lorenz goose-imprinting theory applied to males. According to the Kirsch and Rodman theory, if you are heterosexual, then you carry two genes for heterosexuality; you pair with a female and have moderate reproductive success, since some of your offspring are cannibalized by your neighbors. If you are homosexual in the theory, then you carry two genes for homosexuality, you pair with a male, but you do not permit a female to involve herself in your copulations with your mate. In this case, no eggs are laid, and your reproductive success is zero. But if you are bisexual, according to this theory, you are homosexual enough to pair with another male and heterosexual enough to let a female participate in your courtship and lay her eggs every now and then. The chicks have two males to defend them, almost all survive, and your reproductive success is very high.

How does this mesh with the everyone-gets-married theory? In that scenario, if you carry two copies of the heterosexual gene,[28] then you marry and may have extramarital affairs that would cause you to have illegitimate children; these could disgrace your family and make it difficult for you to rear your legitimate children. If you carry two homosexual genes, then you don't get married and could disgrace your family because you don't carry on the family line. But if you carry one of each kind of gene, then you marry, have children, and have extramarital relationships with members of your own sex—with whom you cannot possibly have illegitimate children.

The final step of the theory comes from standard population genetics, which says that *whenever heterozygotes have a reproductive advantage, it is inevitable that both kinds of homozygotes will continue to be produced*—even if one kind of homozygote is much worse off than the other, reproductively speaking. In the present example, the pure homozygotes are called "homosexual" and "heterosexual," and the principle of heterozygote advantage in population genetics says that

---

[28] I am, of course, using the phrase "heterosexual gene" as a shorthand for the terms I used in the previous paragraph. Genes themselves are neither heterosexual nor homosexual.

they will inevitably be produced if the heterozygote—the bisexual—has the highest reproductive success. (Just how it happens that the heterozygote has the highest reproductive success is not important to the population-genetic theory; this is a fact that has to be observed, or plausibly worked out, as in Lorenz's example.)

It is easy to see why this would be the case. Suppose that all the homosexuality genes had almost died out. Then most people would be entirely heterosexual—and would also be having legitimate and illegitimate children right and left. The few people who had one homosexuality gene would do better, because they wouldn't be disgracing their families.[29] So the gene that helps save them from disgrace—the homosexuality gene—will spread. Likewise, if the heterosexuality gene was about to die out, people carrying it would tend to have higher reproductive success than those who were only producing homosexuals.[30]

One of the disadvantages of this theory, obviously, is that it is the most biologically deterministic of any of those I've discussed. It has very deterministic versions of "homosexuality genes" and "heterosexuality genes" but is merely the simplest of a *class* of theories that assume that a balance of heterosexual and homosexual tendencies might be most adaptive. Any one of these might be closer to the truth. In short, this class of theories assumes that bisexuality is biologically the best sexual orientation, evolutionarily speaking, and that both homosexuality and heterosexuality are reproductively inferior. *Any* such theory qualifies as a "Kirsch and Rodman theory" as long as there is some genetic predisposition for bisexuality that requires heterozygosity.

Another disadvantage of this theory is that it doesn't apply as well in societies that strongly disapprove of homosexuality. Obviously, if bisexual tendencies help you avoid the social shame of illegitimate births, you don't want to substitute the social shame of being discovered in homosexual liaisons. But there are many societies in which homosexuality is taken completely in stride, even as illegitimacy is

[29] Some readers will notice that I have slightly changed the terms of the everyone-gets-married theory for this discussion. All other things being equal, someone who has some illegitimate children will have a higher reproductive success than someone who has no illegitimate children; "some" is a bigger number than "none." But all other things are not equal—and maybe in this case they are never equal. In some societies, illegitimate children are no big problem, and so refraining from having them *is* a reproductively altruistic act. In other societies, illegitimate children *are* a big problem, and so refraining from having them might not be altruistic; it is just common sense. For a better discussion of this fine point, see Weinrich 1987.

[30] If this line of argument sounds familiar, that's because it is analogous to the case of sickle-cell anemia that everyone learns about in high school.

strongly disapproved. Classical Athens was such a society, for example. In Athens, it was very important for citizens to avoid sexual relations with slaves, at least in part because heterosexual liaisons with slaves could produce illegitimate children. But homosexual relations among citizens were not frowned on; indeed, they were encouraged.

And even this disadvantage can be turned around in a society like ours in which homosexual relations are strongly disapproved. Recall from an earlier chapter how Minnesota psychologist Eli Coleman studied married homosexual and bisexual men in psychotherapy. He found, as would be consistent with the everyone-marries theory, that these men had sexual relations only with men outside marriage, never with women. But there are presumably other men who are so conflicted about their homosexuality that they are *entirely* celibate outside their marriages (and perhaps nearly celibate within them) and are thus entirely likely to avoid fathering illegitimate children. Of course, these prohibitions apply to married heterosexuals, too, but heterosexuals in societies like ours may have proportionately more affairs than married homosexuals do, because (after all) the sexual attraction involved in heterosexuality is considered normal. It is as if society gained an advantage by inculcating guilt into people; the more guilt it can successfully inculcate, the more its aims can be reached. By permitting yourself to be socialized as a homosexual so guilty that you get married and then are dreadfully guilty about wanting extramarital affairs with members of your own sex, you have managed (a) to pass your genes on to the next generation and (b) to further reduce the chance that you will have illegitimate children. We might call this the "guilt is good for you" theory—although I should point out that it benefits the reproduction of your genes, not your psyche—and that it is even better for your relatives' genes.

DISCUSSION

I do not have the space to discuss in detail the four theories of sexual orientation in sociobiology that assume that homosexuality is maladaptive: that is, that it does not, and did not, in some way help in the reproduction of individual genes predisposing toward one or another sexual orientation. But I would like to comment on the possibility of maladaptation in general—which is very important in understanding *any* sociobiological theory applied to humans.

It is conceivable that homosexuality does not *now* help increase the reproductive success (or inclusive fitness) of homosexuals; after all, there are many maladaptive things that happen in modern life because our environment has changed so much from hunter-gatherer days. (Mind you, for all I know, homosexuality may be *more* adaptive than it was in the past.) But if homosexuality were anywhere near as common in hunter-gatherer days as it is now, then any maladaptive theory has a difficult task.

Recall the discussion about mutational equilibrium above, when I discussed evolutionary models of transsexualism. Transsexualism is so rare that it might be considered an evolutionary "mistake": the result, plain and simple, of genetic factors (mutations, say) that are in the process of being eliminated from the gene pool in every generation. But it is extremely difficult to claim that the same might be true of homosexuality, because homosexuality is so much more common than any mutational equilibrium theory would permit it to be.

But what about the possibility that homosexuality is an abnormality like teeth crooked enough to require braces, say, or diabetes, which is certainly more common than 1 in 10,000? For that matter, what about the common cold, which is an abnormal condition affecting a higher percentage of the population than homosexuality ever does?

These counterexamples are easily answered if you know the proper paths to follow in evolutionary theory. There are diseases that result, purely and simply, from a genetic mistake (a mutation or a recombination of recessive mutations) and that kill their victims, period. In these diseases, something fails to work right, and the result is death all the time or almost all the time. If transsexualism is such a "disease," then it results in what we might call "genetic death" when transsexuals never reproduce and fail to increase the reproductive success of their relatives. There are other diseases, however, that cause death or disability because, in some sense, *your DNA is fighting some other DNA (or RNA) and the other DNA wins.* That's a competitive interaction, not a mistake, and evolutionary theory puts it into an entirely different category. In fact, there is *no* general prediction that evolutionary theory makes about diseases like this except that both the disease-causing organism and the host will get better and better at fighting each other. Which will win in any specific case cannot be predicted; nor can we predict how common such diseases will be.

So much for the common cold; what about diabetes? All the evidence is not in yet, but the physicians I talk to tell me that diabetes seems to be caused by a slow-acting virus. The virus supposedly works by triggering an autoimmune disease in the host, which destroys the part of the pancreas that normally produces insulin. So diabetes need not occur merely at a mutational equilibrium.

Well, what about teeth that need braces? After all, if natural selection is so good at producing efficient structures, why do so many humans have mouths too small for their teeth? Is there a bug that makes teeth crooked? No. Here, the answer apparently is that our diet has changed drastically from the diet we ate as hunter-gatherers. It was as hunter-gatherers, you'll recall, that our physical attributes, including our teeth and the size and shape of our jaw, evolved away from those of other primates.

Well, some recent experiments showed that if you feed a "naturally tough" diet to squirrel monkeys, they chew a lot, and their jaws grow bigger than those of squirrel monkeys fed a diet of soft foods. The teeth of the natural-diet monkeys, for the most past, arranged themselves just fine: nineteen of twenty-two had "no observable occlusal deviations" in the study I'm referring to. But fourteen of eighteen of those given the soft diet exhibited "deviations . . . analogous to common human malocclusions—[including] . . . impacted malerupted premolars and second molars, malaligned crowded premolar rows, and crowded and rotated incisors."[31] In short, if you chew a lot, your jaw is bigger, and you don't need braces. And so in all probability our ancestors must have chewed a lot, a statement for which there is substantial independent confirmation. Grape Nuts, anyone?[32] Similarly, other "maladaptive" attributes may be the result of diet, change in life-style, etc., not natural selection.

Now let's return to the gender transpositions. Assume that homosexuals constitute somewhere between 5 percent and 10 percent of the population and that there are ten different subtypes of homosexuality, using ten different genetic mechanisms (and any number of environmental ones). Some of these subtypes might be very rare ev-

[31] Corruccini and Beecher 1982.

[32] Some critics of sociobiology accuse sociobiologists of explaining away every possible counterexample to sociobiological theory with "just so" stories not too different from those I've just recounted. But for both scientific and literary reasons I'm not going to apologize for using stories to explain things. Stories are powerful tools and have been used throughout human history; they are a natural means of communicating information for our species. And scientifically there is nothing wrong with a story that is backed up by properly gathered scientific evidence, as is the tooth example. Nor will I apologize for telling stories that haven't been proved true yet, since this is something all scientists do. For example, when I read about the latest development in theoretical physics, the most recent theory of quarks and gluons and whatever certainly sounds like a just-so story to me. You mean there's evidence that the such-and-such theory is inadequate? Well, if you just postulate a new kind of particle—one with "color" or "charm" or "top" and "bottom" properties—then the empirical contradiction goes away. See? It all works out, just so. No, the only problem with these stories is when they are accepted as truth without being tested. (That is to be distinguished from another acceptable use of theoretical stories with incomplete testing in which they are used to show a flaw in the logic of another theory. Such stories do not always have to have empirical evidence to back them up, although it is always better if they do.) So, are just-so stories a big problem in sociobiology? Sorry, it just isn't so.

olutionary mistakes, but at least one of them, and probably several, would be at least as common as 1 percent. And 1 percent is far more common than could be explained by any mutational-equilibrium theory.

To people on the street, 1 percent seems pretty rare. But mutational equilibriums are at least *100 times rarer*—1 in 10,000 (or less), rather than 1 in 100 or so. This makes it very unlikely that garden-variety homosexuality is a mutational mistake.[33] This in turn strongly suggests that at some time in our evolutionary history having homosexual desires or acts was in some way adaptive for the people who had them.

Accordingly, if you define "natural" as that which is produced by nature but not a freak error (i.e., not a mutation), then homosexuality is or was at some time or in some circumstances a natural occurrence—even using a strictly orthodox biological definition of "natural." This is not the only definition of "natural," of course, but it is a very biological one—perhaps the most biological one.

This argument probably also holds up for all the other gender transpositions except transsexualism. No one knows exactly how common transvestites and other cross-dressers are, but 1 percent is probably in the right ballpark, give or take a factor of five or so (somewhere between 0.2 percent and 5 percent of the population). So the very most extreme case—let's say 0.1 percent, or one-tenth of 1 percent—is about as low as anyone could claim without being laughed off the pages of the journals. But that figure is still ten times the size of the highest mutational equilibrium levels. Of course, when the cross-dressing is heterosexual, it need not interfere with reproduction at all, and there is no difficulty in explaining it at all from the point of view of reproduction. When the cross-dressing is homosexual, it may well interfere with reproduction, but then it presumably ought to be explained by the kin-selection model above. I'll discuss both these cases more in chapter 14.

In the discussion so far, I have left out the null transposition, heterosexuality. Heterosexuality is the most common gender transposition in our society. It is thus very unlikely that it is due to a mere genetic mistake. The fabled fit between penis and vagina involved in

---

[33] It was precisely this point that got Hutchinson 1959 thinking about his theory, because it was the Kinsey statistics (1948 and 1953) that showed that homosexuality was much too common to be explained simply as genetic pathology. At that time, the moderately maladaptationist heterozygote advantage theory was the only way to resolve this puzzle, because kin selection had not been worked out. But even heterozygote advantage postulates some advantage to the hypothesized homosexuality gene: it's evolutionarily advantageous to get one copy of it (but not two).

many heterosexual acts also suggests that at some time in our evolutionary history heterosexuality did contribute to the propagation of the species, perhaps even significantly so.[34] Of course, the mere existence of a biologically determined structure is not sufficient evidence to conclude that modern humans must or even ought to use that structure in the ways it has been used in the past. If it were, men would not shave off their beards, women would not shave their armpits, and neither sex would wash the natural scents off their bodies and replace them with deodorants designed to counteract the natural odor-trapping functions of pubic and underarm hair. But in all probability modern heterosexuals do use their penises and vaginas in the ways they were used in the past as well as in other ways.

Let's return to the mutational-equilibrium argument. Notice that this argument is very general; it doesn't depend on kin selection or, for that matter, on any specific theory of the causes of the gender transpositions. But some arguments do. What if someone argued that society should accept the gender transpositions because those traits were selected for by natural selection and are thus "natural"? Perhaps that theory will be proved wrong. Wouldn't that demonstrate that they are unnatural?

Of course the answer is no, and by thinking of homosexuality we can see why. Before the theory of kin selection was developed, was homosexuality universally scorned as unnatural? Of course not; there were and are many definitions according to which homosexuality is perfectly natural.[35] If someone claims that homosexuality was selected for by natural selection and so homosexuality is natural, and if their theory proves wrong, that simply means that they no longer can prove to themselves that homosexuality is natural. It does not demonstrate that homosexuality is unnatural. This is a logical fallacy warned against in many elementary logic textbooks ("affirming the consequent," I believe).[36]

Who, after all, dragged nature into the social debate in the first place? It was, of course, the people who thought they had an airtight argument that homosexuality is *un*natural—the argument being that homosexual acts can't conceive children and that conceiving children is

---

[34] Whether that fit remains evolutionarily advantageous today is, of course, subject to question, because it might motivate couples to have more children than they can raise properly.

[35] For example, one professor I know defines natural as "according to the laws of matter and energy"—so if something happens, it's natural. Unnatural acts don't happen, although we can imagine them; for example, something going up that doesn't come down.

[36] Precisely this fallacy was committed in a 1976 article by Stephen Jay Gould, who should have known better.

the be-all and end-all of evolution. The very existence of a plausible theory—kin selection—that says that having your own children is *not* the be-all and end-all of evolution punctures a permanent hole in this argument. Even if a particular version of a kin-selectionist theory is disproved, this unnaturalness argument is demonstrably fallacious unless it can be demonstrated that kin selection in general is wrong or unless every single adaptive theory of the gender transpositions can be proved wrong. And that's a tall order, because some of those theories haven't even been imagined yet!

Moreover, one theory—the everyone-marries theory—calls attention to the fact that there are ways in which a non-reproductive sexual act can be beneficial precisely because it is non-reproductive. Even if this particular theory proves incorrect, it has pointed out another fallacy.

None of this is to argue that sociobiological theories of homosexuality are sociopolitically risk-free. Many people can be deceived by fallacies that sound logical, and so it is always unfortunate, and sometimes tragic, when a scientific theory or experimental finding is twisted by people intent on tricking society into reaching a particular conclusion. Frankly, I would expect gay people to be petrified by a theory that takes, as its initial assumption, the notion that people's behavior arises ultimately from the logic of maximizing reproductive success. That sociobiology has on the contrary produced theories that tend to view homosexuality in a positive, adaptive light is remarkable. Even more remarkable is that they were produced by sociobiology's pioneers—Wilson and Trivers, for example—in the earliest days of the discipline.

There's a reason for this, and that is the importance of sociobiology's central hypothesis: adaptation. Of course, that's where I began this chapter: describing how sociobiology tends to ask what went right with a particular minority's (or majority's) behavior instead of what went wrong. We have thus come full circle. So let's look back over our journey to see where we've been.

14

THE BIG PICTURE

Homosexuality is not a hereditary condition . . . since homosexuals engage in heterosexual intercourse so rarely, it would be hard to produce enough little homosexuals to replenish the supply.

David Reuben, M.D., *Cosmopolitan*, April 1974, pp. 182–183.

I had once been hell-bent on discovering the origins of my lesbianism. It was a passion, one of my favorite hobbies. . . . It doesn't matter anymore why I'm gay. What matters now is how I'm gay.

Regina Kahney, *Gay Community News* [Boston], 20 March 1976, pp. 10–13.

You're not dead inside, honey; you're alive and sick and living in New York like 8 million other people. You're never gonna be normal, but you're special and you can have a hell of a lot of fun.

Craig Russell, as the drag queen Robin Turner, to Hollis McLaren, as mental patient Liza Connors, in *Outrageous!*, the longest-running movie at the Orson Welles Cinema, Cambridge, Mass.

We've come a long way in this book. So far, we've been able to undertake each segment of our trip fairly independently of the next. But now we've got to take in the big picture and see how everything fits together.

This chapter is by far the most speculative one in this book. If the three most important facts about a piece of real estate are location, location, and location, then the three most important things about science are why?, why?, and why? And that's the reason why I've spent so much time explaining things. I want to design a *complete* explanation of the gender transpositions, and of course I haven't finished. The sober types will complain that we don't know enough facts yet, and they're right. That shouldn't stop us from starting to theorize. I am the architect of desire, and I think I can rough out some plans.

My first task is to consider what such a complete explanation would consist of. My second is to illustrate these considerations by building a model of the berdache that might one day become such a complete explanation. My final task is to give answers to the ten puzzles I haven't answered yet from chapter 3—for which it turns out that the berdache model will be helpful.

A SPECIAL WAY OF THINKING

In this chapter, I'll sometimes use a particular method of sociobiological reasoning that can be disorienting. I will be writing as if people make *calculations* of the reproductive effects that particular decisions have on themselves and their kin—their sociobiological costs and benefits, if you will. But we all know that people don't make such calculations consciously. Instead, they are motivated by greed, love, money, power, empathy, lack of tenure, and a variety of other things that seem to have nothing to do with reproduction. So let me make this disorienting logic more sensible by discussing an experiment anyone can perform at home.

Go over to your stove and turn on one of the burners. Let it get good and hot. Now put your hand firmly onto the burner and hold it there for sixty seconds.

Ouch! That's ridiculous! If you were stupid enough to follow my instructions, I certainly hope you pulled your hand away from the burner long before the sixty seconds were up. So now let me ask, *why* did you pull your hand away?

The proximate reason, of course, is the "Ouch!" You have a reflex built into the nerves of your arm and hand that gets you to withdraw your hand from burning-hot objects as soon as you touch them. But why do you have that reflex built in in the first place?

The ultimate answer is that hot stoves touching human hands damage tissue and *damaged tissue, back in hunter-gatherer days, was associated with reduced reproductive success.* It is this ultimate fact that caused the evolution of the circuits that proximately caused you to pull your hand back. Those circuits are capable of making some pretty fine distinctions: for example, sitting *near* a hot fire can be pleasant, even transcendent; sitting *on* a hot fire is neither. (Or, as any reader of "Goldilocks" knows, the soup can be too cold, too hot, or just right.) The process of making these pretty fine distinctions I call *calculations,* and evolutionary biology says these calculations have to be made in the light of our evolutionary past.

As you read this chapter, you'll have to keep in mind scenarios like the following one. Our human ancestors spent a lot of time as hunter-gatherers, for which certain environmental conditions prevailed. Because of the connection back then between burning your hand and reproductive success, hand burning evolved so as to feel bad.[1] Likewise, if we can presume a connection back then between staring deeply into your lover's eyes and reproductive success, then staring deeply into your lover's eyes would have evolved so as to feel good. Obviously, if you tell a pair of lovers that it feels good to stare into each other's eyes because doing so will eventually increase their reproductive success, they'll think you're silly at best and crazy at worst. And in the proximate sense, they'd be right; that's not the conscious reason why lovers do what they do. But in the ultimate sense it is.

Here's how sociobiological anthropologist Melvin Konner, chairman of the anthropology department at Emory University in Atlanta, put it to his pediatrician regarding the joys of rearing a puking, screaming, brand-new packet of reproductive success known as his daughter.

> "Tell me, Doctor" (I said). "You've been in this business a long time. [. . .] She's ruining my life. She's ruining my sleep, she's ruining my health, she's ruining my work, she's ruining my relationship with my wife, and . . . and . . . and she's ugly." [. . .]
> "Why do I like her?"
> The physician [. . .] seemed most unbaffled by the problem.
> "You know"—he shrugged his shoulders—"parenting is an instinct and the baby is the releaser."
> "Doctor," I said. "That's one of the worst clichés from one of my own worst lectures!"

Konner is, of course, well aware of the difference between a proximate explanation and an ultimate one. He knows exactly why he loves his daughter—in the ultimate, evolutionary sense. But he frankly admits in this passage that he hasn't figured out the proximate reason. In fact, figuring out the proximate reason isn't easy—not for Konner and not for Konner's pediatrician. After all, babies *are* ugly, just like

---

[1] Careful readers will notice that I've omitted a step here. Not only must there be an association between a behavior and reproductive success, but there must also be some genetic basis for the behavior—some genetic variability that natural selection can operate upon. Such variability, contrary to popular opinion, probably exists for a wide variety of human behaviors, even trivial ones. For details, see the footnotes in chapter 13.

Cabbage Patch dolls, and it was a surprise when those dolls were a hit.

Notice that if there were a better proximate answer, we might be tempted to overlook the ultimate one. If you could truly say, "I love my infant daughter because if I didn't, my hand would get burned," then a proximate explanation is obvious. The ultimate explanation would look more bizarre, and it would take someone with special insight to see that the proximate answer fell short of being a complete one.

Likewise, there is *no* good proximate answer to the question of why you like staring into your lover's eyes. "It feels good" is as close as you can come, and that's like saying that Cabbage Patch dolls are cute.

Of course, eventually we will be able to answer questions about behavior on *all* levels. We'll know the ultimate evolutionary reason why a particular emotion evolved. We'll know the details of the circuits in the brain that supervise those emotions. We'll know how environmental events make and break the connections in those circuits, and we'll know the physiological mechanisms that connect the environment with the making and the breaking. Until then, however, it's important to keep the various levels of explanation separate in our minds. We're used to thinking at one level in our everyday affairs. Sometimes sociobiologists explain at those levels, but sometimes they don't. This can be disorienting.

More on Imprinting

The response from Konner's pediatrician makes another point, albeit indirectly: Imprinting doesn't just happen in childhood. Konner was not in love with that daughter when he was young; he fell paternally in love with her—imprinted upon her image, according to the pediatrician—when he was an adult. Although it is true that imprinting is probably more common among the young than among the old, that should not prevent us from looking for it later in childhood, or in adulthood. For example, adult gulls imprint on the patterns of spots on their nestlings' heads; this enables them to feed only the nestlings that are their own, and not their neighbors'.[2]

Well, then, what's the difference between imprinting and good old-fashioned learning? Why not just say that the adults *learn* the pattern

---

[2] With the economy typical of an animal that ought to be assumed smart until proved dumb, this imprinting does not take place until just before the nestlings mature to the point where they might start waddling around.

of spots on their nestlings' heads? Why not just say that Konner learned what his daughter looked like?

Because imprinting is a special form of learning; it's weird when judged by the standards of learning things like the names of the fifty states or learning someone's name. In particular, imprinting is not performed consciously, it can have seemingly illogical effects, and it takes place during restricted periods of time.[3]

We will eventually understand how imprinting works physiologically.[4] When we do, we'll be able to answer Konner's question proximately—although I doubt that answering this proximate question will make the behavior any more comprehensible on an intellectual level. And we'll have forged one more link in the chain leading from ultimate explanations to proximate ones.

But of course Konner's love is already explained ultimately: He loves his daughter because his daughter represents reproductive success to him. Or, more precisely, he loves his daughter because processes have operated upon him that were strongly associated with reproductive success in our hunter-gatherer past. As I pointed out back in chapter 1, this is no mystery. The nonreproductive gender transpositions are puzzling to evolutionary biologists because they do not have such an obvious ultimate explanation.

Explanations: What Went Right Versus What Went Wrong

I will soon use this unusual, sociobiological way of explaining things to explain why some American Indian men would become berdaches and why doing so might not be biologically "unnatural" at all. The best explanation, I think, begins with the concept of an alternate reproductive strategy. But at this point I have to repeat a warning I gave you in an earlier chapter, because there's a very bad mistake that's easy to make. Even if you recall this warning, I want to use it to make an additional point.

Let's pretend that we are all females from a species that can reproduce by parthenogenesis. (No sex, please; we just make ova that never split from the diploid to the haploid state.) Let's say we don't know that there are also men in our species, even though we are (unwit-

[3] For example, as suggested in the previous footnote, those adult gulls only imprint upon their chicks' head-spot patterns during a few days, and chicks can only imprint upon the appearance of their mothers during a restricted period of time. Attempts to get chicks or parents to imprint at other times fail.

[4] See Martin 1978 for an example of the hormones involved in imprinting.

tingly) capable of reproducing sexually as well as asexually.[5] And now suppose that we were to encounter a man, then study him thoroughly—but not thoroughly enough.

"What's wrong with this animal?" we might say. "Its breasts are missing; how could it ever feed its children? Its clitoris is too big. It's missing hair from the top of its head, and it's got too much hair everywhere else. It can't even have babies. What went wrong?"

Then those of us who are evolutionary biologists might add, "Is this some weird kind of mutation? Proof that the theory of punctuated equilibrium isn't all it's made out to be? An imaginary beast from a Stephanie Spielberg movie?"

The point is obvious: if we don't know the purposes for which this particular animal was designed—that is, if we don't think about ultimate explanations—we run the risk of thinking that a normal variation is a mistake. *This is true even if the normal variation really is poorer at doing something important to us.* For example, it really is true that these weird male animals can't bear babies. But of course that doesn't really mean that they suffer from a defect in workmanship or materials.[6]

We have to be careful not to make a corresponding mistake about the gender transpositions. For example, to switch my illustration from male/female to heterosexual/homosexual, let's say that we're trying to figure out this strange kind of animal that some of us call *Homo sapiens heterosexualis*. We watch these animals grow up, observe their courtship rituals, and discover that they became heterosexual (in a proximate sense) because they imprinted on members of the other sex during childhood sexual-rehearsal play. So we get out our brain scanners, do our experiments, and discover that a hormone called *corticosterone* is involved in this imprinting process.[7] We inject human babies with anticorticosteroid drugs and discover that they then grow up to become homosexual because they no longer imprint on members of the other sex. Well, this is a great day for science, because we've discovered a cause of heterosexuality, right?

Right. But if we don't know the purposes for which heterosexuality

[5] Just this scenario was used in a Utopian feminist novel from the nineteenth century, reprinted as Gilman 1979.

[6] For a very well reasoned argument to the contrary, see Sims 1982. Sims argues that men are, evolutionarily speaking, hopelessly much more primitive than women and concludes that they must constitute a different species. But men ("beast humans") and women ("true humans") still have to get along. Her solution is for women to "bestialize" themselves—that is, bring themselves down to the men's level. I don't know which cheek Sims keeps her tongue in, but her sense of humor is delightful.

[7] Martin 1978 showed that injecting corticosterone into newly hatched ducklings reduced the "following" behavior characteristic of imprinting in that species and injections of substances that oppose corticosterone chemically increased the following response.

was "designed," then we run the risk of thinking that heterosexuality is a mistake: it's what happens when somebody has "too much" corticosteroid running around in their bloodstream during sexual-rehearsal play. And if someone complains that we're being prejudiced, then we simply reply that no, we're just being scientific; after all, Masters and Johnson have demonstrated how wretched the sex life of these creatures is.

Of course, I can't give you this example with a straight face. In our society, it's homosexuals, transsexuals, and cross-dressers who are, in the opinion of the heterosexual majority, the ones in need of an explanation. But that opinion only has validity when it comes to ultimate explanations, not proximate physiological ones. As I've explained, heterosexual acts are no mystery when it comes to ultimate explanations. But proximately—when it's all that corticosteroid we're talking about—heterosexuality and the other gender transpositions are equally mysterious.

I'm about to plunge into explanations of a lot of behaviors that have baffled scientists for years. As a sociobiologist, I will for the most part be asking what went right with these behaviors, not what went wrong. And when I try to explain something, it's not because I want to single it out to make it seem bizarre or deviant. In fact, my goal is very simple and very imperialistic: I want to explain everything. I will fail, of course, but that's the nature of the beast; it will be worth trying to pursue this impossible dream, anyway.

Alternate Male *Non*reproductive Strategies

The alternate male reproductive strategies I discussed in chapter 13 are a good example of how important it is to keep purposes and ultimate explanations in mind. Recall the red deer, among whom there are two kinds of males: those with antlers and those without (hummels). Recall also that after enough generations, an equilibrium is reached so that the "decision" as to whether to pursue the antlered strategy or the hummel strategy becomes a toss-up for an average red deer male.

But not all deer are average. A deer's individual circumstances could influence the payoffs to be expected from the two strategies. Some males may be too weak or too crippled ever to succeed following the antlered strategy, and they will in some sense have to "settle" for being a hummel. But there can be males becoming hummels for what amounts to simple "economic" reasons, especially at equilibrium, when theory says investment in the two strategies on average will feature equal returns. If these non-"loser" males had reproductive-success accountants, each would be told that it's just plain a better investment for them, this year, not to grow those expensive antlers. It's not that they can't; it's just that they shouldn't bother.

But as I pointed out in chapter 1, there is nothing in evolutionary theory that says that all individuals *have* to have their own offspring. Remember there are species in which the majority of individuals do not reproduce at all (the most fully social species of ants, bees, and termites, for example); it is kin selection (chapter 13) that can explain how such arrangements can evolve under the action of natural selection. So although the examples of alternate strategies that began chapter 13 are indeed alternate *reproductive* strategies (i.e., those pursuing them do try to reproduce), there is no evolutionary reason why males or females pursuing alternate strategies *have* to have their own offspring as long as they act in a way consistent with kin-selection theory. That is, we can consider alternate strategies that are *non*reproductive and *non*heterosexual. Let me now discuss the possibility that such alternate nonreproductive strategies existed in hunter-gatherer groups.

THE BERDACHE AS AN INTERMEDIARY BETWEEN MEN AND WOMEN

I have referred to Walter Williams's book on the berdache in several previous chapters. From the data presented in that book, it is very reasonable to draw the conclusion that berdaches are (or were) pursuing alternate strategies[8]—alternate *nonreproductive* strategies.

According to Williams, one of the most important functions of the berdache was to act as an intermediary between the men and the women in a tribe. This function was explicitly noted by many of his informants and is visible even in the photographs taken of tribes decades ago. For example, if someone were to take a photograph of the people living in a small town in the United States today, I suspect that the residents would, without being told to do so by the photographer, arrange themselves roughly in family groups. Men and women would appear to be randomly intermixed in such a photo, but you could make sense of their arrangement if you knew who was related to whom. This would reflect the fact that many Americans are used to thinking of themselves as members of nuclear-family units, first and foremost.

[8] And perhaps also that "amazons"—Williams's term for particular types of masculine women—were pursuing alternate female strategies, although Williams presents much less information on them.

American Indian social structure was different. Williams reprints a photograph of a Zuñi tribe in which the men and boys all appear on the photographer's right and the women and girls on the photographer's left, a pattern that was apparently common among American Indians. Standing taller than anyone else in the photo, precisely in between the men and the women, is the tribe's berdache, We-wha.[9]

Williams reports, and my own review of the literature confirms, that this intermediate social status of the berdache was widespread. Also widespread was the status of the berdache as an *intermediary*. It received overt recognition in ceremonies in a large number of tribes where, in dance and/or song, the berdache was recognized as the kind of person who would mediate between the sexes. This could be by virtue of himself exhibiting a combination of traits from the two sexes, by virtue of formally recognized customs assigning him such roles, or both. In some tribes, for example, berdaches were matchmakers, helping to hook up eligible boys and girls in marriage.

Williams's conclusion has excellent support from sociobiological theory, which suggests that it could be important to have such a mediator between the sexes. Let me digress for a moment to explain.

The Theory of Matchmaking

The theory that follows is presented sociobiologically, but most of it need not be. All it results in is two conclusions: (1) that men and women on average pursue different reproductive interests and (2) that members of each sex can deceive themselves as to the rightness or reasonableness of their own strategy. If you agree with these conclusions, then you can dispense with the sociobiology, as some have. Here, for example, is a statement of these conclusions, very much in the tradition of Thurber, from a delightful parody by Margot Sims:

> During high school I went steady with a boy named Tommy, and he usually went steady with me too. . . . Tommy and I broke up in April of our senior year because I had stayed home one weekend writing a term paper for him so he could attend a Christian youth conference. When I learned that he had actually spent the weekend drinking with some friends and having sexual relations with two older women, I became angry. Tommy told me I was prudish and nosey and never called me again, even though I wrote him several letters of apology. . . . During the hours I was wait-

[9] Williams 1986, plate 10, following p. 276.

ing by the telephone for Tommy to call, I couldn't help feeling that there might actually be some difference between males and females.[10]

As I have mentioned in previous chapters, sociobiologists often adopt a Thurberesque view of the relations between men and women. Although most sociobiologists admit—indeed, insist—that men and women can pair-bond, they also know that some men would like to bond with more than one woman (i.e., have more than one wife or lover, as in polygyny) and that far more men than women would like to have casual sex—the sort that could result in children that the man might not support.

This is not to deny that some men are happily monogamous; such men will not see any conflict between the reproductive strategy they are pursuing and the strategy their wives are pursuing. But many men, according to most sociobiologists, will find that they want variety in their sex lives. Mind you, there are theories that explain why *women* would be interested in sexual variety, but the sociobiologists who have proposed such theories (theories I happen to agree with) would admit that the variety would be pursued in different ways, for different purposes.[11]

So there would be no sociobiological controversy at all in response to the suggestion that the typical man's reproductive strategy is quite different from the typical woman's reproductive strategy; the only debate would be over just what those strategies are and over what proportions of each sex pursue them. And finally, there would be no controversy over the ultimate cause of the conflicts in these reproductive strategies: women and men usually pursue different strategies because they usually have different reproductive interests.

Sociobiology also has a *general* theory of conflict, whether it be sexual or nonsexual. This theory concludes that when the fundamental interests of two kinds of animals are in conflict, both kinds will, over evolutionary time, get better and better at dealing with the other's strategy. Predators will evolve better strategies to catch prey, and prey will develop better strategies to avoid getting caught. Casanovas will get better at seducing women and then abandoning them, and women will get better at detecting Casanova tendencies and avoiding the men who embody them. Women wanting to confuse men about the paternity of their children will get better at confusing them, and men

---

[10] Sims 1982, preface.
[11] For an exposition, see Hrdy 1981.

worried about investing in children not their own will get better at not being cuckolded.[12]

Sociobiological theory (and other theories, too, for that matter) next predicts that when there is a fundamental conflict of reproductive interests between two groups, one of the strategies each group will probably use in its never-ending battle with the other is *self*-deception. After all, if a man's seemingly being in love with a woman will make her more likely to give in to his advances, what better strategy for a Casanova than to truly believe (*this* time, anyway) that he *is* in love with this fresh female face? After all, if a woman telling her lover that he really is the father of her child will make him more likely to invest in that child, what better strategy for a woman bent on suggesting paternity than if she herself *really does* forget about the other men she was sleeping with at the time of conception?

This argument extends, too, to less specific instances of conflict between the sexes. When a marriage breaks up, just what is an appropriate division of common property? When one partner is unfaithful, just what is an appropriate punishment or restitution? Just what's fair in love? Sociobiology says that women and men will have, on average, different answers to all these questions and that the passion with which they pursue these answers will be heightened by self-deception about the reasonableness of their particular sex's point of view.

The stage is clearly set for a battle royal: a battle in which each side is convinced that its point of view is entirely reasonable and in which many members of each side are to a significant degree *unable* to see the validity in the other side's point of view—because their self-deception mechanisms are working so well.

Enter the arbitrator. When the unions and management disagree, apparently implacably so, there arises a market for an arbitrator: someone who can scout out the points made by both sides and help them reach an accommodation. After all, a strike and lockout that last forever hurt both sides too much.

Likewise, when men's and women's interests disagree, enter the matchmaker or the negotiator. For if men's and women's reproductive strategies are so at odds with one another that no one actually gets it on and has kids, those strategies will have turned out to be foolish indeed, evolutionarily speaking.

There are several important things to point out about arbitrators, matchmakers, and similar sorts of people. First, they must be *seen* to

[12] *Cuckoldry* is when a woman fools a man into believing that a child of hers was fathered by him when in fact it was fathered by someone else.

be impartial by both sides. Second, they won't be seen as impartial for very long unless their interests are set up so as to *make* them impartial. And third, good ones *benefit* from being good at what they do. That is, they take a commission: a commission that each side is willing to pay because it comes out of whatever it is that would have been wasted by shortsighted or even vindictive acts performed by the combatants.

The Berdache as Arbitrator: Evidence

All three of these points seem to apply to the berdache when we view the berdache from any of several perspectives, including a sociobiological one.

First, the formal status of berdaches, as shown by Williams, was one that permitted both sexes to consult them. Berdaches were, at least in some tribes, fully integrated socially into the tribe's matchmaking and conflict-resolution procedures. They almost invariably were viewed as people who mixed both masculine and feminine attributes—a fact that would itself be attractive to someone of one sex having trouble understanding or dealing with the other—and as people who had a special calling to do so. So the first requirement for being a good arbitrator is satisfied by berdaches.

The third point is also satisfied; not only were berdaches often paid for their services (in cash or its equivalent), but they also received less quantifiable benefits. For example, they had a high status in general (some were chiefs in the ruling councils), and many were shamans. Shamans and leaders doubtless received, as doctors and politicians do today, information and intelligence about the true extent of conflicts, weaknesses, and strengths of various individuals and groups. *Such information is valuable*; in particular, in a hunter-gatherer context, viewed sociobiologically, it would be valuable to one's relatives.

The second requirement is also satisfied by the berdache, especially when viewed sociobiologically. The important aspect is parenthood: although some berdaches fathered children before, after, or even during the time they occupied the role, most berdaches did not. Sociobiologically speaking, then, let me ask this: what are the reproductive interests of people who, for whatever reason, do not and will not have children of their own?

Once asked, the question has an obvious answer. If such people's genes appear in the next generation only because of the reproduction of their relatives, then their reproductive interests are the same as those of their relatives taken as a whole.[13]

Come to think of it, most people have roughly *equal* numbers of male and female relatives. If your genes will show up in the next generation only through the reproduction of those relatives, then *it is no longer in your reproductive interests to view the world with the bias otherwise characteristic of your sex.* By withdrawing from reproduction, you withdraw from the benefits of being a successful Casanova or a successfully cuckolding wife. If people seek advice from you about relations between the sexes, since you have ruled out being either a Casanova or a cuckolder, you can adopt a more evenhanded point of view, for it will not be in your interests to deceive yourself about which strategy is more immoral or which sex is being more reasonable. You might possibly help your male relatives be better Casanovas and your female relatives be better cuckolders, but if so, you won't find it to your advantage to help one sex of relative more than the other, because you are equally related to your male relatives as you are to your female relatives.

The conclusion of all this theorizing is simple: it is quite likely that berdaches *really will* be more likely to see the world of reproductive conflict as it really is rather than deceiving themselves in the manner of many of the members of the sex they were born into or of the sex whose roles they perform.

So all three conditions required for effective arbitration or matchmaking may be satisfied in the case of the berdache: berdaches will have reproductive interests that *really are* more evenly distributed between those of average men and those of average women, and accordingly they can *really be* more evenhanded. From society's point of view, formal recognition of such evenhandedness probably *really is* merited and worth granting to berdaches. And if they *really can* help the sexes get along with less wasteful effort, berdaches probably really can extract a benefit for themselves (and their kin) for playing this special role.

The Personality of the Berdache

If this analysis is correct, then it ought to be reflected in the personality, including the sexual behavior, of the berdache. Let's return to

---

[13] Each relative's importance, mind you, being weighted by the degree of relatedness r between the relative and the berdache.

that possibility to see if what we know about it fits the theory I've sketched out above.

One of Williams's major conclusions is that berdaches are—or were—not so much men who *cross* the gender boundary as they are men who *mix* the gender roles of the two sexes. This is exactly what we would expect if a berdache is to be viewed by gender-unmixed women and men (i.e., ordinary heterosexuals) as someone who knows about both masculine and feminine things from personal experience. It is also exactly what we would expect from an individual who is not planning to take either a masculine or a feminine role in reproduction. After all, sexual dimorphism is hypothesized to result from males and females dividing up (over evolutionary time) the tasks needed to rear offspring and the tasks needed to survive. If you are not going to have offspring or pair with a number of the other sex who can be expected to have been trained in one of these two roles, there is less of a need for you to refrain from learning aspects of the other sex's role.[14] That is, some (not all) sex roles exist *for a reason*—rearing children efficiently—and if you're not going to rear your own children, there is less reason for you to restrict yourself by following them. In fact, to the extent that sex roles involve acts that benefit not particular children but society as a whole, it may be good to have people around who can move back and forth between roles men are supposed to play and those women are supposed to play, as environmental factors change the balance of which kinds of roles are more useful to the tribe as a whole at the moment.

Another aspect of the berdache's role is sexual. Williams recounts many instances in which the berdache had sexual relations with the male members of the tribe—several of them, in fact. For example, in the olden days a berdache might accompany men on a war party; nowadays, he might go along on a skyscraper-construction job in a distant city. In both scenarios, he would cook for the men, look after their emotional needs, and help satisfy their sexual needs. (Indeed, Williams tells the story of a modern expedition fitting this pattern precisely.) According to Williams, this role helped reduce prostitution in

---

[14] The comparison I made with dancing in chapter 11 also applies here. Dancing in couples usually requires each member of each couple to adopt a particular role in the dance. In societies in which dancers do not pair off (as in many Indian tribes), separate roles and steps for men and for women often persist. Interestingly, many tribes had *special* roles for berdaches to take in the dances—sometimes even roles that explicitly symbolized the berdache's intermediate status and in at least one case a role that explicitly recognized the berdache's sexual contacts.

Indian tribes and perhaps also reduced conflict over extramarital affairs.[15]

Remember, however, that the role actually taken up by a particular berdache may have been quite different from the ideal role assigned to him by the culture at large (or, mind you, by the anthropologist describing it to us). As I concluded in chapter 5, the range of variation in gender-role behavior among modern berdaches is not much different from the range of behaviors we see today in all the gender transpositions. Let me expand on this possibility.

A man whom scientists nowadays call a heterosexual transvestite is someone who might well have taken up the berdache role had he been an Indian—but then he probably would only have taken up the role from time to time, as the feminine aspect of his persona waxed and waned. Such a man, I suspect, would not have been viewed as being as powerful a berdache in gender matters, because he would (or could) be married heterosexually and benefit from succeeding at the male reproductive strategies. Nevertheless, he could have had valuable insights into women's roles and points of view that ordinary men would not have.

Similarly, a man who moves, as he gets older, from being what scientists now call a "transvestite" to what they call a "transsexual" (another pattern not rare today) would correspond to an Indian who took up more and more aspects of the berdache role as he got older. Since the reproductive interests of men and women converge as they get older, this transformation, too, would make sense evolutionarily.

It is modern drag queens and effeminate gay men, however, who seem to constitute the most likely category (and arguably the most common one) to fulfill the berdache's duties in traditional societies. In previous chapters, I cited examples, taken from Williams, of a couple of Western drag queens who acted uncannily like berdaches and of a pair of berdaches who, upon moving to a big city, acted uncannily like drag queens.[16] Drag queens carry gender mixing to its most integrated extreme and begin doing so at an early age. Characteristically, they are sexually interested in men they consider "normal" (i.e., heterosexual and masculine) and are occupationally interested in stereo-

---

[15] Sociobiologically, the argument for these particular functions is not strong. However, Williams cannot be faulted for this, as he is not a sociobiologist.

[16] I recently discovered an interview with Williams in which he states that although no translation of the term "berdache" into ordinary English is completely adequate, the word "queen" is perhaps the best (see interview conducted by Charley Shively, *Gay Community News*, 18–24 January 1987).

typically feminine jobs such as hairdresser or interior decorator (although rarely, if ever, in those involved in child rearing, such as day-care worker or nanny).

Take all these characteristics of drag queens and mute them and you get a good description of those modern gay men who are mildly effeminate. Drop the effeminate aspects, confine the others to childhood and adolescence, but continue the avoidance of stereotypically masculine roles and you get a good description of most of the rest of modern gay men.[17]

Lesbians and female-to-male transsexuals also fit neatly into this picture under certain circumstances, although we know less about them in history and anthropology.[18] Here is an illustration from among the Nuer tribes in Africa, who were cattle herders (not hunter-gatherers) of the upper Nile, and among whom a bride-price was perhaps the single most important feature of marriage.[19]

Payment of the bride-price from the groom's family to the bride's family was made in installments. As a courting couple proceeded from betrothal to marriage to consummation, each stage was marked by specific ceremonies.[20] When a woman took up the role of a man, she would thereby take on a man's social role—including the obligation to pay a bride-price when she married other women. On the other hand, she received the father's, brother's, uncle's, or son's shares of a bride-price when one of her family's women got married. She ordinarily allowed her wife to have brief affairs with "other" men, just as most male husbands did among the Nuer (who were not particularly monogamous). These genetic fathers received a single head of cattle if their liaisons resulted in a daughter, just as they would have had the husband been a man.

These patterns were described by the famous anthropologist E. E. Evans-Pritchard, who mentioned that a woman who marries as a man was "generally barren." Such a woman often received cattle in return for performing shamanistic magic. So even though the Nuer were not

[17] I will substantiate the psychological aspects of this assertion later in this chapter.

[18] In preparing my Ph.D. thesis, for example, I found only about one-third as many cultures had female-to-male institutions described as male-to-female ones. (See Weinrich 1976, part 2, tables 1 and 2.) Devereux 1937 or 1963 has one of the best descriptions of a female-to-male berdache, in spite of its being heavily psychoanalytic. As this book went to press, I heard that Pueblo lesbian Paula Gunn Allen's book on lesbianism and female gender variations among American Indians was about to be published—an event that should significantly help redress this imbalance. See also Williams 1986, chapter 11.

[19] Evans-Pritchard 1951, pp. 108–109.

[20] Interestingly enough in the light of proceptivity and female choice, if a young woman wanted to propose to a man, her technique would be to go over to his corral and make off with some of his family's cattle.

hunter-gatherers, we nevertheless see an association I will describe in the next section: an association between a nonreproductive orientation, a low sociobiological cost C of nonreproduction (i.e., barrenness), and special shamanistic gifts that benefit relatives in the form of bride-prices received from controlling daughters. Obviously, a woman who takes up such a role enmeshes herself in the power politics ordinarily reserved for men—and would presumably do so only when she feels herself to be among the most politically astute members of the tribe. Western terminology would describe women taking such roles as ordinary lesbians or female-to-male transsexuals.

All these gender transpositions, then, are loosely connected in ways that are sociobiologically important. In particular, they contain elements of what theory predicts would be helpful in acting as a go-between in sex and gender matters: a convincing renunciation of heterosexual reproductive interests and a moderate to significant mixing of the psychological traits associated with both genders.

Having a Berdache as a Relative: Kin Benefits

Some of Williams's most valuable observations sociobiologically are his descriptions of the benefits a family receives by virtue of having a berdache in the family tree.[21] Altruism is often explicitly recognized as part of the role. For example, when visited in a vision by a berdache spirit, a Lakota berdache was told that "the Great Spirit made people like me to be of help to other people."[22] Berdaches often adopt children (see the next section), and although nowadays the adopted ones might not be genetically related to the adoptive parent, in the original settings they often or nearly always would have been because of the interlocking clan structure common among Indian tribes. They were also regarded, according to Williams, as highly intelligent and as especially good teachers of children. Of course, children benefit from good teachers taking an interest in them as unique (and hence special) individuals, and here (as I also suggested in chapter 5) it is not difficult to imagine a merging of the cross-gender berdache pattern with the older/younger pattern commonly attributed to ancient Greece (see chapter 2).

Berdaches could also have special economic roles, sometimes lucrative ones. They were commonly regarded as especially generous, for

---

[21] Williams 1986, chapter 5.
[22] Williams 1986, p. 85.

example, perhaps because they did not have children of their own upon whom they would otherwise bestow their goods. In some tribes (Williams mentions the Navajo), only the berdaches were allowed to take masculine and feminine jobs simultaneously. This allowed certain occupational combinations that could economically be very profitable.[23] More generally, they were able to do women's work with a devotion that genetic women were often unable to achieve. They were stronger, and unburdened by childbearing or child care, so they could spend more time on tasks and undertake the more strenuous ones. Since having and raising children is an expensive, time-consuming, and vital task, it makes sense that those who forego such tasks have more time to excel in crafts and other activities.[24] No sociobiologist would deny the trade-off between reproductive effort and success in another endeavor; having children is expensive.

For completeness, I should also recall the less flattering side of berdachism: berdaches who were insecure enough in their role to insist that they really were women who "menstruated" (they scratched their thighs) or even got "pregnant" and bore "children" who were always "stillborn." There are hints in Williams's book, and in other accounts, that personal problems sometimes had a relationship with taking up the berdache role.

Although I should emphasize that word "sometimes," nevertheless it is striking how often these aspects arise even in accounts passed on by observers not trying to make the berdaches appear pitiable. For example, Williams quotes a French explorer who claimed that the berdaches he met back in the 1680s were "either lunatick or sickly"; Williams then asks, Why might berdaches "be seen as 'lunatick or sickly' and still be respected?"[25] Notice, to his credit, that he does not defensively deny that some berdaches might be lunatic or sickly.

I started to address this subtle issue in my discussion about those antlerless hummels—a discussion that makes sense for berdaches in the light of the kin-selection formula I mentioned in chapter 13. Recall that formula: reproductively altruistic acts can be favored by natural selection whenever the cost C to the berdache of becoming a berdache is less than $r \times B$, where B is the benefit accruing to relatives from the act, and r is a relatedness factor. Both B and C are measured

---

[23] Williams 1986, p. 60.

[24] Note that it does not demean mothers to conclude that nonreproducing berdaches could do women's work better than mothers could; after all, when it comes to having babies, the berdaches fail utterly! Indeed, Williams is careful to point out that far from being jealous of berdaches, Indian women are happy to have competent workers alongside them—workers, moreover, willing to do some of the most strenuous tasks.

[25] Williams 1986, p. 44.

in terms of reproductive success; in particular, you can think of C as the number of children a berdache might otherwise have had were he to have fathered children.

Particular instances of berdachism might in theory, therefore, be thought of as falling into two categories: those in which $B \times r$ is greater than C because B is an unusually large number and those in which $B \times r$ is greater than C because C is an unusually small number. A lunatic or sickly man would in all probability have trouble marrying and raising children. To say that his C is low is just another way of saying that he is not giving up much by deciding not to have children. This man's sociobiological situation resembles that of a hummel who is a hummel because he just can't muster what it takes to grow antlers.

The other category of berdache would be men with particularly exceptional gifts: men who can contribute an especially large benefit to their relatives by virtue of taking up the berdache role. This kind of man has a high B, and the only puzzle to explain would be why such a fortunate fellow wouldn't have his own children. Perhaps this man's sociobiological situation corresponds to that of a hummel who has found an especially productive way to be a hummel, or for whom the calculations simply happen to work out in favor of the hummel option.

For example, it takes certain skills besides an ability to see both men's and women's sides of things to be a good matchmaker. Let's say one of those skills is intelligence. Someone born with the intelligence to be a particularly good matchmaker can garner a considerable amount of goodwill, money, or kin benefit from the skill. But if he is pursuing reproductive success of his own, he simply may not be trusted. Accordingly, there ought to be some cases of high B in which the benefit can *only* accrue in the context of the berdache role. I have often had it pointed out to me, after lectures, that nowadays members of celibate religious orders sometimes function in similar ways; an intelligent priest had better not reproduce to stay a priest, but his role raises the status of his family in ways that, in a hunter-gatherer context, would probably have raised the reproductive success of many of the family's married members.

As another example of a large-B situation, think of a man who happens to be especially good at the skills required to do good women's work. For such a man, it may be especially profitable for him to do such work. If it's hard to do this work well while taking care of a child, then being emotionally attracted to a woman's role, as a drag queen is, might be one route natural selection has taken to motivate the man in question to take up the role.

Think, too, of the women-husbands among the Nuer, who—as I already pointed out—may have been especially politically astute.

If all this theory strikes you as ineffably imprecise, you may have a point. And in that case, you should recall, first of all, Konner's love for his daughter, which is ineffably imprecise. And you might also wish to fall back on the simple but well-tested folk wisdom of a Lakota Indian who told Williams:

> *Winktes* had to assume the [berdache] role, because if they did not, something bad would happen to them or their family or their tribe.[26]

That, after all, is the sociobiological bottom line: you don't have to consciously understand the connection between the cause (taking up the role) and the effect (increased inclusive fitness). If the connection exists, *for whatever unknown reason,* natural selection will act upon it.

The Maiden Aunt, the Bachelor Uncle

It is but a short step from this kind of observation to an example I hinted at briefly in an earlier chapter: maiden aunts and bachelor uncles in American society only a few years ago. They, too, may be non-reproductive, in an ultimate sense, because of kin selection.

The conquest of disease is a very recent phenomenon. Within the memory of millions of people today, the world was a place in which anyone could be snatched away by death with little or no warning. As I can attest from drawing up my own family tree, and as I suspect many other people can, too, only a couple of generations ago the distribution of children across different brothers and sisters in a family was far more uneven than it is now. That is, nowadays most parents expect most or all of their children to grow up, get married, and have just a couple of kids. But not long ago parents had far more than a couple of kids, and usually only a few grew up to have families of their own (large ones, usually). Others died before they could or, more importantly from the point of view of this section, never married; they became bachelor uncles or maiden aunts.

These aunts and uncles often acted as "spare parents" who were willing to step in and help rear their nieces and nephews should a parent die. Williams shows that precisely this sort of adoption went on among berdaches (as I have pointed c˙t earlier). If this went on

[26] Williams 1986, p. 44.

for enough generations (and human mortality of this sort was, of course, the rule for most of history), emotions would have evolved to motivate this kind of adoption. In an ultimate sense, these emotions would have evolved because they increased the aunts' and uncles' inclusive fitnesses through kin selection.

Nowadays, these emotions persist. But because the environment has changed—we no longer live in kin groups where anyone who lives nearby is genetically related to us to some degree—these emotions can operate in ways that no longer maximize inclusive fitness.

Maximizing Inclusive Fitness

This point of view puzzles and irritates some people. Why put people down if their emotions lead them to do something that no longer maximizes their inclusive fitness? Indeed, why drag inclusive fitness and all that hunter-gatherer stuff into it in the first place?

This irritation is understandable but misplaced. We need to understand hunter-gatherers to understand why we have the emotions we do; I'm not suggesting we ought to copy them or that we should do what maximizes our inclusive fitness in today's environment. Following emotions that no longer "maximize our genes"—"adoption emotions," say—will decrease their frequency in future generations. And so what? They make us feel good, they help kids who need to be adopted, so why worry about inclusive fitness at all?

Indeed, worrying about inclusive fitness in modern environments is something that should be done only by people interested in sociobiological theory. Ordinary folk who aren't interested may be excused—including you, and including me when I'm not feeling sociobiological.

MODERN GAY MEN: A CHECKERBOARD PATTERN OF GENDER MIXING

If modern homosexual men are the sociobiological inheritors of the berdache's emotions and strategies, then they should show some of the psychological characteristics of berdaches. So let us investigate, for the next few paragraphs, a topic that entire books have been written about: the psychological characteristics of gay men.

Psychologists and psychiatrists have put together lots of data on modern gay men's cross-gender traits. Most of it, alas, has been gathered in order to prove or disprove the notion that there is something wrong with a man who is feminine and/or unmasculine. But as you know by now, the sociobiological approach is to look into these differences and to ask not what went wrong but what went right.

In chapter 9, I described the "runs-in-families" study designed and supervised by my colleague Richard Pillard, a psychiatrist at Boston University Medical School. This was one of a series of studies he had been involved in that address masculinity and femininity in homosexuals. In the runs-in-families study, for example, we not only asked our subjects about homosexuality in their families but also assessed their sexually dimorphic traits in several categories. A general pattern has emerged from this study that casts light on the gender-mixing hypothesis.

Recall from chapter 1 that there are one-dimensional and two-dimensional measures of psychological masculinity and femininity. We administered such tests to our subjects; one was the California Personality Inventory (CPI), which results in a Femininity scale of the one-dimensional variety. For example, the item "Windstorms terrify me," mentioned in chapter 1, is from this test. The homosexual men, as a group, scored significantly higher on this "CPI Femininity" scale than the heterosexual men did in our study.

Another test we administered to these men was the Bem scale (illustrated by the items "Forceful" and "Sensitive" in chapter 1), and these scores showed a more interesting pattern. Since it is two-dimensional, the Bem scale yields separate scores for masculinity and femininity. The homosexual and heterosexual men did *not* differ, on average, on "Bem Masculinity"; however, the homosexual men *did* score significantly higher on "Bem Femininity." In short, they scored exactly as one would expect if they were gender mixers rather than gender crossers. This is also exactly as one would expect from the periodic table model of chapter 7, which postulates (in a more explicitly sexual sense) that many homosexual men have acquired some of the traits associated with heterosexual men but have not lost some of the traits associated with heterosexual women.

Another test we administered, the Strong-Campbell Vocational Interest Inventory, had very interesting results in spite of the fact that it does not permit a two-dimensional analysis of masculinity and femininity. Men and women on average differ quite a lot in the kinds of jobs that interest them.[27] In particular, some jobs are more appealing to women in our society, some are more appealing to men, and some

---

[27] Please note that the Strong-Campbell test is admirable, in its most recent revision, in doing its best *not* to suggest (to the high school students who typically take it) that boys should answer questions one way and girls another. Nevertheless, whether it's boys and girls, or men and women, who fill in the 325 little circles on their computer-scorable answer sheets with their number 2 pencils, there are strong sex differences on job preferences that emerge from this test.

seem to appeal equally to the two sexes. Which jobs did the gay men in our sampler prefer? The answer: as a group, with exceptions, they preferred the stereotypically "feminine" ones. To be precise, for the jobs that were significantly preferred by heterosexual women according to the test's norms, the homosexual men on average reported higher levels of interest than the heterosexual men did. This trend was so strong that we could "predict" 65–70 percent of the time whether a given subject was homosexual or heterosexual, knowing solely his Strong-Campbell scores![28] For a psychological test—and one not designed with homosexual/heterosexual discernment in mind—this figure is remarkably high.[29]

So when it comes to psychological masculinity and femininity, we see the gender-mixing pattern: modern homosexual men have interests significantly different from those of heterosexual men, with homosexual men on average scoring in a more stereotypically feminine direction on several different tests.

The pattern is completely different when it is abilities, not interests, that are investigated. It turns out that men and women differ, on average, in several tests of psychological abilities. On IQ tests, for example, men typically score better than women do on the subtests measuring visual-spatial skills, but women typically score better than men do on those measuring complex verbal skills. We wondered whether our gay men would score more like men or more like women on these tests.

The answer is: they score more like men; there were very small differences, if any, between the homosexual and heterosexual men on these tests. For three of the five subtests we administered, there were no significant differences at all. For the other two, the differences were of only borderline statistical significance, and the homosexual men scored in a direction that would be considered more masculine on one of them and more feminine on the other. As a matter of fact, in both cases the scores of the homosexual men were higher. If this is evi-

---

[28] Pillard and Weinrich, as yet unpublished results of a discriminant-function analysis. People have asked us if this analysis could be used to screen out homosexuals from the armed forces without the homosexuals themselves knowing they were being screened. We doubt it. Although our gay men on average did score low, for example, on the "Military Activities" interest scale, what kind of gay man would be trying to get into the armed forces in the first place? Obviously, it will be the kind of gay man less typical for our sample— precisely the ones likely to score *high* on Military Activities and just the ones who would have been inaccurately "guessed" as heterosexual in our analysis. Sorry, Sergeant.

[29] Interestingly, we did not do as well with a discriminant-function analysis of the eighty-six heterosexual, homosexual, and bisexual women whose data we have not quite finished analyzing. It is reasonable to suppose that this is because it is only recently that women were commonly assumed to have an occupational preference other than that of mother and homemaker, but we don't know for sure.

dence of anything, given the marginal statistical significance, it is evidence that the homosexual men in our sample had higher IQs but not particularly more "masculine" or more "feminine" IQ patterns. We administered another test of mental abilities, too, and found no significant differences by sexual orientation.

This is a very interesting pattern. It can be summed up in two sentences: when it comes to *interests and personality*, homosexual men score in a more feminine direction (but not necessarily a less masculine direction!) than heterosexual men do on a variety of tests. But when it comes to *abilities*, there are few if any significant differences, and they are not gender related. What does this pattern mean?

The Darker Side, Again

I'll get to the positive side of this pattern in the next section. But I want to discuss briefly other psychological findings from the runs-in-families study that are less flattering.[30]

The fathers of the homosexual men in our sample had a higher level of alcoholism than the fathers of the heterosexual men did. Likewise, the mothers of the homosexual men had a higher level of depression than the mothers of the heterosexuals. In neither case did these percentages approach a majority; for example, five of the heterosexual men had alcoholic fathers, and thirteen of the homosexual men did, and thirteen is nowhere near a majority of the homosexual sample. So there is no way that this finding could fairly be applied to homosexuals in general. But obviously there are people who would like to take a finding like this one and use it to suggest that homosexuality is "caused" by family problems.

Sociobiologically, I want to point out that even if this finding is confirmed by other investigators and even if we accept the general tenor of the interpretation (only for those homosexual men with alcoholic fathers or depressed mothers, mind you), we may still be missing an important point. Back in hunter-gatherer days (or, for that matter, today), what would it have meant to have a parent as psychologically handicapped as this?

It would have meant, obviously, that the family was in trouble; its children will have trouble making their ways in the world. Sociobiologically, what is one characteristic of a family in trouble? In terms of kin selection, this means that their C of not reproducing is probably

---

[30] But if it's flattery you want, you can pursue the intelligence finding by consulting Weinrich 1978 and 1980b.

relatively small for these children. And that means that following a nonreproductive strategy is more likely to be chosen by them.

This simple argument completely turns around the attitude one takes toward our finding. If it is indeed true that alcoholism and/or depression in parents can raise the probability of homosexuality in their children, this need not be viewed as pathology breeding pathology. It can instead be viewed as misfortune (or pathology) breeding an *adaptive* response to the difficulty. After all, it is my impression that people raised by parents with psychological problems are more likely to become psychologists or psychiatrists themselves. That's scarcely a logical argument that a desire to become a psychologist or psychiatrist is pathological.

This one little insight could have a very beneficial effect on those homosexuals who wonder, in psychotherapy perhaps, whether their parents' problems contributed to their own homosexuality. They might be ashamed of their parents' problems, and they might be unhappy that these problems caused the children difficulty. But they should not be ashamed of the steps they may have taken, consciously or unconsciously, to deal adaptively with those problems and difficulties.

The Social Utility of Gender Mixing

So let me return to the pattern that homosexual and heterosexual men don't differ much on sexually dimorphic abilities but often do differ on sexually dimorphic interests. What does this pattern mean?

It can mean any number of things, but sociobiologically it has a very important interpretation. Let's say you live in a society that builds lots of new houses—whether they be expensive condos in gentrifying neighborhoods or simple Indian tepees on the prairie. Let's say you're a man interested in the construction of these new houses. *What aspects* of those houses will interest you the most?

Well, let's say you're a man with a level of visual-spatial ability ordinary for men—namely, a high level. There are many aspects of those new houses that you might get involved in, because houses are three-dimensional and therefore visual-spatial. If you have the stereotypically masculine interest in gross motor activity—in our culture, building, hammering, and sawing—you'll find yourself building those houses yourself or supervising those who do. And so in our culture perhaps you'd be a building contractor.

But let's say you're a man with the same high level of visual-spatial skill but have little interest in gross motor activity. Instead, suppose you have an interest in design. In this case, it's much less likely that you'll find yourself wanting to build these houses; instead, I think you'll find yourself interested in figuring out what they should look like and how they should be arranged. In our culture, perhaps you'd be an architect.

Now mind you, the earliest hunter-gatherers didn't have more than a few occupations (using the term loosely), and neither "architect" nor "building contractor" was among them. Our society has thousands of different jobs, but hunter-gatherers had only two really major ones, hunting and gathering, plus a couple of others that only a few people pursued. But one of those few specialized roles was, of course, the shaman (or medicine man), and I've already indicated why gender mixing was probably important in the performance of a shaman's duties.

As a hunter-gatherer society moves from hunting and gathering to agriculture and all the later stages that anthropologists describe in the development of societies, the number of different jobs will increase. How might Mother Nature go about producing the variability of interests and abilities that would be necessary to fill those jobs with people who enjoy them and are good at doing them?

By now, I suspect, you've figured out my partial answer. If there is any genetic predisposition whatsoever to the different preferences women and men have in occupations (and this is a very reasonable, if unproved, hypothesis) and if these genetic predispositions have anything whatsoever to do with selection pressures among hunter-gatherers for men and women to pursue different reproductive strategies (likewise reasonable but unproved), then *Mother Nature might be able to increase the variety of occupational choices made by a tribe's members by varying the sex-linked interests previously predisposed for men and for women.* That is, the interest that many heterosexual men have in gross motor activity will lead them to become building contractors, and the interest that many homosexual men have in design will lead them to become architects.

The same thing is true of more general personality traits. Every group of human beings needs leaders, followers, introverts, extroverts, tinkerers, musclefolk, therapists, thinkers, doers, and so on—but not too many of any of them. If any of these types of people is more or less likely in a particular sex under particular circumstances, natural selection could produce new versions of such types by having some of them show up in the sex that previously was less likely to show them. If those new versions turn out to be useful (i.e., they are of reproductive benefit to people who have them or to their relatives), then the mechanisms that produced the new versions will be selected for. This is, in effect, the argument given in a previous chapter that natural selection need not produce the same, single trait in all individuals. What the present discussion adds to this idea is the notion of sex linkage of traits and the consequent association of certain traits with gender transpositions.

These comments are obviously speculative, although we have the data to test them from our runs-in-families study. Let me discuss an even more speculative application of these ideas to both men and women: the hypothesis that *taken in groups, people's average occupational choices can reflect their gender-transposition tendencies.* There are, however, exceptions to this hypothesis.

For example, it is common knowledge in the gay community that male-to-female transsexuals, drag queens, and some gay men often are hairdressers or interior decorators. Of course, among heterosexuals these occupations are often preferred by women rather than men. And likewise, some female-to-male transsexuals and lesbians have occupations that heterosexual men prefer more than heterosexual women do. So far, so bad; these observations are the small kernel of truth in the stereotype that members of the transposed transpositions resemble the other sex.

But there are also professions that display a less stereotypic pattern of gender-transposition bias, and a far more interesting one. Lesbians enjoy certain occupations that heterosexual men do not (nursing, supposedly, is one of these), and gay men enjoy certain occupations that heterosexual women are not especially attracted to (e.g., architecture). Even more interesting, there are certain professions that *both* gay sexes disproportionately enjoy (e.g., librarian, teacher, and computer programmer).

Accordingly, we can divide gender-transposition-preferred occupations into two categories: those that can be explained by a *cross-gender* pattern of interests (e.g., truck driver or hairdresser) and those that are preferred by both gay sexes (e.g., librarian). (This division could be made, incidentally, even if the particular suggestions I'm making for particular professions are empirically shown to be the wrong ones.) What if it turns out that these traits correlate in an interesting way with other variables? *Such as the sex of one's homosexual relatives?*

For example, recall from our runs-in-families study that there appear to be three ways in which homosexuality runs in families: one that happens in males only, one that happens in females only, and one that happens in both sexes. What if the first factor is associated with high levels of (culturally defined) feminine interests, the second with (culturally defined) masculine interests, and the third with a type of homosexuality that is not obviously gender-role transposed? The first factor would not be noticed in women, but a man affected by it would be more likely to choose a culturally feminine occupation. The second factor would be overlooked in men, but a woman affected by it would be more attracted to masculine occupations. Although the third factor would affect occupational choice, it would not do so in ways that strike people as gender-transposed. This admittedly far-out hypothesis could be tested; it would receive support if those families in our sample with both gay men and lesbians in them also tended to be those families with a lot of members who wanted to be, say, librarians.

SUMMARY AND CONCLUSIONS

What does all this mean? Simply this. As humans evolved away from other primates, we changed many traits of our species, among them the amount of sexual dimorphism we display on our bodies and in our behavior. Genetics was undoubtedly important in generating this sexual dimorphism back before we got culture, and it no doubt played a role in its reduction *and modification*. Accordingly, as we were evolving, there was "raw material" for natural selection—genetic mutations being selected for, old patterns being selected against, new combinations of traits arising, and so on—that might have turned out to be useful in the new environments human beings were facing and creating through their culture.

As the importance of human culture increased, it would have been important to make sure there were extra variations in the interests the members of a society brought to bear on that society's tasks and problems. Although a division of labor between men and women did evolve (and/or persist), some aspects of that division of labor made sense, evolutionarily speaking, only in the context of reproduction. Accordingly, some of the raw material of evolution might have been put to use in novel ways—and eventually reproductively beneficial ones—*outside* the context of reproduction. And so the stage was set for genetic factors to get involved in producing the gender transpositions.

Obviously, if there are genetic factors involved in producing the gender transpositions and if it is hypothesized that they can persist by virtue of passing on benefits to one's kin, then homosexuality should run in families. As readers of chapter 9 know, apparently it does.[31]

---

[31] Of course, the raw empirical finding does not in and of itself demonstrate that the cause is genetic. Pillard and I suspect that it runs in families, in fact, for both genetic and environmental reasons.

It is kin selection that provides the theoretical basis for this scenario, admittedly a rarefied one not familiar to most students of the human condition. Only if these new gender transpositions somehow could benefit the genes that helped produce them could those genes spread to, say, a 5 percent or 10 percent level in the population. As it happened, the kinship structure of hunter-gatherer bands might have provided just what was necessary for this to happen. The argument I introduced above—that the different reproductive interests of men and women who do reproduce can lead to intersexual strife that is wasteful—suggests that hunter-gatherers could have used the talents of gender-mixed individuals who could see both sides of the sexual fence. It is very reasonable to suppose that berdaches and "amazons" (masculine women) constituted such individuals.

THOSE TEN PUZZLES

It is now time to return to the ten puzzles set out in chapter 3 and deal with the ones that haven't been addressed yet. Several of them have been dealt with, of course, and to refresh your memory in those cases, I'll briefly summarize the solution. Please remember that, as in all science, the solutions I've proposed may turn out to be wrong. In fact, they almost certainly will be wrong in some aspects. But I am enough of an optimist to hope they won't turn out to be very far from the truth.

Puzzle 1: The Technique Puzzle

Recall that in this puzzle, homosexuals in long-term relationships seem to have better sexual technique than corresponding heterosexuals. I'll admit that this puzzle has been done to death in this book. One possible explanation is that Masters and Johnson's homosexual sample was atypical of the homosexual population as a whole, and their heterosexual sample, while also atypical for the general population, was more typical with respect to the sex taboo. To be happily enough homosexual to volunteer for this study, the homosexuals probably had to come to terms with the sex taboo. Erotically, that probably allowed them to communicate sexually very well with their lovers. But to be happily enough heterosexual to volunteer, Masters and Johnson's heterosexuals might *not* have had to come to terms with the sex taboo and thus could have fallen into a script common in Western societies: that men should know, without being told, how to arouse women sexually and that women should not have to enlighten them.

An alternate explanation applies not only to humans but also to animals. Heterosexual acts can result in reproduction, and when it comes to reproduction, the evolutionary interests of males and females are often in conflict. This conflict may "spoil" intercourse in some proportion of sexual encounters between the sexes because not just pleasure but also reproductive success may be at stake in the interaction. When reproduction cannot result from the acts, then pleasure can become the sole matter at issue. Homosexual acts are always free of this distraction; heterosexual encounters often are not. In societies that disapprove of homosexual acts, mind you, such acts have their own distractions. But this simply strengthens the previous explanation: that volunteers among the homosexuals are especially likely to have overcome those distractions.

Puzzle 2: The Erotica Puzzle

The erotica puzzle is that the sexes seem to differ in their *preferences* for erotic stimulation (in explicit erotica and in stories) far more than they differ in their actual *responses* to such stimulation. Women, for example, respond to the explicitly sexual stimuli that men are aroused by—even in a society such as ours in which they are not socialized to do so. And men respond to the romantic stimuli that women stereotypically are aroused by.

I addressed this puzzle in chapter 5 with the limerent/lusty theory. According to this theory, there are two ways of responding to stimuli: autonomously (no specific stimulus needed), in a way I called an "impulse," and only after exposure to specific stimuli, in a way I called a "response." The theory supposes that in most women lustiness is a response and limerence is an impulse, and that in most men limerence is a response and lustiness is an impulse.

So this theory claims that underneath it all, men and women are alike: We all respond to the same stimuli in roughly similar ways. But it also claims that men and women differ in the extent to which they seek out particular kinds of limerent and lusty situations.

Puzzle 3: The "How Common?" Puzzle

How can we explain the different incidences of the various gender transpositions? This puzzle has only been partly addressed. In order to finish it off, we need to extend the periodic-table theory of chapter 7, as I meshed it with the limerent/lusty theory of chapter 6. There are several possible solutions to this puzzle, and below I will give you just this one.

We need to add two more hypotheses about sexual orientation: developmental ones. Recall that when it comes to the genitalia, in prenatal life both male and female fetuses begin with the same genital precursors (labioscrotal folds and a genital tubercle). The periodic-table theory suggests that the same is true of the sexually dimorphic brain circuits that eventually become involved in adult sexuality. Ordinary girls develop into ordinary heterosexual women along a very well traveled developmental pathway: their mount-receiving circuits are facilitated, and their mounting circuits are inhibited. Ordinary boys develop into ordinary heterosexual men along a developmental pathway that involves specific processes that counteract these tendencies: a *masculinization* process (facilitating the circuits involved in mounting behavior) and *defeminization* (inhibiting the circuits involved in mount-receiving behavior).

The Two Hypotheses

The first additional hypothesis is that masculinization happens early— *in utero*, or very early in life—and that defeminization happens later— in late childhood or early puberty. Boys who, in early childhood, do not show the signs of masculinization—sissy boys, for example, who are not interested in rough-and-tumble play—are therefore signaling that they will not undergo the next developmental step that their typically masculine neighbors are undergoing. That is, they do not defeminize at all or do not defeminize until much later (after imprinting; see below).

The second additional hypothesis is that sexual orientation is determined by a poorly understood set of circumstances that depend on one or two things: first, imprinting experiences that happen in childhood (but which do not start becoming evident to those who undergo them until the lustiness circuits are brought into play by the hormonal changes of puberty), and second, the poorly understood matter of the timing of defeminization and its cause.

The imprinting that goes on seems to be of the sort in which familiarity breeds contempt. Sissy boys play with girls, and most girls play with girls; both groups thus eroticize what is not available to them, namely, male companionship. Tomboys play with boys, and most boys play with boys, and these groups both eroticize female companionship. In fact, there are anthropological studies that seem to show this same mechanism operating cross-culturally.[32]

The timing of defeminization, and its mechanism, is the second cir-

---

[32] Werner 1979 and 1980.

cumstance that might also play a role. Richard Pillard suggested in a paper he and I coauthored that *rough-and-tumble play* might be a crucial step in the developmental process for boys. A typical boy is masculinized prenatally and then displays rough-and-tumble play in childhood. Is this rough-and-tumble play part of the boy's defeminization process? Sissy boys don't get interested in rough-and-tumble play, so they wouldn't defeminize. Nonsissy but nonmasculine boys likewise show little interest in rough-and-tumble play, and so they may or may not defeminize. *We propose that sexual orientation is caused by factors that are different from those involved in gender role, but the two processes are loosely linked.* The result would be a pattern in which sexual orientation sometimes really is related to gender role (as in sissy boys who grow up to become gay men) and sometimes really is not (as in nonsissy boys who do the same).

When it comes to cause and effect, there are two theoretical possibilities. If rough-and-tumble play helps to *cause* defeminization directly, then nonmasculine boys will probably not defeminize; if someone had forced them to participate in rough-and-tumble play, then they would have. Another possibility, however, is that rough-and-tumble play merely *signals* that defeminization is on the agenda, developmentally speaking. In this case, forcing these boys to participate in rough-and-tumble play will *not* elicit defeminization. Very imprecise evidence favors the latter alternative. However, there is a hypothesis, described below, that *forcing* boys to act in a masculine way may be involved in the genesis of transsexualism. Let the parent beware.

Developmental Pathways

In our theory, a sissy boy is following a developmental pathway in which it is extremely unlikely that he will imprint upon heterosexual stimuli—so he will be sexually attracted to males, perhaps even before he knows what sexual attraction is. Moreover, he will not defeminize, and he will not have masculinized much, and so he will quite likely be most interested sexually in mount-receiving behavior and perhaps a bit interested in mounting. Such a boy would make a perfect berdache.

A typically masculine boy is on a pathway in which just the opposite is the case. He will probably imprint upon heterosexual stimuli, so he will be sexually attracted to females. Moreover, he will defeminize, and so he will be almost exclusively interested in mounting, sexually speaking.

And a nonsissy but nonmasculine boy is on a pathway in between. He may imprint upon either heterosexual or homosexual stimuli, because many of these boys are loners or play with both boys and girls. He will have masculinized but will not be showing the typical association of masculinization with rough-and-tumble play. Accordingly, he will probably not defeminize. And if not, then he will probably be attracted in adulthood to both mounting and mount-receiving kinds of sexuality. Such a boy might become a berdache, or he might become a gender-typical man who is attracted to berdaches (either as a permanent preference or as an occasional taste).

Those two hypotheses, along with other arguments, can now be applied to the puzzle at hand.

The Puzzle Solved

This theory suggests that homosexuality is more common among men because it results proximately, in this scenario, from slight variations in experiences common to the ordinary development of heterosexuality among males: namely, masculinization and defeminization. It is less common among women because, according to the periodic-table theory, lesbian women must either have been (a) defeminized or (b) masculinized in ways that typical women aren't. (Recall that typical women start unmasculinized and undefeminized and stay that way.) Tomboys have apparently been masculinized at least as far as rough-and-tumble play is concerned and thus are more likely to become lesbians interested in both mounting and mount-receiving. Female-to-male (f–m) transsexuals must have not only masculinized (according to the periodic-table theory) but also managed to become defeminized—*both* of which are unlikely for genetic females. Accordingly, f–m transsexuals should be very uncommon.

Male-to-female transsexuals should also be uncommon either because they have been neither masculinized *nor* defeminized or because they have been defeminized *in spite of* not having been masculinized. It should be clear why the first case is unlikely; both features go against the events ordinary males are programmed to go through. Now if childhood rough-and-tumble play is involved in the causation of typical defeminization, how can we expect the latter to occur in a sissy boy who is completely uninterested in the former? Perhaps transsexualism can happen to men who are *forced* into such macho activities when their sissy personalities resist. The example of Daniel Schreber, recounted in a couple of previous chapters, illustrates the possibility. He had strong transsexual wishes and certainly had a father with very masculine aspirations for his sons, which he very likely imposed upon them.

Hormones

The "how common" puzzle will probably not be definitively solved until the hormones involved in brain masculinization and defeminization processes are better understood. Müllerian-inhibiting hormone (MIH), for example, has only recently been discovered to be present in significant quantities in adult human beings (as opposed to fetuses), and if MIH is around, physiologically speaking, in adulthood, we really don't know what its effects on psychological traits might be. This situation is equivalent, in comparison to the chemical periodic table, to finding out the fundamental physical structure of atoms, molecules, electrons, orbitals, and whatnot. We can't understand the chemical periodic table without understanding the mechanisms of physics, and it will probably turn out to be true that we can't completely understand the sexological periodic table until we understand the physiological mechanisms of desire. After all, it is those mechanisms—the pathways by which insistently stereotypical child rearing might affect masculinization and defeminization, say—that provide the raw material for evolution to act upon.

Puzzle 4: What Is Bi About Bisexuals?

Recall that this puzzle points to the confusion about just exactly what it is that is "bi" about bisexuals. For some people a bisexual is someone who has had sexual relations with both women and men—in which case bisexuals definitely do exist. For other people (e.g., Kurt Freund, who uses the "body shape" definition), a bisexual is someone whose penis responds to photographs of both naked males and naked females—in which case "bisexuality proper" apparently doesn't exist.

This puzzle has been explained in chapter 6—again, by way of the limerent/lusty theory. The theory suggests that body-shape bisexuality requires lusty arousal to both sexes, and thus that bisexuality in this kind of attraction would be minimal or nonexistent. However, limerent arousal is hypothesized to be more likely to key into a person of either sex.

So the typical bisexual woman probably is the kind of person who can fall in love, limerently, with either women or men. Although she may have only one "lusty" type, she may not be particularly aware of what it is or she may find the kind of sexual attraction less salient in her erotic life. The typical bisexual man probably is lustily aroused exclusively by men but has discovered that he can fall in love limerently with women (or with both men and women).

These distinctions are often missed. When bisexual organizations say that touch should not always be interpreted as *sexual* touch (see the last section in Klein and Wolf 1985), it is easy to see limerence asserting itself—albeit in a way that may unduly poise the sexiness of lust against the sexiness of friendship. Since limerence is a form of sexual attraction, limerent bisexuality should give pause to those who would dismiss bisexuality "merely" as a form of closeted homosexuality. At the same time, it can happen that in the rush to embrace human diversity, the existence of certain kinds of people is merely asserted rather than carefully looked into.

Puzzle 5: Pseudolesbian Porn

This puzzle is embodied in the observation that many (if not most) heterosexual men enjoy pornography in which two women thought to be lesbians are engaging in sexual relations with each other. Given that men are socialized to find *heterosexual* relations interesting, how can this be explained? Some arousal might be expected to carry over into the pseudolesbian sphere from heterosexual socialization, but many men report that these images are even *more* arousing than man-with-woman images are—reports that are confirmed when tested with penile plethysmography.

This puzzle was explained in chapter 8. The evidence there suggests quite simply that naked bodies are releasing stimuli for erections in men. That is, the most sexually stimulating pictures for heterosexual men are those with lots of releasers in them (i.e., those with lots of naked women in them), not the ones that are "the most heterosexual" (i.e., those with both naked men and naked women). This problem does not arise with homosexual men, for whom the "most homosexual" stimuli are also the ones with the most naked men; a corresponding statement is true about lesbian women.

The question can be extended to heterosexual women: Are they aroused by images of two men having sexual relations? The answer is more subtle. Some women have told me that they are, but plethysmography has not confirmed this in other samples. Women attending male strip shows certainly are aroused by live, nude male stimuli (not all at once, but one after another), but remember that for most women this arousal is a response, not a conscious impulse. Accordingly it is something that such women have to discover they have, not something they know ahead of time they have, and they may find it easier to deny or resist the temptation that so many heterosexual men do not deny. The whole question of explicitly sexual stimuli created to please women is under active investigation. I'll bet we'll have a lot more information about this topic in a couple of years.

Puzzle 6: The Little-Girls/Teenaged-Male-Buttocks Puzzle

This pair of puzzles has not been sufficiently explained yet. Please note, however, that the explanations below are attempts to explain small and subtle effects. What is most interesting to me is that the plethysmographic technique can detect such small effects in the first place. We should not be too disappointed if the theories explaining them turn out to be not particularly stunning in their breadth.

The teenaged-male-buttocks puzzle is the easier of the two to explain. The explanation, as you might imagine, calls attention to the signal of submissiveness in primates: presenting one's rear. Juvenile males are no threat to the dominance of adult males in a particular group of primates, but adolescent males are. Accordingly, it is as adolescents that primate males will first display high levels of presenting to show submissiveness. And it is when a juvenile becomes an adolescent that an adult male ought to be able first to experience the small amount of sexual arousal necessary to motivate him to mount that male to show his dominance.

Well, here I am, talking about monkeys and how they "sit around [or fail to sit around] on their asses" (as that Harvard professor once said). Why would this trait be expected to survive, even in rudimentary form, in humans?

One explanation, although not compelling, is suggested once we take account of the extended periodic-table hypothesis I discussed in a previous section. Young teenaged boys, according to this extended hypothesis, would be in the final stages of their metamorphosis from already having been masculinized to becoming both masculinized and defeminized. Regarding masculinization-defeminization status, then, they are at a spot of the periodic table where most ordinary gay men are (and will stay). It might therefore be expected that they have not yet gotten rid of mount-receiving propensities, even as they are developing their interests and skill in mounting behavior. Accordingly, they would be more responsive than adult heterosexual men are to mount-receiving in sexual relations with other people (whether those other people be other boys, adult men, or women). Likewise in courtship, they may act more proceptively than they will in a few years. In a society that permits such relationships, they may be at just the right stage for a relationship with an older man (willing to mount) or with a boy about their own age (willing to exchange mounting and mount-

372

receiving). Indeed, it is remarkable how often these patterns show up cross-culturally: ordinary "preheterosexual" boys, who will get married and have children, can form sexually tinged bonds with adult men and/or with each other, and perhaps also with Mrs. Robinson. It is considered perfectly normal in such societies that boys will grow out of these relationships, but very often they will find themselves somewhat attracted to boys or young men once they themselves have grown up. If in some societies, such as ours, these patterns exist but are not reinforced, they may nevertheless show up when sensitive techniques like plethysmography are used.

Now let's move on to naked little girls. First, on both sides of the sexual-orientation fence, there is some degree of continuity. Girls of any age have *some* of the releasers that release erections in heterosexual men, and boys likewise for homosexual men. So I presume that there are some ordinary homosexual men who are (a little) aroused by pictures of naked little boys. The puzzle therefore is Why are there enough fewer of them, or their arousal enough weaker, for the plethysmographic effect to disappear in comparison with the case among ordinary heterosexual men?

My favorite explanation is embodied in the notion that homosexual men often mix sexual and gender roles in matters of sexual arousal and heterosexual men usually do not. Frankly, ordinary heterosexual men like to mount and insert, and frankly, both can be done with little girls, even if ordinary heterosexual men don't want to do so. Ordinary homosexual men often like to mount and insert, and both can be done with little boys—and so far there is no difference between the two sexual orientations. But homosexual men often like to be mounted and inserted into, and frankly, it's rare for little boys to do the mounting and inserting. I know of true pedophiles who like to play doctor with the kids they're attracted to, and I know of pedophilic rapists who like to force kids to be inserted into, and I know of men who prefer adults as sexual partners who trick kids into having sex with them. But I don't know of any man of any preference who really, first and foremost, wants to be inserted into by a very butch first-grader.

So to the extent that ordinary gay men are interested in mount-receiving and to the extent that a naked man's body elicits erections in them because they think of that man as being willing to mount them, they will find naked boys' bodies *un*arousing in a way that goes beyond those bodies merely being sexually immature. Only after those little boys go through the defeminization of puberty will they be attractive to this category of homosexual man.

Puzzle 7: The Exhibitionism Puzzle

This one's tough. There are few good proximate explanations of exhibitionism itself; a vague wave of the hand in the direction of childhood imprinting experiences is about as good as they get. And so it is difficult to explain proximately why nearly no homosexual men are exhibitionistic in the way that heterosexual exhibitionists are. But I think we now understand the importance of developmental pathways in the gender transpositions to solve this puzzle in part.

The main point of the first half of this chapter is that homosexuality and heterosexuality have *functions*—not consciously designed ones, but functions nevertheless. The periodic-table model suggests that they also are *pathways* with a developmental history. With a really good theory, we should be able to see the connection between the pathway leading to a gender transposition and its function. In particular, the pathway leading to reproduction and heterosexuality must *necessarily* involve finding a partner, becoming intimate with him or her by removing your clothes, and then becoming sexually aroused in physical contact.

But by definition, the pathways leading to the nonreproductive gender transpositions do not lead directly to reproduction. Although partners are often sought, of course, they are not as necessary for achieving the effects "designed" for them. So courtship disorders[33] like exhibitionism should be more common among the gender transpositions that can lead to reproduction (simple heterosexuality included) and less common among those that do not. I don't find this a convincing explanation, but I do think it worth pursuing.

One way to pursue it is to follow a lead from the people who use the term "courtship disorder," who view exhibitionism, voyeurism, rape, and toucheurism (touching people indecently in public without their consent) as "short circuits" in the ordinary heterosexual courtship sequence. Since homosexuals court, too, this doesn't at first solve the problem. But it does raise the following question: Are *all* the courtship disorders rarer among homosexuals (not just exhibitionism)? For voyeurism and toucheurism, no one knows. But for rape, the answer may well be yes.

When the Kinsey Institute staff decided, just before Kinsey died, to write a book about the sex offenders they interviewed in the course of their massive study of American sexuality, they adopted a typo-

---

[33] Courtship *disorders* like rape and exhibitionism should be distinguished from courtship *difficulties* such as those discussed in chapter 11. Both homosexuals and heterosexuals have courtship difficulties, but apparently courtship disorders, especially exhibitionism (and, as I will next suggest, rape), are more common among heterosexuals.

logical approach.[34] That is, they divided their subjects into types according to their offense. They wrote separate chapters that covered heterosexual *offenders* against adults (that is, men who committed sex crimes against women), heterosexual offenders against adolescents, heterosexual offenders against children, heterosexual *aggressors* against adults, heterosexual aggressors against adolescents, and heterosexual aggressors against children. Likewise, they had separate chapters for *homosexual* offenders against adults (men who committed sex crimes against men), homosexual offenders against adolescents, and homosexual offenders against children. But *they had no chapters for aggressors against men or boys*—not because such men didn't exist, but because they were very rare in comparison with the corresponding aggressors against females.

This lesser role of physical force in relationships between men than between men and women may also apply to men who have not committed a sex crime. Eugene Kanin, a sociologist at Purdue University, has for decades been studying sexual aggression among heterosexuals. Back in the mid-1970s, he and colleague Stanley Parcell found that then, as twenty years previously, "approximately 50% of a sample of university women report being victims of sexual aggression during the academic year."[35] A decade before, he had asked a randomly selected sample of 400 undergraduate men, "Have you, since entering college, made an aggressively forceful attempt for sex intercourse?"—and 25.5 percent of the 341 respondents said that they had.[36] Mind you, this was not a report of mere miscommunication between the man and the woman; these men *knew* they had used aggressive force.

Although gay men sometimes attempt to force sex, the size of these percentages flabbergasts the gay men I've told them to. The percentages do not flabbergast many heterosexuals. This suggests that when heterosexual men fear being approached by homosexual men, it is to a large extent projection from what they know about heterosexual relationships, even if they are among the 74.5 percent who believe they do not use force themselves.

Interestingly, homosexual women can be surprised to discover this low level of force in male homosexual relationships. Rita Mae Brown, a well-known lesbian author and activist, once got a gay male friend to sneak her into a gay bathhouse. The resulting portrait she painted, in the era before AIDS, was not entirely flattering, but when it came to force, or the lack thereof, Brown was surprised. Wearing a fake

[34] Gebhard et al. 1965.
[35] Kanin and Parcell 1977.
[36] Kanin 1965.

mustache and cruising around in a bathrobe instead of a towel, she was fascinated—and, of course, sexually approached several times. Each time, it was easy to say no. *This dawned on her only gradually.* Finally, she concluded:

> The easiness of refusal is incredible. In heterosexual life and lesbian life a first refusal never sinks in. Men and to a lesser extent, gay women, are geared to pursue you. . . . In the baths, . . . if you say "no" it means "no," that's all, and that simple "no" also protects fragile egos. Sex isn't a weapon here, it's a release.[37]

If it really is true that homosexual men use force in sexual relations less often than heterosexual men do, then this would jibe with the fact that they are scarcely ever exhibitionists—*if* we view exhibitionism and rape as examples of a common category (courtship disorders). If so, then we are on the right track in pursuing the hypothesis that such disorders are disorders in the steps leading to *heterosexual* intercourse. That wouldn't solve the puzzle completely, of course, but it would point us in the right direction.

Puzzle 8: The Approval Puzzle

Most of the approval puzzle has already been explained: it is easy for women to understand why men are sexually attractive, and so they can sympathize with men who are similarly attracted. And vice versa for men and their interests in lesbianism. This is, as I termed it in chapter 3, the cross-gender empathy effect. The lesbian sympathy effect has not been as well explained, however, and I'm not sure I have a good explanation of it.

But part of the explanation probably is simply that ordinary heterosexual men are often sexually aroused by lesbianism. How can men really disapprove of something that turns them on? Some men consider lesbianism decadent, but if so, it's a decadence they enjoy thinking about. This would account for a lesbian sympathy effect among men. A lesbian sympathy effect among women might likewise simply be an effect of the fact that women are more bisexual than men (in any of the ways described in chapter 3).

Puzzle 9: The "Grass Is Greener on My Side" Puzzle

It is depressingly easy for human beings to misunderstand each other, for a variety of reasons. Sociobiology has a theory as to why this hap-

[37] Brown 1977.

pens, as do many other disciplines. I believe that sexual misunderstandings result mostly from the sex taboo, which makes people unable or unwilling to talk about aspects of their sexual life-styles that other people will need to know about in order to avoid assuming the worst. In chapter 15, I will go into this in detail. But for the moment I will describe societies in which homosexuals—even effeminate homosexual men—are not viewed as negatively as they are in ours.

Sociologist Fred Whitam, at the University of Arizona, has done fieldwork in the gay communities of several countries: Guatemala, Brazil, and the Philippines, to name a few. Whitam finds that the extreme hatred of homosexuals called "homophobia," all too common in the United States, is rare in these countries. This surprises Americans, because these countries are regarded as politically conservative, even repressive,[38] and in our country political conservatism is associated with antihomosexual attitudes.

But not in those countries, according to Whitam. Homosexuals are not exactly the national symbols of good citizenship there, but everyone knows about them, jokes about them, has opinions about them, and has had sexual relations with them or know plenty of people who have. *Homosexuals are known quantities,* and like everyone else, they are seen as pleasant when they are pleasant, talented when they are talented, and not when they are not.

For example, some drag queens in these countries host television shows that are hugely popular. Everyone knows that it's a man on the tube in these instances, and few disapprove, because viewers are familiar with similar kinds of people in their own neighborhoods. Nor are sexual approaches from such homosexuals considered vile or particularly distasteful. Plenty of the men in these countries have lost their virginity to a drag queen and are grateful for the experience—even though, if asked, they would probably have preferred to have lost their virginity to a real woman. Having sexual relations with drag queens is not culturally associated with a challenge to a man's masculinity—only taking the receptive role in such relations is—and so people are not as bothered when they see homosexuals approaching their sons, brothers, or husbands. The idea that homosexual men would be a danger to children is seen as ridiculous, just as New York *Times* columnist Russell Baker thought it ridiculous that his being taught by nuns as a boy would make him want to grow up to be a nun. This is so even though there are, I presume, the same kinds of truly danger-

---

[38] Whitam's fieldwork in the Philippines was done during the Marcos regime, for example.

ous persons (lust murderers, kidnappers, etc.) in those countries as there are in our own.

According to Whitam, homosexuals in these countries are physically as safe as any other citizens are. They are not beaten up by "fagbashers," and do not fear being robbed more than other citizens do. They are astonished to learn that in the United States homosexuals sometimes do have to worry about such things. Nor do they face persecution by the police or other state agencies. Whitam claims that homosexuals in these countries face police difficulties only when they organize left-of-center political groups. In these countries, it is left-wing political organizing that brings down the wrath of right-wing regimes, not homosexuality per se.

In the United States, however, homosexuals (including drag queens) are *not* known quantities, and our society puts up considerable barriers to prevent them from becoming so. Happily, such barriers are falling, for reasons I explain in chapter 15.

Puzzle 10: The Pain-and-Pleasure Puzzle

This puzzle has been explained in detail in chapter 10. If a significant amount of sadomasochism results (proximately) from imprinting experiences in childhood, then what will be imprinted upon will be the adult in the role of the punisher and the child in the role of the punished. When the child grows up and these imprinted images are activated by adult hormone levels and interpreted by the adult mind, people imprinted in this way will find pain and submissiveness sexually arousing. Although it is certainly possible for children to find other children to dominate, if such experiences result in imprinting, then there will be a more equal amount of imprinting upon each role. So taken as a whole, there ought to be more masochists and submissives in the world than there are sadists and dominants.

CONCLUSIONS

So we have indeed come full circle. We haven't explored everything there is to see in the sexual landscape—that takes a lifetime—but we've scaled the Mount of Venus and peeked into some of the landscape's more threatening caves. For the purposes of this book, then, our journey is over, and as your guide and architect, I can now reveal to you that I've played some tricks on you along the way.

For example, in this chapter, I've put you, involuntarily, in the role of a parthenogenetic lesbian, a masochistic hand burner, a heterosexual suffering from too much corticosteroid during childhood imprinting, a heterosexual building contractor, and a homosexual architect. That's a lot of role reversal to impose on someone; after all, you're not all of those things any more than I am. The purpose was, of course, to help you see features of the sexual landscape that you might be able to see *only* from particular points of view.

But now recall that the main purpose of this chapter has been to demonstrate that berdaches, as gender mixers, could get a great deal of insight into their tribes' problems by taking on different sexual roles and thus seeing the sexual landscape from more than one point of view. If you found this chapter illuminating, then I presume you agree.

But my last, and perhaps most daunting, task in this book is to convince you that you probably are a sodomite—or, at the very least, ought to want to be one. Yes, it's time to pay a visit (scientists can think of it as a site visit) to Sodom and Gomorrah.

15

CONCLUSIONS

I met with gay-community leaders and my advisory board of physicians, and I told them what I was going to do. I promised them that the regulations would involve [banning] only high-risk sex in the baths, but that I wasn't going to say that in making the announcement, as I wasn't going to talk about masturbation at a press conference.

> Dr. Mervyn Silverman, public health director for the city of
> San Francisco, quoted by Frances FitzGerald,
> *The New Yorker,* 28 July 1986, p. 55.

This article that was in the *Reader's Digest* recently about all this hogwash you should tell your child when he says, "Where did I come from?" And I'm supposed to immediately say, "You came from inside me." . . . I'd have to get a book and read up, because I don't think I'd know about it myself, and I've had three. . . . I might be all wrong, but that's just the way I feel.

> Mother quoted in Sears, Maccoby, and Levin 1957, p. 191.

Joel, sometimes you gotta say, "What the fuck!" . . . "What the fuck" gives you freedom.

> Miles (played by Curtis Armstrong) to Joel (Tom Cruise) in
> *Risky Business,* Warner Brothers.

Fuck 'em if they can't take a joke!

> Bette Midler

The drawing reproduced at the beginning of this book is one that I like a lot. In fact, I liked it even before I realized that it depicts a trip across the sexual landscape. In this chapter, I want to share with you the reasons why.

A few years ago, this drawing would not have seemed funny. In fact, it might not even have been publishable. After all, "sodomy" is named after Sodom itself, and in the fire-and-brimstone version of the story, Sodom and Gomorrah represent the worst sexual decadence possibly imaginable. Although modern biblical scholarship has not treated this version kindly, it is still around, its grip on the imagination firm for most people.[1]

The drawing suggests the grip is loosening. Somewhere, tucked away in a corner of our subconscious, is the sneaking suspicion that Sodom and Gomorrah might have gotten a bum rap. Maybe it was all a mistake and that's why God hasn't done the same to other cities since. Maybe God had only heard rumors.

Maybe, just maybe, citizens in Sodom and Gomorrah gave their children a decent sex education—which their neighboring cities' residents thought scandalous. Perhaps they had overcome the sex taboo and were able to put wine, (wo)men, and song into an appropriate perspective—which their neighbors were too drunk to imagine. Maybe they allowed their childhood sexual-rehearsal play to produce the imprinting it did in hunter-gatherer days—while others beat their children when they caught them playing doctor. Possibly they allowed women to go to male strip shows and not feel guilty afterward—which others thought unnatural. Conceivably, they thought the gender transpositions were no big deal—while others stoned such transposees. And—heaven forbid!—I even heard that the University of Gomorrah had an entire department of sexology offering a wide range of courses to undergraduates and night-school students!

But people choose Scarsdale instead. What a pity!

RESPONSIBLE SEXUAL FREEDOM

There is a wider movement—as yet unrecognized and unnamed—toward responsible sexual freedom. Popular culture shows it spreading, but no one has quite figured out what its goals and principles are.

Responsible sexual freedom should be distinguished from mere license, mere libertarianism, and mere moderation. You don't have to be a sexual radical to want your children to grow up sexually healthy. You don't have to belong to the sexological right wing to want husband and wife to understand each other sexually and enjoy their relationship. You don't have to be a predatory gender transposee to want those children headed toward the gender transpositions to proceed

---

[1] In this argument I follow the lead of Yale historian John Boswell. See Boswell 1980, pp. 92 ff.

toward them at their own speed (even if that's faster than their parents think they are ready for). You don't have to be Ralph Ginsburg to want to talk about sex using words a bit less tongue-tying than "fellatio" and "cunnilingus." Indeed, you don't have to be a Weatherman to want to use a word like "blowing."

I don't know how many outside the baby-boom generation will understand that last sentence. If I have the impression that the movement toward responsible sexual freedom is a baby-boom phenomenon, this may only be because there are so many baby boomers around these days—and they are all starting to talk about how they were raised, sexually speaking.

A Survey

Here are the results of an October 1984 poll conducted by the Milwaukee *Journal*:

> . . . in sexual matters the baby-boom generation, defined as people from 23 to 38 years old, was much more [sexually] permissive than people over 38. For example, 61% of the younger group "approved" of "casual sex," whereas only 28% of the older group did; and 77% of the younger group approved of unmarried people living together, whereas only 39% of the older group did.[2]

Those are remarkable figures in a society in which a 10-percentage-point difference in a presidential election is considered a landslide, and although there are obvious exceptions, these figures suggest that the generation gap is still very wide when it comes to sex. There's other evidence of this, too.

Some Movies

Consider the movie *Risky Business*, directed by baby boomer Paul Brickman. This enormously and justifiably popular movie is not one baby boomers recommend to their parents, because it presents the nice middle-class asexual upbringing they got with an almost vicious black humor.

The plot sounds like something straight out of Sodom and Gomor-

[2] This poll is quoted by Jonathan Schell in *The New Yorker*, 12 January 1987, p. 63.

rah: a sexually innocent high school boy, Joel, is tricked by his friend Miles into phoning in an order for a home visit from a prostitute. This one misstep—taken while Joel's parents are on vacation—leads, as the brimstone follows the fire, to the complete disintegration of Joel's life. The prostitute demands a lot more money than he can possibly come up with, one thing leads to another and another, and once the woman's pimp gets involved, Joel finds himself fighting for his family's house. Brickman's original script called for the movie to end with Joel and his family nearly penniless, his college hopes in ruins—thus preposterously justifying his parents' rules and worries—but the producers interceded and forced a surprise "happy" ending.

Will you forgive me if I tell you that in spite of this the movie succeeds on many levels? At the box office, it made millions and continues to pack 'em in whenever it plays at the revival houses. It is gorgeously photographed. And the symbolism, while not quite on the level of *The Seventh Seal,* could stand being treated by a few undergraduate English honors theses.[3]

There's even a brief subplot involving a gender transposition, and it's done right. The first prostitute Joel gets turns out to be (a) black and (b) a deep-voiced drag queen—perfect evidence, if any was needed, of how little Joel really knew about sex. And she only takes him for seventy-five dollars.

Smooth Talk, directed by baby boomer Joyce Chopra, covers sex undereducation from a daughter's point of view. It's based on a story by Joyce Carol Oates in which a high school girl's ignorance about sex is exploited by a threatening man who enjoys deflowering virgins. Oates hints that perhaps he enjoys doing more sinister things, too. The girl freaks out when this man visits her at home one day (she's alone) but finally hands her virginity over to his manipulations. Oates left you wondering what happened to her, while the movie (like *Risky Business*) ends somewhat more happily: the girl comes home changed, but alive, and less willing to be a kid.

One of the movie's best scenes is when she confronts her more prudent, and prudish, older sister and asks, Have you ever had a boy hold you in his arms and sing you a lullaby? Read you his poetry? That is, behave as boys otherwise never do? Her mother has only told her the bad side of what boys do to girls, and finding out about the

---

[3] I especially like the way Joel's bicycle is tipped over by the winds of puberty, the way the French doors blow open when, for the first time, he embraces a woman the way he's always wanted to, and the way the camera pans quickly from the two of them having s*x on the stairway past photos of Joel as a little boy.

good side makes the warnings quite a bit less effective. Mae West said, "Too much of a good thing can be delightful." And I say, How many parents want their kids to discover this for themselves by way of sex?

Miscommunication flashes across the boundaries of the gender transpositions, too, in *My Beautiful Laundrette,* written by baby boomer Hanif Kureishi. It's the story of a half-Pakistani, half-British young man named Omar who, in South London, starts up a trendy laundrette (of all things) and hires an old school chum named Johnny, now a punker trying to escape from his poor-white-trash street gang. It is a watershed gay movie (and a straight movie, as well), because Johnny and Omar are lovers. What I find exceptionally accurate is its portrayal of the reactions of the heterosexuals in their lives.

The pair-bond between Omar and Johnny turns out to be about as strong as that between Odysseus and Penelope, and yet everyone else acts as if it's nothing. Being slow to catch on to such things is common enough, even nowadays, but even those who do catch on to their relationship never take the two boys seriously—not even as seriously, for example, as they take the trivial marriage proposed for Omar and his cousin, "naughty daughter" Tania. Accordingly, both Johnny's gang and Omar's family make some serious miscalculations.[4] Johnny lets them make their mistakes and then, with an impish grin, lets them in on the secret after it's too late for them to do anything about it. Omar is too spacey to manipulate like this but has the good sense to follow Johnny's lead; in the crucial scene at the end of the movie it is he who leads and Johnny who follows.

Laundrette is fiction, but in real life I have seen the same reaction during sex-education classes coming from people who have just viewed a movie showing two gay men making love.[5] The two men, in their young twenties, had been together about a year when the movie was made. There are almost always a few in the audience who say that they never knew gay men had relationships longer than overnight casual pickups. This is astonishing ignorance. Although homosexuals themselves can have misconceptions about heterosexual life—usually resulting from knowing only their parents' relationship in any detail—

[4] They are like the miscalculation Blanche DuBois makes in *A Streetcar Named Desire*, long before the play's main action takes place. In one scene, Blanche recalls how she found her sensitive husband in bed with a man; she reacted insensitively, he committed suicide, and her life fell apart.

[5] One such movie is *Vir Amat*, filmed by Laird Sutton. Such films, and their heterosexual equivalents, are standard fare during a sex-education seminar for adults called "Sexual Attitude Restructuring." The films are noncommercial—documentary, not pornographic; sensitive, not sensational. Some of them aren't very good, technically speaking, but it's not for lack of trying.

it is rare for these to approach the higher levels of misunderstanding seen on the other side of the coin.[6]

All three of these commercial movies underscore the destructive aspects of the sex taboo. Why is it that our society insists that kids be kept so profoundly ignorant of one of life's most important aspects? Why do *Laundrette*'s heterosexuals keep themselves so ignorant of what was, to Omar and Johnny, the most important fact about their lives? After fourteen chapters, I still don't think I have an answer. Except the obvious one, of course: that sex is dangerous, that sex is spectacular, and so the powers that be had better keep people ignorant or they'll never keep us under control. That's only part of the answer, because of course we keep ourselves ignorant, too. I'll come back to that later.

Up-front Versus Irresponsible

Those of the baby-boom generation are certainly not the first ones to worry about sex. But they are the first ones to grow up with contraception available from the very beginning, and they are arguably the first ones with the freedom and the time—due to the nuclear balance of terror, the Great Society, and Reaganomics—to face an almost predictably prosperous economy and a relatively warfree life.[7] Perhaps this gives them more freedom to think about reworking their sexual arrangements, and their numbers give them the power to make others notice.

But to imply that *only* the baby boomers can do this is to give the generation gap too much credit. True, some old dogs never learn new tricks, but plenty of older people have come around to their own form of sexual liberation. They've seen their children "live in sin," and both parents and children live to tell about it. In fact, the ease with which living together before marriage has been accepted by the younger generation is rivaled only by the ease with which living together after the end of a marriage has been accepted by the divorced or widowed generations.

So how did it happen, in the sexual revolution, that being up-front about sex got confused with being irresponsible about it? If we can answer that question, then we can answer a lot of questions. We will understand why a herm in its natural state is so dangerous, because a

---

[6] Similarly, although both blacks and whites can misinterpret each other, the amount of black misunderstanding of white is dwarfed by the white misunderstanding of black.

[7] Let me stress, about a dozen times, "almost" and "relatively." The recessions baby boomers have experienced are, of course, dwarfed by the Great Depression. And although some of our operations in developing countries have been extremely damaging, they are dwarfed by the two world wars and history's previous record of nearly continuous warfare.

herm is nothing if not up-front. We will understand why openly gay couples seem so disturbing to other people (and not just heterosexual people, I might add). So let me give you some examples of being responsible and being up-front: one short, one long.

Sex Education, the Right to Know, and Political Belief

In Sweden, sex education in the schools is mandatory. Yes, there are in Sweden, as in the United States, sexual conservatives who believe that sex education should be taught only in the home. They have been outvoted by those who believe that sex education is a right: that all children, regardless of their parents' views, have *the right to know* how babies are made, what homosexuals are, how condoms work, and so on, just as they have the right to free choice and free exercise of their own religion even if their parents want them to practice the religion they were brought up in.

In the United States, the sex educators have been cast as liberals, the noneducators as conservatives. But there are liberals who are sexually uptight. And I don't see anything in conservative doctrine that requires that sexual ignorance be the right thing to encourage. It doesn't really improve the look of our finer university marching bands, it doesn't really reduce the federal deficit, and it doesn't really promote our covert operations in developing countries.

So why don't those conservatives get their act together and establish religious sex-education centers? Why doesn't the Catholic Church teach sexual anatomy, sexual physiology, and the details of the rhythm method in the schools they maintain at such enormous cost? If the researchers employed in Catholic hospitals could come up with a better understanding of sexual physiology, it would help make the rhythm method work better and add an extra contraceptive option to couples of all faiths. If marriage is a holy institution blessed by God, then why not exult in this good news and help it out a little bit, sexually speaking? Why doesn't Jerry Falwell copy the idea I put forth in the fake "Sesame Street" press release I wrote for chapter 4 and give sex-education information for married couples in his television appearances?

In short, why *must* sexual conservatism be tied to the sex taboo? Recognizing Communist China was thought to be something only a Democratic president would do until a Republican did it. Teaching a husband to ask his wife about what feels good to her sexually is thought to be something only a liberal would do—until some bright young conservative does it.

After all, until conservatives *do* disentangle the sex taboo from their political views, the liberals will claim that conservatives are acting in a stupid, self-defeating, and hypocritical way—and they'll be right. I have been amazed how Dr. Ruth Westheimer totted up an enormous radio audience, seemingly overnight, in an era that ought to be, were we to believe the Falwell oratory, increasingly unreceptive to her message of sex education for all. But contrary to Falwell's propaganda, America continues, sexually speaking, to liberalize and rationalize its thinking about sex (far too slowly, of course, but that's another issue).

I am happy to report that some conservatives seem to be waking up. As this book reached its final drafts, for example, conservative Surgeon General C. Everett Koop issued his report on AIDS.[8] Widely reported in the press, this report is an impassioned, and quite sensible, argument that the dangers of AIDS require sex education in the schools at much earlier ages than had been thought advisable. Aspects of the report were immediately denounced by the less sensible conservatives in the Department of Education, but the point was made, and it seems to be sticking. As you may have guessed, I would prefer to have sex education in the schools without having to point to something as depressing as AIDS to justify it, but Koop's argument, taken on its own terms, is logical, accurate, and impressive in its willingness to tell the truth. Mind you, it is only when proponents of all political persuasions break the sex taboo that we will have the chance for a truly informed debate about sexual matters.

AIDS and Safe Sex in San Francisco

If we can understand how being up-front about sex got confused with being irresponsible about it, we will also understand the conflict between the gay community's reactions to the AIDS crisis and the straight community's opinion of how it ought to be reacting to it.

Consider Frances FitzGerald's superlative writings about "the Castro" (a gay neighborhood in San Francisco) and its inhabitants' reactions to AIDS. She documented how many heterosexual San Franciscans were shocked that the gay community didn't seem to be doing anything about "the baths" (gay bathhouses visited by homosexual men for sexual purposes). One pregnant journalist told FitzGerald, for example, "The one thing they do know is that AIDS can be sexually transmitted. And yet they won't close down the places where all the sex goes on. It's unbelievable." San Francisco's mayor, Dianne Feinstein, added: "If this were a heterosexual problem, these establish-

---

[8] Koop 1986.

ments would have been closed a long time ago."[9] And FitzGerald documented a lot of the gay community's reactions to the epidemic—those homosexuals who vehemently agreed that the baths should be closed, the enormous percentages of gay men reducing their unsafe sex practices (to an extent that would previously have been thought impossible)—and the fact that many heterosexuals seemed unaware of these changes.

But she seemed to have trouble understanding why so many gays still resisted closing the bathhouses. Her explanation—that the baths were an important symbol to the gay community and could only be relinquished slowly—has a lot of truth in it but is incomplete.

In fact, the main stumbling block was the question of "safe sex," which FitzGerald described but underestimated. It is possible, in fact, to have sex with a person with full-blown AIDS and yet be virtually certain not to contract the AIDS virus.[10] Not a few gay men in San Francisco have done so: lovers of AIDS patients, for example, who understand how important sexual contact is in a disease that can cause its victims to be considered literally untouchable. The point of view FitzGerald didn't describe in enough detail is the one that says that instead of blaming *sex* for AIDS, one should blame *particular sexual practices*.[11] This view suggests not closing the baths but getting safe sex practiced there. After a brief digression, I'll explain why this was important.

The digression is to consider the point of view of people who agree that *in theory* one can have safe sex in a bathhouse but worry that *in practice* it can rarely be guaranteed. This is a legitimate question, but note that it can really be answered only by people who are experts on the baths, in what goes on there, and in how behavior can be changed there. Those most likely to be expert in this way would, frankly, be certain gay bath patrons themselves, and it seems unlikely that Mayor Feinstein would accept their testimony as authoritative.

Yet just this problem occurs in the larger battle against AIDS. Most AIDS education efforts are directed at gay men themselves; the heterosexual world at large does not read enough about them. Even if they did, they would have no way to know, really, if the education was taking hold. Only certain gay men themselves, the scientists con-

---

[9] FitzGerald 1986, pp. 54 and 59.

[10] This is now empirically verifiable through the blood test for the AIDS antibody: if someone without the antibody has safe sex with someone with AIDS, he or she does not become antibody-positive.

[11] In drug-abuse-related AIDS, one should blame not injections but injections with *dirty needles*. In the blood-transfusion cases, one should blame not transfusions but transfusions with *improperly tested blood*.

ducting surveys on this particular question, and a few sensitive outside observers (such as FitzGerald) would know whether the efforts are succeeding. In each of these three cases evidence would originate with gay men and would be of the following form: "Yes, when I went to a gay bar last night, the AIDS Action Committee handed out an information packet with condoms, antiseptic lubricants, and practical information—and people were paying attention to it." "Yes, when I settled in with my lover, we had a long talk about what our sex lives would be like in light of the fact that we didn't know if we had previously been exposed." "Yes, when I went to the baths in New York, there were free condoms everywhere." And so on. Certain gay men know about these things from their personal experience, others from observing their friends, and FitzGerald reported some similar conversations, but how can ordinary heterosexuals be expected to find out about them? Although one could reply that people who don't know what's going on should keep their mouths shut until they do, such restraint is difficult and perhaps counterproductive in a democracy; fools have the right to speak, too, and nonfools have fears they may not have had put to rest. Such debates end only with education.

So let us get back to the question of safe sex and what San Francisco officially did about it in the baths. The matter ended up in the courts, which made precisely the correct distinction: the baths could stay,[12] but the city had the right to regulate what kind of sex took place on their premises. The city's public health director, Mervyn Silverman, had issued such regulations (see the quotation introducing this chapter) but waffled on announcing their safe-sex provisions in public. Accordingly, seven of the nine physician-advisers who had previously supported him abandoned him because, in his words, "I didn't mention 'safe sex.' "

Silverman and those doctors lined up on opposite sides of the sex taboo. Silverman said that he wasn't going to violate the taboo ("I wasn't going to talk about masturbation at a press conference"), and most of his advisers believed he would have to. The fear of AIDS had already been magnified far too much, they thought, by reporters too timid to say exactly what sex acts were known to transmit AIDS,[13] and it didn't make sense for a public health official to encourage them further. When the national press reported that Silverman had banned

---

[12] Homosexual acts themselves were legalized in California several years ago, and the baths are not public accommodations. So it is hard, legally speaking, to claim that they ought to be closed across the board.

[13] It was a milestone—and perhaps a network-television first—when Tom Brokaw uttered the phrase "anal intercourse" on a late-night NBC News documentary about AIDS.

all sex at the baths, the physicians essentially said, "We told you so."

A substantial number of homosexuals, however, misunderstood how obvious the case for closing the baths seemed to most of the rest of San Francisco. And so they interpreted the attack on the baths as the beginning of an attempt to repress homosexual freedoms across the board rather than as a somewhat misinformed but genuine attempt to ensure the public health. On the other side of the fence, of course, were those who thought it was obvious that the baths should be closed; they had no way to understand the opinions of those homosexuals who remained opposed. Many of San Francisco's heterosexuals (including the mayor, Dianne Feinstein) could only conclude that there were too many irresponsible homosexuals out there continuing to have irresponsible sex—and many of its homosexuals (including some of the gay community's leaders) could only conclude that there were too many homophobic heterosexuals out there wanting to continue queer-bashing.

Here's an example to illustrate the dilemma. It so happens that we have a miniepidemic of hepatitis in the United States due to the rise in the use of day-care facilities. With more mothers working, more kids are placed in day care before they are toilet trained. That means more contact with feces, which carry hepatitis—and hepatitis is not a trivial disease.[14] So do we hear proposals to close the day-care centers because they literally are breeding grounds for a serious, far too often fatal, virus? No, we do not; day care is here to stay, and everyone knows it.

Since there really is a medically safe way to have day care without spreading hepatitis, *in and of itself* hepatitis is not enough reason to shut down day care in general.[15] Indeed, if proposals to do so were made, then feminists would interpret them less as public health measures than as political ones, and to a large extent they'd be right.

Likewise, if there really is a medically safe way to have (legal) sex in bathhouses—even with an AIDS patient—without spreading AIDS, then AIDS is not *in and of itself* a good enough reason to shut down the baths across the board. Since such proposals to close the baths were made—albeit not often by people who really knew about safe sex—many gay leaders interpreted them as an attack on rights they had spent a decade or more establishing. It is obvious that day care is

---

[14] Hepatitis B has killed more gay men than AIDS has, for example, although AIDS may eventually outstrip it.

[15] Of course, if a *particular* day-care center were shown to have an unusually high rate of hepatitis transmission and refused to take the proper sanitary steps to cut it down, there would certainly be a reason to close that particular center.

here to stay, but to many homosexuals it is not at all obvious that gay rights are here to stay. And so it was very difficult for these homosexuals to believe that closing the baths would not proceed to closing the bars, then closing off their homes and their lovers. The recent Supreme Court declaration that it is legal for policemen to enter Georgia bedrooms in the enforcement of sodomy laws has hardly reassured them. About half of the states still outlaw sodomy, and a few even single out homosexual sodomy while permitting heterosexual sodomy.

Perhaps I am naive, but I am of the opinion that neither side really understood the other's point of view in the bathhouse matter. Alas, there really are people out to use AIDS as a weapon to force gays back into the closet, and there really are people with AIDS out there having unsafe sex with unknowing partners (sometimes, I presume, in the baths). But neither of those things was really responsible for the frustration experienced by both sides in the debate; rather, a deep misunderstanding was.

Again, this fact may also be related to the "technique puzzle" of chapter 3. Open gays, of the sort who live in the San Francisco Bay area, have usually come to terms with the sex taboo and know in their bones that stopping AIDS does not necessarily require stopping sex. Those heterosexuals who have also come to terms with the sex taboo can agree. But most heterosexuals don't *have* to come to terms with the sex taboo in order to be heterosexual in our society. Accordingly, what sometimes first appears to be a homosexual/heterosexual split on an issue like this is really a split on the sex taboo: most (but not all) of the heterosexuals tacitly endorsing the taboo and most (but not all) of the homosexuals opposing it.

Getting to Know You

This is but one of the difficulties that separate the gender transpositions from each other. We Americans pride ourselves on being a melting pot, and many San Franciscans pride themselves on contributing to a city where straight and gay can understand each other. But we all know the tensions that arise when we have to integrate similarities with differences. There comes that good ol' Western dualism again! How can we integrate sex with love? Gay people with straight people with transpeople? Old with young?

A problem with the age barrier is that age itself is built into the sex taboo. As John Money points out, a powerful aspect of the sex taboo is intergenerational. People of different ages aren't supposed to *think* about sex in each other's presence, much less *talk* to each other about it. This has not only tragic consequences—as when parents deliver too little too late in sex-education information to their children—but also comic ones.

I'm sorry I don't recall who it was who did this study, but some sex educators decided to ask kids about their parents' sex lives, after having asked parents about their kids' sex lives in so many of those studies that demonstrate that sex education at home usually means no sex education at all. How often, they asked, do you think that your parents engage(d) in each of the following sexual activities: Fellatio? Intercourse with Mom on top? Intercourse in the missionary position? And so on. It turned out that the kids underestimated what their parents were doing just as much as parents usually underestimated what their kids were doing.

Perhaps the sex taboo just helps keep the parents one step ahead of the kids. After all, if you and your kid are shopping downtown and you both notice a cross-dresser doing so poorly at cross-dressing that you both figure out instantly what's going on, what do you do when your kid asks you about it? Do you tell your impressionable child that the "woman" you saw was a homosexual? A transsexual? Both those answers could easily be wrong. How can you give a correct answer if you don't know what it is yourself?

So how, *practically* speaking, are we going to get the word out about sex? We have a massive sex-education problem affecting millions of Americans of all ages, races, educations, creeds. And the problem is more than mere dry facts and figures; it has to do with emotions, opinions, and prejudices, which have a stubborn illogic of their own. Where to begin?

Popular Culture

Well, sometimes you just have to say, "What the fuck." This will give us freedom. We can start with education of the most popular sort. The reason why I have been citing popular culture so often in this book is that popular culture is our society's lay educator.

I know a little girl who at first thought Boy George was gross. A few years later she was imitating him (short of doing drugs) and was going around explaining how she *likes* being different—that being just like everybody else is boring. It was Boy George who taught her *emotionally* that she has options. Formal courses in school pale by comparison.

Oldies—whether they be old songs or old movies—tell us where we were, and that's often more of a shock than where we're going. I watch popular but not exactly path-breaking movies like *The Breakfast Club* and *Fame* and wonder if movies like that were around when I was a teenager. I never saw any; was that because they weren't being made yet or because I was unaware of them? Usually, I think it was because they weren't there—at least until *The Graduate*—and that's scary, because they clearly fill a need today's kids want filled. When I was their age, I didn't even know those needs existed, and that's probably why I didn't see *The Graduate* until about two years after it came out.

BAD SCIENCE AND BAD SOCIETIES

The sex taboo also messes up our scientific attempts to figure out the truth—in all the obvious ways, of course, but sometimes in ways that are not. For an obvious example, consider the gender transpositions in other cultures. If anthropologists don't know what ordinary modern lesbian women are really like—in terms of personality, sexuality, bonding, and all that—how can they recognize ordinary lesbian women in other societies if lesbians happen to exist there? The anthropologists are likely to conclude, say, as some have, that "real" lesbianism doesn't exist in society X if there are no women running around looking like men or wanting to be men. But what that observation really means is that there are no female-to-male transsexuals or female cross-dressers in society X, which is not surprising given how rare these categories are in our own. Likewise, if you're doing rat experiments on sexual orientation but you have a poor conception of what human sexual orientation is all about, your rat experiments are going to be in trouble. And so a number of studies—anthropological, physiological, whatever—implicitly confuse the gender transpositions with each other. And it's the sex taboo, at least in part, that keeps people from understanding what the human gender transpositions are really like.

For an unobvious example, consider *gender constancy*, a favorite concept from developmental psychology. Gender constancy is a developmental milestone: the point at which a kid learns that a boy stays male his whole life, a girl female her whole life. Child psychologists experiment to discover at exactly what age the average child makes this connection. One method is to show kids dolls with "anatomically correct" features[16] but with mismatches—like a penis on a

---

[16] The usual meaning of "anatomically correct," by the way, is a euphemism; "genitally correct" or "genitally uncensored" would be more accurate. After all, what is anatomically unusual about these particular dolls is, specifically, their *genitalia*—not necessarily other

doll wearing a dress or no penis on a doll with short hair and a mustache—then ask the kid whether it's a male doll or a female doll. Kids that sort the dolls by genitalia have achieved gender constancy (of a particular type); those that sort by clothing or by hair have not.

To "pass" tests like this, kids have to know that a male is someone with a penis, and a female is someone without one.[17] But penises in our culture are covered up almost all the time, and some children are never told what really makes males different from females. So kids have to learn that the difference between boys and girls is a part of the body everybody keeps a secret. They have to solve a puzzle when grown-ups don't tell them there's a puzzle to solve.[18] Of course, most children eventually do solve this puzzle, as the tests show. But scientifically things are getting skewed by the sex taboo.

After all, has anyone ever studied when children in nudist camps achieve gender constancy? How about children in tropical societies in which everyone goes unclothed? Those kids, I'd bet, achieve gender constancy sooner, because they don't need X-ray eyes to achieve it. And yet Western developmental psychologists go their merry way, hoping to find that achieving gender constancy is (or is not) a universal human milestone—implicitly assuming that they are measuring a simple trait in an ordinary society. In fact, they are measuring a subtle and complicated trait in a very bizarre society, sexually speaking. I must have read dozens of papers on gender constancy, but not one of them raises this issue. And so a peculiar trait of our own society has been made the centerpiece of a supposedly universal issue.

This parochialism is, of course, part of what it means to have a culture. All cultures are parochial, academic cultures included. Indeed, we academics seem to have a different parochialism in every department. Let me discuss the parochialism of extreme environmen-

---

features, like flexible elbows, that are just as "anatomical." It also strikes me as odd what is deemed okay to show on a doll sold openly in Western societies. Barbie dolls have breasts but not nipples. Dolls that are even remotely genitally accurate are considered controversial, while dolls that "wet"—that is, urinate—are considered perfectly normal. Well, why not dolls that vomit? That defecate? That perspire and require the application of little roll-on deodorants from tiny vials that the deodorant companies would no doubt be willing to supply to doll manufacturers? I'd go crazy trying to explain these distinctions to a Martian sociologist trying to understand Western culture in the twentieth century. I do believe, however, that the toy-company executives who risked careers and ridicule to introduce the first urinating doll deserve a medal in the battle against the sex taboo—whoever they may be. Tracking down this matter would be a worthy thesis topic.

[17] In our society, advanced kids—and some grown-ups—know that a woman actually is someone more than just someone without a penis, but frankly this knowledge is rarely used in sex determination by ordinary mortals.

[18] If this sounds like the legend of Santa Claus to you, you're right; kids have to solve a puzzle that grown-ups don't tell them exists. Draw your own conclusions.

talism: the notion that everything is learned, that culture rules all, and that biological predispositions can safely be ignored.

I'll describe two cases: the "sweet tooth is learned in childhood" debacle and the "monkey see, monkey do" fallacy embodied by some of the opponents of the dismal kind of erotica deemed "pornography."

A Sweet Tooth: Learned in Childhood?

In the mid-1970s, a theory appeared and became popular that purported to explain why we humans in Western societies like sugar. Remember it? It supposedly had nothing to do with our physiology, our genetics, or anything like that; it had to do with our childhoods. The theory claimed that we like sweet things because that's what we were given to eat when we were kids.

I remember being irritated by this theory whenever I read of it. Although I'm not a nutritionist, it bothered me because it didn't fit with what little I did know about the human diet. For example, we apparently maintain ourselves accurately at a particular average weight—an average that slowly increases with age, perhaps by a pound or two per year—and in order to do so, we don't need to count calories or weigh ourselves on a scale every day. Usually, all we have to do is eat until we're comfortably full at each meal. Particular brain lesions can tip this delicately balanced mechanism either way, and so can drugs like tobacco and cocaine. So I supposed that although environment may have a clear effect on particular instances of weight gain or loss, it has less to do with it than commonly supposed for the great mass of people—in a society that manages to feed itself well. More to the point, it bothered me that the theory implicitly assumed that liking sugar in childhood was an independent variable—something that was culturally variable and hence had culturally variable effects on adulthood. This seemed to be putting the cart before the horse. Children do not have to be socialized into liking candy bars—although admittedly they can't like candy bars if candy bars don't exist in their environment.

It is always pleasing to have one's snap judgments confirmed, as mine were in this case by a 1979 article in *Science* magazine.[19] It turns out that when you actually try to generate this effect in a mammal (yes, I'll admit it's rats) by feeding sugar to newborns, there is no difference in the adult diet preferences of the sugar-fed rats in com-

---

[19] Wurtman and Wurtman 1979.

parison to control rats not given sugar while growing up. It was at that point that I suddenly stopped seeing references to sugar socialization in childhood. Apparently the theory was dropped because there never was the slightest experimental evidence in its favor.

That it could spread as far as it did, however, was scary, scientifically speaking. It turns out that intense preferences for carbohydrates (sugar is, of course, one form of carbohydrate) may be a form of self-medication for depression.[20] No one really knows why depression is epidemic in our society, but there is now little doubt that biochemistry sometimes figures prominently in its cause and cure. The idea that we crave carbohydrates just because we learned to do so as children thus helped lead us down exactly the wrong path.

Pornography: Monkey See, Monkey Do?

I have similar doubts when I listen to debates about pornography nowadays. For the purposes of this section, let me define pornography as erotic depictions designed to produce sexual arousal in particular kinds of people and not designed to achieve any goal other than sexual arousal. This definition would never work in court, but then again I'm a scientist, not a lawyer or a judge, and I'm about to make a scientific point, not a legal one. Of course, there are intermediate and special cases, but for the most part we all know why pornography is made: the person writing the story or taking the picture intended somebody to become sexually aroused by the results, and very few people (other than sexological scholars) use it for any nonsexual purpose. After all, *Playboy* centerfolds are photographed to arouse heterosexual men, and few if any museums buy copies of those photographs for their permanent collections, no matter how exquisite the lighting of the breasts or the genitalia. (Of course, some other nudes in *Playboy* do not fall into the category of pornography by my definition.)

There are critics of pornography—the Meese Commission is but one—who seem to have an astonishing faith in the principle of "monkey see, monkey do" when it comes to such materials: that viewing or reading pornography will, as the night follows the day, encourage the performance of sex crimes. I have no doubt that such things happen, and I won't even complain (at the moment) if people say that they happen often. But to stop thinking about the issue at this point in the logical analysis is a gross and dangerous oversimplification.

This question is important partly because some critics claim that

---

[20]This is because carbohydrates, when eaten without protein, affect serotonin in the brain, which is related to depression. See papers in Wurtman and Wurtman 1986.

pornography encourages men to attempt having sex with children. When these critics are asked to cite scientific studies demonstrating such links, a heated battle ensues. Regardless of the outcome—and I have seen it go both ways—some critics fall back to a position that says that it really doesn't matter if the studies are inconclusive; if banning pornography prevents *even a single child* from being molested by an adult, they say, then that child will have been well served by the ban.

But what of the other side of the coin? There is evidence—I'll examine its quality in a moment—that *permitting* pornography can reduce child sexual abuse. In Denmark, for example, after legalization of hard-core pornography in the 1960s, child sexual abuse went down by a very substantial percentage, and stayed down—an effect not accounted for by liberalized societal attitudes, increased underreporting, or less diligence on the part of the police (all of which were very carefully checked out in the study). So I ask the critics, If legalizing pornography prevents *even a single child* from being molested by an adult, would that child have been well served by the legalization?

This is a very complicated question, and the tragedy is that almost no one seems to want to know what the real answer is. But if you really do want to reduce child molestation, you should really want to find out what really causes it. Let me sketch the study's explanation for the Danish finding.[21]

The explanation is entirely consistent with everything else we know about child molestation. First of all, sex offenders in general (including child molesters) have on average had *less* exposure to pornographic materials in their childhoods than has the population at large.[22] More importantly, a great deal—not all—of the sexual contacts between adult heterosexual men and girls is committed by men who are not true pedophiles. (True pedophiles are those who are exclusively or predominantly aroused by such contacts.) Instead, much of it is contact by shy or inept heterosexual men who would prefer sex with adult women but are frustrated in their attempts: men who found, usually accidentally at first, that younger women or girls are less competent in resisting their advances. This was the conclusion of the Kinsey study of sex offenders, for example.[23] It is confirmed by some scientists working in criminology and corrections.[24] It has been veri-

---

[21] Kutchinsky 1973.

[22] Goldstein and Kant 1973.

[23] Gebhard et al. 1965.

[24] Groth and Birnbaum 1978, for example, state that heterosexual child molestation is more often substitutional in nature than homosexual child molestation is. The point they were making is that ordinary homosexual men who prefer adults as sexual partners are *less*

fied plethysmographically by Kurt Freund and his coworkers, who do not include a man in their samples of heterosexual pedophiles unless he had been arrested *more than once* for sexual relations with under-aged girls (or admits that he is sexually attracted to them). This is because men who have been arrested only once for such an offense *often* turn out to show ordinary heterosexual arousal patterns when tested plethysmographically.

That is, much heterosexual child molestation is *substitutional* in na-ture: such men apparently can resist contacts with girls if they substi-tute masturbation with pornography depicting their main interest, adult women. Note, however, that the Danish experience of the late 1960s was confined to pornography depicting adults. The argument does not apply as well to child pornography, since those purchasing such ma-terials are more likely to be true pedophiles, who may or may not be able to substitute pornography for the real thing. The argument is im-portant, however, because it shows that the possibility of substitution has to be taken seriously: perhaps it really has worked in some cases.

I said that most people don't really seem to want to know what the real answer is because this is what I see in my own observations of people's reactions to such studies. Let us suppose, for the sake of ar-gument, that the Danish studies were correct. One critic of the Danish work really seemed more intent on showing that rape of adult women increased after what he termed "porno-violence" was legalized,[25] not so much that heterosexual child molestation decreased after pornog-raphy depicting heterosexual relations among adults was legalized. So let us suppose for the sake of argument that these studies also are correct. The point I'm getting at should now be obvious: it may well be that pornography has *varied* effects, some of them noxious and some of them not.

The "monkey see, monkey do" hypothesis assumes that human learning is extremely simple. You see it, you're likely to do it. Or even, you see something taboo, you're likely to do almost anything taboo. It is shockingly naïve in its learning theory and surprisingly ignorant of tests of its predictions. And it tends to be confused by, rather than intrigued by or resigned to, the probability that all of pornography's effects might not be in the same (negative) direction.

The "monkey see, monkey do" theory acquires its force—or, more

---

likely to molest boys than ordinary heterosexual men who prefer adults as sexual partners are likely to molest girls. Of course, it is a different question to ask whether there are more men who *prefer* to have sex with boys or more who *prefer* to have sex with girls. And yet a different question is whether more boys or girls are approached and/or molested.

[25] Court 1984.

accurately, its sense of inevitable correctness—from extreme environmentalism. Ironically, this point of view sees humans as the highest species, claiming that we have risen above aping our primate cousins; yet it turns right around and endorses a theory of learning in pornography that makes oysters look far more in control of their libido.

Extreme Environmentalism and the Sex Taboo

As my models in this book demonstrate, I have no objection to taking account of real or reasonably hypothesized environmental influences on behavior, but the extreme brand of environmentalism excludes biology. It is thus doomed from the start. And it sometimes results in the silliest of statements. I've lost track, for example, of the number of times I've heard parents or talk-show hosts try to account environmentalistically for teenagers' sudden preoccupations with sex. Here's a recent example:

> If there is a surge in teen-age pregnancy, certainly the National Academy of Sciences need not spend $600,000 to ascertain the cause. It need only to look at what the young look at. Sex is publicized and "sold" to our children by the movie industry and TV, network as well as cable.[26]

Note, first of all, how this letter illustrates the sexual aspects of the generation gap by overlooking the possibility that the knowledge kids acquire from the movie industry and TV is worth acquiring. And perhaps its author favors more responsible sex in the media. But more to the point, whatever happened to the good old hormonal theory of puberty? The one that says that children would become interested in sex and romance even if they were *not* socialized to do so by the manufacturers of blue jeans?

This extreme environmentalism, I believe, may even be a *necessary* component of some forms of the sex taboo. After all, sex is spectacularly important, and sex to begin with (though certainly not to end with) is a biological phenomenon with at least one biological purpose. So if you want to deny the importance of sex, you'd better deny the importance of biology.[27]

---

[26] Letter to the editor of *The Wall Street Journal*, 8 January 1987, from Jay Carlisle.

[27] Of course, this denial is not necessary in the case of simple environmentalism, which works perfectly well with a great many other theories of human behavior.

Biologists have no excuse to overlook sex.[28] Other scientists do. After all, if society socializes its children—overtly, anyway—to believe that sex is unimportant, then it makes sense for sociologists to put sex aside in attempts to understand that society—at first, anyway. Such sociologists will turn out to be wrong, of course, because sex is important in any society, but they can be forgiven until they consciously start overlooking empirical evidence that contradicts their otherwise logical hypothesis. For example, this was the case for developmental psychologists trying to find correlations between childhood traits and adult traits; for the most part, they failed to find nontrivial correlations until the sissy-boy studies showed them one from sexology (see chapter 9).

Toward Better Research

Sexologists have no more to be ashamed of in their record of past research than other scientists do in other disciplines. Of course, some sexological studies could have been done better. Of course, sexologists are outsiders in the context of most of academia, and this hampers their work. Of course, the first group of people attracted to an outsiders' discipline may contain a disproportionate number of kooks. But none of that is an excuse for overlooking sexology's strengths and its case for more resources.

Is this a pitch for more money? Yes. I can't think of any other subject that has been more unjustly underfunded for a longer period of time for sillier reasons than sex research. Although I've been arguing this implicitly throughout the book, let me take a moment to tie this grant proposal up into a prettier package.

I've subscribed to *Scientific American* for decades, and I've been pleased to notice that when they publish an article on animal behavior, its authors often mention interesting aspects of the animal's sexual behavior. But I've been disappointed to find that this prestigious scientific magazine has seldom, if ever, published an article focusing specifically on sex. Come to think of it, "human sexuality" would be a great topic for one of their October single-topic issues, wouldn't you think? Or how about an article surveying Americans' attitudes on gay

---

[28] And as a result, biologists have overcome the sex taboo to some extent: botanists discuss pistils and stamens without blushing, and entomologists have no trouble discussing damselfly penises. But biologists as a class escape the sex taboo *only when it comes to their own organisms*: ask them to deal with sex *in humans* and some of them get just as antsy as the rest of our society. Remember the uncomfortable reception Monica Moore received when she presented her studies of human courtship to behavioral biologists (see chapter 11).

rights, similar to the series of articles they've published every few years on whites' attitudes toward blacks? When rumors flew in the press that KGB agents were hanging out in gay bars in Washington, D.C., trying to entrap congressmen who were gay and closeted, why were articles not published about the connection, or lack thereof, between homosexuality and national security? How about an article surveying the gender transpositions by John Money (or any of a number of other experts)? *Scientific American* has been willing to be a leader in many other areas of scientific controversy, but when it comes to sex, other science magazines have beaten them to press.

Similarly, as a rule it is the smaller state colleges, rather than the more prestigious state universities, that first (or ever) offer more than a token course in sex education or human sexuality. And it is Harvard that has lagged behind the rest of the Ivy League in the same way.

Private philanthropy is likewise disappointing. The Playboy Foundation funds some basic sex research, but impressions to the contrary notwithstanding, it is not particularly wealthy. There is a foundation that grants research monies specifically for studies of transsexualism, but for various reasons it has been able to make such grants only intermittently. The only other foundation I am aware of that has supported research into human sexuality is the Rockefeller Foundation, which was the ultimate source of funds for much of the Kinsey research. In fact, the Rockefellers supported various kinds of research into human sexuality for over forty years, right through John D. Rockefeller III's formation of the Population Council in 1952. And for a few years in the 1970s they supported a small staff at the Harvard University Graduate School of Education that conducted a study on how children acquired their knowledge of sexual matters. Alas, the Rockefellers no longer make grants in such areas, and one sexological historian recently wrote that "few families or foundations have stepped forward to pick up where they [the Rockefellers] left off. I am also not certain that any committee of scientists deciding on research projects to fund would be any more likely to fund social science projects on sex than they were 40 years ago"[29]—referring to the fact that Kinsey's research was as close to social science as the scientists of the day were willing to get.

Are times changing? Yes and no. The recent National Academy of Sciences report on AIDS research, for example, called Kinsey's research "quasi-scientific"—a term that obviously distances its author from sex research. It did, however, call for more basic and applied

[29] Bullough 1985 is a detailed account of this funding history.

research on social factors in human sexuality.[30] Although I obviously applaud this conclusion, I wish that they, like Surgeon General Koop, didn't have to fall back on the tragedy of AIDS to reach it and had shown better knowledge of the scope of modern sex research in their report.

I'd like to think that simple naïveté was what got me into this field, but as I look back, I have to admit that's only part of the reason. Another important motivation was that there were (and are) terribly important questions I could investigate, because the sex taboo has scared off a lot of people who otherwise would have gotten there before I did. And I'll admit it's exciting to work on something so terribly important.

Because so many choice questions have been left unanswered for so long, good sex research can be relatively inexpensive. Richard Pillard's and my work on homosexuality running in families was paid for by a pair of very small three-year grants from the National Institute of Mental Health. Kurt Freund and his many distinguished colleagues at the Clarke Institute in Toronto are supported by the ordinary workings of Canada's national health insurance system and that government's associated research councils. John Money has been doing his research on a shoestring budget for decades, given the sheer volume (not to mention quality) of research he's published. If sex research were to receive funds for basic research that amounted to just 1 percent of the annual budget for the Plasma Physics Laboratory at Princeton University (to pick a random, but expensive, project at my alma mater), sexologists would be deliriously happy even if that amount were handed out over the space of ten years.

Is this envy? Of course. It's also anger.

BREAKING THE TABOO RESPONSIBLY

Let me now return to the pure-ignorance hypothesis: that the sex taboo continues because past victims of the taboo—parents—have no choice but to create new victims—their children. Think back to that man dressed as a woman you and your kids saw on the street. How can you explain cross-dressing to them if you don't really know what it is yourself?

Well, Daddy and Mommy, why did the dinosaurs die out? The solution is simple. When you encounter that question about the cross-dresser, why not just answer, "I don't know; let's go to the library

[30] Baltimore 1986.

and take out a good book about cross-dressing and find out"? *Sexual Landscapes,* for example?

Why not? Because you're still trapped by the sex taboo,[31] you don't see how easy—and how hard—it is to break it. When I tell the "Uncle Jim" story from chapter 1, I often get sympathetic reactions; after all, it is difficult to explain rape to a little girl, right? Rape is a complicated thing to explain to anyone. I mean, nowadays it's not just men who rape women; it can be . . . Well, of course sometimes it's hard to tell the difference between rape and . . . Can a husband rape his wife? . . . It's just *so complicated,* right?

No, it's not complicated at all. *Rape is when someone forces someone else to have sexual relations with them against their will.* Uncle Jim knew that at the time, logically, but he was tongue-tied emotionally. He now knows that this italicized sentence is easy to say. You practice saying it now—aloud—or else when your niece asks you what rape is, your response will be the same as Uncle Jim's.

Remember Johnny? The little boy who was playing with his penis and then had to interpret Mummy's very mixed message? The people who reported that incident—Robert Sears, Eleanor Maccoby, and Harry Levin—did an excellent study of child rearing and, much to their credit, did not exclude sex when they did it. They found that a few families *do* give their children good explanations of sexual functioning. But even those families *never told kids about the emotions involved with sexuality.* That is, not one Johnny was told in anything other than mechanical terms—scientific terms, ahem—why sex is the way it is.

For example, if Johnny asked Mummy why his penis was getting hard, *not one* family told their Johnny, "You're feeling sexy; that's why you're acting like that." It's simple, once you think of it, isn't it? Even if you want to tell him that our society says it's inappropriate for a little boy to show off his erect penis at his parents' cocktail party (just as it's inappropriate for him to throw a temper tantrum there), you can connect the behavior to an emotion that he will be feeling throughout his life, and that explains things to him (just as the emotion of anger explains a tantrum). This answer tells Johnny that there is an emotion called sexiness. It tells him that he has this emotion built into him. And if the phrase is delivered with a shrug of the shoulders, it tells him he's not weird to have this reaction. Those are latent messages, not overt ones, but they are very important.

In some hunter-gatherer tribes, latent messages like these are given

---

[31] And the library is, too, of course. Now where *did* we put those "Sesame Street" books about Bert and Ernie getting dressed up as Laverne and Shirley for Halloween?

all the time. Here's what Melvin Konner, an anthropologist and child psychologist at Emory University, had to say about the !Kung:

> When not in the sling, infants are passed from hand to hand around a fire for . . . interactions with one adult or child after another. They are kissed on their faces, bellies, genitals, are sung to . . .[32]

Now Western politicians love kissing babies, but any politician that tries to kiss a baby in all the places where the !Kung routinely kiss theirs will end up in jail, not in office. This is but one symptom of the fact that Western babies, from the moment the first diapers are put on and every time they are kissed everywhere *except* on their genitals, are learning something about the sex taboo.

Kids are nearly never taught—and thus may never learn—these emotional facts about sex. Is it any wonder, then, that they grow up to discover that they are out of touch with their emotions? And that what is really very simple appears to be impossibly difficult? To explain to Johnny why, *scientifically* speaking, his penis got hard, you'd have to lecture him at least the length of this book. Far better to take the emotional route—if only because the emotions really are the proximate cause of things like erections, anyway. But the sex taboo operates insidiously by getting you to interpret Johnny's question as a scientific one. Frankly, let him learn about vasocongestion and the corpora cavernosa when he goes to medical school.

I hope that many times, while you were reading this book, you thought to yourself, Gosh, I never thought of it that way; it's really very simple, isn't it? You're just like Johnny, really: when it comes to sex, very few people have ever explained things to you honestly and straightforwardly. It's refreshing, but it's disorienting, when someone does. Let me assure you that you can get used to it; it's called overcoming the taboo.

But the best reason for sex-educating your children—and everyone else's children—is the same as the best reason for doing sex research. *Preventing people from doing so is living a lie.* Sex is spectacular, sex is astonishing, sex is dangerous, and sex is painfully delightful. Living these simple facts can give you freedom: freedom to travel for miles and miles about the sexual landscape and to be fascinated at every turn.

[32] Konner 1982, p. 302. By the way, that exclamation point is part of the name of the tribe; it represents a linguistic click made with the tongue. And if you want to be thoroughly horrified by Western child-rearing techniques, just read Konner's chapter 13.

REFERENCES

Aaron, William (1972). *Straight: A heterosexual talks about his homosexual past.* Garden City, N.Y.: Doubleday.

Abbott, Sidney, and Love, Barbara (1972). *Sappho was a right-on woman: A liberated view of lesbianism.* New York: Stein and Day.

Akers, Jean S., and Conaway, Clinton H. (1979). Female homosexual behavior in *Macaca mulatta. Archives of Sexual Behavior* 8:63–80.

Alcock, John (1984). *Animal behavior: An evolutionary approach* (3rd ed.). Sunderland, Mass.: Sinauer Associates.

Allen, Clifford (1952). Reviews. [Review of: Cory, Donald Webster. *The Homosexual in America.*] *International Journal of Sexology* 5:236–238.

Bakwin, Harry (1968). Deviant gender-role behavior in children: Relation to homosexuality. *Pediatrics* 41:620–629.

Baltimore, David (1986). *Confronting AIDS: Directions for public health, health care, and research.* Washington, D.C.: National Academy Press.

Bancroft, John H. J.; Jones, H. G.; and Pullan, B. P. (1966). A simple transducer for measuring penile erection, with comments on its use in the treatment of sexual disorders. *Behaviour Research and Therapy* 4:239–241.

Barlow, George W. (1967). Social behavior of a South American leaf fish, *Polycentrus schomburgkii*, with an account of recurring pseudofemale behavior. *The American Midland Naturalist* 78:215–234.

Barrows, Sydney Biddle (1986). *Mayflower madam: The secret life of Sydney Biddle Barrows.* New York: Arbor House.

Bauman, Robert (1986a). The secret life of Bob Bauman. *The Washingtonian* 21(10):98–148.

Bauman, Robert (1986b). *The gentleman from Maryland: The conscience of a gay conservative.* New York: Arbor House.

Bell, Alan P.; Weinberg, Martin S.; and Hammersmith, Sue Kiefer (1981a). *Sexual preference: Its development in men and women.* New York: Simon and Schuster.

Bell, Alan P.; Weinberg, Martin S.; and Hammersmith, Sue Kiefer (1981b). *Sexual preference: Its development in men and women. Statistical Appendix.* Bloomington, Ind.: Indiana University Press.

Bickerton, Derek (1983). Creole languages. *Scientific American* 249(1): 116–122.

Binder, Carl V. (1977). Affection training: An alternative to sexual reorientation. *Journal of Homosexuality* 2:251–259.

Blanchard, Ray (1985). Typology of male-to-female transsexualism. *Archives of Sexual Behavior* 14:247–261.

Blanchard, Ray; Racansky, I. G.; and Steiner, Betty W. (1986). Phallometric detection of fetishistic arousal in heterosexual male cross-dressers. *Journal of Sex Research* 22:452–462.

Boardman, John (1974). *Athenian black figure vases.* New York: Oxford University Press.

Boardman, John (1975). *Athenian red figure vases: The Archaic period: A handbook.* New York: Oxford University Press.

Bogoras, Waldemar (1904). The Chukchee. *Memoirs of the American Museum of Natural History* 11:1–732 [reprinted from vol. 7, part 1, the Jesup North Pacific Expedition].

Bohman, Michael (1978). Some genetic aspects of alcoholism and criminality: A population of adoptees. *Archives of General Psychiatry* 35:269–276.

Bornstein, Marc H. (1975). The influence of visual perception on culture. *American Anthropologist* 77:774–798.

Bornstein, Marc H.; Kessen, William; and Weiskopf, Sally (1976). The categories of hue in infancy. *Science* 191:201–202.

Boswell, John E. (1980). *Christianity, social tolerance, and homosexuality: Gay people in Western Europe from the beginning of the Christian era to the fourteenth century.* Chicago: University of Chicago Press.

Boswell, John E. (1982). Revolutions, universals, and sexual categories. *Salmagundi* 58-59:89–113.

Brackbill, Hervey (1941). Possible homosexual mating of the rock dove. *The Auk* 58:581.

Breland, Keller, and Breland, Marian (1961). The misbehavior of organisms. *American Psychologist* 16:681–684.

Breslow, Norman; Evans, Linda; and Langley, Jill (1985). On the prevalence and roles of females in sadomasochistic subculture: Report of an empirical study. *Archives of Sexual Behavior* 14:303–317.

Briddell, D. W., and Wilson, G. Terence (1976). The effects of alcohol and expectancy set on male sexual arousal. *Journal of Abnormal Psychology* 85:225–234.

Brown, Rita Mae (April 1977). A stranger in "Paradise": Rita Mae Brown goes to the baths. *The Body Politic,* pp. 15–16.

Bullough, Vern L. (1985). The Rockefellers and sex research. *Journal of Sex Research* 21:113–125.

Burley, Nancy (1981). Sex ratio manipulation and selection for attractiveness. *Science* 211:721–722.

Cade, William (1980). Alternative male reproductive behaviors. *Florida Entomologist* 63:30–45.

References

Califia, Pat (15 September 1983). Playing with roles and reversals: Gender-bending. *The Advocate* [San Mateo, Calif.] no. 376:24–27.

Carpenter, C. R. (1942). Sexual behavior of free ranging rhesus monkeys *(Macaca mulatta)*: II. Periodicity of estrus, homosexual, autoerotic and nonconformist behavior. *Journal of Comparative Psychology* 33:143–162.

Carrier, Joseph M. (1971). Participants in urban Mexican male homosexual encounters. *Archives of Sexual Behavior* 1:279–291.

Carrier, Joseph M. (1976). Cultural factors affecting urban Mexican male homosexual behavior. *Archives of Sexual Behavior* 5:103–124.

Chauncey, George, Jr. (1982). From sexual inversion to homosexuality: Medicine and the changing conceptualization of female deviance. *Salmagundi* 58–59:114–146.

Chevalier-Skolnikoff, Suzanne (1974). Male-female, female-female, and male-male sexual behavior in the stumptail monkey, with special attention to female orgasm. *Archives of Sexual Behavior* 3:95–116.

Chevalier-Skolnikoff, Suzanne (1976). Homosexual behavior in a laboratory group of stumptail monkeys *(Macaca arctoides)*: Forms, contexts, and possible social functions. *Archives of Sexual Behavior* 5:511–527.

Chomsky, Noam (1976). On the biological basis of language capacities. In Rieber, Robert W. (Ed.), *The neuropsychology of language: Essays in honor of Eric Lenneberg*, pp. 1–24. New York: Plenum Publishing.

Coates, Susan, and Person, Ethel Spector (1985). Extreme boyhood femininity: Isolated behavior or pervasive disorder? *Journal of the American Academy of Child Psychiatry* 24:702–709.

Coles, Claire D., and Shamp, M. Johnna (1984). Some sexual, personality, and demographic characteristics of women readers of erotic romances. *Archives of Sexual Behavior* 13(3):187–209.

Collias, Nicholas E., and Jahn, Laurence R. (1959). Social behavior and breeding success in Canada geese *(Branata canadensis)* confined under semi-natural conditions. *The Auk* 76:478–509.

Conover, Michael R.; Miller, Don E.; and Hunt, George L., Jr. (1979). Female-female pairs and other unusual reproductive associations in ring-billed and California gulls. *The Auk* 96:6–9.

Constantinople, Anne (1973). Masculinity-femininity: An exception to a famous dictum? *Psychological Bulletin* 80:389–407.

Corruccini, Robert S., and Beecher, Robert M. (1982). Occlusal variation related to soft diet in a nonhuman primate. *Science* 218:74–76.

Court, John H. (1984). Sex and violence: A ripple effect. In Malamuth, Neil M., and Donnerstein, Edward (Eds.), *Pornography and sexual aggression*, chap. 5, pp. 143–172. New York: Academic Press.

Craig, Wallace (1909). The voices of pigeons regarded as a means of social control. *American Journal of Sociology* 14:86–100.

Davenport, Charles W. (1986). A follow-up study of 10 feminine boys. *Archives of Sexual Behavior* 15:511–517.

Davison, Gerald C. (1976). Homosexuality: The ethical challenge. *Journal of Consulting and Clinical Psychology* 44:157–162.

Dawkins, Richard (1976). *The selfish gene.* New York: Oxford University Press.

De Cecco, John P. (1981). Definition and meaning of sexual orientation. *Journal of Homosexuality* 6:51–67.

de Lacoste-Utamsing, Christine, and Holloway, Ralph L. (1982). Sexual dimorphism in the human corpus callosum. *Science* 216:1431–1432.

Devereux, George (1937). Institutionalized homosexuality of the Mohave Indians. *Human Biology* 9:498–527.

Devereux, George (1963). Institutionalized homosexuality of the Mohave Indians. In Ruitenbeek, Hendrik M. (Ed.), *The problem of homosexuality in modern society,* chapter 12, pp. 183–226. New York: Dutton.

Dizick, Missy, and Bly, Mary (1985). *Dogs are better than cats.* New York: Dolphin/Doubleday.

Dover, Sir Kenneth J. (1978). *Greek homosexuality.* Cambridge, Mass.: Harvard University Press.

Duncan, Starkey D., Jr. (1983). Speaking turns: Studies of structure and individual differences. Wiemann, John M., and Harrison, Randall P. (Eds.), *Nonverbal interaction,* pp. 149–178. Beverly Hills, Calif.: Sage Publications.

Duncan, Starkey D., Jr., and Fiske, D. W. (1977). *Face-to-face interaction: Research, methods, and theory.* Hillsdale, N.J.: Lawrence Erlbaum.

Ellison, Peter T. (1984). Book review. [Review of: *Margaret Mead and Samoa: The making and unmaking of an anthropological myth.*] *Ethology and Sociobiology* 5:69–70.

Evans, Richard I. (November 1974). Lorenz warns: "Man must know that the horse he is riding may be wild and should be bridled." *Psychology Today* 8(6):82–93.

Evans-Pritchard, E. E. (1951). Kinship and marriage among the Nuer. New York/Oxford: Oxford University Press.

Fang, Betty (1976). Swinging: In retrospect. *Journal of Sex Research* 12:220–237.

FitzGerald, Frances (28 July 1986). A reporter at large: The Castro-II. *The New Yorker,* 62(23), pp. 44–63.

Freedman, Daniel G. (1979). *Human sociobiology: A holistic approach.* New York: The Free Press/Macmillan.

Freund, Kurt W. (1974). Male homosexuality: An analysis of the pattern. In Loraine, J. A. (Ed.), *Understanding homosexuality: Its biological and psychological bases,* pp. 25–81. New York: Elsevier.

Freund, Kurt W. (1977). Should homosexuality arouse therapeutic concern? *Journal of Homosexuality* 2:235–240.

Freund, Kurt W.; Chan, Samuel; and Coulthard, Robert (1979). Phallometric diagnosis with "nonadmitters." *Behaviour Research and Therapy* 17:451–457.

Freund, Kurt; Langevin, Ron; Chamberlayne, Richard; Deosoran, Anthony;

and Zajac, Yaroslaw (1974). The phobic theory of male homosexuality. *Archives of Internal Medicine* 134:495–499.

Freund, Kurt W.; McKnight, C. K.; Langevin, Ron; and Cibiri, Stephen (1972). The female child as a surrogate object. *Archives of Sexual Behavior* 2:119–133.

Freund, Kurt W.; Scher, Hal; Chan, Samuel; and Ben-Aron, Mark (1982). Experimental analysis of pedophilia. *Behaviour Research and Therapy* 20:105–112.

Freund, Kurt W.; Sedláček, F.; and Knob, K. (1965). A simple transducer for mechanical plethysmography of the male genital. *Journal of the Experimental Analysis of Behavior* 8:169–170.

Freund, Kurt W.; Steiner, Betty W.; and Chan, Samuel (1982). Two types of cross-gender identity. *Archives of Sexual Behavior* 11:49–63.

Friday, Nancy (1980). *Men in love: Men's sexual fantasies: The triumph of love over rage.* New York: Delacorte Press.

Gadgil, Madhav (1972). Male dimorphism as a consequence of sexual selection. *American Naturalist* 106:574–580.

Gallup, Gordon G., Jr., and Suarez, Susan D. (1983). Homosexuality as a by-product of selection for optimal heterosexual strategies. *Perspectives in Biology and Medicine* 26:315–322.

Gebhard, Paul H. (1972). Incidence of overt homosexuality in the United States and western Europe. In Livingood, John M. (Ed.), *National Institute of Mental Health Task Force on Homosexuality: Final report and background papers,* pp. 22–29. Washington, D.C.: U.S. Government Printing Office. (DHEW publication no. HSM 72–9116).

Gebhard, Paul H.; Gagnon, John H.; Pomeroy, Wardell B.; and Christenson, Cornelia V. (1965). *Sex offenders: An analysis of types.* New York: Harper/Hoeber.

Gebhard, Paul H., and Johnson, Alan B. (1979). *The Kinsey data: Marginal tabulations of the 1938–1963 interviews conducted by the Institute for Sex Research.* Philadelphia: W. B. Saunders.

Geist, Valerius (1975). *Mountain sheep and man in the northern wilds.* Ithaca, N.Y.: Cornell University Press.

Gilman, Charlotte Perkins (1979). *Herland.* New York: Pantheon Books.

Goldfoot, David A.; Westerborg-van Loon, H.; Groeneveld, W.; and Koos Slob, A. (1980). Behavioral and physiological evidence of sexual climax in the female stump-tailed macaque *(Macaca arctoides). Science* 208:1477–1479.

Goldin-Meadow, Susan, and Feldman, Heidi (1977). The development of language-like communication without a language model. *Science* 197:401–403.

Goldin-Meadow, Susan, and Mylander, Carolyn (1977). Gestural communication in deaf children: Noneffect of parental input on language development. *Science* 221:372–374.

Goldman, Ronald, and Goldman, Juliette (1982). *Children's sexual thinking: A* comparative study of children aged 5 to 15 years in Australia, North America, Britain and Sweden. London: Routledge and Kegan Paul.

Goldstein, Michael J., and Kant, Harold S. (1973). *Pornography and sexual deviance.* Berkeley, Calif.: University of California Press.

Goodwin, Donald W.; Schulsinger, Fini; Hermansen, Leif; Guze, Samuel B.; and Winokur, George (1973). Alcohol problems in adoptees raised apart from alcoholic biological parents. *Archives of General Psychiatry* 28:238–243.

Goodwin, Donald W.; Schulsinger, Fini; Møller, Niels; Hermansen, Leif; Winokur, George; and Guze, Samuel B. (1974). Drinking problems in adopted and nonadopted sons of alcoholics. *Archives of General Psychiatry* 31:164–169.

Gould, James L., and Marler, Peter (January 1987). Learning by instinct. *Scientific American* 256(1):74–85.

Gould, Stephen Jay (November 1976). So cleverly kind an animal. *Natural History* 85(9):32–36.

Gould, Stephen Jay (August 1983). Sex and size. *Natural History* 92(8): 24–27.

Green, Richard (1974). *Sexual identity conflict in children and adults.* New York: Basic Books.

Green, Richard (1976). One-hundred ten feminine and masculine boys: Behavioral contrasts and demographic similarities. *Archives of Sexual Behavior* 5:425–446.

Green, Richard (1979). Childhood cross-gender behavior and subsequent sexual preference. *American Journal of Psychiatry* 136:106–108.

Green, Richard (1985). Gender identity in childhood and later sexual orientation: Follow-up of 78 males. *American Journal of Psychiatry* 142:339–341.

Green, Richard (1987). *The "sissy boy syndrome" and the development of homosexuality.* New Haven, Conn.: Yale University Press.

Green, Richard; Williams, Katherine; and Goodman, Marilyn (1982). Ninety-nine "tomboys" and "non-tomboys": Behavioral contrasts and demographic similarities. *Archives of Sexual Behavior* 11:247–266.

Groth, A. Nicholas, and Birnbaum, H. J. (1978). Adult sexual orientation and attraction to underage children. *Archives of Sexual Behavior* 7:175–181.

Hanby, J. P. (1974). Male-male mounting in Japanese monkeys *(Macaca fuscata). Animal Behaviour* 22:836–849.

Harcourt, A. H. (1979). Social relationships among adult female mountain gorillas. *Animal Behaviour* 27:251–264.

Harcourt, A. H.; Stewart, K. J.; and Fossey, Diane (1981). Reproduction by the gorilla in the wild. In Graham, C. E. (Ed.), *Reproductive biology of the great apes.* New York: Academic Press.

Hare, E. H. (1962). Masturbatory insanity: The history of an idea. *Journal of Mental Science* 108:1–25.

Hartman, Daniel Stanwood (1971). Behavior and ecology of the Florida manatee, *Trichechus manatus latirostris* (Harlan) at Crystal River, Citrus County. *Dissertation Abstracts International* 32(4):B2442. University Microfilms International order no. 71–24515.

Hartman, Daniel Stanwood (1979). *Ecology and behavior of the manatee (Trichechus manatus) in Florida.* Special publication no. 5. Pittsburgh, Penn.: American Society of Mammalogists.

Hearne, Vicki (18 August 1986). Questions about language. I: Horses. *The New Yorker* 62(26):33–57.

Heiman, Julia R. (April 1975). The physiology of erotica: Women's sexual arousal. *Psychology Today* 8(11):90–94.

Heiman, Julia R. (1977). A psychophysiological exploration of sexual arousal patterns in females and males. *Psychophysiology* 14:266–274.

Hirschfeld, Magnus (1912). Die zwölf Hauptgründe für das Angeborensein der Homosexualität. *Jahrbuch für sexuelle Zwischenstufen* 12:404–418.

Hirschfeld, Magnus (1936). Homosexuality. In Robinson, Victor (Ed.), *Encyclopaedia sexualis: A comprehensive encyclopaedia-dictionary of the sexual sciences*, pp. 321–334. New York: Dingwell-Rock, Ltd.

Hite, Shere (1981). *The Hite report: A nationwide study of female sexuality.* [New revised edition] New York: Dell.

Hite, Shere (1982). *The Hite report on male sexuality.* [Condensed edition] New York: Dell.

Holland, Saba Smith, Lady (1855). A memoir of the Reverend Sydney Smith: By his daughter, Lady Holland. New York: Harper and Brothers.

Hoon, Peter W. (1979). The assessment of sexual arousal in women. *Progress in Behavior Modification* 7:1–61.

Hrdy, Sarah Blaffer (1979). The evolution of human sexuality: The latest word and the last. *Quarterly Review of Biology* 54:309–314.

Hrdy, Sarah Blaffer (1981). *The woman that never evolved.* Cambridge, Mass.: Harvard University Press.

Hunt, George L., Jr. (1980). Mate selection and mating systems in seabirds. In Burger, Joanna; Olla, Bori L.; and Winn, Howard E. (Eds.), *Behavior of marine animals*, vol. 4, pp. 113–151. New York: Plenum Publishing.

Hunt, George L., Jr., and Hunt, Molly Warner (1977). Female-female pairing in western gulls *(Larus occidentalis)* in southern California. *Science* 196:1466–1467.

Hunt, George L., Jr.; Wingfield, John C.; Newman, A.; and Farner, Donald S. (1980). Sex ratio of western gulls on Santa Barbara Island, California. *The Auk* 97:473–479.

Hunt, Morton (1974). *Sexual behavior in the 1970s.* Chicago: Playboy Press.

Hutchinson, George Evelyn (1959). A speculative consideration of certain possible forms of sexual selection in man. *American Naturalist* 93:81–91.

Immelmann, Klaus; Hailman, Jack P.; and Baylis, Jeffrey R. (1982). Reputed band attractiveness and sex manipulation in zebra finches. *Science* 215:422.

It's OK to Say No!–Coloring Book (1984). New York: Playmore/Waldman Publishing. Unpaginated.

Jacobs, Sue-Ellen (1983). Comments [on Callender and Kochems 1983]. *Current Anthropology* 24:459–460.

Jowett, B. (1973). *The Republic and other works by Plato*. Garden City, N.Y.: Anchor Books/Doubleday.

Kalat, James W. (1983). Evolutionary thinking in the history of the comparative psychology of learning. *Neuroscience and Biobehavioral Reviews* 7:309–314.

Kanin, Eugene J. (1965). Male sex aggression and three psychiatric hypotheses. *Journal of Sex Research* 1:221–231.

Kanin, Eugene J., and Parcell, Stanley R. (1977). Sexual aggression: A second look at the offended female. *Archives of Sexual Behavior* 6:67–76.

Kaufman, I. Charles, and Rosenblum, Leonard A. (1966). A behavioral taxónomy for *Macaca nemestrina* and *Macaca radiata*: Based on longitudinal observation of family groups in the laboratory. *Primates* 7:205–258.

Kelley, Ken (May 1978). Playboy interview: Anita Bryant. *Playboy* 25(5): 73–250.

Kety, Seymour S.; Rosenthal, David; Wender, Paul H.; Schulsinger, Fini; and Jacobsen, Bjorn (1975). Mental illness in the biological and adoptive families of adoptive individuals who have become schizophrenic: A preliminary report based on psychiatric interviews. In Fieve, Ronald R.; Rosenthal, David; and Brill, Henry (Eds.), *Genetic research in psychiatry*, pp. 147–165. Baltimore, Md.: The Johns Hopkins University Press.

Kinsey, Alfred C.; Pomeroy, Wardell B.; and Martin, Clyde E. (1948). *Sexual behavior in the human male*. Philadelphia: W. B. Saunders.

Kinsey, Alfred C.; Pomeroy, Wardell B.; Martin, Clyde E.; and Gebhard, Paul H. (1953). *Sexual behavior in the human female*. Philadelphia: W. B. Saunders.

Kirsch, John A. W., and Rodman, James E. (1982). Selection and sexuality: The Darwinian view of homosexuality. In Paul, William; Weinrich, James D.; Gonsiorek, John C.; and Hotvedt, Mary E. (Eds.), *Homosexuality: Social, psychological, and biological issues*, chap. 16, pp. 183–195. Beverly Hills, Calif.: Sage Publications.

Klein, Fred (1978). *The bisexual option: A concept of one hundred percent intimacy*. New York: Arbor House.

Klein, Fritz, and Wolf, Timothy J. (Eds.) (1985). *Bisexualities: Theory and Research*. New York: Haworth Press. Previously published as volume 11, Nos. 1/2, *Journal of Homosexuality*.

Konner, Melvin (1982). *The tangled wing: Biological constraints on the human spirit*. New York: Holt, Rinehart, and Winston.

Koop, C. Everett (1986). Surgeon General's report on acquired immune deficiency syndrome. Washington, D.C.: U.S. Department of Health and Human Services.

Kovach, Joseph K., and Hess, Eckhard H. (1963). Imprinting: Effects of painful stimulation upon the following response. *Journal of Comparative and Physiological Psychology* 56:461–464.

References

Kutchinsky, Berl (1973). The effect of easy availability of pornography on the incidence of sex crimes: The Danish experience. *Journal of Social Issues* 29:163–181.

Lame Deer/John Fire, and Erdoes, Richard (1982). *Lame Deer: Seeker of visions.* New York: Simon and Schuster.

Lane, Harlan (1984). *When the mind hears: A history of the deaf.* New York: Random House.

Langevin, Ron (1983). *Sexual strands: Understanding and treating sexual anomalies in men.* Hillsdale, N.J.: Lawrence Erlbaum Associates.

Lebovitz, Phil S. (1972). Feminine behavior in boys: Aspects of its outcome. *American Journal of Psychiatry* 128:1283–1289.

Lockard, Robert B. (1971). Reflections on the fall of comparative psychology: Is there a message for us all? *American Psychologist* 26:168–179.

Loovis, David (1974). *Gay spirit: A guide to becoming a sensuous homosexual.* New York: Strawberry Hill/Grove Press.

Lorenz, Konrad Z. (1937). The companion in the bird's world. *The Auk* 54: 245–273.

Lorenz, Konrad (1966/1963). *On aggression* [Marjorie Kerr Wilson, trans. Original title: *Das sogenannte Böse: Zur Naturgeschichte der Aggression.*] New York: Harcourt, Brace and World.

MacLusky, N. J., and Naftolin, F. (1981). Sexual differentiation of the central nervous system. *Science* 211:1294–1303.

Magoun, H. W. (1981). John B. Watson and the study of human sexual behavior. *Journal of Sex Research* 17:368–378.

Martin, James T. (1978). Imprinting behavior: Pituitary-adrenocortical modulation of the approach response. *Science* 200:565–567.

Masters, William H., and Johnson, Virginia E. (1979). *Homosexuality in perspective.* Boston: Little, Brown.

McConaghy, Nathaniel (1976). Is a homosexual orientation irreversible? *British Journal of Psychiatry* 129:556–563.

McConaghy, Nathaniel (1978). Heterosexual experience, marital status, and orientation of homosexual males. *Archives of Sexual Behavior* 7:575–581.

McEwen, Bruce S. (1981). Neural gonadal steroid actions. *Science* 211:1303–1311.

McIntosh, Mary (1968). The homosexual role. *Social Problems* 16:182–192.

McNulty, Faith (17 January 1983). Our far-flung correspondents: Peeping in the shell. *The New Yorker* 58(48):88–97.

Mead, Margaret (1961). Cultural determinants of sexual behavior. In Young, William C. (Ed.), *Sex and internal secretions* (3rd ed.), pp. 1433–1479. Baltimore, Md.: Williams and Wilkins.

Mednick, Sarnoff A.; Gabrielli, William F., Jr.; and Hutchings, Barry (1984). Genetic influences in criminal convictions: Evidence from an adoption cohort. *Science* 224:891–894.

Money, John (1980). *Love and love sickness: The science of sex, gender difference, and pair-bonding.* Baltimore, Md.: The Johns Hopkins University Press.

Money, John (1985). *The destroying angel: Sex, fitness and food in the legacy of degeneracy theory, graham crackers, Kellogg's corn flakes and American health history.* Buffalo, N.Y.: Prometheus Books.

Money, John (1986). *Lovemaps: Clinical concepts of sexual/erotic health and pathology, paraphilia, and gender transposition in childhood, adolescence, and maturity.* New York: Irvington Publishers.

Money, John; Annecillo, Charles; and Hutchison, June Werlwas (1985). Forensic and family psychiatry in abuse dwarfism: Munchausen's syndrome by proxy, atonement, and addiction to abuse. *Journal of Sex and Marital Therapy* 11:30–40.

Money, John; Annecillo, Charles; and Kelley, John F. (1983). Growth of intelligence: Failure and catchup associated respectively with abuse and rescue in the syndrome of abuse dwarfism. *Psychoneuroendocrinology* 8: 309–319.

Money, John; Annecillo, Charles; and Kelley, John F. (1983). Abuse-dwarfism syndrome: After rescue, statural and intellectual catchup growth correlate. *Journal of Clinical Child Psychology* 12:179–283.

Money, John, and Athanasiou, Robert (1973). Pornography: Review and bibliographic annotations. *American Journal of Obstetrics and Gynecology* 115:130–146.

Money, John, and Ehrhardt, Anke A. (1972). *Man and Woman, Boy and Girl.* Baltimore, Md.: The Johns Hopkins University Press.

Money, John, and Hosta, Geoffrey (1968). Negro folklore of male pregnancy. *Journal of Sex Research* 4:34–50.

Money, John, and Lamacz, Margaret (1984). Gynemimesis and gynemimetophilia: Individual and cross-cultural manifestations of a gender-coping strategy hitherto unnamed. *Comprehensive Psychiatry* 25:392–403.

Money, John, and Russo, Anthony J. (1979). Homosexual outcome of discordant gender identity/role in childhood: Longitudinal follow-up. *Journal of Pediatric Psychology* 4:29–41.

Money, John, and Weinrich, James D. (1983). Juvenile, pedophile, heterophile: Hermeneutics of science, medicine and law in two outcome studies. *Medicine and Law* 2:39–54.

Money, John, and Werlwas, June (1976). *Folie à deux* in the parents of psychosocial dwarfs: Two cases. *Bulletin of the American Academy of Psychiatry and Law* 4:351–362.

Money, John, and Werlwas, June (1982). Paraphilic sexuality and child abuse: The parents. *Journal of Sex and Marital Therapy* 8:57–64.

Moore, Monica M. (1985). Nonverbal courtship patterns in women: Context and consequences. *Ethology and Sociobiology* 6:237–247.

Morris, Desmond (1952). Homosexuality in the ten-spined stickleback *(Pygosteus pungitius* L.). *Behaviour* 4:233–261.

Morris, Desmond (1954). The reproductive behaviour of the zebra finch *(Poephila guttata),* with special reference to pseudofemale behaviour and displacement activities. *Behaviour* 6:271–322.

Morris, Desmond (1955). The causation of pseudofemale and pseudomale behaviour: A further comment. *Behaviour* 8:46–56.

Morris, Desmond (1964). The response of animals to a restricted environment. *Symposia of the London Zoological Society* 13:99–118.

Morris, Desmond (1970). Author's note, 1969. In Desmond Morris, *Patterns of reproductive behaviour*, pp. 39–41. New York: McGraw-Hill.

Moser, Charles A., and Levitt, Eugene E. (1987). An exploratory-descriptive study of a sadomasochistically oriented sample. *Journal of Sex Research* 23:in press.

Nanda, Serena (1984). The hijras of India: A preliminary report. *Medicine and Law* 3:59–75.

Nestle, Joan (September 1983). Voices from lesbian herstory. *The Body Politic* no. 96:35–36.

Niederland, William G. (1984). *The Schreber case: Psychoanalytic profile of a paranoid personality.* (Expanded ed.) New York: Analytic Press/Lawrence Erlbaum Associates.

Parsons, Elsie Clews (1916). The Zuñi la'mana. *American Anthropologist* 18: 521–528.

Perper, Timothy (1985). *Sex signals: The biology of love.* Philadelphia: ISI Press.

Perrill, Stephen A.; Gerhardt, H. Carl; and Daniel, Richard (1978). Sexual parasitism in the green tree frog *(Hyla cinerea). Science* 200:1179–1180.

Petrie, Marion (1983). Female moorhens compete for small fat males. *Science* 220:413–415.

Pillard, Richard C.; Poumadere, Jeanette I.; and Carretta, Ruth A. (1981). Is homosexuality familial? A review, some data, and a suggestion. *Archives of Sexual Behavior* 10:465–475.

Pillard, Richard C., and Weinrich, James D. (1986). Evidence of familial nature of male homosexuality. *Archives of General Psychiatry* 43:808–812.

Pillard, Richard C., and Weinrich, James D. (1987). The periodic table model of the gender transpositions. I: A theory based on masculinization and defeminization of the brain. *Journal of Sex Research,* 23:in press.

Poole, Kenneth (1972). The etiology of gender identity and the lesbian. *Journal of Social Psychology* 87:51–57.

Radway, Janice A. (1984). *Reading the romance: Women, patriarchy, and popular literature.* Chapel Hill, N.C.: University of North Carolina Press.

Rancour-LaFerriere, Daniel (1985). *Signs of the flesh: An essay on the evolution of hominid sexuality.* Approaches to Semiotics 71. Berlin/New York: Mouton de Gruyter.

Ritchie, John P. (1926). Nesting of two male swans. *Scottish Naturalist* 159:95.

Robinson, Paul (1976). *The modernization of sex: Havelock Ellis, Alfred Kinsey, William Masters and Virginia Johnson.* New York: Harper & Row.

Ross, Michael W.; Rogers, Lesley J.; and McCulloch, Helen (1978). Stigma, sex, and society: A new look at gender differentiation and sexual variation. *Journal of Homosexuality* 3:315–330.

Ruse, Michael (1981). Are there gay genes? Sociobiology and homosexuality. *Journal of Homosexuality* 6(4):5–34.

Ryder, John P., and Somppi, Patricia Lynn (1979). Female-female pairing in ring-billed gulls. *The Auk* 96:1–5.

Sade, Donald Stone (1966). Ontogeny of social relations in a group of free-ranging rhesus monkeys (*Macaca mulatta* Zimmerman). Ph.D. thesis, Department of Anthropology, University of California at Berkeley. University Microfilms International no. 67-05156. *Dissertation Abstracts International* 27(10-B):3379.

Sade, Donald Stone (1968). Inhibition of son-mother mating among free-ranging rhesus monkeys. In Masserman, Jules H. (Ed.), *Animal and human*, pp. 18–38. Vol. 12, *Science and psychoanalysis*. New York/London: Grune and Stratton.

Sagarin, Edward M. (1973). Book review of: Aaron, William (1972). Straight: A heterosexual talks about his homosexual past. Garden City, N.Y.: Doubleday. *Journal of Sex Research* 9:79–81.

Saghir, Marcel T., and Robins, Eli (1973). *Male and female homosexuality: A comprehensive investigation*. Baltimore, Md.: Williams and Wilkins.

Sakheim, David K.; Barlow, David H.; Beck, J. Gayle; and Abrahamson, Daniel J. (1985). A comparison of male heterosexual and male homosexual patterns of sexual arousal. *Journal of Sex Research* 21:183–198.

Sauer, E. G. Franz (1972). Aberrant sexual behavior in the South African ostrich. *The Auk* 89:717–737.

Schäfer, Siegrid (1976). Sexual and social problems of lesbians. *Journal of Sex Research* 12:50–69.

Schäfer, Siegrid (1977). Sociosexual behavior in male and female homosexuals: A study in sex differences. *Archives of Sexual Behavior* 6:355–364.

Schatzman, Morton (1973). *Soul murder: Persecution in the family*. New York: Random House.

Schiavi, Raul C.; Theilgaard, Alice; Owen, David R.; and White, Daniel (1984). Sex chromosome anomalies, hormones, and aggressivity. *Archives of General Psychiatry* 41:93–99.

Schmidt, Gunter, and Sigusch, Volkmar (1973). Women's sexual arousal. In Zubin, Joseph, and Money, John (Eds.), *Contemporary sexual behavior: Critical issues in the 1970s*, chap. 7, pp. 117–143. Baltimore, Md.: The Johns Hopkins University Press.

Schreber, Daniel Paul (1903). *Denkwürdigkeiten eines Nervenkranken*. Leipzig: Oswald Mutze.

Schreber, Daniel Paul (1955/1903). *Memoirs of my nervous illness*. Macalpine, Ida, and Hunter, Richard A. (Trans.) London: William Dawson and Sons.

Schwartz, Mark F., and Masters, William H. (1984). The Masters and Johnson treatment program for dissatisfied homosexual men. *American Journal of Psychiatry* 141:173–181.

Scott, John Paul (1978). Critical periods. *Benchmark Papers in Animal Behavior* 12. Stroudsburg, Pa.: Dowden, Hutchinson and Ross.

Sears, Robert Richardson; Maccoby, Eleanor Emmons; and Levin, Harry (1957). *Patterns of child rearing.* Evanston, Ill.: Row, Peterson.

Seligman, Martin E. P. (1970). On the generality of the laws of learning. *Psychological Review* 77:406–418.

Shore, Elsie R. (1984). The former transsexual: A case study. *Archives of Sexual Behavior* 13:277–285.

Silverstein, Charles, and White, Edmund (1977). *The joy of gay sex: An intimate guide for gay men to the pleasures of a gay lifestyle.* New York: Crown Publishers.

Sims, Margot (1982). *On the necessity of bestializing the human female.* Boston: South End Press.

Sintchak, George, and Geer, James A. (1975). A vaginal plethysmograph system. *Psychophysiology* 12:113–115.

Sisley, Emily L., and Harris, Bertha (1977). *The joy of lesbian sex: A tender and intimate guide to the pleasures and problems of a lesbian lifestyle.* New York: Crown Publishers.

Smuts, Barbara B. (1985). *Sex and friendship in baboons.* Chicago: Aldine.

Sociobiology Study Group (1977). Sociobiology—a new biological determinism. In The Ann Arbor Science for the People Editorial Collective (Eds.), *Biology as a social weapon,* pp. 133–149. Minneapolis, Minn.: Burgess.

Spengler, Andreas (1977). Manifest sadomasochism of males: Results of an empirical study. *Archives of Sexual Behavior* 6:441–456.

Sreenivasan, Uma (1985). Effeminate boys in a child psychiatric clinic: Prevalence and associated factors. *Journal of the American Academy of Child Psychiatry* 24:689–694.

Starkey, Edward E. (1972). A case of interspecific homosexuality in geese. *The Auk* 89:456–457.

Steffensmeier, Darryl, and Steffensmeier, Renée (1974). Sex differences in reactions to homosexuals: Research continues and further developments. *Journal of Sex Research* 10:52–67.

Stoller, Robert J. (1973). Male transsexualism: Uneasiness. *American Journal of Psychiatry* 130:536–539.

Stoller, Robert J. (1982). Transvestism in women. *Archives of Sexual Behavior* 11:99–115.

Swaab, D. F., and Fliers, E. (1985). A sexually dimorphic nucleus in the human brain. *Science* 228:1112–1115.

Symons, Donald (1979). *The evolution of human sexuality.* New York: Oxford University Press.

Tennov, Dorothy (1979). *Love and limerence—the experience of being in love.* New York: Stein and Day.

Thornhill, Randy (1976). Sexual selection and nuptial feeding behavior in *Bittacus apicalis (Insecta: Mecoptera). American Naturalist* 110:529–548.

Thornhill, Randy (1979). Adaptive female-mimicking behavior in a scorpionfly. *Science* 205:412–414.

Tripp, Clarence A. (1975). *The homosexual matrix.* New York: McGraw-Hill.

Trivers, Robert L. (1972). Parental investment and sexual selection. In Bernard Campbell (Ed.), *Sexual selection and the descent of man 1871–1971*, pp. 136–179. Chicago: Aldine.

Trivers, Robert L. (1974). Parent-offspring conflict. *American Zoologist* 14: 249–264.

Trivers, Robert L. (1976). Sexual selection and resource-accruing abilities in *Anolis garmani*. *Evolution* 30:253–269.

Van den Assem, J. (1967). Territory in the three-spined stickleback (*Gasterosteus aculeatus* L.): An experimental study in intra-specific competition. *Behaviour*, Supplement 16:1–164.

Vining, Daniel R., Jr. (1986). Social versus reproductive success: The central theoretical problem of human sociobiology. *Behavioral and Brain Sciences* 9:167–187.

Wade, Nicholas (16 September 1977). NASA bans sex from outer space. *Science* 197:1163–1165.

Waltrip, Bob (March 1965). Elmer Gage: American Indian. *ONE: The homosexual viewpoint* 13(3):6–10.

Weinberg, Martin S., and Williams, Colin J. (1974). *Male homosexuals: Their problems and adaptations.* New York: Oxford University Press.

Weinrich, James D. (1976). Human reproductive strategy (Doctoral dissertation, Harvard University, 1976). *Dissertation Abstracts International.* 1977, 37:5339-B. University Microfilms no. 77–8348.

Weinrich, James D. (1978). Nonreproduction, homosexuality, transsexualism, and intelligence: I. A systematic literature search. *Journal of Homosexuality* 3:275–289.

Weinrich, James D. (1980a). Homosexual behavior in animals: A new review of observations from the wild, and their relationship to human homosexuality. In Forleo, Romano, and Pasini, Willi (Eds.), *Medical Sexology: The Third International Congress*, pp. 288–295. Littleton, Mass.: PSG Publishing.

Weinrich, James D. (1980b). On a relationship between homosexuality and I.Q. test scores: A review and some hypotheses. In Forleo, Romano, and Pasini, Willi (Eds.), *Medical Sexology: The Third International Congress*, pp. 312–317. Littleton, Mass.: PSG Publishing.

Weinrich, James D. (1982). Is homosexuality biologically natural? In Paul, William; Weinrich, James D.; Gonsiorek, John C.; and Hotvedt, Mary E. (Eds.), *Homosexuality: Social, Psychological, and Biological Issues*, pp. 197–208. Beverly Hills, Calif.: Sage Publications.

Weinrich, James D. (1985). Homosexuals, transsexuals, and sissy boys: On the mathematics of followup studies. *Journal of Sex Research* 21:322–328.

Weinrich, James D. (1987). A new sociobiological theory of homosexuality applicable to societies with universal marriage. *Behavioral Ecology and Sociobiology* 8:37–47.

Werner, Dennis (1979). A cross-cultural perspective on theory and research on male homosexuality. *Journal of Homosexuality* 4:345–362.

References

Werner, Dennis (1980). Erratum. *Journal of Homosexuality* 5:333–334.

Whitaker, J. (1885). Swans' nests. *The Zoologist* 9 (3rd series):263–264.

Whitam, Frederick L. (1977). The homosexual role: A reconsideration. *Journal of Sex Research* 13:1–11.

Whitam, Frederick L. (1980). The prehomosexual male child in three societies: The United States, Guatemala, Brazil. *Archives of Sexual Behavior* 9:87–99.

Whitam, Frederick L. (1983). Culturally invariable properties of male homosexuality: Tentative conclusions from cross-cultural research. *Archives of Sexual Behavior* 12:207–226.

Whitam, Frederick L., and Mathy, Robin M. (1986). *Male homosexuality in four societies: Brazil, Guatemala, the Philippines, and the United States.* New York: Praeger Scientific.

Whiting, Beatrice Blyth, and Whiting, John Wesley Mayhew (1975). *Children of six cultures: A psycho-cultural analysis.* Cambridge, Mass.: Harvard University Press.

Williams, Katherine; Goodman, Marilyn; and Green, Richard (1985). Parent-child factors in gender role socialization in girls. *Journal of the American Academy of Child Psychiatry* 24:720–731.

Williams, Katherine; Green, Richard; and Goodman, Marilyn (1979). Patterns of sexual identity development: A preliminary report on the "tomboy." In Simmons, R. (Ed.), *Research in community and mental health,* volume 1, pp. 103–123. Greenwich, Conn.: JAI Press.

Williams, Walter L. (1986). *The spirit and the flesh: Sexual diversity in American Indian culture.* Boston: Beacon Press.

Wilson, Edward O. (1975). *Sociobiology: The new synthesis.* Cambridge, Mass.: Harvard University Press.

Wilson, Edward O. (1978). *On human nature.* Cambridge, Mass.: Harvard University Press.

Wilson, G. Terence, and Lawson, David M. (1976a). The effects of alcohol on sexual arousal in women. *Journal of Abnormal Psychology* 85:489–497.

Wilson, G. Terence, and Lawson, David M. (1976b). Expectancies, alcohol, and sexual arousal in male social drinkers. *Journal of Abnormal Psychology* 85:587–594.

Wilson, G. Terence, and Lawson, David M. (1978). Expectancies, alcohol, and sexual arousal in women. *Journal of Abnormal Psychology* 87:358–367.

Wincze, John P.; Hoon, Peter; and Hoon, Emily Franck (1977). Sexual arousal in women: A comparison of cognitive and physiological responses by continuous measurement. *Archives of Sexual Behavior* 6:121–133.

Wingfield, John C.; Martin, Audrey; Hunt, Molly Warner; Hunt, George L., Jr.; and Farner, Donald S. (1980a). Origin of homosexual pairing of female western gulls on Santa Barbara Island. In Powers, D. (Ed.), *Symposium on the California Islands,* pp. 461–466. Santa Barbara, Calif.: Santa Barbara Museum of Natural History.

Wingfield, John C.; Newman, A.; Hunt, George L., Jr.; and Farner, Donald S. (1980b). Androgen in high concentrations in the blood of female western gulls, *Larus occidentalis*. *Naturwissenschaften* 67:514.

Witkin, Herman A.; Mednick, Sarnoff A.; Schulsinger, Fini; Bakkestrøm, Eskild; Christiansen, Karl O.; Goodenough, Donald R.; Hirschhorn, Kurt; Lundsteen, Claes; Owen, David R.; Philip, John; Rubin, Donald B.; and Stocking, Martha (1976). Criminality in XYY and XXY men. *Science* 193:547–555.

Wurtman, Judith J., and Wurtman, Richard J. (1979). Sucrose consumption early in life fails to modify the appetite of adult rats for sweet foods. *Science* 205:321–322.

Wurtman, Richard J., and Wurtman, Judith J. (Eds.) (1986). *Food constituents affecting normal and abnormal behaviors*. Nutrition and the Brain series, vol. 7. New York: Raven Press.

Yates-Rist, Darrell (1983). The woman who lives inside. *Christopher Street* 7(2):24–35. Issue no. 74.

Young, W. C.; Goy, Robert W.; and Phoenix, C. H. (1964). Hormones and sexual behavior. *Science* 143:212–218.

Zucker, Kenneth J.; Bradley, Susan J.; Corter, Carl M.; Doering, Robert W.; and Finegan, Jo-Anne K. (1980). Cross-gender behavior in very young boys: A normative study. In Samson, J. (Ed.), *Childhood and sexuality*. Montréal: Éditions Études Vivantes.

Zuger, Bernard (1966). Effeminate behavior present in boys from early childhood: I. The clinical syndrome and follow-up studies. *Pediatrics* 96:1098–1107.

Zuger, Bernard (1978). Effeminate behavior present in boys from childhood: Ten additional years of follow-up. *Comprehensive Psychiatry* 19:363–369.

Zuger, Bernard, and Taylor, Patsy (1969). Effeminate behavior present in boys from early childhood: II. Comparison with similar symptoms in non-effeminate boys. *Pediatrics* 44:375–380.

INDEX

Index

Index

Index